FROM
OLD REVELATION
TO NEW

From
Old Revelation
to
New

A Tradition-Historical
and Redaction-Critical Study
of Temporal Transitions in Prophetic Prediction

Simon J. De Vries

WILLIAM B. EERDMANS PUBLISHING COMPANY
GRAND RAPIDS, MICHIGAN

© 1995 Wm. B. Eerdmans Publishing Co.
255 Jefferson Ave. S.E., Grand Rapids, Michigan 49503

Printed in the United States of America

00 99 98 97 96 95   7 6 5 4 3 2 1

Library of Congress Cataloging-in-Publication Data

De Vries, Simon John.
From old Revelation to new: a tradition-historical and redaction-critical study of temporal
transitions in prophetic prediction / Simon J. De Vries.
p.   cm.
Includes bibliographical references and indexes.
ISBN 0-8028-0683-X (pbk.)
1. Bible. O.T. Prophets — Criticism, interpretation, etc. 2. Time in the Bible.   I. Title.
BS1505.6.T5D48   1995
224′.06 — dc20   94-25013
CIP

In Gratitude to
Rev. J. Harold Ellens, Th.M., Ph.D.
Pastor, Scholar, and Healer
Who assisted in the "birth" of this offspring

Contents

PART ONE
THE DISTRIBUTION AND EMPLOYMENT
OF FUTURISTIC TRANSITIONS

PART THREE
FUTURISTIC TRANSITIONS
IN THE TRADITIONING PROCESS   239

Preface

The biblical view of time is a problem that has long held the author's attention. The publication, in 1975, of his book *Yesterday, Today and Tomorrow: Time and History in the Old Testament* has made the writing of the present book inevitable — inevitable not so much in terms of logical consequence as in terms of an unfulfilled task. There were three major parts in that book: Day Past, Day Present, and Day Future. The method of working was to examine every Old Testament passage containing certain time designatives built on the vocable *yôm* in order to determine their respective functions and reconstruct a theology of time and history from the resultant data. However, the third part of the book, that dealing with future time, had neither the extent nor the depth of the preceding two parts. Perhaps this came about through weariness or through a lack of confidence on my part in finding a publisher, should I make the book any longer. Be that as it may, the challenge of dealing adequately with the future aspect has not vanished. That is the reason — or at least the occasion — for the present book.

In order to give a more adequate analysis to Israel's way of speaking and thinking about future time, I have gone over the data once again and have discovered many things that I had not seen before as I broadened my method to include an examination not only of the most common futuristic formula *bayyôm hahû'*, but of a whole range of similar formulas. In examining the role of these formulas in the growth of the individual books, my insight has been that it is the transitional use of these formulas that offers the clue for understanding both eschatological tradition and redactional methodology. The present book is therefore about futuristic transitions, of which there are two kinds, the integral and the introductory. This distinction is very important because integral temporal transitions often reveal something of the "eschatology" of the prophetic writers themselves, while introductory temporal transitions reveal the same thing on the part of the redactors of the prophetic collection.

I have found here a tool for clearing away some of the brush that confuses and inhibits the scholarly discussion about prophetic eschatology. It has been generally realized that substantial sections of each prophetic book contain a greater or lesser number of nonauthentic words, but apart from following obvious clues for relative dating, the students of the prophetic literature have not been able to relate this secondary material significantly to the various stages of redaction that have produced the books as we now have them. In view of the fact that the common method used by redactors in expanding original materials was by simple juxtaposition (laying the new text alongside the underlying text without formal connection of any sort), passages that are connected to their context by a formal transition, such as one of the temporal formulas that are to be discussed in this book, attract our attention and curiosity. What one would have no prospect of accomplishing with respect to expanded texts without a formal connective has been possible here. It has in fact been possible to develop an elaborate analysis of redactional method with reference to syndetically connected passages and to give an explanation of the prophetic ideology involved in this type of expansion. What results from this analysis is a sense of texture, an awareness that prophetic redaction is not a blur or a tangle, but a phenomenon of amazing creativity, perspicuity, and tenacity.

The essential issue in all this is intentionality — the intentionality of the disciple-redactors who spoke as their master spoke, or would have spoken in their new situation. Essentially, predictions introduced by temporal transitions are expressions of an ideology of the continuing relevance of the prophetic proclamation. We receive the impression of unrestrained vitality — of biblical tradition in the making. Biblical revelation is not static but dynamic, rooted in tradition but reaching out for still further visions of the divine purpose.

I have offered small sections of my research for this book in lectures to scholarly audiences, as at the Oriental Institute in Cambridge in 1978 and the Congress of Old Testament scholars in Leuven in 1988, and have benefitted from the ensuing discussions. I am most indebted, however, to individual scholars in the field of prophetic redaction who have done me the honor of reading the manuscript in provisional form; in particular, Professor Ronald E. Clements of King's College in London, Professor Magne Saebø of Oslo, Professor David Carr of the Methodist Theological School in Delaware, Ohio, and Professor Rolf Knierim of the Claremont Graduate School. From each of these very able, but very busy, scholars I have received much appreciated counsel.

In all modesty, I turn this study over to potential readers with the belief that it may prove to serve as a landmark in the study of prophetic eschatology and redactional methodology. My book aspires to stand alongside the recent works of highly respected scholars, such as Robert Carroll and Michael Fishbane, who have written on this challenging subject. Some readers may disagree with me on details, but what will matter is that it offers to open up new vistas in the study of the biblical prophets and their redactors, bringing light on questions that have lingered in obscurity.

Abbreviations

Aram	Aramaic
AUNVAO	Avhandlinger Utgitt av Det Norske Videnskaps Akademi i Oslo
BBB	Bonner Biblische Beiträge
*BHS*mg	*Biblia Hebraica Stuttgartensia,* marginal reading
Bib	*Biblica*
BKAT	*Biblischer Kommentar, Altes Testament*
BWANT	Beiträge zur Wissenschaft vom Alten und Neuen Testament
BZAW	Beihefte zur Zeitschrift für die alttestamentliche Wissenschaft
CBQ	*Catholic Biblical Quarterly*
comm.	commentary
CTM	*Concordia Theological Monthly*
ETR	*Études Théologiques et Religieuses*
EvQ	*Evangelical Quarterly*
FOTL	The Forms of the Old Testament Literature
FRLANT	Forschungen zur Religion und Literatur des Alten und Neuen Testaments
fs.	Festschrift
G, LXX	The Greek Septuagint
Gvar	idem, variant readings
GKC	*Gesenius' Hebrew Grammar,* ed. E. Kautzsch and A. E. Cowley
HAR	*Hebrew Annual Review*
HSM	Harvard Semitic Monographs
ICC	International Critical Commentary
IDB	*Interpreter's Dictionary of the Bible*

Int	*Interpretation*
JBL	*Journal of Biblical Literature*
JSS	*Journal of Semitic Studies*
KuD	*Kerygma und Dogma*
Ms/Mss	Ancient manuscript(s)
MT	Masoretic Text
OTS	*Oudtestamentische Studien*
par	biblical parallel
pc	*pauci,* few
PEQ	*Palestine Exploration Quarterly*
RB	*Revue Biblique*
RQ	*Römische Quartalschrift für christliche Altertumskunde und Kirchengeschichte*
RSV	Revised Standard Version
SBLMS	Society of Biblical Literature Monograph Series
SBS	Stuttgarter Bibelstudien
SBT	Studies in Biblical Theology
SJT	*Scottish Journal of Theology*
ST	*Studia Theologica*
SVT	Supplements to Vetus Testamentum
Syr	Syriac version
TDOT	*Theological Dictionary of the Old Testament*
Tg	Targum
THAT	*Theologisches Handwörterbuch zum Alten Testament*
TLZ	*Theologische Literaturzeitung*
Ug	Ugaritic
VT	*Vetus Testamentum*
WMANT	Wissenschaftliche Monographien zum Alten und Neuen Testaments
YTT	*Yesterday, Today and Tomorrow*
ZAW	*Zeitschrift für die alttestamentliche Wissenschaft*

Transliterations of Hebrew Script

(Daghesh and raphe are not represented)

־	a	א	ʾ
ֳ	ă	ב	b
ָ	ā	ג	g
הָ	â	ד	d
יוָ	āw	ה, ה	h
יֵ	ay	ו	w
יָ	āy	ז	z
ֶ	e	ח	ḥ
ֱ	ĕ	ט	ṭ
יֵ	ey	י	y
ֵ	ē	ך, כ	k
יֵ	ê	ל	l
ֽ	ĕ	ם, מ	m
ִ	i	ן, נ	n
יִ	î	ס	s
ָ	o	ע	ʿ
ֳ	ŏ	ף, פ	p
ֹ	ō	ץ, צ	ṣ
וֹ	ô	ק	q
ֻ	u	ר	r
וּ	û	שׂ	ś
		שׁ	š
		ת	t

Introduction

CHAPTER ONE

The Problem of Futuristic Appendages in the Prophetic Literature

Redactional Expansion as a Creative Element in Composition

Learning how to detect literary seams between original and secondary materials in a biblical passage is as essential in the training of a critical scholar as penetrating the skin with a scalpel is for one learning surgery. To handle every word in a biblical text as part of an undifferentiated mass would be as fruitless for a Scripture scholar as confusing bone with cartilage would be for a surgeon. One must know what one is looking for and be able to recognize it when one sees it. One must see precisely where to cut and must not hesitate to apply the knife.

However, the analogy of surgery has its limits. The anatomical dissector is looking for bad tissue in order to remove it from the good and the healthy. The biblical critic should not presume that in separating secondary from original he is necessarily cutting bad from good. In the post-Wellhausenian criticism many scholars did indeed believe that what they could cut away from the pristine original was relatively worthless, or even positively bad. They practiced their criticism under the dominance of a rigid developmental theory concerning the origins of biblical religion. Limited by the canons of rationalism though inspired by the enthusiasm of romanticism, they searched for a shining, Camelot-like moment in ancient Israel's experience when puerile growth had been sloughed away — allowing a rigorous heroism to emerge — and before decadence had set in. This was essentially the deeply moral and personalistic preaching of the eighth-century prophets. All that came before and after was suspected of defect and decay.

Standing consciously or unconsciously under the logic of this philosophy of history, scholars like Bernhard Duhm labored to relieve the authentic words of the original biblical writers — especially the great prophets — from layers of degenerate accretions. That era has now passed. It is now customary to treat, say, a prophetic book as the residue of an ongoing enthusiastic activity in which some of those who had ministered to one of the original prophets and had preserved his message — and perhaps others who lived after a prophet's lifetime but stood still in his tradition — felt free to arrange, adapt, and expand what had been collected, endeavoring to reshape it into a new, dynamic, continuously relevant form of their master's preaching.

In this light, it would seem that contemporary scholars should no longer be inclined to focus their analytical efforts one-sidedly on the presumed original. The pristine words of one of the great prophets might indeed prove to be linguistically, aesthetically, and spiritually superior, and therefore well worth searching for. But as a witness to spiritual truth within a dynamic, ongoing process of intellectual and religious development, the putative original can claim no inherent superiority over the added-on elements that have brought it to its more complex, canonical shape.

A comparison of three recent major commentaries on Jeremiah shows how widely present-day scholars may nevertheless differ on this issue. William L. Holladay's very detailed treatment in the Hermeneia series aspires to recover the original words of Jeremiah while placing many of his oracles within a precise historical framework, doing little with secondary materials beyond identifying them.[1] Robert P. Carroll's commentary in the Old Testament Library series, on the other hand, assumes a stance of relative literary and historical agnosticism, claiming that nothing original may confidently be isolated out of this complexly redacted book.[2] William McKane's commentary for the International Critical Commentary seems to strike a mediating position, admitting the presumption of an original literary core — but one that has been all but obscured by successive layers of redactional expansion.[3] McKane shows one way out of the impasse, which is to provide perspective on relative proximities to the original within a given passage by defining a "triggering process" that led to specific redactional revisions.[4]

Redaction and the Tradition of Predictive Expansion

Given the fact that individual scholars may have differing assessments of the role that redaction has played in the composition of the various prophetic books, we need to inquire about the techniques and the ideology of the prophetic redactors — at least to ask the question even though we may not immediately discover a clue to what they were up to. This can only be addressed by directly searching into individual texts. It is an error to speculate at random about the redactional process without first determining what each redactor was doing with his received material, and with what purpose. The question of technique cannot be separated from the question of ideology, for technique is in the service of ideology, and ideology comes to expression in technique. The present study is concerned with both, but with special focus on the peculiar linguistic phenomenon of stereotyped temporal transitions having the function of expanding the futuristic images of the underlying materials.

Virtually all secondary expansions within the prophetic literature are concerned for the future, and fall accordingly into the broad category of eschatology. Accordingly, a study of redactional technique will automatically involve questions regarding eschatological tradition. It is on this problem that the present effort intends to create for itself a special place within the current discussion of eschatology in general. It will not presume to offer a comprehensive solution to the problem of eschatology within the broad discipline of biblical theology, nor will it be able to analyze every relevant text. Rather, it aspires to find satisfying answers to one single problem, that of the process of expansion through the use of temporal transitions, anticipating that eventually this may contribute significantly to the solution of the broader problems.

Books, monographs, and articles about Old Testament eschatology continue to appear, and on many problems no consensus has yet emerged. It is no longer possible to accept the verdict of the Wellhausenian school, to the effect that the prophetic forecasts for the future — particularly those of favor and blessing — arose either from idle speculation or from subjectivistic optimism. We now understand that the prophets and their redactors were not speaking only for themselves, but for the believing community to which they belonged. Futuristic aspiration was endemic to Israel's self-understanding; it was an irresistible outgrowth of their traditionally derived and historically orientated belief concerning the electing and covenant-making God who had brought them to the present moment. This much, contemporary scholars are able to agree on. But this conception gives rise to numerous related problems.

There is much current discussion of the problems of prophetic prediction and eschatology. Here is a list of the important clusters of questions concerning Israel's futuristic expectation that continue to require investigation:

(1) Is the term "eschatology" appropriate and adequate? As a term derived from Christian dogmatics, does it really fit the biblical phenomenon of futuristic prediction? In addition, does "eschatology" necessarily require the notion of an end to time and history, or does it allow for two distinct aeons? Are there contending and irreconcilable concepts within the Old Testament eschatological tradition? What is the distinction between biblical eschatology in general and the special form known as apocalyptic?

(2) Why did Israel alone among the ancient Near Eastern peoples develop

a genuine eschatology? Is there any validity to the claim that it developed out of the mythological culture of the age (Gunkel, Gressmann), or to the claim that it arose out of the Israelite cult (Mowinckel)?

(3) Within the biblical tradition, is eschatology to be viewed as an accidental or even erratic phenomenon? In other words, does it represent an authentic and essential aspect of biblical religion, or has it arisen from psychological factors, such as disillusionment (Carroll)? Must optimistic eschatology be viewed as a betrayal of prophetic integrity (Fohrer)?

(4) What is the connection between judgment prophecy and salvation prophecy? Is there an integral association between the two; and if so, what is its theoretical basis? Do judgment prophecy and salvation prophecy stem from opposing, mutually exclusive traditions, or are they to be understood as paradoxically related elements in an organic apprehension of Yahweh's nature?

(5) What is the theoretical basis for a process of expanding reflection on Yahweh's purpose for the future? What understanding of revelation underlies this burgeoning eschatological elaboration? What is the relationship between traditional and speculative images of the future?

(6) How do Israel's understanding of time and history govern eschatological ideology, and what is the connection between historically oriented predictions and the spiritualizing transcendentalism of many late predictions?

(7) How are nationalism and particularism related to universalism within the eschatological tradition? What explains the concern for the gentiles' destiny? In what ways were blessings for the nations linked to blessings for Israel? What caused the cessation of universalistic ideology?

(8) What is apocalyptic in relationship to "normative" biblical eschatology? Are the roots of apocalyptic to be found there, or does this ideology derive from the wisdom tradition (von Rad)? Are there sociological factors in the shift to the apocalyptic mode (Plöger, Hanson)? How are the theocratic model of Yahweh's rule and the apocalyptic mode related to each other? Is the rise of apocalyptic related to the demise of prophetism, and if so, what is the relationship between the two?

In view of the ongoing debate about the suitability and precise bearing of the term "eschatology" in relationship to Old Testament theology, our practice will be to keep it in quotation marks up to that point in our discussion when we will actually be in a position to define it. Among recent efforts to show the present state of research on this question and each of the questions just mentioned, we may make particular mention of an interpretive volume of essays published in Horst Dietrich Preuss's book *Eschatologie im Alten Testament*,[5] which brings the discussion up to 1978. The single effort that has earned general approval in this field of study has apparently been Th. C. Vriezen's 1958 paper on "Prophecy and Eschatology," read to the Leiden Congress of Old Testament scholars.[6] Vriezen's peculiar service has been to rescue Old Testament eschatology from Gressmann and Mowinckel, who had claimed extraneous or nonprophetic sources for it.[7] Vriezen argued that biblical eschatology arose from authentic impulses in biblical religion: it was occasioned by the effort to reconcile the revelation of Yahweh's intention with historical Israel's failure to live up to that intention, coming to a head in the disasters of destruction and exile.[8] Scholars have generally been influenced as well by sections in major studies by Lindblom and von Rad devoted to the question of eschatology.[9] There have been a number of important monographs relating to eschatology, the most important of which have been E. Rohland's *Die Bedeutung der Erwählungstraditionen für die Eschatologie der alttestamentlichen Propheten* (Heidelberg, 1956), relating exodus traditions in Hosea, Zion traditions in Isaiah and Zephaniah, and David traditions in Amos, Isaiah, and Micah to the emergence of eschatology; also S. Herrmann's *Die prophetischen Heilserwartungen im Alten Testament* (BWANT 85; Stuttgart, 1965), making careful distinctions between the expectations of the prophets and those of the prophetic redactors; also H.-P. Müller's *Ursprünge und Strukturen alttestamentlicher Eschatologie* (BZAW 109; Berlin, 1969), proposing a systematic analysis that distinguishes between ultimate *(endgültig)* concepts of salvation that are noneschatological because they apply to present reality and those that are eschatological in a proper sense because they are futuristic, resolving an aporia between what ought to be and what actually is.[10]

What has often been missing in studies relating to biblical eschatology is a fresh and thorough exegesis of the textual material. We perceive the need, and grasp the opportunity, to carry previous study further by selecting for close scrutiny one group of "eschatological" passages that share a dominant and distinctive feature — that of redactional attachment to underlying material through the use of temporal transitions. To be sure, biblical theologians and exegetes have been aware of these transitions and have suggested that at least some of the formulas involved may have an inherently eschatological character.[11] But there has been no systematic effort to analyze passages with these formulas as a special group. Our expectation is that a thorough examination of them will produce insights that may have value for the whole body of predictive literature within the prophetic collection. Each of the questions that we have listed pertaining to eschatology in general will receive attention in our treatment of the various passages containing these formulas. The problems that affect the general study of eschatology pertain to them as well. This suggests that the solutions that we aspire to discover regarding this special group of passages may have relevance for the whole field of study.

The Intentionality of Redaction

Even though critical biblical commentaries normally discuss the evidence for redactional expansion within the books they are treating, it is not often that scholars have offered separate treatments of redactional ideology and technique. To be sure, some significant studies have recently been devoted to this question. We may mention such efforts as those of James A. Sanders in his book *Torah and Canon*,[12] and in related writings. It will be especially useful to our purpose at this juncture to take special note of several publications that we consider to be especially important in providing a background of understanding for the discussion of this topic.

1. Von Rad: The "reactualization" of tradition

Added editorially under the title "Postscript" to the English translation of von Rad's *Alttestamentliche Theologie*[13] is an essay published elsewhere by von Rad under the title "Offene Fragen im Umkreis einer Theologie des Alten Testaments."[14] This not only aptly summarizes this great scholar's methodology, but provides as well the essential rationale for an understanding of the ideology underlying the redactional process in general, and of the prophetic redaction in particular.

   This is how von Rad clarifies that the approach to "Old Testament theology" exemplified in the works of Köhler, Eichrodt, and now of himself, emancipates biblical studies both from historicism and from the absolutist claims of religion-phenomenology. As he sees it, a self-conscious confessional intentionality unifies the strongly heterogeneous content of Scripture through the pattern of type and antitype, along with the theme of promise and fulfillment. The ancient biblical traditions, though generally preserved in their primitive form, have received actualization in novel and seemingly arbitrary ways as the various writers and redactors found new ways of representing Israel's growing understanding of Yahweh's being and work. "It was . . . only when an old tradition was actualized that [Yahweh] was made a present reality to his chosen people" (414). Figures in the ancient narratives became relevant for ongoing history as they were treated as types of larger realities. As they came to stand in the biblical text, they invited new interpretations giving them a wider illumination because each new experience of Yahweh's power stood within the tension of promise and fulfillment. "If Old Testament theology allows itself to be guided by the ceaseless process of the handing on of tradition. . . , if it takes seriously this openness to the future which again and again directs the reader's eye to divine fulfillments . . . , then the material itself would bear it from one actualization to another, and in the end would pose the question of final fulfillment" (428).

Von Rad articulates an insight that has relevance for predictive material as well as for narrative, for redactors as well as for composers, and for every stage of literary development and level of theological reflection. The essential claim of his article is that the holy writings that claim to convey authoritative revelation do not regard the revelational experience as once for all — as finished and done with — but as a continuous and dynamic force reaching toward a fuller understanding of God's ways in the world.

This concept is basic to all of von Rad's exegetical and theological writings, and it must be an essential assumption for our study of prophetic redaction. It is especially evident in those redactional expansions that are introduced by temporal formulas — chiefly *bayyôm hahû'*, "in/on that day" — that the prophetic redactors wished to expand and reinterpret revelation once given, seeking now a broader, and also deeper, apprehension of the divine presence and purpose in Israel's historical experience.

2. Carroll: Socio-psychological forces in predictive reinterpretation

Robert Carroll's recent book *When Prophecy Failed, Cognitive Dissonance in the Prophetic Tradition of the Old Testament*[15] has enriched current discussions of prophetic tradition with respect to the problem of the fulfillment or nonfulfillment of prophetic prediction. Though the title and subtitle highlight the most innovative — and at the same time most controversial — facets of Carroll's book, its main contribution is in providing a wealth of insight into all the factors stimulating the development of interpretive tradition, of which "cognitive dissonance" is only one. Part I, by far the longest section, provides a stimulating discussion of the prophetic traditioning process as a whole; Part II explains the theory of cognitive dissonance in its general application and evaluates its impact upon the prophetic traditions in particular; Part III studies the reinterpretation of prophecy as coming to expression in Isaiah and Second Isaiah, then in Haggai and Zechariah; and it goes on to discuss particular problems such as prophetic conflict, the divine deception of a prophet, and the rise of apocalyptic — all important factors that modified the effect of cognitive dissonance upon prophetic prediction in Holy Scripture.

We look particularly at Parts I and II because they are the most suggestive for the question that we intend to take up. Carroll's intent in Part I is essentially to provide the general background against which to evaluate the effect of cognitive dissonance upon the Old Testament, but the main outcome of his discussion is to narrow the scope of its applicability. As Carroll states it, the "domain assumption" of biblical prophecy is that Israel's god Yahweh controls history; and that since history presents negative as well as positive experiences for Yahweh's people, prophecy is by necessity dialectic, ever balancing the No of doom with the Yes of salvation. Most predictions are for the near future and are general rather than particular in their focus. Human response is always a factor in shaping both the predictions and their eventual reinterpretations. Even those predictions that remain unfulfilled are influential in stimulating new predictions. The effect of partial fulfillment — particularly of oracles of doom — is to enhance the status of the prophet who has uttered them, while strengthening the expectation of the complete or eventual fulfillment of all predictions, including oracles of salvation.

One of the important purposes of the literary recording of prophecy, according to Carroll, was to broaden and extend the scope of its applicability. "The preservation and transmission of prophecy were not done for antiquarian reasons but because the prophets were seen as astute analysts of their time. . . . The critique of society retained . . . elements of warning for later communities but the interpolation of salvation oracles into the traditions turned them into words of hope for the hard-pressed communities of the postexilic age" (55). But because of the uncertainties of the future, the prophets who had been called to announce the future stood at risk of being proven either wrong or irrelevant.

Carroll goes further in Part I to discuss the intentionality of prophetic prediction. He points out that a given prophet's language may be quasi-magical, or that it may embody nonliteral language borrowed from the cult. Certainly prophetic speech makes wide use of symbolism, the general effect of which is the refraction of the message. Prophetic prediction may be either absolute or contingent; and it may be explicitly or implicitly conditioned on the repentance of the hearers. It may also be posited on a prior question, one known to the prophet and his immediate hearers though hidden from modern interpreters without careful investigation. Furthermore, a prophetic prediction may be performative. "The success or failure of various prophetic performatives would . . . be related to [the prophets'] ability to persuade the community to follow them rather than to a capacity for seeing the future before it came into being" (71). "There is a multiplicity of levels at which questions and answers were posed and answered in the traditions. There are the obvious surface ones that constitute part of the texts themselves and then the deeper questions to which the traditions were answers in the first place" (79).

Against the background of this very rich exposition, Carroll explains the theory of cognitive dissonance as outlined chiefly by Leon Festinger. This dissonance is seen most clearly in the impact of disconfirming facts upon the ideology of fadists such as the flat-earth theorists or the expectations of chiliasts. The ideology or the expectation in question must be explicit and it must be shared by the group, who are first distressed as they see their concept threatened or even refuted by the facts, then devote themselves with great zeal and energy to creating rationalizations of one sort or another. This confirms their group solidarity while attentuating the validity of their predictions. The opposite reaction, conversion, may possibly occur; but this requires a breaking away from the group.

After expounding this theory, Carroll endeavors to evaluate its applicability to prophetic prediction in sacred Scripture. He thinks he can discern elements of cognitive extension or reinterpretation in the hermeneutical systems of various groups of ideologists, particularly the theocratic model of Chronicles, the dualistic futurism of the apocalypticists, the realized messianism of the early Christians, and the nomism that came to general prominence in postexilic and postbiblical Judaism.

In numerous ways this valuable study will serve to inform and enrich the study on which we are about to embark, even though Carroll's exegetical treatments of particular passages in this volume and in his separate treatments of Jeremiah[16] have taken no special note of the phenomenon that we will be studying — that of predictive expansions introduced by temporal transitions. To be sure, his suggestions concerning ideological impulses toward the reinterpretation of prophecy must play an important role in our own treatment. Regarding the specific techniques of redaction, however, he has little directly to contribute. He tends to concede a very large role to redactors but has not entered into a detailed analysis of compositional or of redactional procedures.

A final critique of Carroll's work would be that the decisive role he claims for cognitive dissonance seems out of proportion to its general applicability. While we, on our part, would certainly wish to allow for a large measure of disappointment and even dismay at the apparent nonfulfillment of specific predictions, we would prefer to place emphasis on the impulse toward creative newness, based on a growing prophetic awareness of who Yahweh is and what he does. We must certainly not overlook this dynamic force in evaluating the process of revelational self-renewal. The theological element has always been decisive.

We shall discover in our projected study that the creative impulse was certainly one of the most important factors, if not the most important factor, towards the expansion of previous prophecy, particularly when this has occurred through the use of new materials introduced redactionally by the use of temporal formulas. In the Old Testament the future is often announced as something quite new while remaining congenial to past tradition. The prophetic redactors intended to remain faithful to former revelation even though they felt themselves free to expand the scope and refocus the intent of that revelation. Von Rad's emphasis on the repatterning of old tradition in terms of new levels of applicability will be proved to be fully justified in the results of our own study.

3. Fishbane: Mantic exegesis

Very much a confirmation of Carroll's treatment, though written independently of it, is the even more extensive discussion of nonfulfillment in Michael Fishbane's much-admired *Biblical Interpretation in Ancient Israel.*[17] The analysis of what Fishbane calls "mantic exegesis" occupies in fact a comparatively narrow space within his book (84 pages) in proportion to his treatment of "legal exegesis" (189 pages) and "aggadic exegesis" (162 pages), yet what he writes about it is often detailed and will require careful attention on the part of students of prophetic tradition. To some extent his treatment lacks focus because he does not distinguish carefully between classical prophetism and apocalyptic.

Fishbane offers a number of insightful distinctions with regard to the biblical documents that carry out the mantic exegesis that he describes. The one that is all important, and is applied consistently throughout the book, is that between the *traditum* (the text that has been inherited or received) and the *traditio* (the interpretation given it among those to whom the text had been committed).

Eventually, a given exegetical *traditio* may itself become part of the *traditum*. The *traditum* of dreams, visions, and omens (all involving visual phenomena) and that of predictive oracles (involving aural phenomena) is always prospective, but the exegetical *traditio* that interprets it is essentially retrospective. Cognitive dissonance arises when valued oracles have not been actualized, when their manifest meaning is cast in doubt or they appear to have been refuted by events. Thus the major hermeneutical problem is about the manifest rather than the esoteric meaning of prophetic prediction. Reinterpretive exegesis aims to prolong the validity of the old predictions while establishing their interpretive closure in a more precise determination of how they are to be activated.

Fishbane briefly notes the casual explications, classifications, or codes that do not actually transform the underlying material; these may be of several varieties: open-ended, homiletical, and cryptographic. His main concern, however, is for the techniques that do transform the underlying material.

The transformational types of exegesis involve the adaptation, application, or revision of old predictions. Certain predictions that seem vague and imprecise receive later specification; e.g., 2 Sam 7:11-15 within Kings, Chronicles, and Psalm 89. On the other hand, precise and particular predictions may be reused and revised. Fishbane discusses anachronistic interpolations, the deuteronomistic innovations, and the specific intimations of exile. He finds particularly illuminating a comparison of Jer 33:14-16 with 23:5-6 (parallel passages that will be extensively analyzed in our study); the very self-conscious reinterpretations found in Isa 16:13-14 and Ezek 38:17; and the diverse applications of the seventy years of exile motif, including Jer 25:9-12, Isa 23:15-17, 2 Chr 36:18-21,[18] Zech 1:12, and Dan 9:2, 24ff. He also discusses the technique of making a collage out of a number of ancient predictions, seen in Dan 9:4-20, Isa 10:20-23, and throughout Deutero- and Trito-Isaiah. He continues his discussion with an analysis of generic transformations, e.g., from blessings and curses to oracles or from oracles to nonoracles.

In a concluding section (pp. 506-24) Fishbane points up what he considers to be the most significant results of his study of mantic exegesis. He stresses that the problem of validity arises not at the point of issuance but in the eventual course of nonfulfillment. Initially, because oracles in themselves are clear, exoteric communications, the matter of dissonance lies in the background while the predictive element stands in the foreground. In those ideological circles where the predictive quality of the divine forecasts was a major concern and the verification of the original prediction was at stake, nonfulfillment was dealt with in a number of ways: either it was announced that the fulfillment had been temporarily delayed, it was revised, or it was simply consigned to the mystery of God's secret wisdom. In any event, the essential need was to impose rational order upon the apparent disorder of history. What was at risk was not only the validity of particular prophecies standing in the biblical text, but the very rational order of God's universe.

Fishbane next discusses the various forms in which reinterpretive exegesis of the mantic type comes to manifestation. There is no single *Sitz im Leben;* reinterpretive elements are generally made to conform to the form of the materials to which they are attached. As *ad hoc* expansions, they tend to be isolated and atomistic.

The sum of Fishbane's analysis is that mantic exegesis arises for a particular purpose, and at the same time opens up a new horizon of understanding. "Particularly characteristic of mantology is the acute consciousness of the present-future horizon of the divine communications received. On the one hand, predictive communications, given in the present, express an as yet unrealized *future* fulfilment; on the other hand, the proleptic disclosure of a future means that the recipients of these communications already anticipate this final closure in the *present.* . . . Where the expected closure does not occur as predicted, exegesis may emerge in order to prolong the original divine voice. . . . Waiting, revising, and decoding are . . . the dynamic components of the mental matrix of mantological exegesis" (521; F's emphasis).

It hardly seems adventitious that Fishbane has touched upon only a very few of the predictive passages that we will be taking under study here. He does not mention the phenomenon of special temporal formulas used as transitions, even though he might legitimately have taken some passages of this type as elements of rationalization to be placed alongside such blatantly revisionist passages as Isa 16:13-14 and Ezek 38:17.

Although the present study will be influenced by Fishbane's treatment with respect to the ideology that lies behind the effort to revise prophecy, it will not be possible for us to agree with Fishbane any more than with Carroll with respect to the claim that cognitive dissonance is the single most important factor in the production of revisions. As detailed as Fishbane's treatment may be at times, it deals with only a handful of relevant passages.

Furthermore, it is to be noted that apocalyptic plays a role in his analysis entirely out of proportion to its role within the Old Testament as a whole. Fishbane lumps together apocalyptic and prophetic prediction. This is a serious mistake because apocalyptic ideology is quite different from the ideology of classical prophecy.[19] Even while augmenting the transcendental factor, apocalyptic tends to be thoroughly rationalistic. That it gives a large place to the problem of nonfulfillment is to be understood in the nature of the case. Fishbane is certainly correct when he argues that this type of prediction is concerned not so much for the validity of particular prophecies as for the rational order of God's universe. But without careful special study it is simply unacceptable to apply this ideology in retrospect to the parallel phenomenon of classical prophetism.

Fishbane's cover-term "mantic" disguises this distinction, if not in intent, then in effect. Classical prophetism is far more intuitive than is apocalyptic, and it demands to be interpreted independently of it. It may be argued whether or not apocalyptic may be viewed as erratic or even errant; but there can be no question but that it is based on an entirely different ideology than that of classical prophetism.

In our final evaluation, we would insist that there are at most no more than a very few classical prophetic predictions that show clear evidence that "cognitive dissonance" was a dominant factor. We may recall the insight of Gerhard von Rad as a necessary corrective here: that the urge to say more, and still more, about Yahweh's work in the awaited future must have been a far more important force than the subjectivistic factors of disappointment and disillusionment that have been placed in the foreground by Carroll and Fishbane.

4. Clements: Literary composition and the theology of prophecy

Ronald Clements has recently published an article that is particularly relevant for the present study, "Prophecy as Literature: a Re-appraisal," appearing in a collection of special essays.[20] Clements anticipates some of the things we will have to say in the present study, though also without special attention to the phenomenon of temporal transitions. He begins by remarking that the writing down of previously given oral prophecy resulted immediately in its interpretation. Redactors and editors were already engaging in an interpretive process as they created connections and interrelationships between the materials they had received. Unavoidably they were extending and enriching the prophetic tradition. Thus the insights into the divine nature and purpose that the individual prophecies communicated were gradually given a larger degree of coherence and consistency. The redactors were concerned to show that diverse prophecies have come from the same Deity, and that these reveal a consistent and unchanging nature.

This was the rationale and function of the prophetic schools, whose existence is clearly indicated in books such as Isaiah, Ezekiel, and Amos, and may be inferred for most or all of the others.

Clements goes on to discuss one special effect of the eventual canonical shaping of the prophetic books: the tendency to place oracles of blessing and hope at the end of a given series of doom oracles. The message of each prophet is now placed in comparison with the messages of other prophets in order to draw a consistent picture of the divine being and purpose.

The editors of the prophetic collection are more concerned to show the larger prophetic context than to clarify the historical situation of the individual prophecies. The oracles of doom now have a didactic purpose — that of warning the present generation of further apostasies. At the same time, the oracles of blessing have the effect of confirming faith in a God whose purpose extends beyond present calamity and doom.

These editorial interests led on to the more elaborate secondary systems of interpretation, that of emerging Christian typology and eschatology, and that of Jewish midrash and mishnah. It was now believed that a given prophecy could refer to an event in the far distant future — that of an entirely new spiritual era. "Prophecies could be regarded as held in suspense, so that the time of their fulfillment could be regarded as not finally determined, or they could be regarded as susceptible of more than one fulfillment" (73). Oracular prophecy was thereby superseded by a theology of prophecy, the final effect of which was to provide an ideological basis for each of the above-mentioned derivative systems.

It would be difficult to find a more incisive explication of the ideology of prophetic redaction than what is offered here. Although Clements's essay does not enter into the question of the methods and techniques of that redaction, it will be extremely valuable to us as we turn directly to an examination of temporal formulas employed as a special redactional device. As we intend to show, the employment of these particular formulas at points of transition reveals much indeed about the ideology of those who first preserved and later extended the prophetic heritage.

The Study of Futuristic Transitions

No literary analysis goes far enough when it stops with isolating the original from successive layers of redaction. Nor does it go far enough when it traces the distinct original and secondary literary materials within the orbit of their individual tradition histories. The literary critic must go beyond the "what" and the "how" to explain the "why." He must ask, "Why were early materials expanded? What ideologies and intentionalities are reflected in the tendency toward expansion?" Broad elements of the answers to these questions have been suggested in the works of the previously mentioned scholars, but it is necessary to draw the circle tighter, to make the questions more precise.

An effective diachronic approach will reveal the biblical text as multi-dimensional, and will furthermore take seriously every compositional and redactional stage or level on its own terms. If this precludes a one-sided concentration on a presumptive original, it precludes also a one-sided concern for the "final," canonical product, for every single stage, from earliest to latest, must be brought into focus if the text is to become vibrant and alive in its organic fullness.

We need to view the redactional process comprehensively,[21] to study its techniques as clues to the peculiar ideologies of those involved in it, and to integrate this firmly into our understanding of literary structures and our reconstruction of tradition history.[22] It is important also to acknowledge that redactors did not work mechanically, but participated creatively in the dynamic growth of Scripture through the application of a number of special methods.

There are essentially four distinct ways in which a literary text may be modified following its initial composition: (1) by the rearrangement or revision of its verbal content; (2) by the internal insertion of additional words; (3) by the appendage of an attached supplement; or (4) by the loose juxtaposition of related material. Each of these methods has entered into the process by which redactors have expanded the prophetic corpus. Skill, insight, and care must be exercised in analyzing the method — and, by extension, the intention — of the redactor or redactors in question.

It is the third method, that of appendage through the use of temporal transitions, that will attract our special attention in the projected study. Appendage as we are defining it is quite different from simple addition by way of asyndetic attachment. Addition is asyndetic; appendage is syndetic.

Appendage requires a formal linking device of one sort or another. Such linkage may be fairly elaborate, as when it is constructed as the narrative framework for a collection of pregiven materials. One prominent form of framework composition involves the use of dating formulas, whose main purpose is to relate narrated events sequentially, often adding historical con-texting as an additional element of interpretation.[23] Less ambitious is the technique of linking secondary material to earlier elements through the use of formulaic transitions, which regularly stand at the head of the new material.

A very common type of formulaic transition involves a temporal word or phrase — the phenomenon that we are taking up in this special study. Temporal transitions may introduce events that are past or events that are future, joining them to other past or future events, either sequentially or synchronically. The object of the present study is specifically to analyze those temporal formulas that are futuristic, and more specifically those that appear within the corpus of prophetic prediction that has been preserved in the Old Testament. A particular concern will be to explain the development of those idealistic forms of futurism that are customarily referred to as "eschatological," in differentiation from the more proximate and pragmatic forms or prediction.

This search calls for a detailed analysis of all transitional temporal formulas within the Old Testament that refer to future time. The locutions that we have found to be important in this function are the following:

- *(wĕ)'attâ,* "(and/so) now"
- *'āz,* "then"
- *(wĕhāyâ) bayyôm hahû',* "(and it will happen) on/in that day"
- *bayyāmîm hahēm,* "in those days"
- *bā'ēt hahî',* "at that time"
- *hinnēh yāmîm bā'îm,* "behold, days are coming"
- *'aḥar* and *'aḥărê-kēn,* "afterward," "later"
- *bĕ'aḥărît hayyāmîm,* "in the sequel of days."[24]

We shall exclude from our study the occurrence of the above expressions (1) when they are used for past rather than future time, and (2) when they do not function specifically as transitions. At certain points other uses, such as identifying time when, will be brought into the discussion, but only for the purpose of comparison. Other use of expressions of time must carefully be kept separate from the transitional function.

A further distinction of considerable importance will be that between integral and introductory position. Certain of the above-mentioned transitional formulas appear either organically and integrally within compositional units or at the beginning of redactional supplements, attaching these as appendages to the underlying material. The latter function has been defined as the item of special concentration in the present study and will receive major attention; but we need to study the other function as well, both for structural and for ideological comparison.

It has not been well understood by biblical scholars that each of the formulas in question does in fact possess a distinctively different meaning and function. In the main, one looks in vain for helpful analysis of these formulas in the commentaries. They rarely discuss them when they occur, and when they do, they are inclined to dismiss them as egregious glosses.[25] So likewise the essays in literary criticism. It is true that a very few of the above expressions occasionally appear as (or in) literary glosses; but, as will be shown in what follows, this is far more rare than has been imagined.

One special study of the expression *bayyôm hahû'*, a 1936 monograph by the Norwegian scholar P. A. Munch, while helping to identify secondary versus original occurrences of this expression, has partially confused the problem by insisting that this familiar expression always means "then," and nothing more.[26] One asks what the distinction might be from *'āz,* also translated "then"; as will be shown, *'āz* and *bayyôm hahû'* are by no means synonymous. In my book *Yesterday, Today and Tomorrow,*[27] I have pointed out an especially crucial shortcoming in Munch's methodology, that of undertaking an analysis of futuristic *bayyôm hahû'* while neglecting to make a parallel investigation of its past usage. The fact is that this expression occurs far more often in past narration than in futuristic prediction. My book tried to correct Munch's oversight by first analyzing the past usage; it went on to analyze the cognate time-designatives *hayyôm* and *hayyôm hazzeh,* which refer to the present, along with *bayyôm hahu'* in reference to the past — all of which is essential as a preparation for the eventual study of the futuristic use of *bayyôm hahû'* and the range of related expressions. Apart from the specifically philological aspects of this investigation, this is important also for a sound biblical theology because the Old Testament's projection of the future may be understood only in the light of its interpretation of the past and present.

The conclusions of my book remain valid, but there is need for a fresh analysis of futuristic *bayyôm hahû'* within the context of a parallel investigation into the whole range of similarly functioning time expressions, particularly those that refer to the future, and especially those that refer to the future as foretold by the prophets.

It is necessary to resist the notion that temporal transitions are used casually, even interchangeably, in Scripture. In view of the cavalier methods and apparently casual attitude of many Bible translators, it is not surprising to see these expressions drop into obscurity in the translation process. They may be (1) rendered quite literally as the translator fails to discern any distinctive import in them (as often in KJV, RSV, NRSV, and NEB), (2) paraphrased with unlicensed abandon,[28] or (3) ignored altogether.

Scholars who do recognize the distinctive meanings of these expressions may nevertheless be quite arbitrary in dismissing them from the presumptive original text. But our intended investigation will show that these expressions are in fact almost always integral to the text. Careful scholarship is well advised not to arbitrarily set them aside; the fact that they do stand in the text is a challenge to ask why they are there.

Looking specifically for the intention of the various composers and redactors who have made use of these expressions, we may recognize a deliberate syndetic link to the underlying material. It does in fact make a difference when a redactor does not simply juxtapose new material to the old material. We would be rash indeed if we were to suppose that the use of these expressions is casual or even downright careless. If a temporal transition in a particular passage involves no special intentionality on the writer's part, why then, we must ask, did that writer not simply leave it out, which certainly would have been easier?

The extended analysis that follows in the successive chapters of this book leads eventually to the conclusion that many redactors, as well as composers, using these expressions for making transitions did indeed employ them with a special purpose, and they did this with important differences in mind. What precisely these distinctions were will be exhibited in a fresh analysis of each of the individual passages where the various expressions occur.

For the reason stated, it will be important to identify and explain integral usage in distinction from introductory usage.[29] Also, while observing how temporal transitions are made, it will be important to take note of the material contents or *topoi* that have been linked together by these distinct types of transitions.

Although individual items linked together by temporal transitions will be interpreted from within their specific historical and ideological contexts, we shall refrain from involvement in an extensive search for the putative "original" author — which would be precarious in any case because materials from a given prophet may actually have emerged from different periods of time in the context of different situations in the prophet's life; also because a prophet may in some cases have been his own redactor.

In the extended study that is projected it will be of little use simply to marshal figures and draw generalizations. Our serious endeavor to bring new light into the problems of eschatological ideology and redactional procedures must ask and attempt to answer a long list of questions. A great amount of detail must be analyzed and incrementally used for still further analysis.

Our study will be organized into three Parts, each of which will include separate chapters devoted to individual subjects or special areas of study, as follows:

Part I. The distribution and employment of futuristic transitions:

    Chap. 2: Integral transitions ʿattâ and ʾāz

    Chap. 3: Integral and introductory *(wĕhāyâ) bayyôm hahû'*

    Chap. 4: Integral and introductory *bayyāmîm hahēm(mâ), baʿēt hahî', hinnēh yāmîm bā'îm, 'aḥar/'aḥărê-kēn,* and *bĕ'aḥărît hayyāmîm/haššānîm*

Part II. Futuristic transitions in the growth of the prophetic books:

Chap. 5: Introduction

Chap. 6: Isaiah

Chap. 7: Jeremiah

Chap. 8: Ezekiel

Chap. 9: The preexilic minor prophets

Chap. 10: The postexilic minor prophets

III. Futuristic transitions in the traditioning process:

Chap. 11: Redactional levels

Chap. 12: Themes in the expansion of tradition

Chap. 13: The tradition of expanding revelation.

Since evidence from a large number of relevant passages will be addressed in this study, it will not be feasible in every case to provide a complete and final discussion of a given passage in a single place within this book. The discussion of important passages may have to be traced progressively from place to place as they are treated from one viewpoint and then from another. The reader may find it useful to consult the special index of passages treated. Any measure of inconvenience this may cause will be more than compensated in the larger fullness and widened perspective of an ongoing review as individual passages are subjected to continuing analysis in the light of incrementally expanding insights.

PART ONE

The Distribution and Employment of Futuristic Transitions

CHAPTER TWO

Time-designatives Occurring Mainly as Integral Transitions

We begin this chapter with a detailed examination of predictive passages that contain the temporal transitions mentioned above. One will see that none of these formulas is in itself a technical term for the so-called "eschaton," as does become the case in the writings of the Qumran sect.[1] Most of these expressions may refer to the past as well as the future, but we have selected for study only the passages where they refer to future or present/future events, as seen from various perspectives of time and circumstance.

Temporal *'attâ* and *wĕ'attâ,* "Now" and "So Now"

1. Introduction

a. Root meaning and extended meaning

Whatever its etymology and cognate affinities, we may agree with Ernst Jenni that the Hebrew word *'ēt* and its derivative *'attâ* never refer to time in the abstract but to time that is specified or narrowly qualified.[2] In fact, the purely temporal use of *'attâ* and *wĕ'attâ* must be seen as a development from, or extension of, a primary situational use in which the time element comprises only a special part of the general situation out of which an event emerges.[3]

It is important to distinguish occurrences of *'attâ* and *wĕ'attâ* used in a strictly temporal sense (cf. Ger. "jetzst") from the same expressions used in a logical or situational sense (cf. Ger. "nun," "nunmehr"), to which we may give the name "situation formula." Strictly temporal "now" and "so now" occur in an initial or other emphatic position when the present time is being

23

contrasted to another time. It is when these expressions function as transitions, integral or introductory, and not when they serve merely as time identifiers, that they provide important evidence for the redactional processes under study here.[4]

b. The situation formula

Situational (i.e., nontemporal) ʿattâ and wĕʿattâ are highly formulaic, and require careful identification to prevent temporal ʿattâ and wĕʿattâ from being confused with them. Examining their occurrences in narrative, liturgical, communicative, and didactic literature, one observes that they provide a logical or situational link between (1) a narrative, description, or definitive statement indicating the background or premise and (2) an appropriate and consequent command, appeal, petition, admonition, exhortation, rhetorical question, or definitive declaration based upon it. Used formulaically in this manner, situational ʿattâ and wĕʿattâ appear foremost in a clause or sentence that draws an appropriate action out of the situation that circumscribes it. The effect of this formula is more emphatic when other conjunctions are added: gam ʿattâ (1 Sam 12:16; Job 16:19); wĕgam ʿattâ (Joel 2:12), ʾak ʿattâ (Job 16:7), rĕʾēh ʿattâ (1 Chr 28:10). Another way is to repeat (wĕ)ʿattâ in a pattern of ascending emphasis (e.g., 1 Sam 23:21-22, 25:26-27, 26:19-20; 2 Sam 2:6-7). But a somewhat looser structure may make the situation formula even more emphatic, as when a speaker (or new speaker) is introduced without the formal premise element (Exod 6:1; 1 Sam 27:1; Isa 33:10; Ps 20:7 [E 6]; 2 Chr 29:31).

A more formal usage is seen in the use of these expressions as a stereotyped introduction to a unit of wisdom instruction, as in Prov 5:7, 7:24, 8:32 (cf. CD I:1, II:2.14). In direct communication between two persons there may be no special indication of the situation and wĕʿattâ leads directly to the matter of main concern. This may happen in the messenger speech, as at 1 Sam 25:7 and 2 Sam 2:7. It also occurs in the relatively sophisticated genre of the letter. Biblical examples are at 2 Kgs 5:6 and 10:2; extrabiblical examples appear in the Arad letters,[5] at Lachish,[6] and at Wadi Murabbaʿat (DJD II, 27:1) In these documents the prescript (name of addressee and/or blessing) leads directly to the situation formula and then the body of the letter.

What concerns us especially here is that situational ʿattâ, or, more commonly, wĕʿattâ, appears in a sizeable list of prophetic passages, including passages of prophetic discourse within narrative pericopes. The occurrences are as follows: Isa 28:22, 30:8, 33:10 tris, 43:1, 44:1; Jer 7:13, 18:11, 26:13, 27:6, 42:15, 22, 44:7; Ezek 7:8, 43:9; Hos 8:13; Joel 2:12; Hag 1:5, 2:4, 15; Mal 1:9, 2:1.

In every instance it may be seen that the situational transition introduces the special effect of a more general situation. In Isa 28:22 advice not to scoff proceeds from an awareness of Yahweh's decree. In Isa 30:8 the prophet is commanded to write the preceding woe-oracle (vv 9ff.) in light of the pro-Egyptian party's reputation for rebellious perversity.[7] In Isa 33:10 *(tris)* Yahweh emphatically announces his imminent rising to help, posited on Israel's desolation. In Isa 43:1 and 44:1 the promise of the divine presence is expressly affirmed within the situation of wrath.

In Jer 7:13 a threat to the Jerusalem temple is posited on the visible wreckage of the former shrine at Shiloh.[8] In Jer 18:11 a call to repentance proceeds from an awareness of the respective effects of repentance and of nonrepentance. In Jer 26:13 a call to repentance proceeds from Jeremiah's assertion of his divine appointment. In Jer 27:6 the appointment of Nebuchadrezzar devolves from the fact of Yahweh's supremacy over men and animals.[9] In Jer 42:15, 22 death in Egypt is posited on the foregoing warning of the effects of disobedience. In Jer 44:7 an impassioned complaint arises from the waste and desolation that is to be seen *bayyôm hazzeh,* "at this very day" (time identifier).

Ezek 7:8 has situational *'attâ* announcing wrath *miqqārôb,* "soon," as a consequence of an "end" already here (cf. temporal *'attâ* in v 3; see below). In Ezek 43:9 the complete banishment of idolatry is posited on awareness of the continuing punishment for it.

In Hos 8:13 Yahweh's remembrance to punish Ephraim proceeds from her persistence in cultic sin. In Joel 2:12 a command to repent stands within the context of the awesome day of Yahweh described in vv 1-11.[10] In Hag 1:5 and 2:15 *wě'attâ* introduces a call to consider the effects of the people's reluctance to rebuild the temple, together with their symbolic uncleanness. In Hag 2:4 a summons to courageous rebuilding arises within the situation of the former temple's ruin. In Mal 1:9 the hypothetical offering of an unworthy offering to Yahweh is set in contrast to the hypothetical offering of a similar gift to the governor. In Mal 2:1, finally, a summons to a new Levitical covenant is based on the foregoing curse upon priestly venality.[11]

c. Excluded temporal use

In addition to *'attâ* and *wě'attâ* when used specifically as a situation formula, we set aside from consideration nonformulaic temporal uses of *'attâ* and *wě'attâ;* that is, those that do no more than identify present time ("now," "and now"). Within the prophetic literature, those are found at Isa 37:26, 43:19, 48:7, 49:19; Jer 27:16; Hos 4:16, 5:3, 8:8, 10, 10:2-3; Mic 5:3 [E 4], 7:4, 10; Zech 9:8; and Mal 3:15.

The occurrence at Jer 32:36, a non-Septuaginal gloss, is omitted from
our consideration because the temporal transition, *wĕʿattâ lākēn,* establishes
an erroneous connection between an already complete judgment speech in
32:27-35 and the standard introduction to a new speech in 32:37-41.

2. Temporal transitions

Each occurrence of *(wĕ)ʿattâ* as a purely temporal transition requires analysis.
As will be seen, the transition formula occurs solely in integral position within
the pericope to which it belongs.

1 Sam 2:30. In an oracle spoken to Eli by a man of God, a historical
review (vv 27-28) and a complaint (v 29) lead to the nullifying of Yahweh's
previous declaration of benign intent. This is secured by the oracle formula,
nĕʾum YHWH (otherwise called the "prophetic utterance formula") in favor
of a new divine declaration, introduced by *wĕʿattâ* and a second oracle formula
(v 30) concerning Yahweh's present intention based upon the Elides' con-
temptuous attitude. All this is preparation for further announcements and
predictions (vv 31-36) for punishing the Elides and establishing a *kōhēn
neʾĕmān,* "faithful priest(hood)." For further details see below in our treatment
of the *hinnēh yāmîm bāʾîm* formula in v 31.[12]

1 Sam 15:1. Wĕʿattâ and a summons to hear Yahweh's word, which
follows in vv 2-3, provide a temporal sequence between the event of Samuel
anointing Saul, posited upon Samuel's transcendental authority, and his communication of a special summons to holy-war action laid on Saul.[13]

2 Sam 7:8 par 1 Chr 17:7. Wĕʿattâ and a command to speak provide a
temporal transition from an extended rhetorical question concerning the absence of previous commands for the building of a shrine (vv 5-7) and an
extended announcement concerning a new and special divine plan for David's
"house" (vv 8-16).[14]

2 Sam 12:10. Structurally similar to 1 Sam 2:27-36, Nathan's oracle to
David in 2 Sam 10:7-12 has first an historical review (vv 7-8), then a complaint
about David's murder of Uriah (v 9), and finally, introduced by *wĕʿattâ,* a
statement of the situation that now pertains (v 10); an announcement of
David's punishment, introduced by the messenger formula, follows in vv
11-12.

Isa 16:14. A section of oracles against Moab in Isaiah 15–16 concludes
with the redactional notation of 16:13-14, indicating that the foregoing declaration comprised the word that Yahweh spoke concerning Moab *mēʾāz,* "in
the past." Apparently because such prophecy has not yet been fulfilled, the
prophetic redactor writes a temporal *wĕʿattâ* followed by the statement that
Yahweh has also said a new word for the present standing in contrast to "back

then" *(wĕʿattâ);* it pertains to a fulfillment that is to follow "within three years," i.e., the transitory "years of a hireling."[15]

Isa 48:16. In a summons to assembly, vv 14-16, in which Yahweh appears as the initial speaker, calling attention to his sovereign intentionality *mērōʾš,* "from the beginning," parallel to *mēʾēt hĕyôtāh,* "from when it came into existence," a prophetic spokesman announces the sending of the divine spirit upon himself in the immediate future *(wĕʿattâ,* "but now, at this time"), contrasting this with the past situation as just described.

Jer 4:12. From among various possible interpretations of Jer 4:1ff., it seems best to view vv 13-17, concluding with the oracle formula *nĕʾum YHWH,* as an original continuation from vv 5-8. Vv 9-10, beginning with *wĕhāyâ bayyôm hahûʾ* and the oracle formula, has been introduced by an early redactor (see below in Chapter Three on *bayyôm hahûʾ),* while a second redactor has appended 4:11-12, intended as epexegesis to vv 9-10 (note the repeated phrase "to this people and Jerusalem"). Although it seems evident that the grim word about "a hot wind" is to be spoken at a proximately future date (see below in the section on *bayyāmîm hahēm),* the time word *ʿattâ* draws attention back to the present moment, in which a speaker indicated by the emphatic *gam ʾănî,* "as for me," is speaking (impf. of *dbr;* contrast the impf. of *ʾmr,* v 11.[16]

Jer 14:10. Secondarily attached,[17] a short Yahweh-speech radically modifies the foregoing liturgical lament (vv 2-9) in a partial quotation from Hos 8:13; as in that passage, *ʿattâ* shifts from a series of perfect verbs, defining the present situation of guilt and rejection, to an announcement, with a verb in the imperfect, of the people's juridical state as they are, and will be, confronted with Yahweh's judgment.[18]

Ezek 7:3. The day of Yahweh poem of vv 2-4 makes the startling announcement that Israel's judgment has already come; temporal *ʿattâ* emphatically points to the present moment as the beginning of the outpouring of Yahweh's wrath.[19]

Ezek 19:13. Vv 10-14, secondary to the *qinah* over the princes of Judah in vv 1-9, constitute a dirge or mock lament (= taunt) with a "then"/"now" pattern similar to that of 26:17-18, 27:3-9, 26-35, 28:12-19.[20] *Wĕʿattâ* introduces the resulting desolation, in temporal sequence from the foregoing plucking up, casting down, drying out, and burning up of the strong stem (= ruler) that sprouts from a fruitful mother.[21]

Ezek 26:18, 27:34 LXX. In a "then"/"now" sequence, *ʿattâ* in 26:18 leads to mention of a trembling on the part of *hāʾiyyîn* (the "isles" or "seacoast") that is to result from Tyre's imminent vanishing, v 17.[22] In a similar dirge against Tyre found in 27:1-9, 25b-36, *ʿattâ* is read by the LXX in place of MT's meaningless *ʿēt,* creating a "then"/"now" sequence from Tyre's former vaunting glory to its eventual wreck at sea.

Ezek 39:25. In the redactional summary to Ezekiel's original book, vv 23-29,[23] the first two verses summarize Yahweh's true purpose in allowing the exile to occur, while *laken* with the herald formula, followed by ʿ*attâ*, introduces Yahweh's new purpose for those who are to return, in temporal sequence from their present desolation, vv 25ff.[24]

Hos 2:12 (E 10). Wěʿattâ introduces a climactic divine act of judgment, that of uncovering the unfaithful wife's lewdness in the sight of the very paramours whom she was unable to find in her desperate search according to v 9 (E 7); in the author's intent the temporal transition marks an essential sequence from a provisional to an ultimate form of divine chastisement.

Hos 5:7. V 7a summarizes the standing charge against Ephraim/Israel (identified as contemporaneous in v 3 with nontransitional *wěʿattâ*) while ʿ*attâ*, foremost in v 7b, introduces the menacing penalty that is to appear sequentially — as well as consequentially — from it.[25]

Hos 7:2. Temporal ʿ*attâ* at the beginning of v 2b brings into sequence Yahweh's frustrated intent to be kind to Israel, stated in the circumstantial clauses at the end of 6:11 and the beginning of 7:1, and the discovery of Israel's treacherous deeds.

Hos 13:2. The time of Ephraim's former exaltation and authority, leading to its death for baalistic apostasy (v 1), is put in temporal contrast to the increase of guilty behavior introduced by nontransitional *wěʿattâ* at the beginning of v 1.

Amos 6:7. Lākēn introduces the announcement of punishment for the guilty persons denounced in the participial clauses of vv 1, 4-6, while foremost ʿ*attâ*, together with the prepositional phrase *běrōʾš gōlîm*, "at the head of the exiles," draws a close temporal connection between this sinning and the threatened banishment.

Amos 7:16. This passage is similar to 1 Sam 15:1 in that Amos's repartee in v 14 serves like the declaration that Yahweh had sent Samuel, who was to anoint Saul in order to establish his prophetic authority for communicating revelation. It would be erroneous to identify *wěʿattâ* in either of these passages as primarily situational. As this time-word in the Samuel passage places the anointing and the command to "hear" (that is, obey) the sound of Yahweh's words in temporal sequence with each other, v 15 in the Amos passage affirms a foregoing election and a divine command to prophesy as prior in sequence to Amos's demand that Amaziah now listen to his word of denunciation.

Mic 4:9, 10, 11, 14 (E 5:1). The fourfold appearance of foremost temporal ʿ*attâ* in Mic 4:8–5:3 (E 4) (*wěʿattâ*, v 11, *kî* ʿ*attâ*, v 10) makes compositional unity for the entire section likely. In each place the temporal transition introduces one or another kind of calamity coming upon the "daughter of Zion": death of a king/counselor, v 9; exile to Babylon, v 10; the assembly of hostile nations, v 11; Jerusalem put under siege, v 14. Out of each calamity triumph emerges (4:10c, 12-13), leading to the climactic promise of a ruler from Bethlehem (5:1 [E 2]), whose greatness to the ends of the earth is for a "now" that is already present in the writer's expectation (if. 5:3 [E 4]). On the probability that the reference to Babylon in v 10 reflects the tradition of 2 Kgs 20:12-19 par Isa 39:1-8, it is more reasonable to ascribe this entire pericope to the prophet Micah than to place it in the late seventh century or in the postexilic period.[26]

Nah 1:13. An oracular promise, vv 12-13, contrasts the present destitution with the coming end of affliction and the bursting of bonds, between which events *wĕʿattâ* stands as a temporal transition.

Zech 8:11. Here time relationships are structural to the whole: *kĕyāmîm hārîʾšōnîm* in v 11 points to the negated remote past; *lipnê hayyāmîm hahēm* in v 10 defines the difficult recent past; *bayyāmîm hāʾēlleh* in v 9, together with *bĕyôm yuśśad bêt YHWH,* points to the problematic present; *wĕʿattâ* in v 11 introduces an imminent future of peace and prosperity, in contrast both to past and present.

Dan 10:20. The "one having the appearance of a man" (v 10), engaging in dialogue with Daniel, concludes his speech with a leading question; a transitional *wĕʿattâ* then introduces an announcement of intentionality for a proximate future (fighting the prince of Persia) preparing the way for a more remote future (causing the prince of Greece to come). The present of Michael's speaking and the future events of the angel's announcement disguise an actual event within the writer's past, a *vaticinium ex eventu.*[27]

3. Conclusions

A number of observations may be made concerning our analysis of *ʿattâ* and *wĕʿattâ* when used as temporal transitions. First of all, it is important to take note that within prophetic speech all occurrences prove to be integral to the pericopes within which they are found. An instance of integral occurrence within secondary literary material is that of *ʿattâ* in the editorial conclusion to Ezekiel's original book at 39:23-29, where it bridges the gap from a past judgment (continuing its effects into the present) to a coming future blessing grounded in the fact that exiled Israel has now fully paid for her sins and awaits therefore a glorious restitution. Except in this single passage, temporal *ʿattâ* always belongs to original materials.

a. Private oracles

It is noteworthy that five (six, counting a literary parallel) of the passages where these temporal transitions are found contain private oracles. In 1 Sam 2:30 this is addressed to Eli; in 1 Sam 15:1 it is addressed to Saul; in 2 Sam 7:8 par 1 Chr 17:7 it is addressed to David; in 2 Sam 12:10 it is again addressed to David; and in Amos 7:16 it is directed to the priest Amaziah. Only in 2 Sam 7:8 par 1 Chr 17:7 is the oracle a word of blessing, and even here it comes within the context of an implied rebuke laid upon the addressee. Elsewhere the word is an announcement of judgment based on the addressee's dereliction of divine appointment (2 Sam 12:10), on a new revelation superseding a previous revelation (1 Sam 2:30), or on the speaker's special authority, established by previous appointment as Yahweh's spokesman (1 Sam 15:1; Amos 7:16). The message is brought in every instance to an institutional representative, either a king (Saul, David) or a priest (Eli, Amaziah).[28]

b. Collective judgment oracles

The remaining passages with temporal *ʿattâ* and *wĕʿattâ* belong to the prophetic canon and are addressed either to Israel (also Judah as Israel or Jerusalem representing Israel/Judah)[29] or to the foreign nations. In view of the fact that prophecies of judgment have the greater number of these transitions, it is instructive to note their positioning with relation to the formal elements belonging to this genre, namely, accusation and announcement (older terminology: invective and threat). The possibilities are as follows:

(1) The transition is integral to the accusation, Hos 13:2;
(2) The transition introduces an announcement without a foregoing accusation, Isa 16:14; Jer 4:12;
(3) The transition introduces the announcement following an accusation, Ezek 26:18, 27:34 LXX ("then"/"now" taunt pattern); Hos 5:7, 7:2;
(4) The transition is integral to the announcement following an accusation, Jer 14:10; Ezek 7:3; Hos 2:12 (E 10); Mic 4:9, 10, 11, 14 (E 5:1).

From this it can be seen that temporal *(wĕ)ʿattâ* most often appears inside either the accusation or the announcement. Thus it is a minority of passages in which it marks the cause-and-effect transition from Israel's sin to its punishment, making it virtually equivalent in function to that of the previously identified situation formula. The main move within the majority of judgment passages is from one sin to another, worse sin ([1] above) or from one act of judgment to another that is even worse ([4] above). This pattern may be compared with the pattern found with situation formulas as they appear within oracles of judgment, where situational *(wĕ)'attâ* may introduce the announcement following an accusation (Jer 18:11, 27:6, 42:15, 22; Hos 8:13) or may be integral to the announcement (Isa 28:22, 30:8, 43:1, 44:1).

c. Patterns of occurrence

Within the prophetic collection, temporal *'attâ* and *wĕ'attâ* are fairly widely distributed, appearing in all books except Joel, Obadiah, Jonah, Habakkuk, Zephaniah, and Malachi. This may be compared with the list of situational passages, which are found in all books except Obadiah, Jonah, Micah, Nahum, Habakkuk, Zephaniah, and Zechariah. Isaiah prefers the situational use of *(wĕ)'attâ* to the temporal (five of seven passages), as does Jeremiah (six of eight occurrences). But Ezekiel prefers the temporal use to the situational (five of seven occurrences), as do Hosea (four of five occurrences), Micah (all), Nahum (one passage), and Zechariah (one passage). In the remaining prophetic books only situational *(wĕ)'attâ* is found (Joel once, Amos twice, Haggai and Malachi, thrice each).

d. Temporal relationships in collective judgment passages

Within the collective judgment passages, we discover five distinct patterns for sequencing events by use of temporal *(wĕ)'attâ:*

(1) The move is between past events disguised as present and future *(vaticinium ex eventu):*

Dan 10:20b, from Michael's query regarding Daniel's comprehension to the beginning of his fighting with the kings of Persia and Greece.

(2) The move is from the past into the present:

Isa 48:16b, from revelation "from the beginning" and "from the time it came to be" (v 15) to new revelation in the present;

Ezek 19:13, from the stem's withering (v 12) to its transplantation to dry soil;

Ezek 26:18, 27:34 LXX, from Tyre's glory and pride to its wreck at sea;

Hos 13:2, from Ephraim's former guilt and punishment (v 1) to its present continuing sinfulness.

(3) The move is from past situations having consequences reaching into the present, to an imminently ensuing future:

Jer 14:10b, from the people's waywardness and divine rejection (v 10a) to Yahweh's remembering to punish their sins;

Ezek 7:3, from the arrival of the predicted "end" (v 2) to the outpouring of Yahweh's wrath;

Ezek 39:25, from Israel's former exile (vv 23-24) to its imminent restoration and return;

Hos 2:12 (E 10), from the warning and shaming deprivation of Gomer (vv 8-11 [E 6-9]) to her ultimate ruin;

Hos 5:7b, from Israel's treacherous wantonness (v 7a) to famine and death;

Hos 7:2b, from the sin against revelation (v 2a) to disclosure in judgment;

Amos 6:7, from idle luxury (vv 4-6) to exile;

Nah 1:13, from the cessation of Israel's affliction (v 12) to the breaking of its bonds;

Zech 8:11, from poverty and turmoil (v 10) to peace and restoration.

(4) The move is to one past/present calamity after another:

Mic 4:9–5:3 (E 4), from Zion's loss of a king, exile, hostile confrontation, and siege to its ultimate deliverance.

(5) The move is from a generalized past/present to a moderately remote future (specified in terms of duration):

Isa 16:14, from a judgment on Moab announced but not fully realized (v 12) to its loss of glory and population.

(6) The move is in a reverse direction, viz., from a moderately remote future (introduced by $bā\ \!^\circ\!ēt\ hahî^\circ$) back to the prophet's present:

Jer 4:12b, from a destroying wind (vv 11-12a) to Yahweh's declaration of contemporary judgment.

It can readily be seen that the second category of movement is the normal one; the other patterns are unusual and eccentric. The third type of movement is peculiar to Micah, while the fourth and fifth, involving a logical sophistication beyond the naive and experiential pattern of the majority of passages, are seen only in redactional epexegesis. The expectation is for specific and concrete events except where symbolical elements are introduced in their place.

e. Formulas of revelational authority

Wherever the formula *nĕ°um YHWH* or its equivalent strengthens the transition formula, it marks a change that is particularly momentous. With temporal *(wĕ)°attâ* this occurs in three of the private oracles on our list (1 Sam 2:30, *wĕ°attâ nĕ°um YHWH;* 1 Sam 15:1, *wĕ°attâ šĕma° lĕqôl dibrê YHWH;* Amos 7:16, *wĕ°attâ šĕma° dĕbar-YHWH*); and in redactional Isa 16:14 *(wĕ°attâ dibber YHWH lē°mōr . . .).* We have seen that in 1 Sam 2:30 a new revelation

supersedes an older one and that both in 1 Sam 15:1 and in Amos 7:16 there
is a foregoing declaration of special appointment to the prophetic office; thus
these formulas of revelational authorization are appropriately employed. In
Isa 16:14 older revelation concerning Moab is being superseded (or supplemented) by a new revelation. With temporal *(wĕ)ʿattâ* as well as with *wĕʿattâ*
as a situation formula,[30] this particular form of strengthening is the exception
rather than the rule. This should be compared with the virtually stereotyped
appearance of the oracle formula *nĕʾum YHWH,* which often follows the
temporal formulas *bayyôm hahûʾ, bayyāmîm hahēm(mâ), bāʿēt hahîʾ, hinnēh
yāmîm bāʾîm,* and *ʾaḥărê-kēn* (see the special sections on these formulas
below).

Temporal *ʾāz,* "Then"

1. Introduction

Within prophetic discourse the time-word *ʾāz* usually indicates the transition
from a proximate future to one more remote, but it can also mark the logical
consequence in a purely cause-and-effect relationship. Though we are directly
concerned only with futuristic occurrences of *ʾāz* within the prophetic collection, a clear grasp of its futuristic function depends upon a survey of its use
in reference to the past as well. It proves in fact to be far more frequent when
referring to the past than to the future.

a. Past usage

For balance, we must take a brief glance at *ʾāz* when used as a past transition.
Transitional *ʾāz* may refer to the past in two special kinds of biblical literature:
narrative and liturgical. It creates a past synchronism first of all when it inserts
into an ongoing narrative an archaeological note or explanatory remark. This
occurs in Gen 4:26, 12:6, 13:7; Exod 4:26; Num 21:17; Deut 4:41; Josh 8:30;
2 Sam 21:17, 21:18 par 1 Chr 20:4; 2 Sam 23:14 par 1 Chr 11:16 *bis;* 1 Kgs
8:12 par 2 Chr 6:1; 1 Kgs 9:24, 11:7, 16:21; 2 Kgs 8:22, 15:16; Jer 32:2;
1 Chr 16:7. It puts separate episodes into narrative sequence in Exod 15:1;
Josh 10:33, 22:1, 31; Judg 8:3, 13:21; 1 Kgs 8:1 par 2 Chr 5:2; 1 Kgs 9:11,
22:50 [E 49]; 2 Kgs 12:18, 13:19, 14:8, 16:5; 1 Chr 15:2; 2 Chr 8:12, 17,
24:17.[31] In liturgical or literary materials referring to past events, transitional
ʾāz may indicate either a synchronism or a sequence between past events: Gen
49:4; Exod 15:15; Judg 5:8, 11, 13, 19, 22; Ps 40:8 [E 7], 89:20 [E 19], 119:92,

126:2; Job 28:27.[32] We list these occurrences not only for the identification of excluded passages, but to provide a paradigm for occurrences of *'āz* as a futuristic temporal transition.

b. Nonpredictive futuristic usage

In addition to past usage, we must carefully set aside occurrences of *'āz* that are only apparently predictive. Futuristic *'āz* creates transitions in other than prophetic discourse. It may create a sequence within narrative discourse, as at Gen 24:41; 1 Sam 6:3; 2 Sam 2:27, 5:24,[33] 19:7 [E 6]; and 2 Kgs 5:3. It creates a liturgical sequence in Ps 2:5, 19:14 [E 13], 51:21 [E 19], 56:10 [E 9], 69:5 [E 4], 96:12 par 1 Chr 16:33; Psa 119:6. It also creates a formal sequence of "then"/"now," or of "if"/"then" in parenetical passages: Lev 26:34 *bis*, 41 *bis*; Deut 29:19 [E 20]; Josh 1:8; 1 Kgs 3:16; 1 Chr 22:13; also in wisdom instruction at Prov 2:5, 9, 3:23. This is similar to its function when it introduces the apodosis of a past or future hypothetical condition, as in Job 3:13b, 9:31, 13:20, 22:26, 33:16; this is a peculiar Joban construction similar to *kî 'attâ* when introducing an apodosis (Job 3:13a, 6:3, 7:21, 8:6, 13:19, 14:16). Finally, it creates a cultic future sequence (or consequence) in cult-legislative passages at Exod 12:44, 48, and Josh 20:6.

Comparison with the use of transitional *'āz* in these categories can aid our understanding of futuristic transitional usage within prophetic discourse, to which we now direct our attention.

2. Integral transitions[34]

Isa 33:23. Within what is probably late anti-Egyptian epexegesis (vv 21aβb, 23) to a postexilic liturgy (see above on the threefold *'attâ* in v 10), a taunt similar to that of Ezek 32:12-15 (see below on v 14) leads sequentially to the effect *('āz)* of Egypt's haplessness, viz., its vulnerability to being plundered even by the lame.[35]

Isa 35:5, 6. In a panorama of blessing inspired by the poems of Second Isaiah, a summons for the weak and fearful to witness God's imminent coming (vv 3-4) leads via a double *'āz* to a declaration that handicapped persons (the blind, deaf, lame, dumb) will do that which is not normally expected of them, viz., see, hear, leap, and sing. These marvelous actions are to follow sequentially from the predicted event of God's coming.

Isa 41:1. The coastlands/peoples who see and hear of Yahweh's deed mentioned in vv 2-4a are here summoned to listen, renew strength, and approach; and after that *('āz)* they are to speak in judgment.[36]

Isa 58:8, 9. A rhetorical question (vv 6-7) defines the humanitarian behavior that should rightfully accompany true spiritual fasting, the result of which *('āz)* will be light, healing, righteousness, glory (v 8), and Yahweh's accessibility in prayer (v 9). This declaration is conditional and at the same time parenetical, defining a future condition that would result from a hypothetical change in behavior on Israel's part.

Isa 58:14. The parenesis of vv 13-14 is in the form of a hypothetical statement in v 13, in which the *'im*-clauses define true sabbath observance, then by two clauses, the first of which is introduced by *'āz,* describing the effects of its performance, first for Israel and then for Yahweh; this is finally guaranteed by a grounding clause in the form of a special conclusion formula, *kî pî YHWH dibber,* "for the mouth of Yahweh has spoken."[37]

Isa 60:5. A command to witness the return of the exiles in v 4 leads to the new and consequent event, introduced by *'āz,* of Israel's joyous witnessing of abundant tribute.

Jer 22:22. Kî *'āz* introduces the effect of an exile predicted for Lebanon in the first part of this verse; consequence as well as sequence is implied.

Jer 31:13. In this late passage, the dancing and merriment that *'āz* introduces at v 13 follows in sequence from, and as a consequence of, the imminent joys predicted in v 12, which themselves proceed from an already experienced ransoming and redemption, v 11.

Ezek 32:14. *'āz* is distinctly temporal in introducing the prospect of purification and abundance for the "waters of Egypt." This appears as an exception to and exemption from the general devastation of all living things predicted in vv 12-13. It may reflect a change of mood similar to that of Ezek 29:13-14. The drastic shift from a judgment to a salvation theme, in what is to come later than the already future judgment of Egypt, requires the recognition formula, "then they shall know that I am Yahweh," and a special editorial interpretation strengthened by the oracle formula (v 16).[38]

Mic 3:4. *'āz* introduces what is in effect an announcement of judgment on certain oppressors mentioned in the third-personal plural, who have to be the same as those described in the accusation of vv 2-3, also in the third-personal plural, following the foregoing second-personal summons to hear and reprove. Following a series of asseverative perfects, v 4 proceeds with three futuristic imperfects followed by a "because" *(ka'ăšer)* clause with the perfect.[39] Most commentators want to take the clause with *'āz* as a protasis to an apodosis in the next two verbal clauses, but there is no certain evidence that *'āz* ever occurs as a transition to the protasis in a conditional clause or sentence. The entire verse may better be seen in temporal sequence from vv 2-3, indicating an imminent future developing directly out of the present. *Bā'ēt hahî'* has been glossed by a later scribe into the text to assure this futuristic bearing.

Hab 1:11. '*āz* does not provide a sequence to a future event, but rather draws a before-and-after sequence in relation to the events set forth in vv 9-10. The move is from a description of what has been and is presently customary on the part of the threatening Chaldeans, to a statement of the effect of their hostile behavior.[40]

Zeph 3:11. In a second redactional addition to Zephaniah's original judgment oracle against Jerusalem, vv 1-8, a salvation saying for what is presumably the same city (second personal feminine) first states the negative condition of non-shaming, followed by a "because" clause; an asseverative or adversative *kî* with *kî* '*āz* next introduces an act of Yahweh that is intended as sequential (removing the exultant and haughty; cf. vv 3-4) from this negative condition.

3. Introductory transition

Zeph 3:9. Here *kî* '*āz* introduces the earliest redactional addition to Zeph 3:1-8. It is likely that the styling with asseverative or adversative *kî* is the mark of the same redactor as in v 11, but the order of composition remains unclear. In any event, '*āz* clearly points to a future event that is subsequent to the act of divine judgment predicted in the material to which it is attached.

4. Conclusions

a. Patterns of occurrence

Within the prophetic canon, futuristic transitions with '*āz* appear only in Isaiah (8x), Jeremiah (2x), Ezekiel (1x), Micah (1x), Habakkuk (1x), and Zephaniah (2x). Jer 22:22, Mic 3:4, and Hab 1:11 may claim to belong to the original prophet in question, hence these occurrences should be dated to the preexilic or early exilic periods. Isa 41:1 and Jer 31:13, on the contrary, are late exilic, while Isa 35:6, 7, 58:8, 9, 14, 60:5, Zeph 3:9, 11 are all early postexilic. From very late in the postexilic period come the occurrences referring to Achaemenid Egypt at Isa 33:23 and Ezek 32:14.

b. Temporal relationships

There are three patterns of sequencing with the transitional use of futuristic '*āz*:

(1) The move is from the present to a proximate future:

Mic 3:4, from outrageous injustice (vv 1-3) to the withdrawal of revelation;

Hab 1:11, from the Chaldeans' derision of enemy cities (vv 6-10) to their irrepressible conquest of other nations, including Judah.

(2) The move is from the proximate future to a more remote future:

Isa 33:23, from Egypt's haplessness (v 22) to its utter defenselessness;

Isa 35:6-7, from Israel's restrengthening and recompense (vv 3-4) to the healing of the blind, the deaf, the lame, and the dumb;

Isa 41:1b, from the "coastlands'" preparation (v 1a) to their participation in a council of judgment;

Isa 60:5, from the return of sons and daughters (v 22a) to a joyful witnessing;

Jer 22:22b, from Lebanon's exile (v 22a) to its shameful confounding;

Jer 31:13, from return and restoration (vv 10-12) to universal rejoicing;

Ezek 32:14, from Egypt's desolation (v 13) to a purification of Egypt's waters;

Zeph 3:9, from the day of final wrath on Jerusalem (v 8) to universal purification and worship;

Zeph 3:11, from the removal of shame on the day of restoration (vv 9-10) to a removal of the proud.

(3) The move is hypothetical, from an "if" to a "then":

Isa 58:8-9, from social righteousness among those who fast (vv 6-7) to the restoration of light, healing, righteousness, and glory (v 8), together with Yahweh's renewed accessibility (v 9);

Isa 58:14, from a reverent sabbath-keeping (v 13) to spiritual restoration, assured by the declaration, "for the mouth of Yahweh has spoken."

In summary, it may be said that with the exception of Mic 3:4 and Hab 1:11, where concrete historical images are employed, the expectation announced in new predictions introduced by integral 'āz is cast in highly symbolic language. (See Chapter Twelve for the significance of this conclusion.)

CHAPTER THREE

Bayyôm hahû', "on/in that day"

1. Introduction

We come now to the backbone of our study, an analysis of the widely distributed futuristic formula of transition, *bayyôm hahû'*, "on/in that day," which Hugo Gressmann far too hastily identified as a special eschatological *terminus technicus,* which P. A. Munch wished to restrict to the meaning, "then," and about which I published my book, *Yesterday, Today and Tomorrow.*[1] Before concentrating on *bayyôm hahû'* as a futuristic transition, we should summarize past usage for general comparison and then set aside futuristic occurrences that are not transitional in function.

a. The analogy of past and present usage

After treating in my book each passage where past *bayyôm hahû'* appears, I was able to put all occurrences in tabular form, using categories similar to those to be employed in the present study.[2] Concern for economy of space will allow no more than general statistics by way of summary. *Bayyôm hahû'* when referring to the past falls into the following categories in proportion as indicated:

1) Glosses: editorial or scribal, 7; redactional, 1;
2) Transitions for incorporating literary supplements: of interpretive comment, 3; of independent material, 5; of narrative expansion, 7;
3) Concluding formulas: secondary transitions, 3; secondary time identifiers, 1; original epitomes, 17; secondary epitomes, 2;
4) Transitional formulas between narrative episodes: incorporating second-

ary material as a separate episode, 4; original transitions at the beginning, 14; at the middle, 2; at the ending, 13;

5) Narrative elements in nonnarrative pericopes: deuteronomic, 4; prophetic, 3; epitomizing synchronism, 1.

I did much the same with the cognate formulas *hayyôm*, "today," *bayyôm hazzeh*, "(on) this day," and *bĕʿeṣem hayyôm hazzeh*, "on this very day," placing the occurrences into separate categories of use, with the following resulting statistics:[3]

1) Time identifiers, 44;
2) Epitomes, 60;
3) Appeals and commands, 21;
4) Identifying characterizations, 108.

The effect of this survey will be to sharpen our impression of frequent use of highly formulaic time-designatives with reference to the past and present. We expect to find parallel locutions referring to future time, which may be other than the historic future.

b. The nonformulaic futuristic use of bayyôm hahû'

Paralleling a cultic/gnomic present indicated by the time-designatives *hayyôm*, *bayyôm hazzeh*, and *bĕʿeṣem hayyôm hazzeh* (Exod 12:17; Lev 8:34, 16:30, 23:21, 28, 29, 30) is what I have called a cultic/gnomic future.[4] This does not refer to an historical event but rather to a sequence within a formal procedure within typical situations. This is found in cult legislation at Lev 22:30, 27:23; Num 6:11; and Ezek 45:22; in cultic instruction at Exod 13:1-16; in casuistic law at Deut 21:23; and in wisdom instruction at Ps 146:4.[5] It should be obvious that this is not a true future and hence should be excluded from a study of prophetic prediction.

Another futuristic use of *bayyôm hahû'* that must be excluded from the present study is its nonformulaic employment as a simple time identifier.[6] Instances of this are to be found at Exod 8:18 (E 22); Deut 31:17 *bis;* 1 Sam 8:18(1); 1 Kgs 13:3, 22:25 par 2 Chr 18:24; Isa 3:7, 5:30, 19:21, 29:18, 30:23; Jer 25:33 (LXX *beyôm YHWH*); Hos 2:20 (E 18); Zech 2:15 (E 11), 6:10, 12:8(2). It is relatively easy to spot these because the time-designative appears in the secondary rather than primary position within a given syntactical structure. Furthermore, a simple time identifier is never preceded by futuristic *wĕhayâ* or followed by the prophetic utterance formula *nĕʾum YHWH*, as is commonly the case when the time-designative functions as a transitional formula. The function of a time-identifying *bayyôm hahû'* within a syntactical unit is to make an identifying characterization or to specify the time of a verbal action.

c. Epitomes

We must also set aside the remarkable formulation that I have designated as "epitome."[7] This occurs with some frequency when *bayyôm hahû'* refers to a just-narrated past event (see the listing mentioned in section a above). This is a remarkable phenomenon never previously noted. As I have defined it, an epitome is a succinct distillation and summation on the part of an authoritative interpreter (the speaker/writer) regarding the central significance of a past event. But its equivalent also appears when such an interpreter addresses the present moment (designated by *hayyôm* or its equivalents) or an event in the future (with *bayyôm hahû'*). The futuristic passages where such an epitome occurs are Deut 31:18; 1 Sam 8:18(2); Isa 2:11, 17, 10:27, 20:6, 27:1, 52:6; Amos 2:16, 8:3; Obad 8; Zech 9:16 and 14:21.[8] In an epitomizing declaration, it is usual for *bayyôm hahû'* to appear at the very end of the pericope, as in the Samuel passage and in Isa 2:11, 17, in the Amos passages, and in Zech 14:21. In Isa 10:27, Isa 20:6, and Zech 9:16 it is placed laconically in the middle. In Obad 8 it is preceded by the interrogatory particle *hălō'*. Two passages, Isa 10:27 and 27:1, have it at the beginning (in the first passage with foregoing *wěhayâ*), not because it is a transitional formula but because of its parallelism with a foregoing time word.

d. Scribal glosses

We must set aside, finally, those futuristic passages where *bayyôm hahû'* occurs as (or within) a scribal gloss. These do not count as introductory transitions, or as integral transitions within redactional supplements, because they have no organic connection with the syntactical structure of the particular text in which they are found. Virtually all these glosses are found in Jeremiah's relatively difficult text. They fall into three categories:

1) Unsupported in LXX: *bayyôm hahû'* in Isa 4:1; Jer 49:26, 50:30; the phrase *wěhāyâ lipnékā bayyôm hahû'* at the end of Jer 39:16;[9] all of Jer 48:41b (glossed in from 49:22);
2) Disturbing the poetic meter: Jer 49:22; Zeph 1:9;
3) Disturbing the syntax: Ezek 24:26.[10]

Except in the Ezekiel passage, the position chosen by the glossator is never the foremost, and in Jer 39:16, 49:26, 50:30 it falls at the conclusion. With regard to function, we may say that it never serves other than as a nonformulaic time identifier. Within the insertions at Jer 48:41, 49:22, 26, and 50:30 it is fairly certain that the glossator in question was attempting to emulate the commonly attested genre of "casualty report," which often contains an epitome using *bayyôm hahû'* or its variant: *bā'ēt hahî'*. I have described this phenomenon in my book *Yesterday, Today and Tomorrow*.[11]

With these identifications of extraneous phenomena, the slate is cleared for a systematic study of the historically futuristic *bayyôm hahû'* when occurring as a formal transition. There are two distinct uses: integral and introductory. We shall treat each category separately in what follows.

2. Integral transitions

An important distinction that needs to be made respecting *bayyôm hahû'* in futuristic passages, either as an integral or as an introductory transition, is whether it provides a synchronism with an event mentioned in the material to which it is attached, or creates a sequence from it. This particular time-designative is fully temporal and never situational (though, of course, a situational background is often implicit). As might be expected, integral transitions tend to create a sequence from a first event to a second.

For the sake of convenience, we take up first a single passage within this category in which as an integral transition *bayyôm hahû'* creates a synchronism with the event of the underlying material. We will follow this with a lengthy list in which it creates a sequence from such an event.

a. Synchronisms

Ezek 38:14, 19. Several expansions to the original Gog apocalypse have *wĕhāyâ bayyôm hahû'* as introductory transitions (see below on 38:10, 18, 39:11). However, *bayyôm hahû'* is preceded in 38:14 by the interrogative particle combined with the negative particle *(hălō'),* and by *'im lō'* ("if not"), followed by what amounts to the protasis in a conditional sentence in v 19, this being a common ellipsis for the standard oath form. In v 14, following the formula of commissioning and the messenger formula, Yahweh is in effect asking menacing Gog whether the following is not true: that he is aware[12] that Israel is now dwelling securely, that he has departed with numerous allies, and that he is about to attack Israel. In v 19, wrathful Yahweh is quoted as swearing "on that day" — the day mentioned in v 18 — that there should be a tremendous earthquake. Thus we have here two unusual and especially emphatic ways of explicating the impact of the coming day of judgment on Israel's cosmic enemies.

b. Sequences

Isa 22:20, 25. The private oracle of Isa 22:15-25 is a random block of original Isaianic material containing two successive redactional expansions, each of which creates a sequence from the earlier to the later.[13] The original oracle, against Shebna and referring to Yahweh in the third person, is in vv 15-18. A first redactor added vv 19-23, referring to Yahweh in the first person; it announces that Shebna is deposed, and then, with *wĕhāyâ bayyôm hahû'* as transition, that Eliakim is to be called and empowered with authority. A second redactor added vv 24-25, expanding and reinterpreting the image of a peg, *yātēd:* heavy weight is to be placed on that peg (Hilkiah) with the consequence (initial *bayyôm hahû'*) that it shall give way and fail in its purpose. This final stage of redaction is given double validation as revelation, first by addition of the oracle formula *(nĕ'um YHWH ṣĕbā'ôt)* following the temporal transition, and at the end by the formula of conclusion *kî YHWH dibber,* "for Yahweh has spoken." Each redactional addition is in fact a *vaticinium ex eventu,* purporting to predict a proximate future that is actually past/present in the redactors' observation or experience.

Isa 31:7. A prose expansion, vv 6-7,[14] to a preexilic warning against reliance on Egypt and Assyria, vv 1-5, 8-9,[15] constitutes an urgent appeal to postexilic Israel not to revolt against Yahweh because of Yahweh's coming day of purging, underscoring this in a grounding clause (v 7) introduced by *kî* and *bayyôm hahû'.* The transition formula with *kî* is integral to the expansion but intends to create a sequence between the event of the turning to Yahweh mentioned in v 6 and the event of the throwing away of idols in v 7, appropriate to Yahweh's act of dread, vv 4-5. This turning is for the present and imminent future and is to be motivated by foreknowledge of what lies beyond it in the proximate future.

Ezek 24:27. The questions of the dating and geographic setting of the entire book of Ezekiel depend on the recognition (1) that the synchronism between the exile's arrival and the end of the prophet's dumbness are correctly dated in the MT of 33:21-22 (see our discussion in Chapter Eight); (2) that it is a redactor who created confusion in 24:25-27 by making the day of removal from Jerusalem synchronous with the exile's arrival in Chaldea; and (3) that *bayyôm hahû'* in v 26 (see Section 1.d above) and *'et happālîṭ* in v 27 are explicative glosses making this synchronism even more emphatic. With these glosses removed, initial *bayyôm hahû'* in v 27 creates an imaginary sequence (within a single day) between the deportation from Jerusalem and the opening of the prophet's mouth.[16]

Hag 2:23. In a private oracle to Zerubbabel, vv 20-23, Yahweh first announces (*'ănî* followed by the participle and a connected sequence of *waw*-consecutive perfects) the world-shaking events which are presently occurring; then transitional *bayyôm hahû'*, followed by the oracle formula, introduces the divine act that is to follow from this (*lqḥ* niph. impf.) with an act consequent upon it (*śym* perfect consecutive) as a signet,[17] all of which is then underscored by a grounding clause stating the fact of Zerubbabel's divine election, followed by another oracle formula at the end.[18]

Zech 12:4. Of ten occurrences of *bayyôm hahû'*, with or without preceding *wĕhāyâ*, within the late postexilic pericope, Zech 12:1–13:6, all are introductory transitions which will be treated below, except a time identifier creating an identifying characterization in secondary position at 12:8b and an integral transition, *bayyôm hahû'*,[19] followed by *nĕ'um YHWH* in 12:4a, concluding the original Yahweh-speech in 12:1b-2a, 4a. (For further details, see in Chapter Ten.) Yahweh's terrifying of the enemy nations is thus placed in sequence from the nations' attack upon Jerusalem.

3. Introductory transitions

a. As liturgical rubrics

Traditional prophetic material has at certain points been adapted for liturgical use by the insertion of formal rubrics with *bayyôm hahû'*, introducing either hymns of victory or laments, as the case may have required. Although syntactically *bayyôm hahû'* serves as a time identifier within a verbal clause, the entire rubric is designed as a transition to new redactional material brought into service with a specific liturgical purpose. In each instance the relationship between an event in the underlying passage and the new event is one of synchroneity and not of sequence. Those in Isaiah reflect a very late stage of the book's redaction. (For further discussions of these particular passages, see our following treatments of the respective books where they occur.)

Isa 12:1, 4. Isa 12:1-6 actually constitutes an editorial conclusion to the early collection, chaps. 5–11, and it is probable that 11:10, 11, and 12-16 — all postexilic — were not in the collection when this conclusion was added.[20] This means that it is the salvation saying in 11:1-9 that provided the original focal point for the attachment of 12:1-3, 4-6. In Isa 12:1 the rubric is *wĕ'āmartā bayyôm hahû'*, "and you (2ms) will say on that day," appropriate to the following hymn of individual praise. In 12:4 the rubric is in the plural, *wa'ămartem bayyôm hahû'*, appropriate to the following collective hymn of praise.[21]

Isa 25:9, 26:1. Within the very late "little apocalypse" of Isaiah 24–27, 24:21-23 and 25:6-8 are intrusive but appear to belong together, while 25:1-5 and 10b-12 must be seen as still later insertions. Probably it is to this conflate text that the praise saying of 25:9, introduced by the formal rubric *wĕ'amartā bayyôm hahû'*,[22] and that of 26:1-6, introduced by the rubric *bayyôm hahû' yûšar haššîr hazzeh bĕ'ereṣ yĕhûdâ* ("on that day this song shall be sung in the land of Judah"), have been attached.

Isa 27:2. The love song of Isa 27:2-5 was evidently employed as liturgy.[23] In any case *bayyôm hahû'* at the beginning creates awkward syntax in connection with the love song's modified substantive and imperative, as compared with passages where it is simply in anacrusis (see the following section on transitions in anacrusis).

Mic 2:4. Attached to a Mican woe-oracle in vv 1-3 is a collective mock lament that is introduced with the formal rubric *bayyôm hahû' yiśśā' 'alêkem māšāl wĕnahâ nehî [ ] we amar . . . ,* "on that day one shall take up concerning you a saying and shall lament with a lament [ ] and will say. . . ."[24] The lament next cited is intended less as an explication of *'et rā'â,* "an evil time," in v 3 than as a call for an appropriate (quasi) liturgical response. V 5, introduced by what would otherwise be a second connective *lākēn* within the passage, must be taken as the redactor's conclusion drawn from the lament. "For it will be an evil time *(kî 'ēt rā'â hî')*" is best seen as a concluding epitome with vv 1-3. (For further comments on this difficult text, see in Chapter Nine.)

Zeph 3:16. A whole series of redactional additions (vv 9-10, 11-13, 14-15; cf. 19, 20) have altered Zephaniah's word of bitter judgment in vv 1-8 in terms of countervailing salvation. Vv 14-15 is a victory hymn for Zion and may have been used in the liturgy of the postexilic temple. A second victory hymn is introduced in vv 16-18 with the liturgical rubric *bayyôm hahû' yē'āmēr lîrûšālaim,* "on that day it shall be said to Jerusalem."[25]

b. As anacrusis in poetry

Closely related to the liturgical rubrics just observed is *bayyôm hahû'* when inserted redactionally to introduce new poetic material. It almost always expands existing poetry, and it as often predicts punishment as promises salvation. It is striking that in this group of sixteen passages, ten have preceding *wĕhāyâ,* while eight have a following oracle formula. In each of these passages a rough synchronism is created between the event of the underlying material and the new event or condition of the addition.[26]

Isa 17:4. An original oracle against Damascus, concluded by the oracle formula (vv 1-3), is expanded as an early oracle against Israel, likewise concluded by the oracle formula (vv 4-6).[27] The transition formula, *wĕhāyâ bayyôm hahû'*, stands in anacrusis at the beginning of the expansion.

Isa 24:21. *Wĕhāyâ bayyôm hahû'* in 24:21 and the conclusion formula in 25:8 frame an incremental unit of epexegetical expansion (24:21-23, 25:6-8)[28] to an expansive day-of-Yahweh poem, 24:1-20. The recognition that the temporal expression stands in anacrusis facilitates scanning this material as poetry in long meter. It is the "eschatological" images within this expansion (cosmic forces subdued, a universal feast of inauguration, an end to death and sorrow) that are responsible for the widely accepted name "little apocalypse" given the section, Isaiah 24–27.

Isa 28:5. The woe-oracle against the *'aṭeret gē'ôt,* "proud crown," of Ephraim's drunkards in Isa 28:1-4 resembles Amos's denunciations and must come from a relatively early period, if not from Isaiah's own hand. A redactor, probably already in the seventh century, deliberately composed a paean to Yahweh's *'aṭeret ṣĕbî,* "glorious crown," in vv 5-6. The thematic verb *hyh* itself indicates a condition rather than an event; hence the transition formula is *bayyôm hahû',* which stands in anacrusis and without foregoing *wĕhāyâ.*[29]

Jer 4:9. A Jeremianic prophecy of punishment on Jerusalem (4:5-8, 13-17, with closing *nĕ'um YHWH*) has been severed in two by the early expansion in vv 9-10, introduced by *wĕhāyâ bayyôm hahû'* in anacrusis and *nĕ'um YHWH.*[30] A cry of alarm urging last-hour repentance is strengthened by the assurance that leaders of every class will be immobilized by terror (on vv 11-12 see Chapter Two in the section on *'attâ*), followed by what is probably a report of these leaders' complaint that they have been deceived by the prophets of peace, v 10. Though the rhythm is uneven, parallelism marks this expansion (without its introductory formulas) as poetic. This particular redactional expansion may in fact be the prophet's own reinterpretation of his own prophecy, occasioned perhaps by Nebuchadrezzar's return in 598, after he had first spared Judah (605). This passage will come under further review in later sections of this book.

Jer 30:8. The redactor who collected Jeremianic oracles for the "book of consolation" in Jer 30:5–31:22 placed first in order a short day-of-Yahweh poem (31:5-7), but its effect was immediately blunted by the insertion of a poetic salvation oracle in 31:8-9, introduced by *wĕhāyâ bayyôm hahû'* and *nĕ'um YHWH ṣĕbā'ôt,* predicting something that is thematically quite unrelated to the imagery of the day of Yahweh, viz., transfer of vassalship back to Yahweh and the raising up of David as king. In this expansion the rhythm is uneven, but a rough parallelism is apparent once the transition formula in anacrusis is identified. The formula *wĕhāyâ bayyôm hahû'* is in fact rare in

Jeremiah, being found elsewhere only at 4:9 (cf. original *bayyôm hahû'* without preceding *wĕhāyâ* at 39:17).[31]

Hos 2:18 (E 16), 23 (E 21). The best explanation for the composition of Hos 2:18-22 (E 16-20) and 2:23-25 (E 21-23) is that they represent parallel streams of interpretive expansion upon the Hoseanic poem of vv 3-17 (E 1-15).[32] Each consists of parallelistic poetry (in the first with somewhat uneven meter) and each has identical formulas of transition in anacrusis: *wĕhāyâ bayyôm hahû'* with *nĕ'um YHWH.* Since the second addition directly expands the imagery of vv 16-17 (E 14-15), while the first develops the implications of true covenanting, it is evident that the second does not expound the first expansion, but rather the original poem, thereby turning Israel's judgment into salvation, as in 2:1-2 (E 1:10-11).

Joel 4:18 (E 3:18). Among random sayings of judgment on the nations and of salvation for postexilic Israel (vv 9-17), the idyllic prediction of v 18, in poetic form with *wĕhāyâ bayyôm hahû'* in anacrusis, predicts a condition of abundant fruitfulness.

Amos 8:9, 13, 9:11. As we shall see, Amos 8:11-12 and 9:13-15 come from widely separated stages of redaction even though they both begin with *hinnēh yāmîm bā'îm* in anacrusis, followed by the oracle formula. In attempting to sort out the wide-ranging expansions that have been attached to original material in chaps. 8 and 9 of Amos, it is important first to set aside those pericopes that cannot be from Amos or his immediate disciples; and second, to discern, if possible, internal links between them. Scholars are virtually unanimous in placing 9:11-12 as well as 9:13-15 in the late preexilic or early exilic period. The remaining materials follow the main themes of Amos's own preaching, though somewhat freely. One discerns that additions lacking a temporal transition are in the closest compositional proximity to original core materials, which appear in two collocations, 8:4-6, 7-8 and 9:2-4, 5-6, 9-10; in distinction, materials introduced by temporal transitions appear in the two appended collocations, 8:9-10, 11-12, 13-14 and 9:11-12, 13-15. Furthermore, 8:11-12 appears to extend the imagery of 8:9-10, while 8:13-14 expands vv 11f.'s theme of famine and thirst. This last pericope, introduced by *bayyôm hahû'* without the oracle formula, very likely dates from after the fall of Samaria in 722 B.C.E. because the scene of prophetic denunciation has shifted to Beer-Sheba, but 8:9-10, introduced by *wĕhāyâ bayyôm hahû'* and the oracle formula, is thematically related to original material at 5:18-20. 8:11-12 was probably composed after 8:9-10 but before 8:13-14. Little more can be said with assurance except that all the expansions in Amos 8 are certainly preexilic; also that 8:11-12 clearly reflects the ideology of the deuteronomistic school. A negative conclusion is that none of the temporal transitions under study here offers itself as belonging to any one particular redactor.

Mic 4:6. Bayyôm hahû' in anacrusis, followed by *nĕ'um YHWH,* attaches a Yahweh-speech promising restoration for the afflicted remnant, vv 6-7a,[33] to what is probably an early postexilic prediction of salvation in vv 1-5 (on it and its parallel in Isa 2:2-5, see the following section on *bĕ'aḥărît hayyāmîm*).

Mic 5:9 (E 10). Wĕhāyâ bayyôm hahû' in anacrusis, followed by *nĕ'um YHWH*, introduces a stern oracle against idolatry in the land similar in language and ideology to Isa 2:6-8, which is certainly preexilic. Like Mic 5:4-8 (E 5-9), vv 9-14 pertains to Judah's period of subjugation to the Assyrians. Both Judah and Assyria are exposed to Yahweh's coming wrath.[34]

Zeph 1:10, 12 LXX. The "day of Yahweh" is the recurrent theme of Zeph 1:2-18. The collector of the prophet's messages has added words referring to Yahweh's acts in the third person (vv 7, 13, 14ff.) to reports of Yahweh's direct speech (vv 8-9, 10-11, 12), using a temporal transition including the word *yôm* at strategic points.[35] From the reference to Yahweh's grim sacrifice in v 7, a transition is provided in the words *wĕhāyâ beyôm zebaḥ YHWH*, "and it shall happen on the day of Yahweh's sacrifice." In v 10 *wĕhāyâ bayyôm hahû'* in anacrusis, followed by *nĕ'um YHWH*, introduces an especially dramatic announcement of terror upon Jerusalem. In v 12 initial *wĕhāyâ bayyôm hahû'* (LXX)[36] in anacrusis makes the transition to Yahweh's speech in vv 12-13.

Zeph 3:11. As has been noted, Zeph 3:9-10 and 11-13 introduce late attachments to the book of Zephaniah. Twice the locution *kî 'āz* (9, introductory; 11, integral) introduces an announcement of Yahweh's intervention in order to remove something offensive in the attitude and behavior of the returned exiles. *Bayyôm hahû'* in anacrusis in v 11 introduces a prediction of the addressee's status as this is to be affected by the second purgation.

c. Introducing prose additions

The passages containing liturgical rubrics with *bayyôm hahû'* have proven to be late, while passages with *(wĕhāyâ) bayyôm hahû'* in anacrusis have proven in most instances to be relatively early. When we take up the long list of passages in which the transition formula introduces prose attachments to (almost always) poetic passages, these generally turn out to be late. Very often it will prove all but impossible to detect anything more than a synchronous (in distinction from sequential) relationship between the event of the under-lying material and the new event of the redactional supplement.

1 Sam 3:12. We must first turn to a passage that lies outside the classical prophetic collection. In the narrative of a dream revelation to young Samuel, Yahweh announces that he is about to do startling things; the familiar formula of imminent action is employed (v 11). In my book *Yesterday, Today and*

Tomorrow, I argued that the original text had its continuation in vv 13bα2β-18, with chap. 4 as the narrative of fulfillment.[37] Initial *bayyôm hahû'* in v 12 introduces an interpretive remark, possible by a Zadokite redactor, but more probably by the Deuteronomist, announcing that in this divine action all the predictions ("from beginning to end") of 2:27ff. would be fulfilled (see further in the following section on *hinnēh yāmîm bā'îm*). Inasmuch as the downfall of the Elides was an accomplished fact at the time of the redactor, this is in fact another example of *vaticinium ex eventu.*

Isa 2:20. Isaiah's day-of-Yahweh poem in 2:12-17, with epitomizing *bayyôm hahû'* at the conclusion, has received epexegesis in the form of two distinct but similar expansions, vv 18-19 and vv 20-21.[38] In the second, initial *bayyôm hahû'*[39] places human response into synchroneity with Yahweh's awesome day.

Isa 3:18. Initial *bayyôm hahû'* introduces a redactional list of adornments (vv 18-23) that Yahweh intends to confiscate from the proud women denounced in Isaiah's oracle of vv 16-17, 24, 4:1.[40] The expansion may very well be preexilic.[41] The image of predicted mutilation and the image of predicted confiscation are seen as synchronous with each other.

Isa 4:2. The deprivation announced in Isa 3:18-23, with introductory *bayyôm hahû',* and the image of polyandry in 4:1, also with *bayyôm hahû'* as time-identifier in secondary position, are made synchronous with Yahweh's plague upon the haughty women in Isaiah's own oracle in 3:16-17, 24 (see above). In the late prose expansion of 4:2-6, which is a promise of eschatological bliss, the temporal or conditional clause in v 4, introduced by *'im,* presupposes the already occurring cleansing of Zion's daughters. Thus initial *bayyôm hahû'* in v 2 contemplates an event in sequential relation to what precedes it.[42]

Isa 7:18, 20, 21, 23. It seems certain that four separate expansions to 7:10-17, introduced by *wĕhāyâ bayyôm hahû'* (vv 18, 21, 23) or *bayyôm hahû'* (v 20), are not original. They collectively explicate the ominous *yāmîm,* "days," threatened in the Isaianic words of v 17; yet their style, content, and historical bearing would clearly place them together in the same general period (734-701 B.C.E.), when Assyrian domination was a serious menace but not a fully realized fact.[43] V 21 is at least susceptible to the interpretation that it predicts an ironic judgment. Vv 18-19 and v 20 speak of Yahweh's action, while v 21 and vv 23-25 present panoramic scenes of desolation. The first, third, and fourth expansions carry images from nature, while the second (alone with introductory *bayyôm hahû'*) has the homely image of shaving. The most likely explanation for the creation of this collocation is that a single preexilic redactor preserved distinct traditional sayings from the early Isaiah school appropriate to the situation, intending each of them as an illustration of the judgment referred to in vv 16-17.[44] This complex of expansions will be more fully discussed in Chapter Six.

Isa 10:20. Postexilic redactors[45] have placed expansive materials, vv 20-23 and vv 24-27a, at the end of Isaiah's oracle against the king of Assyria in vv 12-19. Both are prose additions within poetry.[46] Vv 20-23, introduced by *wĕhāyâ bayyôm hahû'* (referring back to epitomizing *bĕyôm 'eḥād* in v 17) is notably contemplative and discursive. The phrase *šĕ'ar 'ēṣ*, "remnant of trees," in v 19 has led the redactor to meditate in these verses on the survival of a remnant *(šĕ'ar)* from Jacob, recognized as remarkable in the light of Yahweh's universal judgment. The judgment of Israel, the judgment of Assyria, and the rescue of Israel's remnant (vv 20ff.)[47] are all to occur synchronously as the realization of Yahweh's comprehensive intention.

Isa 11:10, 11. A single late redactor may be responsible for successive expansions in vv 10 and 11 to the probably exilic "stump of Jesse" poem in 11:1-9.[48] Though each of them begins with *wĕhāyâ bayyôm hahû'*, they were probably composed together from traditional material as the redactor in question contemplated the universal attractiveness of Jesse's "root" (*šōreš*, not *ḥōṭer*, "shoot," or *nēṣer*, "branch," as in v 1), and then an additional *(yôsîp . . . šēnît)*[49] recovery of Israel's remnant from far-flung territories not mentioned in 10:20-22,[50] to which the second expansion apparently alludes.

Isa 17:7, 9. As we have seen, *wĕhāyâ bayyôm hahû'*, standing in anacrusis, has provided a transition between a preexilic oracle against Damascus (vv 1-3) and a preexilic expansion directed against Israel (vv 4-6). Postexilic prose expansions to this combined text (vv 7-8, 9)[51] are each introduced by *bayyôm hahû'*. The first predicts humankind's conversion from idol worship. The second is an unfocused reflection upon v 7; it is more likely postexilic than exilic because widespread devastation did continue in certain areas after the return. Though vv 7-8 and v 9 express different concerns, it is more likely that a single redactor has added them together than that a second redactor would have predicted punishment (v 9) as an expansion of a first redactor's prediction of salvation (vv 7-8), or that vv 7-8 was inserted between vv 1-6 and v 9,[52] for both would involve procedures without parallel elsewhere within the materials under study.

Isa 19:16, 18, 19, 23, 24. Bayyôm hahû' in v 21 is a mere time identifier creating an identifying characterization of the converted Egyptians. All remaining occurrences in this section introduce prose expansions to a reworked oracle against Egypt (vv 1b-15),[53] providing first a transition to an announcement of woe (vv 16-17) and next transitions to announcements of weal (vv 18ff.). One should note that vv 16-17 take up the theme of terror upon Egypt introduced in v 1, specifying that Judah should be the instrument of this terror rather than Yahweh himself. This is certainly late religio-political propaganda, but not so late as the increasingly universalistic expansions that follow. Vv 18, 19-22, 23, and 24-25 presuppose the conditions of the Persian period,[54] or possibly even of the Hellenistic. Each is likely from a new redactor endeavoring to outdo the startling announcement that precedes it.[55] References to five cities including Heliopolis in v 18, to an altar and a pillar in v 19, and to a highway between Egypt and Assyria in v 23 give some of this material the character of *vaticinium ex eventu;* the rest is predictive, highly speculative eschatology. One future day (tantamount to the "day of Yahweh" for Egypt) offers expanding evidence of Yahweh's presence in the land of Egypt (and also in Assyria), bringing even the inclusion of these erstwhile enemies within the covenant of salvation (vv 24-25).[56]

Isa 23:15. An oracle against Tyre, 23:1-12, has received two late prose expansions in vv 15-16 and in vv 17-18.[57] The second, an ideological correction to the first, is introduced by the temporal expression *wĕhāyâ miqqēṣ šib'îm šānâ,* "and it will happen at the end of seventy years," borrowed from v 15. *Wĕhāyâ bayyôm hahû'* at the head of v 15 expands the event of Tyre's ruin, predicting a period of forgottenness[58] commencing at the time of this event and ending in the performance of a taunt song that commemorates this forgottenness (v 16).

Isa 27:12, 13. Each of two prose verses within this section is introduced with *wĕhāyâ bayyôm hahû',* and the second is a literalizing explication of the metaphor of gathered grain in the first. Here it is more likely that successive redactors were involved than that the second prophecy is an afterthought added by the same redactor. Thematically, they are each remote from the theme of judgment on postexilic Samaria appearing in vv 6-11.[59]

Ezek 29:21. The same exilic redactor who added predictions of weal for "the house of Israel" at the end of the Tyre-Sidon collection (28:24, 25-26) has composed similar material in 29:21 for the original end of the Egypt collection in the book of Ezekiel.[60] Initial *bayyôm hahû'* synchronizes Yahweh's reward for Nebuchadrezzar (equivalent to his judgment on Egypt), vv 17-20, with symbols of restoration for Israel.

Ezek 30:9. In the exilic period epexegesis introduced by *bayyôm hahû'* expanded Ezekiel's oracle against Egypt in 30:6-8 so as to include the anguish of the Kushites in consequence of their hearing about "the day of Egypt's doom" (cf. Isa 18:1).

Ezek 38:10, 18, 39:11. Ezek 38:1–39:22 is proto-apocalyptic, though structured as a prophecy of punishment. Its original core in 38:1-9, 39:1-5, 17-20[61] has been expanded by a series of redactors employing *wĕhāyâ bayyôm hahû'* (38:10, 18, 39:11) as temporal transitions[62] (*'im lō' bayyôm hahû'* in 38:19 is integral to the expansion of which it is a part; see above). The assumption of each successive redactor is that the event of each expansion is synchronous with Gog's attack, scheduled in 38:8 for a remote period identified in the unparalleled phrase *bĕ'aḥărît haššānîm,* "in the sequel of years" (see the following section on this time expression and our extensive discussion in Chapter Eight).

Hos 1:5. This verse is not poetry but prose.[63] An early redactor has drastically altered v 4's ominous announcement interpreting the naming of the child Jezreel, exchanging a geographical symbol for one that is purely political. *Wĕhāyâ bayyôm hahû'* in v 5 synchronizes the breaking of Israel's bow with the end of Jehu's dynasty, scheduled in v 4 for *'ôd mĕ'aṭ,* "in just a little while." Since this was probably added after the events, it involves another *vaticinium ex eventu.*

Zech 3:10. Zechariah 3 intrudes into the night-vision cycle (1:7–2:17 [E 13], 4:1ff.). It seems likely that the stereotyped eschatological imagery of v 10, introduced with *bayyôm hahû'* and the oracle formula, was added to this chapter prior to its insertion into this context.[64] It synchronizes a condition of paradisaical hospitality with the event of Joshua's investiture and the removal of the returnees' corporate guilt.

Zech 12:3, 6, 8(1), 9, 11, 13:1, 2, 4. In sorting out redactional stages signalized by the temporal formula in the baroque apocalyptic passage, Zech 12:1–13:6, we first set aside *bayyôm hahû'* occurring as a mere time identifier in 12:8(2), as well as the integral *bayyôm hahû',* followed by *nĕ'um YHWH,* in 12:4a (see the preceding section on integral occurrences). The latter concludes an original day-of-Yahweh (holy war) oracle in 12:1b-2a, 4a, promising the rebuff of a foreign attacker.[65] All other occurrences of *(wĕhāyâ) bayyôm hahû'* in this passage introduce redactional expansions at two or more distinct levels. Here we observe the remarkable tendency already encountered in Ezekiel 38–39, viz., a proliferation of the temporal formula as a marker of incremental epexegesis. The apocalyptic vision tends to go on and on, integrating the fulfillment of rival aspirations for Yahweh's final day of decision.[66] For further analysis of this pericope, see our extended discussion in Chapter Ten.

Zech 14:6, 8, 9, 13, 20. Remarkably similar in compositional processes, but diverging somewhat in ideology, is the great apocalyptic prognosis of Zechariah 14. We must first set aside *bayyôm hahû'* serving as a time identifier (in secondary position) in v 4, together with epitomizing *bayyôm hahû'* at the very end of v 21. This leaves a collage of expansions, many of them introduced by the temporal transition, reflecting various interests; they have apparently been introduced in successive redactional stages. This passage as well will be thoroughly analyzed in Chapter Ten.

4. Conclusions

As I have argued in *Yesterday, Today and Tomorrow,* the most elemental distinction in understanding the Bible's concept of time is that between quantitative and qualitative.[67] The first approach to the phenomenon of time uses

the day-interval as a primary unit of measure, applicable to arranging distinct
time-periods within a chronological sequence. The second regards each day
as a unique experience, identified according to its dominant and most distinctive quality. This amounts to what some writers have called *kairos,* i.e., time
as an opportunity for decisive choice and action on the part of God or of
man.[68] This is the concept that prevails in Israel's historiographic, parenetic,
and prophetic literature. In speaking of the future — our present concern —
Israel's prophets made predictions that were to be fulfilled on particular
"days" lying directly ahead, proximately or remotely future.[69] It is especially
the familiar transition *(wĕhāyâ) bayyôm hahû'* that points to fateful moments
in the encounter between God and humankind.

a. Temporal relationships

As has been done with *'attâ* and *'āz,* we may sort out occurrences of
futuristic *(wĕhāyâ) bayyôm hahû'* according to a variety of time relationships in which a new event expands or modifies the event of the material
to which it is attached. Except where clear sequencing is expressed or
implied, the two events are to be interpreted as roughly synchronous with
each other:

(1) The move is from a present and/or imminent future event to another
imminent event:[70]

> 1 Sam 3:12 (introductory synchronism in prose addition), from the cap-
> ture of the ark (v 11) to punishment on Eli's house *(vaticinium ex
> eventu);*
> Hag 2:23 (integral sequence in primary source), from worldwide turmoil
> to Zerubbabel's investiture.

(2) The move is from one event or situation to another within the
proximate future:

> Isa 2:20 (introductory synchronism in prose addition), from the terror
> of Yahweh's day (vv 12-17) to universal human panic;
> Isa 3:18 (introductory synchronism in prose addition), from the shaming
> of Zion's haughty daughters (v 17) to the confiscation of their
> adornments;
> Isa 7:18, 20, 21, 23 (introductory synchronisms in prose additions), from
> judgment on Ahaz and his people (vv 14-17) to Egyptian and
> Assyrian plagues, shaving by the Assyrian "razor," meager diet,
> and the desolation of tillable land;
> Isa 12:2, 4, 25:9, 26:1, 27:2 (synchronizing liturgical rubrics), from
> events of cosmic judgment and renewal to appropriate acts of
> praise;

Isa 17:4 (introductory synchronism with the transition in anacrusis),
from judgment on Syria (vv 1-3) to famine in Ephraim;

Isa 22:20, 25 (integral sequences in double redaction), from the deposition of Shebna (v 19) to the investiture of Eliakim; from the
overburdening of Eliakim (v 25) to his collapse *(vaticinium ex
eventu);*

Isa 23:15 (introductory synchronism in prose addition), from lament
over Tyre's destruction (v 14) to the beginning of her seventy years
of forgottenness;

Isa 28:5 (introductory synchronism in prose addition), from judgment
on Ephraim's drunkards to glory, justice, and strength for the holy
remnant;

Isa 31:7 (integral sequence in redaction), from Israel's repentance (v 6)
to the purging of idols;

Jer 4:9 (introductory synchronism with the transition in anacrusis), from
foreign invasion experienced as divine wrath (vv 5-8) to the
leaders' dismay;

Ezek 24:27 (integral sequence in redaction), from a new exile's report
of Jerusalem's fall to the opening of Ezekiel's mouth;

Ezek 29:21 (introductory synchronism in prose addition), from the capture of Egypt as Nebuchadrezzar's reward (vv 19-20) to the spring-
ing up of a "horn" and the renewal of prophecy;

Hos 1:5 (introductory synchronism in prose addition), from vengeance
for Jezreel's "blood" (v 4) to defeat in the valley of Jezreel *(vaticinium ex eventu);*

Hos 2:18, 23 [E 16, 21] (introductory synchronisms with transitions in
anacrusis), from a wilderness renewal (vv 16-17 [E 14-15]) to a
new naming and a renewed intimacy; and from this to a new
fruitfulness in the land;

Amos 8:9 (introductory synchronism with the transition in anacrusis),
from upheaval in Israel's land (v 8) to darkness and mourning;

Amos 8:13 (introductory synchronism with the transition in anacrusis),
from a famine of Yahweh's word (vv 11-12) to the languishing of
the young and strong;

Mic 2:4 (synchronizing liturgical rubric), from an evil time of judgment
on oppressive landowners (v 3) to appropriate lament at their ruin;

Mic 5:9 [E 10] (introductory synchronism with transition in anacrusis),
from victory for the remnant of Jacob to defeat in battle and a
purging of idolatry;

Zeph 1:10, 12 LXX (introductory synchronisms with transitions in
anacrusis), from punishment on Jerusalem's leaders (vv 8-9) to the
sounds of siege and the plundering of the complacent.

(3) The move is from a proximate future to a remote future (although the text indicates no sequence, in each instance the redactor thinks of an era far removed from that of the underlying material):

Isa 4:2 (introductory synchronism in prose addition), from a plea for plural marriage consequent upon imminent calamity (v 1) to an age of renewal and purging;

Isa 17:7, 9 (introductory synchronisms in prose additions), from judgment on Syria (vv 1-3) and Ephraim (vv 4-6) to the renunciation of idolatry and the desertion of strong cities;

Isa 19:16, 18, 23, 24 (introductory synchronisms in prose additions), from Egypt's loss of wise counsel (vv 1-15) to terror of Judah, Egyptian allegiance to Yahweh *(vaticinium ex eventu),* Egyptian repentance because of Yahweh's altar *(vaticinium ex eventu),* a highway enabling Yahweh's worship from Egypt to Assyria *(vaticinium ex eventu),* and divine blessing on Egypt and Assyria;

Jer 30:8 (introductory synchronism with the transition in anacrusis), from anguish on Yahweh's imminent day of judgment (v 4) to the restitution of loyalty to Yahweh and David;

Amos 9:11 (introductory synchronism with the transition in anacrusis), from the death of sinners (vv 9-10) to the Davidides' return to world dominance;

Zech 3:10 (introductory synchronism in prose addition), from Joshua's investiture and the removal of guilt (v 9) to luxuriating hospitality.

(4) The move is from one event or situation to another within the remote future:

Isa 10:20 (introductory synchronism in prose addition), from eventual punishment on the king of Assyria (vv 16-19) to the survival of a believing remnant;

Isa 11:10, 11 (introductory synchronism in prose additions), from righteousness and peace through a "stump of Jesse" (vv 1-9) to the exaltation of the "root of Jesse" and Israel's second return;

Isa 24:21 (introductory synchronism with the transition in anacrusis), from terror upon the earth (vv 17-20) to the commencement of Yahweh's universal reign;

Isa 27:12, 13 (introductory synchronisms in prose additions), from a lament over the "fortified city's" fall (vv 7-11) to the regathering and return of the exiles;

Ezek 30:9 (introductory synchronism in prose addition), from the "day" of Egypt's doom (vv 6-8) to terror upon Kush;

Ezek 38:10, 14, 18, 19, 39:11 (introductory synchronisms in prose additions), from Gog's attack (vv 7-9) to his aggressive intent, his siege on Yahweh's people, the arousal of Yahweh's wrath, and the counterattack of nature's forces;

Joel 4:18 (E 3:18) (introductory synchronism with the transition in anacrusis), from Yahweh's dwelling on Zion (v 17) to the ripening of nature;

Mic 4:6 (introductory synchronism with the transition in anacrusis), from walking in the name of Yahweh forever (v 5) to the restoration of "lame" Israel;

Zeph 3:11 (introductory synchronism with the transition in anacrusis), from the return of a cleansed diaspora (vv 9-10) to the exaltation of the humble;

Zeph 3:16 (synchronizing liturgical rubric), from the return of Jerusalem's king (vv 14-15) to appropriate exultation;

Zech 12:4 (integral sequence in primary source), from a fruitless attack on Jerusalem (v 2) to battle panic upon those attacking it;

Zech 12:3, 6, 8(1), 9, 11, 13:1, 2, 4 (introductory synchronisms in prose additions), from the city's invincibility (vv 2-3), to Jerusalem felt as a heavy stone, Jerusalem seen as a fire, Jerusalem protected by a supernatural shield, destruction on the attacking nations, mourning as for Hadad-rimmon, a cleansing fountain, the cutting off of idols, and reproach upon the prophets;

Zech 14:6, 8, 9, 13, 20 (introductory synchronisms in prose additions), from Yahweh's day upon Jerusalem (vv 1-5) to continual summer and continuous day, living waters issuing from Jerusalem, recognition of Yahweh as one, panic on besiegers, and comprehensive holiness.

b. Vaticinium ex eventu

The vision of a coming future is not always a true prediction but, in fact, an actual past/present disguised as future. Occurrences of *vaticinium ex eventu* introduced with *(wĕhāyâ) bayyôm hahû'* are found in 1 Sam 3:12, Isa 19:18, 19, 23, 22:20, 25, and Hos 1:5. In a few passages we find a somewhat similar phenomenon: a future that is part of a special design or program (Isa 19:24's projection of an extra-Israel covenant and those verses in Zech 12:1–13:6 that either encourage Judah's rivalry with Jerusalem or that urge the violent repudiation of prophecy) or anticipate an appropriate liturgical response (Isa 12:1, 4, 25:9, 26:1, 27:2, Mic 2:4, Zeph 3:16).

Excursus on Revelational Authority in *Vaticinium ex Eventu*

Predictions of the future that are actually based on past events or conditions are fairly common within the prophetic corpus and provide the stock-in-trade of apocalyptic. They are also found among prophetic predictions that contain temporal transitions. The fact that the formulas under study explicitly equate the predicted event with the future event of the underlying material may seem to accentuate a serious apologetic problem. Interpreters seem to be faced with the unwelcome alternative of either crediting the forecaster with proleptic clairvoyance or of blaming him for culpable misrepresentation. Neither alternative provides the right answer. To understand this puzzling phenomenon, we must attempt to enter into the prophets' conception of Yahweh's judging and creative action in history.

Among the passages that will be taken under study here and in the following sections, the element of *vaticinium ex eventu* appears either as the premise or as the consequence of predicted action. The temporal moves are as follows:

1) From the past disguised as present to another past disguised as future: Dan 10:18–11:1, with *'attâ* as transition in 10:20;

2) From a present event to another present event disguised as imminently future: 1 Sam 3:12-13abα[1], with *bayyôm hahû'* as transition in v 12; Isa 22:19-23, with *wĕhāyâ bayyôm hahû'* as transition in v 20; Isa 22:24-25, with *bayyôm hahû'* as transition in v 25;

3) From a present event to another present event disguised as proximately future: 1 Sam 2:27-36, with *wĕ'attâ* in v 30 and *hinnēh yāmîm bā'îm* in v 31 as transitions; 2 Kgs 20:17-19 (par Isa 39:5-8), with *hinnēh yāmîm bā'îm* as transition in v 17 (v 6); Jer 16:16-18, with *wĕ'aḥărê-kēn* as transition in v 16;

4) From a present event disguised as proximately future to another event in the proximate future: Dan 11:2–12:4, with *ûbā'ēt* twice as transition in 12:1;

5) From a present event disguised as proximately future to an event in the remote future: Hos 3:1-5, with *'aḥar* as transition in v 5;

6) From an event in the proximate future to a past or present event disguised as remotely future: Isa 19:18, with *bayyôm hahû'* as transition; Isa 19:19-22, with *bayyôm hahû'* as transition in v 19; Jer 21:3-7, with *'aḥărê-kēn* in v 7 as transition; Jer 46:25-26, with *'aḥărê-kēn* as transition in v 26b; Jer 49:6, with *'aḥărê-kēn* as transition; Jer 49:39, with *wĕhāyâ bĕ'aḥărît hayyāmîm* as transition.

Certain facts with regard to these passages are important to note. First, they are insignificant in number when compared with the vast majority of the passages on our list that do not have the element of *vaticinium ex eventu*. Second, they have to do with concrete historical events that would have been verifiable in reports or records available to the writers. Third, they occur in three specially proscribed types of material: (1) apocalyptic resumés of a series of historical events leading to Yahweh's final action (the Daniel passages); (2) primary source material from preprophetic or early prophetic passages (1 Sam 2:27ff., 2 Kgs 20:17ff. par, Hos 3:1ff.) or from early redaction (1 Sam 3:12f., Isa 22:19ff., 24f., Jer 16:16ff., 21:7); (3) late postexilic favoring oracles for foreign nations (Isa 19:18, 19ff., Jer 46:26b, 49:6, 39).

For those who venerate the Scriptures, the proper question is not, Must one believe that the events referred to actually were foreseen by the prophets or the prophetic redactors who announced them?; but, What is the most adequate as well as the most honest way of apprehending their own self-understanding? One does a great disservice to biblical exegesis as a responsible scientific discipline when one comes forearmed with a philosophical-theological construct into which such passages will be forced to fit.

Exegesis may not be made subservient to the demands of the objectifying supernaturalism that looks for propositional revelation in Scripture. The biblical God does not communicate factual information to those who receive his revelation; he communicates the reality and the truth of his ineffable presence in their destiny, which they as fallible human beings, existing in contingency and creaturely imperfection, may seek to communicate to God's people, employing by necessity the framework of the conceptual and linguistic potentialities of an enlightened but finite human spirit.

The single greatest service of modern critical methodology lies in its undiverted attention to the meaning and intention of the biblical text within its own temporal, situational, and conceptual context. This must remain dominant in our interpretation of *vaticinium ex eventu*. Either the authors of the passages we have mentioned got their information from known facts or they had a special trunkline into the future. On the face of it, the former option is by far the most probable because it stands in congruity with the epistemological system that has brought us all other kinds of knowledge. Over against the claim of some that it might nonetheless be *possible* for the prophets to have received knowledge from such a source (for "all things are possible with God"), one must insist that this is certainly not possible for the kind of God who reveals himself in the Bible.

A serious approach to the biblical understanding of time and history[71] reveals that for the people of the Bible, time exists only as a conceptual abstraction for relating the qualitative human experience of God's purposeful presence in all the moments of his encounter with humankind and that therefore the future remains open for God as it is for us. The future is not predetermined in some kind of cosmic blueprint, but remains exposed to the infinite potentialities of God's encounter with humankind, and of humankind's encounter with God.

So much for the possibilities; the probabilities emerge in the scrutiny of individual texts. What, for instance, is the more probable, that the person who composed the narrative of a confrontation between the "man of God" and Eli in 1 Sam 2:27ff. already knew from tradition that Hophni and Phinehas should die on the same day, and from experience that the priestly house of Eli should come into disrepute — or that he learned these details supernaturally? Which is the more probable, that the writer of 2 Kgs 20:16ff. (the Deuteronomist) knew from tradition and from contemporary experience that the royal treasury should become booty to the Neo-Babylonians and that Hezekiah's "sons" should become eunuchs in the palace of Babylon — or that he learned these details from futuristic clairvoyance? These particular examples of *vaticinium ex eventu* reveal, in fact, a special purpose for this type of prognostication common to the genre also in nonbiblical sources: that of political (or religio-political) propaganda.[72]

May we not infer from these examples that a kind of religious propaganda was similarly at work, for instance, in the composition of Jer 21:7, a literary expansion that is clearly demarcated from its matrix in vv 4-6?[73] Although this verse is secondary with relation to its context, there is no reason to deny that Jeremiah himself may have written it as an interpretive reflection on the original prediction in vv 3-6. He had reported in the previous context Yahweh's announcement that he was about to give victory to the besieging Babylonians and would bring great pestilence on (not necessarily all) "the inhabitants of this city" (v 6); but after the event of 586 Jeremiah came to know that the king and the survivors of "pestilence, sword, and famine" had also been smitten by the sword, and he naturally wished to include this in his prediction, not so much as an afterthought than as a broader perception of Yahweh's purpose. If it was his disciple who added this information, which is equally likely — the effect would be the same.

This happens to be one of the passages on our list. This *vaticinium ex eventu* is introduced by a temporal transition that we have not yet studied, *wĕʾaḥărê-ken* (the following *nĕʾum YHWH* guarantees that it is also — perhaps more emphatically — divine revelation). But exactly the same situation pertains in a similar passage found in the book of Ezekiel at 12:1-16, a prediction that has been expansively rewritten — probably by the prophet himself — to make it applicable to the same king (Zedekiah) and the same event (that king's flight and capture). Walther Zimmerli's definitive commentary on Ezekiel in the series Biblischer Kommentar zum Alten Testament (acknowledged as one of the best ever written) makes the process of composition and redaction in this passage all but certain, and it is necessary to assume from Zimmerli's brilliant analysis that Ezekiel did revise his former predictions in the light of what subsequently followed. In a separate article on the phenomenon of recomposition in Ezekiel,[74] Zimmerli calls special attention to this passage, among similar others in the book, as an example of how the prophet actually did this. He did this by interpolating words as well as sentences, based upon knowledge of subsequent developments, pertaining to a final or more definitive aspect of the future event in question (Ezekiel carried out this practice, and apparently his disciple-redactors as well).

The passage contains a symbolic-action oracle communicating the dread of the people's imminent deportation to Babylon; it includes Yahweh's instruction to the prophet (vv 1-6), a narrative report of compliance (v 7), and Yahweh's subsequent instructions concerning how Ezekiel was to explain this symbolic act to the curious people (vv 8ff.). In the original version Ezekiel was to say to the people, "I am a sign for all the house of Israel. . . . They shall dig through the wall and bring [their baggage] out through it . . ." (vv 11-12). But this was rewritten soon after the event of 586 to include the words, "Thus says Yahweh: This oracle concerns the prince in Jerusalem and all the house of Israel who are in it (v 10). . . . And the prince who is among them shall lift his baggage on his shoulder in the dark and shall go forth in order not to be seen by any eye (12, LXX)" — and then all of vv 13-16, which mentions his being caught in a snare, his being brought blind to Babylon to die, and the devastation of his army — all of which actually did occur following Jerusalem's capture according to 2 Kgs 25:5-7 par Jer 52:8-11.

Although the process of recomposition is more complex in this Ezekiel passage than in Jer 21:1-7, exactly the same literary procedure is involved. A prophet and/or his disciples may feel free to expand and alter, perhaps drastically, a previous prediction in order to communicate the broader and more ultimate significance of the predicted event. This is no intrusion; in fact, the formula *nĕ'um YHWH* does the identical thing in Jer 21:7 that the herald formula, *kōh 'āmar [ădōnāy] YHWH*, does in Ezek 12:10: it underscores revelational authority. It is only reasonable to surmise that the same conception pertains generally in *vaticinium ex eventu* predictions wherever they occur within the prophetic writings. Information that is derived from subsequent events becomes part of the same authoritative revelation from Yahweh. The explanation of this is that the prophet views new information from the viewpoint of divine intentionality; what subsequently happens, or what was previous unknown to the prophet but has now become known to him, is legitimately included in his announcement of the future.[75]

Interpreters of the Old Testament should keep in mind that the religion of ancient Israel did not have a special place for futuristic prediction; in fact, the omen-interpretation and the soothsaying that were so common outside Israel, and especially in Mesopotamia, were sternly suppressed (Deut 18:10-

14). The Israelite prophet was not primarily a prognosticator of the future;[76] rather, he was one who was privileged to receive and empowered to communicate that ultimate dimension of reality which lies above and beyond all earthly phenomena, that which lies within the secret counsel of God. The major test of authentic prophecy was not, in fact, its fulfillment (in spite of Deut 18:22), but internal evidence that what the prophet was announcing was consistent with Yahweh's being and purpose as previous made known.[77] Furthermore, we must take seriously the fact that prophetic language is essentially parenetic, urging an appropriate response on the part of the hearers, and not primarily designed for communicating information. In the deepest sense, prophecy was "fulfilled" when the people obeyed it — and when, if they refused to obey, Yahweh then proved that he was who he said he was in his divine acts of judgment and of salvation.

c. The preponderance of synchronisms

It should be apparent that the redactor's future day cannot always be comprehended within the compass of a single twenty-four-hour period. Thus the chronological future, with strict limits of time, is treated as irrelevant. Yahweh's final day is opened up to allow the experience of a variety of eschatological anticipations. This follows directly from the tendency seen in virtually all the introductory occurrences to settle for an undefined synchronism between the event of the underlying material and that of the redactional expansion. This is contrary to the tendency of the integral occurrences that we have studied, which is to define the two events in close sequence with regard to each other.

d. The wĕhāyâ bayyôm hahû' variation

It is in this connection that we must ponder the frequency with which the wāw-consecutive perfect wĕhāyâ precedes the temporal phrase bayyôm hahû'.

Bayyôm hahû' appears alone in transitional position in the following passages: 1 Sam 3:12; Isa 2:20, 3:18, 4:2, 7:20, 17:7, 9, 19:16, 18, 19, 23, 24, 22:25, 25:9, 26:1, 27:2, 28:5, 31:7; Ezek 24:27, 29:21, 30:9, 38:14, 19; Amos 8:13, 9:11; Mic 2:4, 4:6; Zeph 1:12 LXX, 3:16; Hag 2:23; Zech 12:4.

Wĕhāyâ bayyôm hahû' appears in Isa 7:18, 21, 23, 10:20, 11, 17:4, 22:20, 23:15, 24:21, 27:12, 13; Jer 4:9, 30:8; Ezek 38:10, 18, 39:11; Hos 1:5, 2:18 (E 16), 23 (E 21); Joel 4:18 (E 3:18); Amos 8:9; Mic 5:9 (E 10); Zech 12:3; 9, 13:2, 4, 14:6, 8, 13.

Wĕhāyâ bayyôm hahû' is found in only one out of seven integral occurrences, in none of the liturgical rubrics, in eleven out of seventeen redactional anacruses, and in twenty-one out of forty-three redactional prose additions. The only significant groupings that we can discern are of *bayyôm hahû'* in redactional expansions at Isa 2:20–4:2 and Isa 19:16-24, and of occurrences of *wĕhāyâ bayyôm hahû'* in Hosea 1–2. The Jeremian biographer preferred *bayyôm hahû'* (Jer 39:17), while the Jeremian redactors preferred the form with *wĕhāyâ* (4:9, 30:8). *Wĕhāyâ bayyôm hahû'* is repeated with some consistency in earlier redactional materials at Isa 7:18, 21, 23 and in the postexilic additions at Isa 10:21, 11:10-11, and 27:12-13. Altogether the longer form occurs in twenty of the forty-three prose additions, virtually all of which are postexilic.

We need to pay special attention to the syntax involved respectively in the use of *bayyôm hahû'* and of its variant, *wĕhāyâ bayyôm hahû'*. Leaving aside occurrences of the former in formal rubrics (see above), we find that futuristic *bayyôm hahû'*, when used as a transition, whether integral or introductory, is always followed by a verb in the imperfect. The temporal formula is in fact a prepositional phrase defining the time of the action or event of the main clause. But when *wĕhāyâ* precedes, we have in effect a complete clause consisting of verb and prepositional phrase. It is not surprising that this clause is always attached asyndetically to what precedes it; i.e., that the *waw*-consecutive perfect is not governed by the foregoing imperfect or its equivalent, as is the general rule for continuing a sequence of actions.[78] It is striking, however, that such a clause may be followed not only by a second new clause with *wāw*-consecutive perfect, developing verbal action in sequence from *wĕhāyâ* (Isa 22:20, 23:15; Hos 1:5; Amos 8:9; Mic 5:9 [E 10]), but also by a noun clause (Isa 11:10; Zeph 1:10) or an imperfect. The last would be expected where a negative particle precedes (Isa 10:20; Zech 14:6), but in the large majority of passages (Isa 7:18, 21, 23, 11:11, 17:4, 24:21, 27:12, 13; Jer 4:9, 30:8; Ezek 38:10, 18, 39:11; Hos 2:18 [E 16], 23 [E 21]; Joel 4:18 [E 3:18]; Zech 12:3, 9, 13:2, 4, 14:6, 13) there is no structural element to cause a reversion to the imperfect, according to normal usage. Neither the intervening prepositional phrase nor an occasional oracle formula affects this structure syntactically.[79]

This seems, all the same, to be the dominant pattern with initial *wĕhāyâ* whenever a *kî*-clause or a prepositional phrase intervenes before a main verb predicting the future; i.e., with circumstantial clauses (Isa 10:12, 16:12; Jer 3:16, 5:19) or phrases (Jer 51:63), or with other kinds of temporal clauses (1 Chr 17:11; cf. par 2 Sam 7:12) or phrases (Isa 14:3, 23:17, 66:23; Jer 3:16, 12:15, 25:12; Zeph 1:8). In this list, only Isa 14:3; Jer 5:19; and Zeph 1:8 have a following *wāw*-consecutive perfect; all the others are followed by an imperfect, only twice (Isa 16:12; Jer 3:6) with an intervening negative particle.[80]

This makes it clear that *wĕhāyâ* may be related asyndetically to the main verb, whether it is *bayyôm hahû'* or another temporal or circumstantial element that intervenes. *Wĕhāyâ bayyôm hahû'*, when followed by a noun clause or an imperfect, is strictly formulaic, and might appropriately be rendered by a following colon (:) indicating a major break or pause. However, this is also the case with *bayyôm hahû'* when standing alone in anacrusis at the beginning of a poetic passage, and it may be inferred that this is the intent as well where it introduces prose expansions.

Since the verb *hyh* means "be" or "become," we would expect that *bayyôm hahû'* with preceding *wĕhāyâ* must introduce a condition that arises in the process of becoming, or that is already fully established;[81] in other words, that an entirely new order of being is contemplated and not just a new event. This proves to be the case. In our list, the material introduced by the temporal formula with foregoing *wĕhāyâ* may explicate an ongoing condition (Isa 17:4-6; Joel 4:18 [E 3:18]; Amos 8:9-10; Zech 13:4-6, 14:6-7, 8), a condition reflected in successive actions or events (Isa 7:23-25, 10:21-23, 11:10, 23:15-16; Jer 4:9-10; Hos 2:18-22 [E 16-20), actions or events producing certain conditions (Isa 7:18, 21-22, 11:11, 22:20-23, 24:21-23, 27:12, 13; Jer 30:8-9; Ezek 38:18-23, 39:11-16; Hos 2:23-25 [E 21-23]; Mic 5:9-14 [E 10-15]; Zeph 1:10-22; Zech 13:2), and only rarely a bare event (Ezek 38:10-13; Hos 1:5; Zech 12:3, 9, 14:13-14).

Thus the coming "day" stretches all boundaries of time, producing a condition that will continue indefinitely. However, this conception is not confined to passages with *wĕhāyâ*, for many passages with simple *bayyôm hahû'* show an even stronger tendency toward establishing permanence.[82]

It is remarkable also that the main verb is from the root *hyh* in a number of passages where *bayyôm hahû'* occurs without foregoing *wĕhāyâ:* Isa 4:2, 17:9, 19:16, 18, 19, 23, 24, 28:5; Zech 13:1, 14:9, 20. It may be surmised that this possibility arose as very late usage, for all these passages are postexilic. It is even more striking to observe the anomaly that arises when *wĕhāyâ bayyôm hahû'* is followed by a main verb from the root *hyh,* an apparent pleonasm. This occurs in Isa 7:23 and Zech 14:6, 13. Isa 7:23-25 is a preexilic insertion, hence we would not expect this phenomenon here, as we do in the apocalyptic verses from Zechariah 14. In the Isaiah passage, however, the phrase *yihyeh kol-māqôm* means "every place shall become," reflecting an ongoing action and not the static conditions predicted in the other passages with *hyh*.[83] It should be noted, incidentally, that in passages where Yahweh is the subject of the verb *hyh,* he is spoken of in the third person and only in such formal descriptions as amount to theological confessions (Isa 28:5-6, Zech 14:9b).

e. The oracle formula

Finally, we make some observations concerning the appearance of the oracle formula *ně'um YHWH*.[84] It is striking that it occurs in three of the six integral occurrences at Isa 22:25, Hag 2:23, and Zech 12:4; also that the first two of these belong to private oracles.[85] They mark the oracular materials to which they pertain as especially solemn and emphatic. The oracle formula with the conclusion formula at the end marks Isa 22:25 as the definitive final word regarding Eliakim.

Among passages with introductory *(wěhāyâ) bayyôm hahû'*, it is those that have the transition in poetic anacrusis that have *ně'um YHWH,* not only the most often, but as the dominant form. It appears in anacrusis in Jer 4:9, 30:8; Hos 2:18 (E 21); Amos 8:9; Mic 4:6, 5:9 (E 10); and Zeph 1:10 — thus in eight of fifteen passages, all of which are preexilic. We may be certain that in each instance the redactor in question intended to draw special attention to the prediction and to identify it with the sign of emphatic authority.

Among the numerous prose additions that we have examined — all of which are late — the oracle formula is added only in Zech 3:10 and 13:2. In each of these passages, the redactor in question intended to mark the event with finality and unique authority, no doubt because the eschatological bliss that the first predicts and the elimination of idols that the second predicts were central elements in the respective ideological programs that they espoused. More of this later, when we have opportunity to examine these passages within the book of Zechariah as a whole (Chapter Ten).

CHAPTER FOUR

Other Temporal Formulas Occurring as Integral and as Introductory Transitions

Bayyāmîm hahēm(mâ), **"In Those Days," and**
bā'ēt hahî', **"At That Time"**

1. Introduction

a. Styling

The time-designative *bayyôm hahû'* in futuristic reference pertains to a single crucial day, however much this may need to be expanded to include a number of coming events or situations. Judging from the frequency of its occurrence, this is the normative formula for the transition to more ultimate predictions. As an alternative styling, two parallel formulas of time came into special use: the plural *bayyamîm hahēm(mâ)* "in those days," and *bā'ēt hahî',* "at that time." As has been seen in our study of *'attâ* and *wĕ'attâ,* the word *'ēt* has the primary meaning of "situation," for which "time" is to viewed as an extension. Hence the phrase *bā'ēt hahî'* might in fact refer to a situation extending over a relatively long duration. The parallel formula *bayyāmîm hahēm(mâ)* refers literally to time as a duration; that is, the definite or indefinite multiplication of single "days" into a greater extent of time.

Because this more complex conception of time relationships is commensurate with either formula, we shall treat them together at this point in our study. A special reason for doing so is that in a number of postexilic passages (Jer 3:17 LXX, 33:15, 50:4, 20; Joel 4:1 [E 3:1]) the two time-designatives appear together in a combinational formula, always in the identical sequence: *bayyāmîm hahēm(mâ) ûbā'ēt hahî'.* Rather than assume that the redactors in question were indulging in an idle piling up of synonyms for effect, or were engaging in some arcane expression of style, we should acknowledge a probable intent to specify within a single phrase both time and circumstance: "in those days — even in that situation."

Futuristic transitions with *bayyāmîm hahēm(mâ)* are found in Jer 3:18, 5:18, 31:29, 33:16, and Zech 8:23; those with *bā'ēt hahî'* are found in Isa 18:7, Jer 3:17, 4:11, 8:1, 31:1; Zeph 3:20; those with the combination of the two are in Jer 3:17 LXX, 33:15, 50:4, 20; Joel 4:1 (E 3:1); Dan 12:1.[1] We immediately observe some interesting contrasts. Neither formula, when used as a futuristic transition, occurs with foregoing *wĕhāyâ*. Also, there are five integral occurrences and twelve that are introductory. All but one integral passage (Dan 12:1) produce synchronisms rather than sequences. Securely attested *nĕ'um YHWH* occurs only in redactional prose additions. The book of Jeremiah alone has eleven of the seventeen total passages containing these two formulas.

b. Past usage

As has been the case with *'āz* and *bayyôm hahû',* both *bayyāmîm hahēm(mâ)* and *bā'ēt hahî'* appear also with reference to the past, designating always a past time-period or special situation, rather than the "day" (i.e., the sharply delimited occurrence) of a specific event. Although we must set these aside in our present review, they are mentioned here for comparative purposes.

Of the twenty-five passages with past *bayyāmîm hahēm(mâ),* three occur in epitomes (Judg 17:6, 18:1(1), 21:25), eleven are integral transitions (Exod 2:23; 1 Sam 28:1; 2 Sam 16:23; 2 Kgs 10:32, 15:37; Esth 1:2, 2:21; Dan 10:2; Neh 6:17, 13:15, 23), five, counting parallels, are redactional transitions (Judg 18:1(2), 19:1; 2 Kgs 20:1 par Isa 38:1 par 2 Chr 32:24; Ezek 38:17) and six are mere time-identifiers (Gen 6:4; Exod 2:11; Judg 20:27, 28; 1 Sam 3:2; Ezek 38:17).

Past *bā'ēt hahî'* is more frequent: of its fifty occurrences, six are in epitomes (Deut 1:18; Judg 12:6; 1 Chr 21:28; 2 Chr 13:18, 35:17), eighteen (nineteen) are integral transitions or part of such transitions (Deut 1:9, 16, 3:18, 21, 23, 10:1, 8; Josh 6:26, 11:10, 21; Judg 21:14, 24; 1 Kgs 8:65 par 2 Chr 7:8; 2 Kgs 24:10; Esth 8:9; Neh 4:16 [E 22]; 2 Chr 16:7, 28:16), and eight (nine) are used as redactional transitions (Gen 21:22, 38:1; Josh 5:2, 1 Kgs 11:29, 14:1, 2 Kgs 16:6, 18:16, 20:12 par Isa 39:1). In addition, past *bā 'ēt hahî'* is a mere time identifier in ten (eleven) passages (Deut 2:34, 3:4, 8, 12, 9:20; Judg 11:26, 14:4; 2 Kgs 8:22 par 2 Chr 21:10; Ezra 8:34; 2 Chr 16:10) and a part of an identifying characterization five times (Num 22:4; Deut 5:5; Judg 4:4; 1 Chr 21:29; 2 Chr 30:3). In Amos 5:13 it occurs as a frequentative present *(= 'ēt rā'â).* Both formulas when referring to the past may appear in initial position as well as within the body of a sentence.

c. Nonformulaic futuristic use

In taking up futuristic occurrences, we again need to set aside those that occur as scribal glosses. These occur at Mic 3:4, Zeph 3:19, and Zech 8:6. We also set aside *bayyāmîm hahēm(mâ)* in Joel 3:2 (E 2:29), where it is either part of an identifying characterization modifying "menservants and maidservants" or a time indicator modifying the verb. We also pass by the identifying characterization in the striking deuteronomistic locution *'ăšer yihyeh(û) bayyāmîm hahēm,* "who will be (in office) in those days," creating a hypothetical future (Deut 17:9, 19:17, 26:3; Josh 20:6). Although both our formulas appear in past epitomes (see above), neither serves in an epitome when referring to the future.

2. Integral transitions

Jer 31:1. This verse, beginning with *bā'ēt hahî'* and *nĕ'um YHWH,* is a redactional summary of the reassuring oracles that follow in vv 2ff.[2] It stands back to back with a truncated summary (30:23-24) of 23:16-20 (see below in our section on *bĕ'aḥărît hayyāmîm*), placed here probably by the same early redactor, who intended that the storm of Yahweh's wrath, scheduled for a future time designated as *'aḥărît hayyāmîm,* "following days (years)," and Yahweh's continuing affirmation of the covenant should be seen as synchronous events.

Jer 33:15, 16. Jer 33:14-16 is a late postexilic replication of the late preexilic passage Jer 23:5-6 (on the latter passage see Chapters Seven and Eleven). The divine promise concerning the "righteous branch" has been severed from the introductory transition *hinnēh yāmîm bā'îm* and the oracle formula (see our following section on *hinnēh yāmîm bā'îm*) to make way for the circumstantial clause "when I shall fulfill the promise I made to the house of Israel and the house of Judah," and a new temporal transition is inserted. This is the rare formulation *bayyāmîm hahēm ûbā'ēt hahî',* "in those days and in that situation" (see above), which is found only in late passages. In the place of the original *bĕyāmâw,* "in his days," the redactor has written a second *bayyāmîm hahem.* It is quite apparent that the promise has been severed from the historical present and imminent future, and pushed into an indeterminate, remote future. The future events introduced by the transitions in vv 15 and 16 are meant to be synchronous with the fulfillment of the divine promise in v 14.[3]

Dan 12:1 bis. Though not prophetic in a strict sense, this passage is included in our survey because it is predictive. The major break in Daniel's final vision (11:2–12:4) lies at 11:40, where the *vaticinium ex eventu* breaks off and true prediction begins. This moment is signalized with a temporal transition special to Daniel's kind of apocalyptic ideology: *ûbā'ēt qēṣ,* "and at the time of the end." The apocalypticist had obviously not yet arrived at this moment as he wrote; it was to usher in the imminent final act of world history. Yet this event would require more than a single "day"; indeed, it must be wide enough temporally (11:40-45) to include the last campaigns of the "contemptible person" (11:21). In sequence from these happenings there will be two synchronous events: the arising of Michael and an accompanying *'ēt ṣārâ,* "distressful time," for the faithful people, signaled in 12:1a by foremost *ûbā'ēt hahî'.* In sequence from this arising and this trouble is the deliverance promised in v 1b, following a second *ûbā'ēt hahî'.*

3. Introductory transitions

a. Formal rubrics introducing citations

Jer 4:11. We have shown in our treatment of *'attâ* in v 12 that vv 11-12 are epexegetical to vv 9-10, introduced by *wĕhāyâ bayyôm hahû'.* The formal rubric *bā'ēt hahî' yē'āmēr le' . . . ,* "at that time it shall be said to . . . ," purports to introduce a current saying about the hot wind of judgment (11aβ-12a). The citation has independent power for future fulfilment. V 12b, with emphatically temporal *'attâ,* introduces the prophet/redactor as speaking independently of this citation for the present — until the time of fulfillment shall have arrived (see above on *'attâ, bayyôm hahû'*). In any event, the future reciting of this citation is made synchronous with the coming dismay of the leaders (vv 9-10). The Jeremianic oracle in vv 5-8, 13-17, the initial expansion in vv 9-10, and this secondary expansion have all arisen within the late preexilic period, indicating an intense redactional activity within Jeremiah's intimate circle.

Jer 31:29. Vv 29-30 constitutes an exilic insertion into an early exilic redactional cycle of independent sayings introduced by *hinnēh yāmîm bā'îm* (vv 27-28, vv 31-34, vv 38-40) (see the following section on this formula). Introduced by the formal rubric *bayyāmîm hahēm lō' yō'mĕrû 'ôd,* "in those days they shall no longer say . . . ," it cites a popular saying only for the purpose of negating and refuting it (v 30). The nonfulfillment of this saying is synchronous with Yahweh's predicted sowing and planting (vv 27-28). It is very likely that this secondary redactor was influenced by Ezek 18:2.[4]

b. Introducing prose additions

Isa 18:7. A vast temporal chasm separates two events involving Egypt in Isaiah 18, at least roughly synchronized in v 7 with the transitional formula *bāʿēt hahîʾ*. It seems all but certain that the original woe-oracle involving Kush concluded with the figure of pruning in 18:4-6, without the prose epexegesis of v 7. Transitional *bāʿēt hahîʾ* — here unique in the book of Isaiah — contemporizes God's summoning of Kush to bring his announcement to Egypt, lyrically described in v 2b, with a prediction that the latter nation, described in v 7 with the same lyrical language, should bring homage to Yahweh in Zion.[5] Though difficult to date through lack of historical information, the ambassade of the Kushites could very well have been projected for Isaiah's own time, while the participation of the Egyptians in the worship of Yahweh is a late postexilic ideal (cf. Isa 19:16ff.). Including other late insertions at vv 3 and 6b, the redacted form of this passage suits the conditions of the postexilic period. Elsewhere in Isaiah *bayyôm hahûʾ* is the preferred redactional formula of transition, hence this addition must stand outside the normative Isaianic scribal tradition. The selection of *bāʿēt hahîʾ* for this purpose in an isolated passage may have come out of reflection upon the fact that Egypt's gift-bringing in v 7 has been made synchronous with the alerting of all nations (v 3) in an already composite text, rather than with Kush's ambassade to Egypt.

Jer 3:17, 18. Jer 3:15-18 contains four prose sayings (styled as Yahweh's address to Israel in vv 15-16 but in v 17 referring to Yahweh in the third person) that sever the original connection of poetic materials in vv 14, 19-20.[6] In v 16, which is probably exilic, *wĕhāyâ* with a circumstantial clause concluding with *bayyāmîm hahēmmâ* as a time-identifier, and underscored by *nĕʾum YHWH,* introduces a famous — now to be refuted — liturgical fragment mentioning the lost ark. Together with v 15, it has attracted two competing postexilic sayings concerning the gathering of the nations to Jerusalem (v 17)[7] and the return of a reunited people to the land of their ancestral heritage (v 18). Although vv 15 and 16 are in fact notably earlier than the materials in this composite passage, the respective events have been made synchronous with one another. Because of the varying time-designatives, it does not seem likely that v 17 and v 18 have come into the redacted text together. Rather, we may have here an illustration of what William McKane calls "triggering,"[8] in which elements deriving from an early stage of redaction attract later additions. Although the *topoi* of vv 17 and 18 are different from each other and from those of vv 15-16, they are nevertheless related ideologically. V 16 is a *vaticinium ex eventu;* the following verses are true, idealizing predictions.

Jer 5:18. Directly indicating modification and reinterpretation,[9] the unique transition in Jer 5:18, *wĕgam*[10] *bayyāmîm hahemmâ,* followed by *ně'um YHWH,* introduces prose epexegesis to v 10 (cf. 4:27) in which it is affirmed (v 18) that the devastations of vv 15-17 are to be a severe loss and destruction, but not a complete ruin. Implying the question of purpose, v 19 then goes on to ask and answer the question why.[11] The fact that words spoken about Israel/Judah in vv 10ff. are directly interpreted as applicatory to the persons addressed in vv 18-19 implies that the events of these verses, including foreign bondage, are synchronous with the devastation predicted in vv 10ff. Nevertheless, this prose addition is another *vaticinium ex eventu,* composed in awareness of — and pastoral concern for — the bondage that followed upon the devastation.[12]

Jer 8:1. In a pattern similar to that used in chap. 44, Jeremiah's exilic redactors, seen at work in chaps. 7–8, have added a number of prose pieces, 7:16-20, 21-26, 30-34,[13] and 8:1-3. All of these verses critique the now-ruined Jerusalem cult. The oracle in 8:1-3, introduced by *bā'ēt hahî'* and *ně'um YHWH,* seems unusually severe in announcing a dishonorable death that, *contra* Ezekiel (cf. 33:10-11, 37:1-14), is nevertheless to be preferred to exile. Yahweh's demand in Ezek 33:10 that the exiles should not resign themselves to spiritual death makes it seem likely that Jer 8:1-3 exaggerates and misconstrues a condition to which the redactor in question had already succumbed. The ideology of a stark alternative between life and death (cf. Deut 30:15-20) and the strong polemic against idolatry make deuteronomistic influence all but certain in this passage.

Jer 50:4, 20. Scholars have seen reason to question the authenticity of the prophecies against Babylon in Jeremiah 50–51 in the fact that the prophet had steadfastly identified that nation as the ordained instrument of Israel's well-deserved punishment (see chaps. 25, 29, 40, and compare Ezekiel's policy of silence). Nonetheless, it seems arbitrary to deny outright the possibility that at least some of the judgment oracles in these chapters may be original. This does not hold for words of salvation for Israel in these chapters, however, for they must be seen in the context of expectation for an imminent return in which antecedent punishment for Babylon is a premise rather than a matter of anxious concern. Separate sayings introduced by the special formula *bayyāmîm hahēm ûbā'ēt hahî',* followed by *ně'um YHWH*[14] (50:4-5 and 50:20), predict that, first, the weeping and reunited people should return to Zion synchronously with Babylon's imminent downfall (vv 2-3); and second that, synchronously with punishment on the king of Babylon and with northern (!) Israel's restoration to its native terrain (vv 18-19), the surviving remnant both in Israel and in Judah would be examined for purity and then pardoned (v 20). Apart from the remoteness of the possibility that Jeremiah may have actually spoken these words, the situation would require a date in the last years of the exile or in the early postexilic period, before the return to Zion had actually begun, much as in Zechariah (cf. 2:10-16 [E 6-12]).[15]

Countering the hypothetical possibility that vv 4-5 constitutes an integral continuation from vv 2-3 is the consideration that v 4a is almost certainly prose within a loosely poetic context. In v 20 there is rough parallelism, but the rhythm is uncertain; in any event the shift from concern for northern Israel alone in v 19 to a concern for both Israel and Judah in v 20 is too drastic to make an integral connection likely.[16] Both additions are probably from the same redactor, who uses the double formula in his transitions for predicting the events of future days together with a new situation.

Joel 4:1 [E 3:1]. The complex phrase in Joel 4:1, *kî hinnēh bayyāmîm hahēm ûbā'ēt hahî',* followed by a circumstantial clause, "When . . . ," introduces an apocalyptic expansion in vv 2-3 that is styled as a first-person Yahweh speech. The conjunctive *kî* shows that it has been designed to expound the markedly eschatological material that precedes it, even though the word *hinnēh* is constitutionally disjunctive. The double time-designative may emulate late redactional usage in Jeremiah, but has different spelling *(hahēmmâ* for *hahēm).* The plural of *yôm* is not at all commensurate with the singular *yôm YHWH haggādôl wĕhannôrā',* "Yahweh's great and terrible day," in 3:5 (E 2:31), but is rather designed to cover the synchronous events of a universal outpouring of a prophetic spirit and the heavenly portents that are to occur before the coming *(lipnê bô')* of Yahweh's final day (3:1-5 [E 2:28-32]), along with the survival of true worshipers at Mount Zion. To Joel's redactor these constituted both an indefinite period and a complex situation, coordinate with the restoration of Judah/Jerusalem's restoration and preparatory to the summoning and judging of the nations. The ultimate world-event is to be the "great and terrible day of Yahweh"; preceding it is to be a series of events scheduled for *'ahărê-ken* (3:1 [E 2:28]) and tantamount to the supplementer's "when I restore the fortunes of Judah and Israel" mentioned in 4:1 (E 3:1). This is the world's penultimate day, synchronous with "in those days and in that situation."

Zeph 3:20. Meter is sufficiently regular in Zeph 3:19 to reveal that *bā'ēt hahî'* in that verse is a gloss. *Bā'ēt hahî'* is an introductory transition at the beginning of the following verse (20),[17] which is prose and not poetry. This secondary expansion upon v 19 extends the list of salvific events to include return, renown, and restoration, which are to be synchronous with them, not in sequence from them.

Zech 8:23. Zechariah 8 appears to be composed of a series of summary paraphrases of separate oracles by Zechariah collected by his immediate disciples (see Chapter Two in the section on *wĕ'attâ* in v 11). Each is introduced with the messenger formula (vv 2, 3, 4, 6, 9, 14, 20, 23). Expanding the image of a future *('ôd)* worldwide conversion to Yahweh (vv 20-22) is v 23's lively description of Judaism's special role in this conversion, which is made synchronous with it by an initial *bayyāmîm hahēmmâ.* The plural is appropriate because the predicted return is to consist of numerous individual conversions.

4. Conclusions

a. Formulaic variations

It is a relatively insignificant matter that Jer 3:16, 5:18; Joel 4:1 [E 3:1] (cf. the time identifier in 3:2 [E 2:29]); and Zech 8:23 are among the passages whose temporal transitions exhibit the longer spelling, *bayyāmîm hahēmmâ*, while all other occurrences have the shorter spelling. The fact that virtually all (except Neh 13:15, 23) past occurrences also have the shorter spelling is an indication that this is definitely the older and better established tradition. It is striking that within Jeremiah, with its multiple layers of redaction, this difference in orthography manifests itself as an indication that individual redactors working upon it used distinct spellings. The shorter spelling, *bayyāmîm hahēm,* appears in 31:29, 33:15-16, 50:4 and 20, but these passages vary in date. The short spelling is no direct indication of lateness, but rather a mark of comparative antiquity. The respective spellings must be given their relative dates on the basis of affinities with the original or earlier forms of the redacted text.

It is interesting that all but five combinational occurrences introduce redactional additions, twice in formal rubrics introducing citations. This last is a definite peculiarity of the Jeremianic redaction, in striking contrast to the regular appearance of *bayyôm hahû'* in rubrics introducing liturgical fragments, peculiar to Isaiah, Micah, and Zephaniah (see in Chapter Three).

The five integral occurrences of our two formulas either appear within redactional materials that create a bridge between separate collections (Jer 31:1) and expand earlier oracles (Jer 33:15-16), or belong to an apocalyptic vision (Dan 12:1 *bis*). In other words, there are no original occurrences of either *bayyāmîm hahēm(mâ)* or *bā'ēt hahî'* as an integral transition.

Though it is not clear why *bayyāmîm hahēm(mâ)* or *bā'ēt hahî'* has been chosen in these passages rather than *bayyôm hahû',* some sense may be discerned in the combination of the two formulas at Jer 33:15, 50:4, 20; Joel 4:1 (E 3:1) (the last with foregoing *kî hinnēh*). The evident purpose is to establish both a before-and-after (temporal) connection and a cause-and-effect (situational) connection between what precedes and what follows. This is perhaps what we might expect in the relatively sophisticated historical thinking of later writers. A lengthened period of time and a complex situation allow for events or conditions that are either synchronous with, or sequential from, other events or conditions. It is striking that three of the four passages with the combinational formula involve sequences from what is presupposed to that which is newly announced. In Jer 50:2-3, 4-5 there is a sequence from Babylon's fall to reunited Israel's return. In Jer 50:18-19, 20 there is a sequence from Babylon's fall and northern Israel's restoration, on the one hand, to a reunited Israel's purging, on the other. In Joel 3:1-5 (E 2:28-32), 4:1-3 (E 3:1-3) there is a sequence from the signs of the coming day of Yahweh and the summons of the world to judgment. The only other passage with an integral transition (Dan 12:1) is apocalyptic; though it has only *bā'ēt hahî'*, it has it twice, first as a synchronizer and second for sequencing.

b. Vaticinium ex eventu

Virtually all passages with these particular transitions are true predictions. The redactors in question were projecting the future through intuitive inspiration, not from facts already known. The two exceptions are Jer 5:18-19, predicting an exile that was, in fact, part of the redactor's experience (see the question why, with its answer) and also Jer 8:1-3 (predicting the peoples' acceptance of death). Nevertheless, the predictions at Jer 3:17-18 presuppose the *vaticinium ex eventu* of v 16, while the dual predictions in Dan 12:1 presuppose the *vaticinium ex eventu* of 11:2-39.

c. Temporal relationships

Even though transitional *bayyāmîm hahēm(mâ)* and *bā'ēt hahî'* introduce events or conditions that are to coincide roughly in time with that of the underlying material (whether synchronously or in sequence), these are placed into a varying pattern of time relationships (compare in Chapter Two with regard to *bayyôm hahû'*). Summarizing our foregoing analysis of the individual passages, we may categorize the various temporal moves as follows:

1) The move is from an actual present disguised as proximately future *(vaticinium ex eventu)* to a genuinely proximate future:

Jer 3:17-18 (introductory synchronisms in prose additions), from a condition of prosperous renewal despite loss of the ark (v 16) to the submissive gathering of the nations to Jerusalem *(bā'ēt hahî')* and the reunification of Israel and Judah in the ancestral homeland *(bayyāmîm hahemmâ);*

Jer 50:4 (introductory synchronism in prose addition), from Babylon's ruin (vv 2-3) to the return of repentant Israel and Judah *(bayyāmîm hahēm ûbā'ēt hahî');*

Jer 50:20 (introductory synchronism in prose addition), from Babylon's

ruin and Israel's restoration (vv 18-19) to Israel's and Judah's
pardon and purging *(bayyāmîm hahēm ûbāʿēt hahîʾ);*

Dan 12:1 *bis* (integral sequences to synchronic events), from the end of
a "contemptible person" (11:40-45) to Michael's appearance and
a period of trouble *(ûbāʿēt hahîʾ bis).*

2) The move is from one event to another within the proximate future:

Isa 18:7 (introductory synchronism in prose addition), from universal
ruin (vv 3-6) to Egypt's bringing of tribute to Yahweh *(bāʿēt hahîʾ);*

Jer 4:11 (synchronism in formal rubric introducing citation), from the
people's and Jerusalem's complaint (v 10) to the reassurance of a
destroying wind yet to be experienced *(bayyāmîm hahēm);*

Jer 5:18 (introductory synchronism in prose addition), from a calamitous
invasion (vv 15-17) to survival in servitude *(wĕgam bayyāmîm
hahēmmâ);*

Jer 8:1 (introductory synchronism in prose addition), from general death
and desolation (7:33-34) to the exhibiting and embracing of the
tokens of death *(bāʿēt hahîʾ);*

Jer 31:1 (integral sequence in redactional transition), from Yahweh's
ruinous anger (30:23-24) to reaffirmation of his covenant *(bāʿēt
hahîʾ);*

Jer 31:29 (synchronism in formal rubric introducing citation), from the
replanting of Israel and Judah (vv 27-28) to the placing of responsibility on culpable individuals *(bayyāmîm hahēm);*

Jer 33:15-16 (integral synchronisms in redactional recasting of 23:5-6),
from the fulfillment of promises to Israel and Judah (v 14) to the
appearance of a "branch" who will bring justice *(bayyāmîm hahēm
ûbāʿēt hahîʾ);*

Zeph 3:20 (introductory synchronism in prose addition), from praise on
the day of deliverance (v 19) to return with restoration *(bāʿēt
hahîʾ).*

3) The move is from one event to another in the remote future:

Zech 8:23 (introductory synchronism in prose addition), from a coming
to Yahweh from many cities (vv 20-22) to a request to accompany
each Jew on the part of ten foreigners *(bayyāmîm hahēmmâ).*

4) The move is from a series of synchronous, proximately penultimate
events to other penultimate events prior to the ultimate event:

Joel 4:1 (E 3:1) (introductory synchronism in prose addition), from the
outpouring of the spirit, cosmic portents, and salvation for the
faithful (3:4-6 [E 2:30-32]) to Judah/Jerusalem's restoration and
the gathering of the nations for judgment *(kî hinnēh bayyāmîm
hahēmmâ ûbāʿēt hahîʾ)* prior to *(lipnê bōʾ)* the "great and terrible
day of Yahweh."

Two things invite our special attention as we compare the transitions *bayyāmîm hahēm(mâ)* and *bāʿēt hahî'* with *bayyôm hahû':* (1) the inventory of images is markedly reduced and (2) the new happenings tend to be cast as a permanent state or condition, rather than as a concrete event. The most common images are those of Judah's and Israel's return, cleansing, renewal, and reunification.

d. The oracle formula

A final word needs to be said about the appearance of the oracle formula *nĕ'um YHWH,* with *bayyāmîm hahēm(mâ)* and *bāʿēt hahî'.* The main thing to be noted is that it appears only in Jeremiah, legitimizing an expansion of 5:18, 8:1, 50:4, 20; cf. 3:16 or an emphatic contradiction to (31:1) the underlying event. Jer 5:18, with its unique formula *wĕgam bayyāmîm hahēmmâ,* adds a rationale for Israel's chastisement. 8:1, with *bāʿēt hahî',* intensifies the image of death by articulating the nation's acceptance of it as final. 31:1 offers Yahweh's continuing fidelity to his covenant as the foil to the outpouring of wrath on Israel — the most portentous move within this book's fierce and variegated portrayals of imminent destruction. 50:4 and 20, with *bayyāmîm hahēm ûbāʿēt hahî',* explain Babylon's downfall as the opportunity for the nation's restoration.

Hinnēh yāmîm bā'îm, "Behold, Days Are Coming"

1. Introduction: Syntactical analysis

Hinnēh yāmîm bā'îm, followed by a verb in the *wāw*-consecutive perfect, is a transition formula found almost exclusively in Amos and Jeremiah. Having no possibility of referring to the past, it is temporally and situationally futuristic. The plural *yāmîm* is employed rather than the singular *yôm* because it is a new, ongoing condition or situation that is predicted, not a singular event. The only formal attribute of the *yāmîm,* "days," during which this condition or situation shall occur is that they are "coming" (active participle, pl), that is, in the very process of becoming a present reality.

According to Isa 7:17, the finite plural of the verb *bw'* may apply to future days that Yahweh shall yet bring forth (hiph. impf. 3ms) as well as to days that have already come in the past through Yahweh's permission (qal perf. 3ms); but the participle refers to an incipient and continuous process of becoming, both in the case of the plural and in the case of the singular *yôm,* which is used predicatively in Isa 13:9 and Mic 7:4,[18] attributively in Jer 47:4, and both predicatively and attributively in Mal 3:19 [E 4:1].

The initial deictic particle *hinnēh* in this special formula of transition points emphatically to the factuality and actuality of this coming to new reality. In terms of structure and function, the temporal formula *hinnēh yāmîm bā'îm* must be seen as the counterpart of a special and widely employed prophetic formula for announcing Yahweh's imminent action. This has *hinnēh* inflected with the first personal singular suffix, followed by an active participle from a wide variety of verbs.[19] An appropriate name for this locution might be "imminent action formula"[20] because it stands at the beginning of Yahweh's announcement of his immediate or imminent act or action. Although the temporal formula *hinnēh yāmîm bā'îm* is less directly personal, it too announces the event or situation that is to follow in the imminent future. The oracle formula that follows it in sixteen of twenty occurrences assures its authority as an expression of revelational intention.

As we shall see, it makes a great deal of difference whether *hinnēh yāmîm bā'îm* is integral to a given pericope or provides an introductory link to a redactional expansion. The integral use is slightly more common than the introductory use.

2. Integral transitions

a. From summons/command to announcement of judgment

2 Kgs 20:17 par Isa 39:6. Following repartee between Isaiah and Hezekiah concerning the latter's behavior toward the Babylonian envoys, a prophet legend introduces Isaiah's oracle commencing with a summons to hear, to which *hinnēh yāmîm bā'îm* next appends an announcement of what is to happen with the treasures that the king has vaingloriously displayed, as well as with the princely posterity.[21]

Jer 30:3. Following a distinct break in the text, vv 1-3 stand as a formal introduction to the new collection of optimistic oracles in chaps. 30–31. The messenger formula leads to a command for Jeremiah to write "all the words which I have spoken to you," referring almost certainly to the oracles that are to follow (the "book of consolation," 30:5–31:22) rather than to the foregoing collection of narrative materials to which this has been attached. The command to write is followed by an unusual grounding clause with *kî,* "for" (elsewhere only in Amos 4:2), and the formula under study, appearing to make the announcement of return and repossession of the land a basis for all else that Jeremiah proclaims.[22] This astonishing prediction is authenticated by *nĕ'um YHWH,* following the transition formula. It seems certain that an early redactor, rather than the prophet himself, composed this introduction. This crucial passage will be more fully discussed in Chapter Seven.

b. From accusation (invective) to announcement (threat)

1 Sam 2:31. *Wĕ'attâ* followed by an aphorism concerning whom Yahweh honors and despises in v 30 (see in Chapter Two), which in effect constitutes an accusation against the house of Eli, precedes an announcement of the coming fate of all Elides, introduced by the integral transition *hinnēh yāmîm bā'îm.*[23]

Jer 7:32. Within the epexegetical expansion of vv 30-34, the accusation of abominations in the temple (v 30) and in Tophet (v 31) leads to a transition with *lākēn* and *hinnēh yāmîm bā'îm,* introducing the announcement in vv 32-34 of a change of name that will be symbolic of the all-encompassing death that is to come upon idolaters. The prediction of altered circumstances is strengthened by a following oracle formula.[24]

Jer 19:6. The motifs of renaming and of all-encompassing death make epexegesis in Jer 19:1-9 roughly parallel to 7:30-34, in spite of notable compositional variations between them.[25] It is noteworthy that the peculiar locution *lākēn hinnēh yāmîm bā'îm,* followed by *nĕ'um YHWH,* remains the same in the parallel verses, 7:32 and 19:6. The function of providing the transition from accusation to announcement in an oracle of judgment also remains the same, establishing structural as well as linguistic connections between the two passages.

Jer 48:12, 49:2. Again the peculiar locution *lākēn hinnēh yāmîm bā'îm* provides a transition from what amounts to an accusation against Moab in 48:11 and the announcement of Yahweh's intervention in 48:12-13. Jer 49:1-2 concerns Ammon rather than Moab: the full formula with *lākēn hinnēh yāmîm bā'îm* and *nĕ'um YHWH* provides the transition in 49:2 from an accusation that Milcom has dispossessed Gad to the announcement that through battle and fire Israel shall dispossess Rabbah.[26]

Jer 51:47, 52. The idiosyncratic formulation *lākēn hinnēh yāmîm bā'îm* again appears integrally at the head of separate announcements of divine punishment in what purports to be a judgment oracle against Babylon, but which is in effect a salvation saying for the returning exiles, following sequentially from the announcement. Summonses to flee in the manner of Second Isaiah and Zechariah intervene in vv 47-49[27] and vv 50-51 to separate this dual announcement from the taunt that stands at the beginning of the literary unit commencing in v 41. In v 52, though not in v 47, *nĕ'um YHWH* follows the transition.[28]

Amos 4:2. Although the foregoing occurrences belong to secondary materials, the distinctively styled occurrence in Amos 4:2 is unquestionably original. The accusation against the proud Samarian women in v 1 leads directly in vv 2-3 to an announcement of judgment, introduced by a statement of divine swearing and concluding with *ně'um YHWH,* while *kî* followed by *hinnēh yāmîm bā'îm* introduces the content of Yahweh's oath. The prepositional phrase *'alêkem* (masculine!) specifies the object of divine wrath in the days that are coming.

3. Introductory transitions

a. As anacrusis in poetry

Amos 9:13. In poetic imagery that is strongly reminiscent of "eschatological" language in Jeremiah, a condition of replanting and fruitfulness is predicted in what is intended as the ultimate redactional correction to the harsh words of Amos's book. Expanding the content of "that day" in the redactional verses immediately preceding it, vv 11-12 (see in Chapter Three), it employs the temporal transition under study as it stands in anacrusis, followed by the oracle formula; it is striking that this formula appears once again at the end of the unit (and thus of the entire book!).

b. As introduction to prose additions

Jer 9:24 (E 25). Hinnēh yāmîm bā'îm followed by *ně'um YHWH* introduces a terse and unspecific announcement of judgment on the countries neighboring Judah; there is no discernible literary connection with vv 16-21 (E 17-22) or the wisdom saying of vv 22-23 (E 23-24), leaving this announcement without a foregoing accusation.[29] On this crucially important passage, see in Chapters Six and Nine.

Jer 16:14 par 23:7. Lākēn hinnēh yāmîm bā'îm followed by *ně'um YHWH* introduces a citation, similar to those of Jer 7:32 and 19:6, that is in effect a late announcement of salvation counteracting or extending the foregoing exile. Among occurrences of the introductory transition, this doublet is unique in recording a foregoing *lākēn,* implying a preceding accusation that neither context actually contains. The fact that the LXX places 23:7-8 after 23:40 shows that it was originally connected to words of dire doom, both in 16:13 and in 23:40.[30]

Jer 23:5 par 33:14. The formula of transition, *hinnēh yāmîm bā'îm,* followed again by *ně'um YHWH,* introduces an announcement of Yahweh's benevolent purpose for the Davidides and for Jerusalem; this is attached to a

foregoing salvation oracle for the scattered flock in 33:12-13.[31] In view of the
significant revisions that appear in 33:14-16 over against the undeniably older
text of 23:5-6, it seems likely that 23:1-4 and 23:5-6 were already joined to
each other before they came to serve as the basis for the revision of 33:14ff.[32]

Jer 31:27, 31, 38. Attached to the "book of consolation," Jer 30:5–31:22
(see above on Jer 30:3 and 31:29), are three early additions to the book:
31:27-28, 31:31-34, and 31:38-40. Each of these has the identical introductory
transition *hinnēh yāmîm bā'îm,*[33] followed by *nĕ'um YHWH.* Each unit is a
complete salvation oracle announcing radically altered, permanent conditions
for the "house of Israel and house of Judah" (vv 27f., 31ff.) and Jerusalem
(vv 38-40). The *communis opinio* identifies these units as redactional,[34] but
William Holladay defends the authenticity of vv 31-34, ascribes vv 27-28 to
a close disciple of Jeremiah,[35] and dates vv 38-40 to the time of Nehemiah.[36]
As will be argued in Chapters Six and Nine, although each of these three units
recasts a thematic element that is typical of the prophet, they have not actually
been composed by him. It is apparent at least of vv 27f. and vv 31ff. that they
reflect the situation of the early exile, hence Jeremiah could very well have
written them; but they embody too drastic a change in ideology to be directly
ascribed to the prophet. Hence they must be ascribed to close disciples. All
three have been inserted in the text by a single early redactor. The stereotyped
introductory formula in each unit is the work of this redactor as he strove for
congruence of form in order to enhance an effect of finality in this threefold
addition to the collection of Jeremiah's oracles of hope.[37]

Amos 8:11. An early redactor (certainly not the one of 9:13-15) expanded
the reference to *yôm mar,* "a bitter day," in v 10 (itself part of a redactional
addition beginning with *wĕhayâ bayyôm hahû'* and the oracle formula in v 9)
with use of *hinnēh yāmîm bā'îm* and *nĕ'um [   ] YHWH* in anacrusis.[38] The
transition formula has the effect of expanding a single day of darkness and
mourning into an indefinite period of spiritual famine and futile searching,
while the attached oracle formula authenticates this prediction as divine revelation, specially needed within the context of a predicted withholding of
revelation.

4. Conclusions

a. Integral versus introductory patterns

That its position is most typically integral, even though it usually appears in
secondary materials, is to be concluded both from the predominant appearance
of *hinnēh yāmîm bā'îm* in this position and from the fact that it is only in this
usage that it is original (1 Sam 2:31; 2 Kgs 20:17 par Isa 39:6; Amos 4:2).

Nevertheless, this formula has proven to be readily adaptable when used as an introductory transition. The important difference between these two classes of usage is that a close connection to foregoing material appears only when this formula is integral. In 2 Kgs 20:17 par it follows a summons to hear, and in Jer 30:3 it follows a command to write. In 1 Sam 2:31; Jer 7:32, 19:6, 48:12, 49:2; and Amos 4:2 it provides the bridge between the accusation and the announcement within a prophecy of judgment. And in the remarkably innovative passage, Jer 51:41-53, the formula appearing in vv 47 and 52 connects a taunt, followed by a recurrent summons to flee, to a double announcement of Babylon's judgment. In all the introductory transitions, on the other hand, *hinnēh yāmîm bāʾîm* often appears asyndetically, with a connection far less obvious to foregoing materials. It should be noted that in passages with the introductory transition it is a rule that the new condition or situation should be one of expanded blessing (Jer 16:14 par 23:7, 23:5, 31:27, 31, 38, 33:14; Amos 9:13).

b. The Jeremianic doublets[39]

It is noteworthy that the book of Jeremiah has the majority of the occurrences of this formula; it is in fact all but unique to this book. But it seems even more remarkable that this book contains two sets of parallel passages with it (16:14 par 23:7, 23:5 par 33:14) as well as a third set in which the announcement of judgment is virtually identical, even while the contexts of the respective announcements show independent development (7:30-34, 19:4-9). All Jeremianic occurrences appear either as introductory redactional transitions or as integral transitions within redactional pericopes. The possibility of some authentic derivation of the one from the other must be left open. In fact, the appearance of real or virtual doublets may make authentic derivation more probable, for only a tradition having some probability of connection to the historical Jeremiah would be likely to have produced close variants of this sort. For instance, a comparison of the obviously late 33:14-16 with its model in 23:5-6 makes Jeremianic authorship rather likely for the latter (see especially the substitution of the vague "in those days" for explicit "in his days").

Nevertheless, redactional continuity is notoriously problematical in Jeremiah. It is often difficult to discern whether it is original material that is being expanded or material from a foregoing stage of redaction. When it can be shown that both parallel passages within a given set expand material that is close to the original, as is the case with Jer 7:30ff. and 19:3ff., it is virtually certain that neither expansion actually contains authentic material. On the other hand, when similarly introduced expansions have been arranged in a set, as is the case with 31:27-28, 31-34, 38-40, ascription to a single redaction becomes very likely, even as the possibility of authenticity becomes highly unlikely.

c. The styling with lākēn

If *hinnēh yāmîm bāʾîm* is formally asyndetic with relation to foregoing materials, the styling with *kî* draws a close causal connection with the foregoing. On the other hand, when *lākēn* (occurring only in Jeremiah) precedes this formula as an integral transition or precedes it as an introductory transition, the connection is made stronger at the expense of the syntax, which grows notably awkward (7:31, 16:14, 19:6, 23:7, 48:12, 51:47, 52). The strongly disjunctive *hinnēh* does not go well with the strongly conjunctive *lākēn*. The combination is striking, and it does not seem unreasonable to suggest that a single redactor may be responsible for all occurrences with *lākēn*. The combination may indeed be a mark of relative lateness — which must nevertheless in all instances be independently corroborated from the content. But this in turn makes likely a relative earliness of redaction in the passages without *lākēn,* even though there is no direct basis for assigning all passages without it to an individual redactor.

In spite of the fact that *lākēn* intends to introduce a consequence of foregoing events or situations — here as quite generally elsewhere in the Old Testament — it should be seen that it does not make such a consequence less temporal than in passages where it does not occur. In matter of fact, the list of integral occurrences of *hinnēh yāmîm bāʾîm,* which places the coming events or conditions in close temporal sequence with what precedes, has foregoing *lākēn* in four passages, as compared with four passages without and two passages having it (Jer 51:47, 52) that draw what precedes and what follows into a situational rather than a temporal connection. In none of the redactional occurrences (with *lākēn* only in Jer 16:14 par 23:7) is a temporal sequence evident. It is only possible in the former passage, because the coming events or conditions have no direct precedence from what is implied in the context. The connection may be called situational, but only in a loose way. It would be more appropriate to call the transition synchronic, a form of connection that predominates in the use of most of the temporal formulas remaining for discussion.

d. Vaticinium ex eventu

Depending on the relative dating of individual passages within the books in question, coming events or conditions introduced by *hinnēh yāmîm bāʾîm* are scheduled either for a proximate or for a remote future. It seems irrelevant that the expression *yāmîm bā'îm,* "coming days," implies in itself that what is predicted is immediately emergent; it makes no difference whether the connection is integral or introductory. In point of fact, it is rather clear that in two (three, with the parallel) of our passages what is described as imminent is in fact reserved for a fairly distant future that is in fact already present in the writer's observation and experience. This is certainly the case with 2 Kgs 20:17 par Isa 39:6, where Isaiah predicts an exile to Babylon that is still future for Hezekiah, but is clearly past in the composer's experience and observation. It is certainly true also in 1 Sam 2:31, predicting a rejection of the house of Eli that has already occurred in the experience of the redactor.

That 2 Kgs 20:14-19 par Isa 39:1-8 and 1 Sam 2:27-36 are both anti-dynastic, and that each forecasts a future corresponding to the writer's actual present, argue for some kind of ideological affinity between them. Both have, in fact, been touched up by the deuteronomistic redaction from prophetic legends originating respectively in the time of Samuel and of Hezekiah (in spite of dissenting voices, most scholars agree that the Isaiah doublet was copied into the text from 2 Kings at a time when the original Isaiah corpus was already complete).

In the original Hezekiah narrative, only "some of your sons" (*mibbānékā*) were to go to Babylon along with all the treasure that the envoys had seen. But if Hezekiah's own actual children were intended, this would have to have come only through a political-military disaster which Hezekiah himself would have experienced; hence he would not have been able to say, "Why not, if there will be peace and security in my days?" It has to have been the deuteronomistic redactor, therefore, who shaped the story as it now stands, intending the prediction as a cryptic allusion to his own situation, that of the exile following 586 B.C.E.[40] It seems reasonable to argue that the deuteronomistic redactor was responsible also for the transitional formula *hinnēh yāmîm bā'îm,* which pertains, then, to this redactor's present rather than to Hezekiah's immediate future.

It is somewhat the same with regard to the Samuel passage. As Martin Noth has argued,[41] three narrative traditions have been intertwined in 1 Samuel 1–3: a birth story, a narrative of prophetic denunciation against Eli, and a story of revelation to the boy Samuel. But the anti-Eli material does not appear in the text as originally composed. Most scholars agree that the deuteronomistic redactor has touched up this material,[42] and this is especially evident in 2:34-35, where a "faithful priest" is predicted. However, there are several other problems here, the most serious of which is that Eli is roundly denounced in v 29 for greed even though it is the sons who are guilty according to vv 12-17, and in vv 22-25 Eli deplores what they were doing. One should note also the vacillation in terminology in the references to "your father's house" over against "your house," which has probably arisen from the fact that in the early form of this tradition the concern may have been only for Eli's immediate family ("your house"), whereas in the deuteronomist's recasting the concern is with Eli's dynasty ("your father's house"); cf. 1 Kgs 2:27b. It is more than probable that already at the predeuteronomistic stage, the predicted calamity for the Elides and the ascendancy of the Zadokite priesthood were already accomplished facts. This would also be true if the definitive form of the text could be shown to date from the immediate post-Solomonic period rather than from the period of Josiah.

e. Deuteronomistic antecedents

This analysis has special importance in a search for a *terminus a quo* for the use of the temporal transition, *hinnēh yāmîm bāʾîm*. Amos 4:2 is unquestionably original to the prophet, but here the words do not yet appear as a stereotyped formula. In all the remaining passages we get the impression that it is stereotyped. All passages on our list without a preceding *lākēn* (1 Sam 2:31; 2 Kgs 20:17 par Isa 39:6; Jer 9:24 [E 25], 23:5 [of which 33:14 is a late modification], 30:3, 31:27, 31, 38; Amos 8:11, 9:13) can be dated in the light of the foregoing discussion to roughly the fifty-year period from 625 to 575 B.C.E. Jeremianic passages with the peculiar *lākēn* styling are almost certainly younger and must come from a late redactor.

We have pointed to the likelihood that deuteronomistic influence may be the common link between 1 Sam 2:27ff.; 2 Kgs 20:12ff.; and Amos 8:11-12 and 9:13-15, on the one hand, and the above-mentioned Jeremiah passages, on the other (particularly the notable array, 31:27-28, 31-34, 38-40). To speak of a common influence does not demand a single redactor, deuteronomistic or otherwise. All that can confidently be claimed is that this locution was current in closely related religious circles during the period mentioned. In any event, it is striking that the two occurrences in preprophetic narrative texts are found using this locution as a sham future, thus producing in each passage a *vaticinium ex eventu;* viz., a prediction arising from awareness of an event already past or present. This is important, for such sham futures will appear again with use of some of the temporal formulas yet to be discussed, particularly *bĕʾaḥărît hayyāmîm*, as in Deut 4:30 and 31:29 (see the excursus on revelational authority in the *vaticinium ex eventu* in Chapter Three).

f. Temporal relationships

In surveying futuristic time relationships produced by the transition *hinnēh yāmîm bā'îm*, it is useful to keep the more numerous integral occurrences separate from those that are introductory because the former create sequences while the latter involve no other than synchronisms. Sequential temporal moves are as follows:

1) The move is from the past influencing the present, to a proximate future (accusation-to-announcement pattern):

> Jer 7:32, 19:6 (both with *lākēn*), from cultic abominations (7:30-31; 19:4-5) to the change of Tophet-Hinnom's name to "valley of slaughter";
>
> Jer 48:12 (with *lākēn*), from Moab's security and well-being (v 11) to her destruction and shaming (image of shattered vessels);
>
> Jer 49:2 (with *lākēn*), from Ammon's dispossession of Gad (v 1) to warfare and dispossession in the cities of Ammon.

2) The move is from the present to the proximate future (summons-to-announcement pattern):

> Jer 30:3, from a command to the prophet to write (v 2) to Israel's restoration and return;
>
> Amos 4:2, from exploitative luxuriation on the part of rich women (v 1) to their dispossession and exile.

3) The move is from the present to another present disguised as proximately future *(vaticinium ex eventu):*

> 1 Sam 2:31, from Yahweh's resolve to dishonor those who despise him (v 30) to disaster upon the Elides;
>
> 2 Kgs 20:17 par Isa 39:6, from Hezekiah's prideful display (2 Kgs 20:12-15; Isa 39:1-4) to plunder and exile.

4) The move is retrograde, from a remote future to a proximate future (summons to flee–announcement pattern):

> Jer 51:47, 52 (both with *lākēn*) from a summons for Israel to return (vv 45-46, 50-51) to Babylon's fall.

Passages with introductory rather than integral transitions produce either a sequence or a synchronism. The move is from one event in the proximate future to another event in the proximate future in the case of sequences, and from a proximately future event to a remotely future event in the case of synchronisms:

5) The move is from one event to another in the proximate future (all synchronisms without *lākēn*):

> Jer 23:5, from new shepherds (v 4) to the gathering of the exiles in peace and security under the "righteous branch" of David;
>
> Jer 31:27, 31, 38, from Judah's restoration (vv 23-25) to replanting for Judah and Israel; to a new covenant, a new spirituality, and a new state of forgiveness; to a rebuilt wall with sacred precincts;
>
> Jer 33:14, from new flocks throughout the land (vv 12-13) to the ful-

fillment of Yahweh's promise in the coming of David's "righteous branch";

Amos 8:11, from the darkness of mourning (vv 9-10) to a famine of Yahweh's revelation;

Amos 9:13, from the rebuilding of David's "booth" and renewed conquest (vv 11-12) to the land's prolific fruitfulness.

6) The move is in sequence from a proximate future to a remotely future event (with *lākēn hinnēh yāmîm bā'îm* as transition):

Jer 16:14 par 23:7, from forsakenness in exile to a new way of swearing concerning Israel's "exodus."[43]

Noteworthy here is the predominance of integral sequences marking the transition from one time-frame to another; also the phenomenon of *vaticinium ex eventu* in the predictions found in preprophetic narrative discourse (1 Sam 2:31, 2 Kgs 20:17 par); also the peculiar reverse sequence in Jer 51:47, 52. A sense of definite sequence is seen in the item-5 passages, where *hinnēh yāmîm bā'îm* without *lākēn* is an introductory transition formula.

g. The oracle formula

It may be conjectured, finally, that the styling with *ně'um YHWH* makes a special effort to ensure divine authentication. The original occurrences on our list, 1 Sam 2:31, 2 Kgs 20:17 par, and Amos 4:3, have no need for the special validation sought by the use of the oracle formula because divine authority is already entirely secure. But this is almost a stereotyped element in virtually all the remaining passages, though with some textual uncertainty. We may conjecture that this is needed in the redactional materials in which *hinnēh yāmîm bā'îm* is integral (Jer 7:31, 19:6, 48:12, 49:2, 51:52) or introductory (Jer 9:24 [E 25], 16:14, 23:5, 7, 31:27, 31, 38, 33:14; Amos 8:11, 9:13) because the announcement is of something that constitutes a fresh, innovative interpretation of Yahweh's will.

As a final note it may be pointed out that in the roster of passages with *hinnēh yāmîm bā'îm* we detect a definite pattern of temporal convergence near to, and within, the period of Babylonian exile — the only significant exception being Amos 4:2, unquestionably original to the prophet and dating from the eighth century. Although it cannot be proven, it is not unreasonable to conjecture that this locution came to prominent use in popular speech in the time of Amos. Under the influence of this locution, the deuteronomistic school and the early Jeremianic school came to employ it, most particularly with reference to the coming (or currently experienced) event of the exile. The styling with foregoing *lākēn* appears to be original only to Jeremiah's exilic redactors, who used it integrally in their own compositions at 30:3, 48:12, 49:2, 51:47, 52, and elsewhere in their additions to earlier strata within the book (7:31, 16:14, 19:6, 23:7).

'aḥar, "Afterwards," and *'aḥărê-kēn,* "After This"

1. Introduction

When used as transitions, *'aḥar* and *'aḥărê-kēn*[44] create sequences between the event of the underlying material and a new event to follow. This is true whether the transition is integral or introductory. In this respect these transitions are like integral *bayyôm hahû', bayyāmîm hahēm,* and *bā'ēt hahî',* which almost always create sequences, in contrast to their introductory use, which usually creates synchronisms.

Although we are directly concerned only with *'aḥar* and *'aḥărê-kēn* as futuristic transitions within the prophetic literature, other types of futuristic usage may be noted, along with the numerous past transitions — by far the more common.

As past time identifiers, both forms are used in initial position before introductory temporal or circumstantial clauses. As past transitions, we note the following forms:

wĕ'aḥar, "and afterwards," Gen 10:18, 30:21, 33:7, 38:30; Exod 5:1; Josh 24:5; Judg 1:9; 1 Chr 2:21;

'aḥar zeh, "after this," 2 Chr 32:9;

'aḥar haddābar hazzeh, "after this thing," 1 Kgs 13:33;

'aḥar haddĕbarîm hā'ēlleh, "after these things," Gen 18:5, 39:7, 40:1; 1 Kgs 17:17, 21:1; Esth 2:1, 3:1; Ezr 7:1;

wayhî 'aḥar, "and it happened afterwards," Gen 22:1; Job 42:7;

wayhî 'aḥarê haddĕbarîm hā'ēlleh, "and it happened after these things," Gen 22:20, 48:1;

'aḥărê-kēn, "after this," Josh 10:26; Judg 16:4; 1 Sam 24:6 (E 5); 2 Sam 2:1, 8:1 par 1 Chr 18:1; 2 Sam 10:1 par 1 Chr 19:1; 2 Sam 13:1, 21:14, 18 par 1 Chr 20:4; 2 Kgs 6:24; Jer 34:11; Job 3:1; 2 Chr 20:1, 24:4;

wĕ'aḥarê-kēn, "and after this," Gen 23:19, 25:26, 45:15; Exod 34:32; Josh 8:34.

Futuristic occurrences of transitional *'aḥar* and *'aḥărê-kēn* outside the prophetic corpus, with a number of variations, fall into three special categories, as follows:

1) Discourse: *'aḥar* in Gen 18:5, 24:55, *wĕ'aḥar* in Judg 7:11, 15:7, 19:5;

Ps 73:24; Job 18:2; *'aḥar-kēn* in 1 Sam 10:5, *(wĕ)'aḥarê-kēn* in Gen 32:21 (E 20); Exod 3:20, 11:1, etc.;
2) Gnomic literature: *'aḥar* in Prov 20:17, 24:27;
3) Cult legislation: *wĕ'aḥar* in Lev 14:8, etc.

There is no significant difference between the integral and the introductory use of these locutions, whether as past or as futuristic transitions.

The introductory futuristic transitions in prophecy that we have to deal with directly are relatively few; we find *'aḥar* in Hos 3:5, *(wĕ)'aḥarê-kēn* in Isa 1:26; Jer 16:16, 21:7, 46:26, 49:6, and *wĕhāyâ 'aḥarê-kēn* in Joel 3:1 (E 2:28). As previously, our method of approach is to separate the integral from the introductory occurrences.

Before we turn to these passages, we must comment on the appearance of the unique expression *'aḥărê hayyāmîm hahēm,* "after those days," in the famous passage, Jer 31:33. This passage will not be specially dealt with here since this formula functions as a time-identifier rather than as a transition, except to note that since the covenant of vv 33-34 is equivalent to that of vv 31-32, this expression is not to be understood as in sequence from the "coming days" mentioned in the opening formula at v 31 (see above on *hinnēh yāmîm bā'îm*), but as parallel to and synchronous with them. For further discussion, see our extensive treatment of this pericope in Chapter Seven.

2. Integral transitions

Isa 1:26. Dating possibly from before 701 B.C.E.,[45] the dirge of Isa 1:21-27 first announces a purging (vv 24-25) and then a restoration of judges and counselors to their former condition *(kĕbārišonâ . . . kĕbattĕḥillâ)* (v 26a), in consequence of which *('aḥărê-ken)* Jerusalem is to receive new honorific titles (cf. Isa 62:2-4, 12; Zech 8:3).[46]

Jer 16:16. Jer 16:1-13 probably is Jeremianic; vv 16-18, introduced by *wĕ'aḥarê-ken,* constitutes an early epexegesis upon it since intervening vv 14-15 are a postexilic insertion (see above on *hinnēh yāmîm bā'îm*). Depicting the Egyptians as fishers and the Babylonians as hunters, this is almost certainly a *vaticinium ex eventu* for the reason that the before-and-after sequencing could have been known only from past and present experience. Nevertheless, there is every reason to view this as from Jeremiah himself, or otherwise from his immediate school of disciples.[47]

Hos 3:5. 3:1-5 is styled as Hosea's own first-person report of his difficulties with a woman symbolizing wayward Israel, with vv 4-5 as an interpretation of the prophet's words of chastisement and assurance in v 3. *Bĕ'aḥărît hayyāmîm* at the end of v 5 is an interpretive gloss that is quite superfluous following initial *'aḥar,* and *'et dāwid malkām* is another gloss incompatible with any situation pertaining during Hosea's lifetime. Apart from these glosses, v 5aαbα constitutes a futuristic prediction based on the *vaticinium ex eventu* of v 4. A known, fictionally future event thus leads to a new event that is sequential from it in time, as well as consequent from it situationally.

3. Introductory transitions

a. As anacrusis in poetry

Joel 3:1 (E 2:28). The Joelian salvation sayings in 2:20-27 develop traditional images, but the famous prediction of the outpoured divine spirit, falling upon all conditions and classes of humankind, in 3:1-2 (E 2:28-29), is a late redactional expansion in poetic form introduced by the phrase in anacrusis, *wĕhāyâ 'aḥărê-kēn.* The form with *wĕhāyâ* is unparalleled; it introduces a condition rather than an event and is subsequent to, as well as consequent upon, the foregoing blessings.[48]

b. Introducing prose additions

Jer 21:7. The redactional attachment of this verse to vv 1-6 is another example of what William McKane calls "triggering."[49] The foregoing words probably constitute an accurate report of what Jeremiah might have said in response to Zedekiah's inquiry, and what he now predicts is a logical deduction from the contemporary situation. v 7, introduced by *wĕ'aḥarê-kēn* followed by *nĕ'um YHWH,* continues with a redactional *vaticinium ex eventu* from the early exile period based on previous and current knowledge of Zedekiah's personal fate (see our special discussion of this passage in the excursus on *vaticinium ex eventu* in Chapter Three).

Jer 46:26, 49:6. The brilliant poetry of 46:14-24 (probably Jeremianic) is followed by a generalizing prose summary in vv 25-26a,[50] but this is counterbalanced by the very late prose addition in v 26b, a *vaticinium ex eventu* affirming restoration for Egypt as a place of habitation; this also must have been occasioned by previous knowledge and not by intuitive inspiration. This interpretation is made even more likely by the fact that vv 25-26 are missing in the original LXX. Introductory *wĕ'aḥarê-kēn* creates a sequence, while concluding *nĕ'um YHWH* underscores that this is indeed Yahweh's ultimate intent regarding Egypt. A parallel reversal is affirmed in the *vaticinium ex eventu* of Jer 49:6, an addition to two oracles against Ammon,

49:1-2 (probably Jeremianic; see above on *hinnēh yāmîm bā'îm*), 3-5. *Wě'aḥarê-kēn* produces a sequence to this quasi-prediction, once again emphatically affirmed as Yahweh's final purpose with a concluding *ně'um YHWH*. It seems significant, however, that this verse is also missing in the original LXX (see our following treatment of Jer 49:39).

4. Conclusions

a. Patterns of occurrence

One is struck by the wide range in time of composition among the seven passages with the futuristic transitions, *'aḥar* and *(wě)'aḥărê-kēn*. The three integral occurrences, probably original in Isaiah (1:26), Jer (16:16), and Hosea (3:5), respectively, are very early (eighth to seventh century) while those that function as introductory transitions are relatively late; Jer 21:7 is early exilic, while Jer 46:26, 49:6 and Joel 3:1 (E 2:28) are postexilic. All seven occurrences create sequences from one event or condition to another. It is noteworthy that a variety of composers and redactors are involved.

b. Temporal relationships

The different temporal relationships involved in the use of these transitions are the following:

1) The move is from a proximate future to a remote future (genuine prediction):

Isa 1:26b, from the removal of corrupt officials at the time of Yahweh's wrath (vv 24-26a) to a symbolic renaming of Jerusalem;

    Joel 3:1 (E 2:28), from an abundance on the day of true fasting (vv 23-27) to the penultimate events preceding Yahweh's "great and terrible day" (see above on Joel 4:1 [E 3:1]).

2) The move is from a proximate future to a present disguised as a remote future *(vaticinium ex eventu):*

    Jer 16:16b, from the sending of "fishers" (the Egyptians, v 16a), to the sending of "hunters" (the Babylonians);

    Jer 21:7, from Yahweh's war against Jerusalem (vv 4-6) to Nebuchadrezzar's unpitying execution of Zedekiah and all survivors;

    Jer 46:26b, from the deliverance of Egypt to Nebuchadrezzar (v 26a) to Egypt's repopulation;

    Jer 49:6, from terror upon the Ammonites (vv 3-5) to the restoration of their fortunes.

3) The move is from a present disguised as a proximate future *(vaticinium ex eventu)* to a remote future:

> Hos 3:5, from a time without political leaders or a formal cult (v 4) to Israel's return and conversion.

The disguising of the present as future is a phenomenon that has been seen in early passages with *hinnēh yāmîm bā'îm* and that will be seen to surface also in most passages with *bĕ'aḥărît hayyāmîm,* the formula next to be examined.

Bĕ'aḥărît hayyāmîm (haššānîm), "In the Sequel of Days (Years)"

1. Introduction: nonformulaic usage

This formula is like *'attâ* in that it has no past usage; but while the latter refers only to the imminent future, this refers to what is obstensibly a distant future. The fact is that, probably and sometimes certainly, it refers to a sham future that is an actual present, producing a *vaticinium ex eventu,* as above with *'aḥărê-kēn.* The form with *haššānîm* is an idiosyncratic variant that appears only in primary material within an apocalyptic prediction at Ezek 38:8.

Examining certain nonprophetic occurrences, E. Lipiński has argued that *bĕ'aḥărît hayyāmîm* is no special eschatological *terminus technicus,* and this is confirmed by our own examination.[51] However, all but a very few occurrences of this formula are time identifiers, not transitions. These time identifiers are almost always in final position, appearing in four distinct constructions: (1) redactional introductions to traditional material (Gen 49:1; Num 24:14); (2) additions to deuteronomistic parenesis (Deut 4:30, 31:29); (3) epexegesis to a prophetic oracle (Jer 48:47);[52] (4) introduction to a vision report in late apocalyptic (Dan 2:28, 10:14). There is something remarkably consistent in these passages: they all refer to a sham future, that is, one that is presented as remotely future but is actually present or past in the speaker's experience.[53] There is a resulting expectation that occurrences of this formula that are transitional will also present a sham future, as will be largely fulfilled in the following analysis.

2. Integral transitions

Jer 23:20 par 30:24. The warning against false prophets in Jer 23:16-20 (21-22) may very well be Jeremianic,[54] dating to prior to 586, when its grim predictions were in fact fulfilled. But 30:23-24 is an early exilic extract from it, juxtaposed with 31:1 to serve as a redactional bridge to the collection of oracular material that begins at 31:2 (see the preceding section on *bayyāmîm hahēm(mâ)* and *bāʿēt hahîʾ*). All of Jer 23:16-20 is in poetic form, with the structure: parenetic appeal, 16a; motivation, 16b-17; rhetorical question, 18; vision report, 19-20a; explanatory comment, 20b. *Bĕʾaḥărît hayyāmîm,* set forward in v 20b for emphasis, draws a sharp contrast between the present situation, in which the people are left in uncertainty, and the eventual situation in which they will realize the truth of Jeremiah's words as events fulfill his prediction of doom.[55] It might be tempting to seek another *vaticinium ex eventu* here, but this would require identifying 23:20b as a virtually unparalleled gloss (cf. Ezek 38:17) in which an annotator enters into an imaginery dialogue with unspecified readers. Jeremiah's answer to the present ambivalent situation is fulfillment in the imminent future. For further discussion of this crucial passage, see our treatment in Chapter Seven.

Ezek 38:8, 16. The original non-Ezekielian oracle in 38:1–39:22 commands a mythical Gog to make ready (38:7). *Miyyāmîm rabbîm* in v 8 has drawn a sequence to the new move of mustering; in parallel with it is the unique formula *bĕʾaḥărît haššānîm,* "in the sequel of years," an integral transition to the mention of the marching that is to follow from the mustering. As I have argued elsewhere,[56] this may in fact be the most momentous passage for the early origin of apocalyptic, for it predicts an event that is to follow in sequence from an event that is still future in Ezekiel's own eschatological expectation, namely, Israel's restoration to its ancestral land.

3. Introductory transitions

a. Aṣ anacrusis in poetry

Isa 2:2 par Mic 4:1. Although scholars debate the nature of the interdependence between the two summarizing introductions found in Isa 2:2-5 and Mic 4:1-5, most agree that each is relatively late, certainly no earlier than the end of the exile.[57] In Isaiah the unit follows an editorial title (2:1) and precedes an authentic Day of Yahweh poem in vv 6ff. In Micah it begins an entirely new cycle of authentic material mixed with secondary material in chaps. 4–7, following the acknowledgedly authentic collection in chaps. 1–3. As we shall argue, the Isaiah passage belongs earlier in the overall redactional process than the Micah passage, making it likely that the Micah passage has been drawn from a model similar to, if not identical with, the text in Isaiah.[58]

It is the material in vv 2-4 in the Isaiah passage and in vv 1-3 in the Micah passage that shows a tight parallelism; there is also a thematic unity between Isa 2:5 and Mic 4:5, but sufficient divergence as well to indicate that these respective verses were independent attachments. Once it is recognized that the temporal formula stands in anacrusis, one may see that the dominant meter in each passage is 3:3, entirely in couplets.[59] There is great likelihood that the peculiar formulation with wĕhāyâ (elsewhere only at Jer 49:39) has been influenced by the frequent appearance of wĕhāyâ preceding bayyôm hahû'. This formula assumes an entirely altered situation, to come at a time remote from that of the composition of the original poem, namely, the restoration period after the exile. The reestablished temple is already in place; it is only the people's coming to that temple that constitutes genuine prediction. The wĕhāyâ formulation is appropriate because it is a permanent new condition, rather than a unitary historical event, that is being announced. In any case, the promise is not so much for restored Israel as for the once-tumultous enemies of Israel/Judah, eventually coming to Jerusalem to be judged by Israel's law.

b. Introducing a prose addition

Jer 49:39. We have previously identified redactional additions among Jeremiah's collection of foreign oracles containing temporal formulas that are either transitions (46:26b) or time identifiers (48:47). We must take note of the fact, however, that 46:26, 48:45-47, and 49:6 are not reproduced in the translation of the LXX. A good reason for viewing these sections as missing also from the proto-Hebrew text, and not mere Septuagintal omissions, is that each passage is — or concludes with — a salvation saying drastically reversing an oracle of judgment.

It is different, however, with the Elam oracle in 49:34-39. Even though the LXX transfers it to the front of the series, separating the two parts of the introductory formula at v 34 (MT), it does reflect this material entire. The likelihood is that this unique oracle concerning Elam — without the redactionally appended salvation saying in v 39 — concluded an original collection of Jeremianic words that probably consisted of 25:15-16a, 27, 46:2-12, 13-24, 47:1-7, 49:34-38, 51:59-64.[60] This was placed in an early redaction at the end of the separate scroll of judgment against Israel that concluded the report of Jeremiah's sermon to the exiles in 25:1-13. To this 49:39 was subsequently added, but before 46:26b, 48:47, and 49:6 came into the text.

This interpretation would make 49:39 unique as a salvation saying in the pre-Masoretic text. The formula wehayâ bĕ'aḥărît hayyāmîm in 49:39 is not only different from parallel formulas in the other three non-Septuagintal salvation sayings, but is rare and unique, being found elsewhere only at Isa 2:2 par Mic 4:1.

Rather than agreeing with the majority of scholars that the promise to reverse Elam's fortunes is mere eschatological speculation, we are inclined to agree with Claus Rietzschl's view that a concrete historical event, giving new confidence to the postexilic Jews, was in view, such as the establishment of Darius's capital in Susa in the year 494.[61] This would mean that the redactor of the Elam unit was in fact predicting an event that had already happened, making this promise of renewal another *vaticinium ex eventu*.

4. Conclusions

a. Patterns of occurrence

As we have noted, four distinct classes of material employ a nontransitional *bĕʾaḥărît hayyāmîm* to introduce a future that is, in verity, already past and/or present. Among the transitional passages just surveyed, on the other hand, the integral occurrence at Jer 23:20 stands out in that it contemplates a genuinely predictive future in stark contrast to the present.

All the remaining passages either reproduce the *vaticinium ex eventu* effect (the prose addition at Jer 49:39; cf. Jer 46:26, 49:6) or create a related sort of temporal transposition (in Isa 2:2 par Mic 4:2; Ezek 38:16). The introductory rubrics in the Isaiah and Micah passages actually do predict an eschatological bliss that is perhaps nascent in the present time of the temple's renewal, but that remains nevertheless a matter of hope and hypothesis. The verses in Ezekiel assume that what is still future (return from the exile) has already occurred, and the temporal transition in each case creates a move that is future with respect to this event, remaining in the hypothetical future. One should take special note of the fact that none of the passages in question employs the oracle formula. Perhaps this is because the new event or situation is recognized as a logical and necessary development from the real or implied present, obviously already certain in the divine intention and therefore not requiring special validation.

b. Temporal relationships

Several distinct patterns of time relationships are assumed in the employment of this formula, always involving a sequence from one event or situation to another; as follows:

1) The move is from the present and/or imminent future to a remote future:

Jer 23:20b, from false prophecy producing a storm of divine wrath (vv 16-20a) to an eventual acknowledgment of it as real and true;

Jer 30:24b, from a storm of divine wrath (vv 23-24a) to an eventual acknowledgment of it as real and true.

2) The move is from a proximate future to a present disguised as a remote future *(vaticinium ex eventu):*

Jer 49:39, from wrath on Elam (vv 35-38) to the restoration of its fortunes.

3) The move is from an implied present to a remote future:

Isa 2:2 par Mic 4:1, from Israel's implied restoration to Jerusalem's restoration as a center for the teaching of torah and the practice of strife-avoiding justice.

4) The move is from a remote to a still more remote future:

Ezek 38:8, from the assembly of Gog's host (v 7) to an invasion of the restored land of Israel.

In all these patterns there is a clear sequence from the first event or situation to the next. In one remaining passage there is synchronization but no clear sequence:

5) The move is from one event to a parallel event in the remote future:

Ezek 38:16, from the coming of Gog (introduced by the query *hălō' bayyôm hahû'* in v 14) to Yahweh's bringing of Gog for his own vindication *bĕ'aḥărît hayyāmîm.*

The nonsequential parallelism between *bayyôm hahû'* in Ezek 38:14 and *bĕ'aḥărît hayyāmîm* in v 16 is similar to that between *hinnēh yāmîm bā'îm* in Jer 31:31 and nontransitional *'aḥărê hayyāmîm hahēm* in v 33. There is no true progression, only coordination.

Quite different is the uniquely original occurrence of *bĕ'aḥărît hayyāmîm* in Jer 23:20. The temporal move here is from a present/imminent future to a genuinely predictive and at the same time more remote future; this carries over into the partial redactional replication of it at Jer 30:23-24. In contrast especially to the artificiality of the apocalyptic construction in Ezekiel 38-39, we identify here the characteristic stance of classical prophetism. The present moment of confrontation contains the kernel of the imminent future, while presaging a more remote future in which all ambiguity will be removed — but always (as here) with an expression of passionate parenetic concern for a real present in which the divine word, communicated through the true prophet, seeks to move a wayward people to responsible choice and action.

Excursus on Special Futuristic Transitions in Daniel

Daniel is, to be sure, no prophetic book; but because it does contain quasi-predictive material it will be useful to record here a number of expressions for future time that are used in this book in addition to the already observed *wĕʿattâ* in 10:20 and the twofold *ûbāʿēt hahî* in 12:1. This is less for the purpose of completeness than to point up differences between the use of the formulas that have been analyzed here and this book's special repertoire of temporal expressions. It will also serve the purpose of bringing out some important differences between them and the various temporal transitions found in other early apocalyptic writings, such as Isaiah 24–27, Ezekiel 38–39, Joel 2–3, and Zechariah 12–14.

What can immediately be seen is that all the temporal transitions in Daniel are integral and therefore elemental to its structure. For the purpose of contrast, we shall list the formulas that serve as temporal transitions separately from those that are mere indicators of time when.

Here is a list of additional integral transitions in Daniel referring to future time:

    2:39, *ûbotrāk* (Aram), "and after you"

    2:44, *ûbĕyômêhôn* (Aram), "and in their days"

    8:23, *ûbĕʾahărît malkûtām*, "and in sequence from their rule"

    9:26, *wĕʾaharê haššābuʿîm šiššîm ûšĕnayim*, "and after the sixty-two weeks"

    11:6, *ûlĕqēṣ šānîm*, "and at the end of some years"

    11:13, *ûlĕqēṣ hāʿittîm [šānîm]*, "and at the end of those times [years]"

    11:14, *ûbāʿittîm hahēm*, "and in those times"

    11:29, *lammôʿēd*, "at the appointed time"

    11:40, *ûbāʿēt qēṣ*, "and at the endtime."

In all the above transitions a sequence from the earlier to the later is created, even with *ûbāʿittîm hahēm* in 11:14. The only futuristic synchronism is that between two events introduced by the two occurrences of *ûbāʿēt hahî* in 12:1 (the appearance of Michael in a time of severe trouble and the deliverance of the faithful from it).

To supplement these temporal transitions, the book of Daniel contains a rich supply of futuristic time identifiers, as follows:

    2:29, *dî lehĕwēʾ ʾaharê dĕnâ* (Aram), "what was to happen after this"

    8:17, *lĕʿēt qēṣ*, "for the endtime"

    8:19, *bĕʾahărît hazzāʿam*, "in sequence from the wrath (wrathful time)"

    8:26, *lĕyāmîm rabbîm*, "for numerous days (years)"

    9:26, *wĕʿad qēṣ*, "and toward the end"

    10:14, *bĕʾahărît hayyāmîm*, "in the sequel of the days (years)"

    10:14, *layyāmîm*, "for days (years)"

11:24, *wĕʿad ʿēt,* "and for a time"[62]

11:35, 12:4, 9, *ʿad ʿēt qēṣ,* "until the endtime"

12:13a, *laqqēṣ,* "until the end"

12:13b, *lĕqēṣ hayyāmîm,* "until the end of the days (years)"

To supplement all this, Daniel employs additional expressions for durations of time; these are found in 8:14, 9:25 *bis,* 27 *bis,* 10:13, 11:20, 33, 12:1a, 7, 11. In addition, there are a few verses in which an expression for a particular time or period occurs as a substantive of futuristic time (9:24, 27, 12:11-12).

It is evident that for Daniel the identification of future times and the measurement of durations are of paramount importance. Further evidence of this mentality is the occurrence of several expressions for past time, especially the dating formulas in 2:1, etc. As we have seen, for authentic prophecy, transition formulas, and time identifiers are employed for putting various events into proper temporal relationship with one another. For apocalyptic, times as such have acquired an ontological independence in which they — not the events marked by them — are the major subject of concern.

PART TWO

Futuristic Transitions in the Growth of the Prophetic Books

CHAPTER FIVE

Introduction

Preliminary Considerations

1. Methodological observations

It will be apparent to anyone who has paid close attention to our foregoing analysis of the employment of a variety of temporal transitions within the prophetic literature that there are important differences between them, and that they do each have a definite function. They attach new expectations in a variety of ways to the pronouncement communicated in the underlying material, whether that be the presumed original or secondary material, added in the process of literary expansion.

As has been noted, the habit of textual scholars has been to place little or no importance on the appearance of these transitional formulas. But we have shown that careful exegesis dares no longer pass them over or assume them to be casual elements in a merely conventional speech-pattern, devoid of independent significance or intentionality. One has to object that if these expressions had little significance or intentionality when first inserted into the text, there can be no cogent reason for their being there. Why did the supplementers or redactors bother at all to use them? They could just as well have juxtaposed new materials without them, as has happened in the great majority of cases; but instead they did use them in the passages that we have examined, and we must assume that the effects they intended were deliberate. They do indeed create a more complex and more sophisticated nuancing of the awaited future with relation to the event or situation of the underlying material.

To anyone arguing that the redactors in question may nevertheless have employed these transitional formulas without independent ideological reflection, we may say two things: (1) that one certainly cannot prove the case one way or the other, for it is hazardous to speculate about what might or might not have been in the presumptive redactor's mind; and (2) that in spite of this these words stand, after all, in the text, that they do have meaning and function within the collocation of words to which they belong, and that as scholars living centuries afterward we can and must deal only with what is before us. We need to shift the debate from what might or might not have been in the mind of an ancient writer to what appears in the Hebrew text as presently available to us. And in order to make sense of this text, we must assign significance to the words and other linguistic elements that we are able to observe.

The question is not whether we should do this, but how. Having given independent examination to each occurrence of the various temporal transitions as they appear in the Hebrew Bible, we must now take the data derived from this examination and submit it to various tests in search for a further clarification of their meaning and function.

As has been stated, the present study avoids direct participation in the debate over originality and authenticity. In cases where we have stated an opinion that a particular text is original, this usually reflects the common view, and what is meant is that there is no good reason for denying that the passage in question might be original. Apart from this, our major effort will be toward showing how the text grew after it was composed. We are well aware that it is almost always impossible to trace the path of a given text all the way back to the original spokesman or writer. In virtually every text, some element of redaction has entered in; also in the recording of certain words by a prophet's disciples, or even by the prophet himself. Our assumption must be that every word has been, or may have been, subject to alterations of one kind or another — even when verbatim reproduction was the original intention.

This is why we prefer to use the term "primary" in distinguishing between the underlying material in a given passage and the attached material. "Primary," as we shall use it, refers to basic literary blocks within a book; in some passages this may be presumed to be original to the prophet whose name the book bears, but in other passages (e.g., those drawn from "Second Isaiah") it may belong to the creator of a whole new literary complex attached to an older trunk, adding to the eventual canonical shape of the book in question.

This "primary" material is what we will eventually be setting aside in our search for redactional intentionalities — not because it is irrelevant but because it will have fulfilled its purpose of providing us with a control group of occurrences with which to make a valid comparison. A positive element is that a number of the formulas that we have studied have been found both in primary and in redactional passages. From this we draw the immediate conclusion that few, if any, of these formulas are in themselves the clear marks either of originality or of redaction.

As we eventually place the respective occurrences of the various formulas into a redactional framework, it will be on independent considerations, not because we have thought it possible to date the formulas as such. True, usage may in some cases suggest a narrow time-frame, as is the case with *hinnēh yāmîm bāʾîm* (especially when prefaced by *lākēn*) and with regard to the florid combination *bayyāmîm hahēm ûbāʿēt hahîʾ*. But one is most impressed by the observation that the dominant locution *bayyôm hahûʾ* (also with foregoing *wěhāyâ*) has been found in a wide variety of books and over a broad range of time.

It is probably significant in this connection that the *(wěhāyâ) bayyôm hahûʾ* formula occurs far more often as a redactional introduction than as an integral transition; but it seems especially significant that certain books, or parts of books, that are rich and varied in content, such as Jeremiah and Second Isaiah, use it rarely or lack it altogether. As a transitional formula, *(wěhāyâ) bayyôm hahûʾ* occurs only three times throughout the long and complex book of Jeremiah, but dozens of times in Isaiah. In Isaiah it is restricted to the first thirty-one of this book's sixty-six chapters. While it appears as a distinctive peculiarity of the Isaianic redaction in the early portions of the book, it is not used at all in Second- or Third-Isaiah, in those chapters that stand under the direct influence of these compositions, chaps. 32–35, or in the bridging collection of prophet narratives, chaps. 36–39. When we take notice of the fact that a considerable proportion of the occurrences in Isaiah 1–31 are from late — even very late — expansions, this comparison becomes even more suggestive. Many expansions within Isaiah introduced by this formula are in fact far younger than the Second- or Third-Isaiah collocations that have been appended to the book. This strongly suggests that chaps. 32–66 were attached to the original corpus of Isaiah only after a rather extended period of previous redactional development.[1]

The fact that *(wěhāyâ) bayyôm hahûʾ* is seldom integral and very often introductory demands that this formula should stand at the center of our attention as we strive to get a grasp on the redactional processes involved in the employment of all the formulas under study. We may learn much as well from comparing the introductory with the integral occurrences of the less-employed formulas, whether it be those that have only the integral function *(wěʿattâ/ ʿattâ and ʾāz)* or those in which there is a fair balance between the two functions *(bayyāmîm hahēm, bāʿēt hahîʾ, hinnēh yāmîm bāʾîm, ʾaḥărê-kēn,* and *běʾaḥărît hayyāmîm)*. Also deserving attention are the ways in which sequences and synchronisms have been formed. In addition, we must attend to the peculiar function of *hinnēh yāmîm bāʾîm* as a transition within prophetic oracles to the formal accusation, the summons to hear, or the instruction to the announcement, particularly when prefixed by *lākēn*. Finally, we must study the impact of stereotyped appendages, whether a foregoing *wĕhāyâ* or a following *nĕ'um YHWH*.

2. Evidence from cluster arrangements

In Chapters Two through Four, we have scrutinized each passage in which the various temporal transitions occur. To avoid being entirely bewildered by how to proceed with the abundance and variety of materials that have come to light, it may be helpful at this point to make a tentative probe of how these formulas are interrelated by surveying those passages that contain futuristic transitions in clusters. Our question will be, What was the organizing principle that drew such collocations together? From this we may be able to extrapolate insights that will prove useful in the more comprehensive analysis of the respective biblical books that is to follow.

a. Clusters of integral transitions

Most of the integral occurrences under study are in passages that are unrelated to one another, but there are a few exceptions that may prove to be of special interest. In each instance, the writer responsible for the primary material in question (not necessarily the original prophet; see above) links together two or more elements by the repetition of a specific temporal formula. The purpose will be immediately apparent.

Variations of the *'attâ* formula in Mic 4:9, 10, 11, 14 (E 5:1) relate preliminary experiences of peril and deliverance to an anticipated final deliverance under a new Davidic prince, who is to be expected not from the ruling family in Jerusalem but from the ancestral clan at Bethlehem (5:1-3 [E 2-4]).

In the late salvation hymn of Isaiah 35, a second strophe at vv 3-4 urges the proclamation of divine restrengthening for the weak, feeble, and fearful; the repetition of initial *'āz* in vv 5-6 emphatically defines in parallel couplets the immediate results: new sight and new hearing, new leaping and new singing.

It is rather different in the late admonitory poem of Isaiah 58. Rhetorical questions about true fasting in vv 6-7 draw the immediate consequences expressed in vv 8-9, where repeated *'āz* introduces the images of light, healing, righteousness, and glory for those who heed the admonition; in v 14 a further *'āz* stands as the apodosis of a prediction of spiritual exaltation over against the protasis in v 13, urging true sabbath observance.

In the same vein, *lākēn hinnēh yāmîm bā'îm* in Jer 51:47, 51 introduces separate strophes that express rejoicing over the imminent overthrow of Baby-

lon's idols in sequence from two other strophes (vv 45-46, vv 50-51) in which
the resulting (not preliminary!) departure of the exiles is enjoined.

These passages each proclaim salvation, which is for the sixth-century
exiles to Babylon in the Isaiah and Jeremiah passages, but for the early
seventh-century Jerusalemites in the Micah passage.

A singular announcement of punishment is laid upon Jerusalem's nobility of the late seventh century in the day-of-Yahweh oracle of Zeph 1:7-13,
in which two new strophes introduced by *bayyôm hahû'* at v 10 and at v 12
(LXX) contain divine declarations specifying first the panic, then the ineluCTA-
bility, of an imminent calamity.

We take note, finally, of the cluster appearance of integral *(wĕhāyâ)*
bayyôm hahû' in two redactional supplements at Isa 22:20, 25. Isa 22:15ff. is
an intriguing private oracle — almost certainly authentic — in which words
of divine rejection for Shebna have received two successive redactional supplementations, each time with integral *(wĕhāyâ) bayyôm hahû'*. Though the
same redactor may be involved, they were surely not written at the same time,
for vv 19-23 announce Hilkiah's replacement of Shebna and vv 24-25 announce the former's collapse.

b. Clusters of introductory transitions

Each of the above integral occurrences within primary materials has originated
from a singular composer for each passage, but it is otherwise with the integral
redactional occurrences in Isa 22:20, 25, as well as in clusters where transition
formulas introduce a redactional supplement or expand a redactional supplement from within. In about half of these clusters, a single redactor is responsible, but in those that remain different redactors are at work.

We are immediately impressed by a number of interesting clusters in
Isaiah in which introductory *bayyôm hahû'* or *wĕhāyâ bayyôm hahû'* occurs.
First of all, there is the remarkable array of liturgical rubrics in Isa 12:1-2,
4-6, 25:9-10a, 26:1-6, and 27:2-5. Although the first two attach directly to the
late salvation poem of 11:1-9 and the latter three appear within or at the end
of the "little apocalypse" in chaps. 24–27, there is a strong likelihood that
they all come from the same interpolator,[2] someone living in the Persian period
who intended to utilize the respective contexts to which these rubrics attach
for liturgical praise in a late community of Jews enjoying relative security
and prosperity. Here it is a common theme and purpose that makes likely the
supposition of a single redactor for the entire series.

In chap. 7 of Isaiah, four successive prose additions, introduced by
(wĕhāyâ) bayyôm hahû' at vv 18, 20, 21, and 23, modify the announcement
of judgment in vv 14-17 in terms of the nation's experience of destitution

subsequent to the arrival of the Assyrians. Although some scholars would assign these prose additions to separate levels of redaction,[3] it is not at all likely here that a succession of individual redactors would have added their own little pieces to a growing collection. We have argued, on the contrary, that this is a collection from various tradition sources drawn together by a single redactor. Little should be made of the fact that v 20 is at variance with the other occurrences in employing the simple *bayyôm hahû'* since, as has been shown, little ideological significance is to be discerned in the variation from one formula to another. Thus in Isa 7:18-25 the variation of formulas is quite casual.

We see no reason for identifying separate redactors, furthermore, in each of two further Isaianic clusters, those found at 11:10-11 and 17:7-9. Although the topology involved in these two passages differs from occurrence to occurrence, each reflects roughly the same contemporary situation, and in general the same ideology. Each collocation is from a different redactor, to be sure, because as a collocation 11:10f. reflects a postexilic situation while 17:7ff. reflects a situation during the exile. The first collocation attaches to exilic material in 11:1-9 while the second collocation attaches to late preexilic material in 17:1-6. Each of the two redactors involved — otherwise than in 7:18-25 — is consistent in using either *bayyôm hahû'* or *wěhāyâ bayyôm hahû'* as the formula of introduction. It seems likely that the collocation in 17:7-9 is like the expansion with *wěhāyâ bayyôm hahû'* in 10:20-23 in predicting improved conditions for certain Israelite survivors — not those of the Assyrian occupation, but those of the Neo-Babylonian occupation, its antitype.

It is again different with regard to the five transitional occurrences found in Isa 19:16-25. As has been stated, this chapter's unparalleled chain of prose additions, dating from very late in the postexilic period (probably the latest of all our occurrences, as well as of collocations), reveals a process of epexegetical reflection in which each new addition appears to outdo what precedes it in idealism for God's ultimate plan and purpose regarding the Egyptians in whose land many Jews had found a home during the Persian and Hellenistic periods.[4] In this chapter there has been no mere joining of materials from various ancient traditions, but a process of supplementation involving a successive redaction. This process is not to be thought of as casual, but as deliberate and intensely ideological.

It is probable that two separate redactors are responsible for still another cluster appearance of *wěhāyâ bayyôm hahû'* in Isa 27:12-13, even though each verse concerns the same subject, the return of the exiles. This is because v 12 has to do only with the Egyptian diaspora and is styled as an address to the people, whereas v 13 speaks of the people in the third person and concerns both the Egyptian and the Assyrian (i.e., Babylonian-Persian) diaspora.

Jer 3:16-18 has an idiosyncratic cluster in which *bayyāmîm hahēmmâ* (vv 16, 18) and *bāʿēt hahîʾ* (v 17) alternate. The rare occurrence of the longer spelling *hahēmmâ* in these verses (elsewhere in Jeremiah only at 5:18; also at Joel 4:1 [E 3:1] and Zech 8:23) is evidence that they derive from a redaction distinct from that which produced the spelling *bayyāmîm hahēm* (Jer 31:29, 33:15-16, 50:4, 20). Nevertheless, Jer 3:16, 17, and 18 are not homogeneous in their composition. Vv 15-16, using *bayyāmîm hahēmmâ* only as a time identifier rather than as a formula of transition, represent an exilic expansion. This expansion has attracted postexilic epexegesis in v 17, introduced by *bāʿēt hahîʾ*, proclaiming the gathering of the nations to Jerusalem; and this in turn has led to v 18's further epexegesis, introduced by *bayyāmîm hahēmmâ*, assuring Israel/Judah's reunification and repossession of the land; probably the temporal formula was introduced here under the influence of the same formula in v 16.

Jer 4:9-10, 11-12 is a mixed redactional cluster. As we have interpreted this passage, *wĕhāyâ bayyôm hahûʾ* followed by the oracle formula in v 9 introduces a first expansion interpreting a military attack in terms of the leaders' consternation. A second expansion cites a saying about a hot wind that is to come to fulfillment *bāʿēt hahîʾ*, "in that time/situation," the realization of which confirms the "now *(ʿattâ)*" of the prophet's legitimation as a spokesman of judgment. Although "in that day" and "at that time" point equally to the proximate future (equivalent to the proximate future of the coming attack), it is highly unlikely that the same redactor was responsible for placing the two in close proximity. A reasonable explanation is that a disciple may have recorded Jeremiah's own sentiments in vv 9f., but that subsequently another disciple, or the prophet himself, recorded the more immediate and personal comment of vv 11f.

Another cluster involves the peculiar formula of Jeremiah's redaction, *(lākēn) hinnēh yāmîm bāʾîm*. This is the introductory formula used in the separate prose additions at Jer 23:5-6, 7-8, each of which has a doublet elsewhere in the book, namely, at 33:14-16 and at 16:14-15, respectively. The distinctive topology in each set of doublets is an indication of separate sources, but it is unlikely that a single redactor would have introduced 23:5f. with the formula *hinnēh yāmîm bāʾîm* while introducing vv 7f. with the competing formula — the same with foregoing *lākēn*. This problem is eased by consideration of the fact that the LXX places 23:7f. at the end of the chapter, thus dissolving the cluster. In any event, it is striking that the transition formula in question has been copied intact in each instance.[5] Essentially we are dealing here with an atomistic procedure in which separate redactors have added unrelated materials to an underlying text.

Another remarkable collocation of expansions with *hinnēh yāmîm bāʾîm* is found in Jer 31:27-28, 31-34, 38-40. The material derives from authentic Jeremianic tradition but must be ascribed to the school of the prophet's early disciples. Eliminating several alternatives, our foregoing discussion has settled on an explanation to the effect that a single redactor within this school was responsible for drawing these materials together and attaching them together to original material in Jer 30:1–32:25, the purpose being to produce a fully rounded synopsis of the prophet's favorable message concerning Yahweh's new day of salvation.

There is a loosely connected series of expansions with *we'aḥărê-kēn* in Jer 46:26, 48:47, 49:6, extended to include *bĕ'aḥărît hayyāmîm* in 49:39. Our previous probing has arrived at the conclusion that redactional 49:39 stood at the end of an initial collection of Jeremianic oracles against the nations, assigning those sections having the remaining occurrences to a later redactor.

The succession of expansions to the original Gog apocalypse in Ezek 38:1-9, 39:1-5, 17-20 is best explained as the product of a whole school of redactors. As in Zech 12:3–13:4 and 14:6-20, *wĕhāyâ bayyôm hahû'* in Ezek 38:10, 18, 39:11 serves as a device for attaching still more new material to the expanding apocalyptic vision (one should observe the integral transitions with *bayyôm hahû'* in 38:14, 19). The apparent intent is not as in Isaiah 19 — to expound the foregoing — but simply to give expression to a burgeoning ideology. Inasmuch as the original Gog apocalypse needs to be dated, at the earliest, to the late exilic period, these expansions must have arisen sometime during the postexilic period — earlier rather than later. A parallel process was involved in new supplementations with *(wĕhāyâ) bayyôm hahû'* found in Zech 12:3, 6, 8(1), 9, 11, 13:1, 2, 4, 14:6, 8, 9, 13, and 20. Our preliminary discussion of this material in Chapter Three has taken note of a variety of concerns motivating a series of expansions within the respective apocalyptic circles responsible for them. These passages will be more thoroughly analyzed in the following chapters.

Quite a unique situation is that of the two additions with *wĕhāyâ bayyôm hahû'* in Hos 2:18-22 (E 16-20) and 2:23-25 (E 21-23). As has been argued, they each develop a distinct theme from the original Hoseanic poem about a faithless wife, but independently of each other. It is probable that an early disciple-redactor drew them from separate tradition sources to give expression to the theme of a divine mercy that counteracts severe judgment.

We have previously commented in some detail on the process that created the redactional expansions with either *(wĕhāyâ) bayyôm hahû'* or *hinnēh yāmîm bā'îm* in Amos 8:9-10, 11-12, 13-14, 9:11-12, 13-15. They represent at least two phases of redactional activity, one preexilic and another exilic. The individual pericopes were atomistically attached, first to the authentic collection, then to previously added redactional material.

All of Zephaniah 3 following v 8 consists of a cluster of redactional materials introduced by a temporal formula: introductory *kî 'āz* in v 9a; *bayyôm hahû'* in anacrusis at v 11 (with an occurrence of *kî 'āz* at v b); then the liturgical rubric *bayyôm hahû' yē'āmēr lîrûšālaim,* introducing vv 16-18; and finally *bā'ēt hahî'* in v 20 (*bā'ēt hahî'* in v 19 is a gloss). Though all of this material follows the theme of marvelous success for restoration Jerusalem, the variation of introductory formulas, as well as the diverse subject matter in each section, is again clear indication of an atomistic redaction in which individual sayings were accreted like filings to a magnet.

c. Conclusion

This analysis of temporal transitions that occur in clusters suggests a variety of possibilities for those — yet to be examined — that do not appear in clusters.

Integral occurrences have their own special patterns, which are as follows:

1) In primary materials:

Introducing separate strophes within poems: Mic 4:9, 10, 11, 14 (E 5:1), Isa 35:5-6, 58:8-9, Jer 51:47, 52, Zeph 1:10, 12;

Leading to the apodosis of a conditional sentence: Isa 58:14;

2) In redactional materials:

Appearing in additions made by successive redactions: Isa 22:20, 25.

Transitions in clusters with temporal formulas that introduce redactional additions also display a variety of patterns:

Marking a systematic redaction in an array of passages: Isa 12:1, 4, 25:9, 26:1, 27:2;

Marking the collection of thematically diverse materials from various sources on the part of a single redactor: Isa 7:18, 20, 21, 23, 11:10, 11, 17:7, 9, Jer 31:27, 31, 38, Hos 2:18 (E 16), 23 (E 21);

Marking thematically similar materials added in incremental epexegesis, carried out by a succession of redactors: Isa 19:16, 18, 19, 23, 24; Jer 3:17, 18, 4:9, 11, 46:26, 48:47, 49:6, 39; Ezek 38:10, 18, 39:11; Amos 8:9, 11, 13;

Marking thematically similar materials added atomistically by separate redactors: Isa 27:12, 13; Ezek 38:14, 16, 19; Amos 9:11, 13; Zeph 3:9-20; Zech 12:3-13:4, 14:6-20;

Not belonging to an actual cluster within the original text: Jer 23:5, 7.

This should be enough to remind us not to expect one, or even just a few, redactional patterns within the prophetic books as a group. It will be necessary to approach each individual book without prior presupposition regarding the levels of composition and redaction to which the various occurrences of futuristic transitions must be ascribed. Our following discussion of these transitions as they appear in the respective prophetic books will proceed in the light of this foregoing discussion. If this analysis of clusters has done anything worthwhile, it must be that it will have alerted us to the remarkable imagination and astounding creativity on the part of the Israelite prophets and their redactors that we may expect to encounter as we extend our analysis still further.

Futuristic Transitions outside the Prophetic Corpus

In preparation for taking up the individual prophetic books, we add to the above introductory observations the following brief analysis of parallel materials from outside the prophetic corpus, which occur either in private oracles recorded in the narrative collection or in apocalyptic vision.

Primary transitions	Redactional transitions
1. Integral	
a. In narrative discourse	
1 Sam 2:30 *wĕʿattâ nĕʾum YHWH*	
2:31 *hinnēh yāmîm bāʾîm*[a]	
15:1 *wĕʿattâ šēmaʾ lĕqôl dibrê YHWH*	
2 Sam 7:8 par 1 Chr 17:7	
wĕʿattâ	
12:10 *wĕʿattâ*	
2 Kgs 20:17[b] par Isa 39:6	
hinnēh yāmîm bāʾîm	
b. In apocalyptic visions	
Dan 10:20 *wĕʿattâ*	
12:1(1) *ûbāʿēt hahîʾ*	
1(2) *ûbāʿēt hahîʾ*	
2. Introductory	
a. In expansion of private oracle	
1 Sam 3:12 *bayyôm hahûʾ*	(prose addition)

a. pcMss add *nĕʾum YHWH*
b. G^var add *nĕʾum YHWH*

1. Private oracles

The list of futuristic transitions in narrative discourse requires little commentary beyond what has been said in the preceding chapters on each individual passage. Once they are assembled in one place, it is a simple matter to observe how they compare with one another. All the occurrences in narrative discourse are integral except in the redactional expansion at 1 Sam 3:12. Furthermore, each of these belongs to a private oracle, always announcing a judgment on particular individuals that is extended also to the families or dynasties which they represent; the exception is in 2 Sam 7:8 par 1 Chr 17:7, where divine blessings for the Davidic "house" are announced. In each instance the prophet who delivers the message speaks not only for Yahweh, but as Yahweh. The formula used is *wě'attâ* or *hinnēh yāmîm bā'îm*, even though 1 Sam 2:30-31, 2 Sam 7:8 par, and 2 Kgs 20:17 par predict what is actually past/present for the composer *(vaticinium ex eventu)*. The formula is *bayyôm hahû'* in the redactional gloss at 1 Sam 3:12, implying an event somewhat removed from the situation of the narrative context, but in fact reflecting the redactor's past/present — another *vaticinium ex eventu*. The formula *wě'attâ* in 1 Sam 15:1 is like that of Amos 7:16 in moving from a narrative statement of the prophet's direct authorization to the announcement of grim judgment upon an institutional official found resisting the prophet's authority.

In spite of the fact that the narrative passages (including Amos 7:12-17, to be discussed in Chapter Nine) show remarkable similarities in structure and function, it is clear that there is no compositional affinity among them. The pattern of occurrences is random within each book and shows no programmatic significance in the role played by the normative redaction — in this case that of the deuteronomistic historian. The special significance of the mutual similarities among these passages must accordingly be form-critical; they reflect the *Sitz im Leben* of confrontation between exemplars of institutional authority and the spokesmen for a superior authority derived directly from God. This is true also with regard to the announcement of divine favor in 2 Sam 7:8-16, where Yahweh rejects David's misguided initiative before announcing the divine alternative.[6]

2. *Apocalyptic*

The three temporal transitions in Daniel imply, first an imminent future, and second a remote future, as measured from the present situation in which the divine intention is announced; but these move in actuality to what is already present for the apocalypticist *(vaticinium ex eventu)*.

CHAPTER SIX

Isaiah

Primary transitions	Redactional transitions
1. Integral	
1:26 *'aḥăre-kēn*	
16:14	*wĕ'attâ dibber YHWH lē'mōr*[a]
22:20	*wĕhāyâ bayyôm hahû'*
22:25	*bayyôm hahû'*
31:7	*kî bayyôm hahû'*
33:23	*'āz*
35:5 *'āz*	
35:6 *'āz*	
39:6[b] *hinnēh yāmîm bā'îm*	
41:1 *'āz*	
48:16 *wĕ'attâ*	
58:8 *'āz*	
58:9 *'āz*	
58:14 *'āz*	
60:5 *'āz*	
2. Introductory	
2:2[c]	*wĕhāyâ bĕ'aḥărît hayyāmîm* (anacrusis)
2:20	*bayyôm hahû'*[d] (prose addition)
3:18	*bayyôm hahû'* (prose addition)
4:2	*bayyôm hahû'* (prose addition)
7:18	*wĕhāyâ bayyôm hahû'* (prose addition)
7:20	*bayyôm hahû'* (prose addition)
7:21	*wĕhāyâ bayyôm hahû'* (prose addition)
7:23	*wĕhāyâ bayyôm hahû'* (prose addition)

10:20	*wĕhāyâ bayyôm hahû'* (prose addition)
11:10	*wĕhāyâ bayyôm hahû'* (prose addition)
11:11	*wĕhāyâ bayyôm hahû'* (prose addition)
12:1	*wĕ'āmartā bayyôm hahû'* (liturgical rubric)
12:4	*wa'ămartem bayyôm hahû'* (liturgical rubric)
17:4	*wĕhāyâ bayyôm hahû'* (anacrusis)
17:7	*bayyôm hahû'* (prose addition)
17:9	*bayyôm hahû'* (prose addition)
18:7	*bā'ēt hahî'* (prose addition)
19:16	*bayyôm hahû'* (prose addition)
19:18	*bayyôm hahû'* (prose addition)
19:19	*bayyôm hahû'* (prose addition)
19:23	*bayyôm hahû'* (prose addition)
19:24	*bayyôm hahû'* (prose addition)
23:15	*wĕhāyâ bayyôm hahû'* (prose addition)
24:21	*wĕhāyâ bayyôm hahû'* (anacrusis)
25:9	*wĕ'āmar*[f] *bayyôm hahû'* (liturgical rubric)
26:1	*bayyôm hahû' yûšār haššîr hazzeh* (liturgical rubric)
27:2	*bayyôm hahû'*[g] (liturgical rubric)
27:12	*wĕhāyâ bayyôm hahû'* (prose addition)
27:13	*wĕhāyâ bayyôm hahû'* (prose addition)
28:5	*bayyôm hahû'* (anacrusis)

a. Contrast *mē'āz* (v 13)
b. Par 2 Kgs 20:17
c. Par Mic 4:1
d. Cf. epitomizing *bayyôm hahû'* (v 17)
e. Explicating *yāmîm 'ăšer lō'-bā'û lĕmiyyôm sûr 'eprayim mē'al yĕhûdâ* (v 17)
f. MT; 1QIs[a] Syr *wĕ'āmartā*
g. Note epitomizing *bayyôm hahû'* (v 27)

Redaction and Ideology in Isaiah

1. The historical setting of the book

Isaiah is like the Pentateuch and the Psalter in the remarkable length of its compositional process.[1] Assuming that its superscription (1:1) is correct, this extended from the last year of Uzziah's reign, 740-739, until the period of the Persian rulership in Egypt — possibly even into the third century B.C.E. There are four major compositional blocks: chaps. 1–35, chaps. 36–39 (drawn from 2 Kings 18–20), chaps. 40–55 (Deutero-Isaiah), and chaps. 56–66 (Trito-Isaiah).

Defense of the unity of the book has been given up except in the most conservative circles because it is clearly evident that the work of "First Isaiah" (also called "Isaiah of Jerusalem") and the work of Deutero- and Trito-Isaiah ("Second and Third Isaiah") are relevant only to drastically different historical situations. Chaps. 1–31 have meaning in the historical context of the success of Assyrian aggression in Palestine during the reigns of Tiglath-pileser III (745-727), Shalmaneser V (727-722), Sargon I (722-705), and Sennacherib (705-681). On the contrary, Deutero-Isaiah has no significance except in relation to conditions obtaining during the time of Cyrus's military campaigns commencing in 550, down to the capture of Babylon in 539, and Trito-Isaiah reflects an era of spiritual disillusionment following the return of the exiles and the rebuilding of the temple. It is likely that numerous redactional elements were added to the corpus of (first) Isaiah during the lengthy periods of Assyrian and Neo-Babylonian ascendancy, and that others were added during the Persian, or even early Hellenistic, periods, the fifth and fourth centuries. Hermann Barth has argued that a definitive new recension of the early Isaianic collection appeared during the years of Assyria's collapse, before and after the fall of Nineveh in 612.[2] There is also good reason to believe that new materials were added to this collection in the late years of the exile to Babylon, but independently of Deutero-Isaiah.

It has been assumed throughout this study that readers are well acquainted with the details of Israelite and Jewish history. It is important to note that the content of (first) Isaiah's prophecies arose as responses to a series of disruptive political events. These were Tiglath-pileser III's invasion of the northern part of the Israelite kingdom (742), the Syro-Ephraimite war against Judah (734-732), the capture of Samaria (723/22), Sargon's western campaigns, and Sennacharib's conquest of Judah and siege of Jerusalem (701). The urgent concern of Isaiah's ministry was, first of all, to inculcate a radical faith in Yahweh for the troubled times of Ahaz's and Hezekiah's reigns, which fell during this chaotic period.[3] Although Isaiah did utter words of stern censure upon unfaith and unprincipled political action, his main concern was to give king and people alike a model of transcendent purpose amid the alarms around them.

2. The present state of research

Siegfried Herrmann in his important book on salvation prophecy[4] distinguishes the forms of optimistic expectation in the four great literary blocks, Isaiah, Jeremiah, Ezekiel, and Deutero-Isaiah. He argues that Isaiah, on his part, held out three specific hopes for the nation: (1) that a faithful remnant would survive every calamity coming upon the nation; (2) that the Davidic house would produce an ideal ruler who would reign in true righteousness; and (3) that Zion/Jerusalem would be preserved.[5] These major eschatological themes are restricted, to be sure, to chaps. 1–31 of his book, those that also contain Isaiah's complete repertoire of introductory temporal transitions. Various scholars, however, have questioned whether all of these themes — or indeed any of them — were actually proclaimed by the original prophet. Each theme has been augmented within a preexilic school of disciples, though the literary core of the book surely goes back to "Isaiah of Jerusalem." The point from which we wish to take our departure in analyzing the appearance of futuristic transitions is at any rate a corpus of materials originating in the eighth and seventh centuries that do develop, authentically or redactionally, the themes that have been mentioned. It is our position that by the time of Josiah (reigned 640-609) the scroll of Isaiah's prophecies already proclaimed the beliefs that the city would be saved, that the Davidic lineage would yet reach its ideal, and that some few out of the guilty nation would be saved.

For us to enter at this point into a complete discussion of composition and redaction in Isaiah would be both futile and pointless: futile because the scholarly literature on Isaiah is vast, pointless because the redactional expansions that are formally introduced by temporal formulas certainly were not produced in the initial stages of the shaping of this book.

The trend of recent Isaiah studies has been to concentrate on the history of redaction rather than on isolating "authentic" materials. As we would expect, individual scholars disagree on details, but the trend is unmistakable. Three works in particular claim our attention, those of H. Barth, J. Vermeylen, and M. A. Sweeney. Each calls for brief comment.

Hermann Barth offers an impressive argument in his book *Die Jesaja-Worte in der Josiazeit* (1977)[6] to the effect that the definitive redaction of proto-Isaiah appeared at the time when the Assyrian empire was at the point of collapse, and Isaiah's warnings about Assyria as the instrument of Yahweh's judgment on the kingdom of Judah needed to be reinterpreted in terms of his more ultimate purpose regarding Assyria.[7] This was a time of high optimism. Painstakingly, Barth traces this redaction from passage to passage, identifying in the process three distinct literary elements: (1) the pre-existing corpus of Isaianic materials; (2) Isaianic materials independently transmitted, but now newly incorporated into the text; and (3) materials composed by the redactor as the framework for his inclusions.[8] Barth extends this process backward and forward, detailing the growth of the early collection on the one hand, and on the other hand, further expansions and redactional alterations made during the exilic and postexilic periods.

We cannot accept Barth's identifications in every detail, and certainly he seems to be overly restrictive with regard to the extent of authentic Isaianic material.[9] It is striking that he assigns virtually all the new materials containing temporal transitions to a succession of redactors ranging in time from the eighth century to the late postexilic period. No effort has been made to interpret the phenomena under study here as anything special. Expansive materials with temporal transitions may be formally different from those without them, but Barth recognizes no ideological distinction among them.

If thoroughness balanced with discriminating succinctness generally characterizes Barth's book, J. Vermeylen's two-volume work, published in 1977-78, is the very model of prolixity. The title suggests an important difference in perspective from that of Barth: *Du prophète Isaïe I XXXV, miroir d'un demi-millénaire d'expérience religieuse en Israël.*[10] In the first volume of this work, Vermeylen calls up for review every individual passage within Isaiah 1–35. Then, in the second volume, he examines parallel materials in Isaiah 56–66 and elsewhere within the Old Testament[11] and goes on to delineate seven separate compositional-redactional stages. These are: (1) the first collection of Isaiah's oracles; (2) the collection and redaction from Manasseh's reign to the exile; (3) two separate deuteronomistic redactions during the exile; (4) eschatological rereading in the middle fifth century; (5) a redaction promoting the conversion of the impious; (6) another redaction promoting vengeance on the impious; and (7) a final redaction in the Hellenistic period promoting the proselytizing of the heathen, animosity toward the Samaritans, the return of the diaspora, and apocalyptic expectation.[12] Although Vermeylen does identify minor redactional activity during Josiah's reign, he does not conceive of a definitive recension occurring during this period. In matter of fact, no level is definitive. Each redaction was essentially an independent rereading of an expanding body of Isaianic literature.[13] The important thing to take note of here is that, like most other scholars, Vermeylen sees no special significance in the use of the temporal formulas under study here.

Another impressive effort to delineate redactional stages in the growth of Isaiah is Marvin A. Sweeney's monograph *Isaiah 1–4 and the Post-Exilic Understanding of the Isaianic Tradition* (1988).[14] In preparation for a form-critical analysis of Isaiah 1–39 for the series The Forms of the Old Testament Literature (FOTL), Sweeney first examines the structure of the entire book of Isaiah, including Deutero- and Trito-Isaiah.[15] He then proceeds to a detailed study of chaps. 1–4, where he finds evidence for a series of redactions that he believes have also played a major role within the whole body of the book.[16] Although it contains authentic words from Isaiah, with supplements from the seventh-century Isaianic school, chap. 1 has been placed as a summary prologue to the entire book, as edited in the latter half of the fifth century. For chaps. 2–4 Sweeney also identifies authentic material while defining three successive redactions, as follows: (1) a seventh-century redaction that reinterpreted the prophet's predictions concerning the Assyrian menace as the cosmic Day of Yahweh; (2) a late sixth-century redaction that supported the rebuilding of the temple while reinterpreting the Assyrian oracles to apply to the now defunct Chaldean empire; (3) a late fifth-century redaction whose intent was to counteract religious disillusionment and indifference during the age of Ezra-Nehemiah and Trito-Isaiah. Sweeney goes beyond identifying materials in Isaiah 1–4 that have direct affinities with late compositions to argue for a definitive editing of the entire book in this period. Sweeney, like most scholars, takes little notice of temporal transitions.[17]

Commentaries on Isaiah that adopt the historical-critical viewpoint generally enter as well as they can, within the limits of editorial policy, into a discussion of redaction history, and they should all be consulted for their individual contributions. The single recent commentary that has enjoyed sufficient space, both for an extensive and for an intensive discussion of individual questions, is that of Hans Wildberger in his Isaiah volume on chaps. 1–39 in the series Biblischer Kommentar zum Alten Testament (X/1-2). As a guide to our ensuing treatment, we may summarize this scholar's reconstruction of the complex process of composition, collection, and expansion, though without necessarily endorsing its details. Along with the above-mentioned monographs, it may serve as a guide to current trends in Isaiah research:

I. Original collections of authentic materials within the major blocks:
  A. From the period of the Syrian-Ephraimite war:
    2:6–4:1, concerning Jerusalemite politics
    5:1-24, 10:1-3, concerning social iniquity and corruption
    5:25-29, 9:7-20, warnings of the Assyrian menace
    6:1–9:6, memorial following the Assyrian invasion
  B. From the Sargonic period
    10:5-8, 13-15a, 27-34, 11:1-9
  C. From the time of Sennacherib
    chaps. 28–31
  D. Following Isaiah's death[18]
    1:2–2:4(5), editorial transition
II. Foreign oracle collection, chaps. 13–23
  A. Basic blocks from the Isaianic school
    13:1-22, late exilic
    14:4b-20, time of Nebuchadrezzar
    15:1–16:2, 6-11, late kingdom period
    20:2-5, fall of Ashdod
    23:1-14, time of Esarhaddon
  B. Short commentaries added in chaps. 13, 14, 15–16, 21, 23, all early postexilic
  C. Interpolation of authentic Isaianic materials into the *massa* collection[19]

    14:24-27, 29-32, 17:1-6, 10-11, 12-14, 18:1-2, 4-6, 19:1b-4, 11-14, 22:1-14, 15-19

III. Exilic and postexilic expansions

    A. Judgment recension (short comments neutralizing early salvation sayings)

        2:10-11, 20-21, 3:9bβ, 5:15-16, 6:13abα, 10:10-11, 14:21, 22-23, 15:9, 16:12, 28:13, 19, 29:8-9, 30:32

    B. Salvation recension (early postexilic)

        1:27-28, 2:5, 22, 3:10-11, 6:13bβ, 7:15, 21-22, 10:12, 11:10, 14:2-6, 25, 16:1, 3-5, 17:7-8, 23:17-18, 28:1-4, 5-6, 30:29, 32, 31:6-7

IV. Late postexilic expansions

    A. New salvation recension, 500-450

        4:3-5a, 10:21-23, 24-26, 29:17-22 (23-25), 30:18-26, 32:1-5 (6-8), 9-14,[20] 15-20

    B. Final redaction, *ca.* 400

        19:16-25, chaps. 24–27, 33–35, 36–39; 11:11-16 (with thanksgiving hymns, 12:1-6, 25:1-5, 26:1-6

    C. Subsequent pre-Hellenistic additions

        4:5b-6, 8:8b, 10:27, 11:11b, 13b, 29:11-12, 34:16a.

Like other commentators on Isaiah, Wildberger has relied on three major lines of evidence: (1) linguistic and compositional data, (2) historical allusions, and (3) the development of theological and other ideological concepts. He has not effectively come to grips with the special transitional formulas under study here, nor has he shown any awareness of any significance in their frequency and special patterning within this major prophetic book.

Integral Transitions in Isaiah

We need not be long detained with an examination of Isaiah's integral futuristic transitions because they do not occur in primitive collections of Isaianic material except in 1:26, which the original superscription in 2:1 shows to be outside the main corpus consisting of chaps. 2–31.[21] Many scholars believe that 1:21-26 is from Isaiah himself because of its concern with social righteousness within the city of Jerusalem. This is probably correct. The formula *'aḥărê-kēn* is entirely natural within a structure of parallel opposites, that is, the present prevalent wickedness *versus* the primeval — now to be restored — ideal of institutional justice (v 26a). The proximate future is to see the outpouring of Yahweh's wrath on the perverters of justice; beyond that is a remote event in which Jerusalem's new names will exemplify its return.

In any case, this contrasting of epochs does not prove to be typical for Isaiah's preaching. Although numerous Isaianic oracles are juxtaposed throughout the initial collections, being often subjected to redactional supplementation (with or without temporal connectives), most of them do without any further integral temporal transitions. Where the very few do occur is significant: it is in scattered redactional comments within — and only within — chaps. 2–33 and in supplemental materials belonging to Deutero- and Trito-Isaiah. The integral transitions within redactional expansions in chaps. 2–33 are by no means homogeneous and reflect a wide range of time and ideology.

Attached to the redactionally isolated Isaianic oracle against Shebna in 22:15-18 are the successive redactional expansions of vv 19-23 and vv 24-25, each of which has integral *(wĕhāyâ) bayyôm hahû';* each refers to what is a proximate future from the viewpoint of the redactor in question, although each is in fact a *vaticinium ex eventu.* These expansions arose within the immediate school of the prophet's disciples. The first expansion announces judgment on Shebna but honor for Hilkiah, while the second announces judgment for the latter as well. *Wĕhāyâ bayyôm hahû'* is appropriate as the transition in v 20 because the downfall of Shebna is the main event, while the investiture of Hilkiah results in an ongoing condition in consequence of it; also because *bayyôm hahû'* in v 25, secured as transcendentally certain by a following *nĕ'um YHWH,* is viewed as a decisive new event.

The three remaining passages on the list of redactional occurrences with integral transitions are postexilic.

To a late kingdom-period oracle against Moab in 16:1-12, previously expanded, a redactor in the early Persian period has added the self-conscious editorial comment in vv 13-14, stating that Moab's previous judgment, still unrealized, is presently *(wĕ'attâ)* in the process of fulfillment, to be brought to conclusion within a three-year period of some significance to the redactor, though unknown to the modern exegete.

As has been shown, 31:1-5, 8-9 speaks of a weakness on Egypt's and Assyria's part that had remained unknown to those relying on them for help; this may contain an authentic core, but reflects the anxieties of the late preexilic period. An early postexilic redactor called in vv 6-7 for true repentance on the part of the *bĕnê yiśrā'ēl,* "the Israelites" (in Isaiah a postexilic expression),[22] grounded in the redactor's belief that 2:20's prediction *(kî bayyôm hahû')* was about to be fulfilled.[23]

The postexilic liturgy in 33:1-22, 24 was expanded by a redactional comment in v 23, stating the addressee's (probably Egypt's) present weakness and consequent *('āz)* susceptibility. This leaves us with a number of primary integral transitions with *'āz* (35:5, 6, 41:1, 58:8, 9, 14, 60:5) or *wĕ'attâ* (48:16); the passages to which they belong are certainly all postexilic. They all point

to an imminent future. Materials drawn from 2 Kings in chaps. 36–39 reproduce *hinnēh yāmîm bāʾîm* (39:6 par 2 Kgs 20:17), ostensibly pointing to the
distant future, but in fact producing another remarkable *vaticinium ex eventu*.

Thus every one of the integral occurrences in Isaiah is in supplemental
material, except for that in 1:26. It is therefore certain that Isaiah himself was
not in the habit of announcing an age far off, removed from the present and
imminent future that were his urgent concern.

Introductory Transitions in Isaiah

Except for *wĕhāyâ bĕʾaḥărît hayyāmîm* in 2:2 and *bāʿēt hahîʾ* in 18:7, the
regular and frequent futuristic formula for introducing redactional expansions
in the book of Isaiah is a construction with *bayyôm hahûʾ*. This is the more
striking because Isaiah himself never uses *bayyôm hahûʾ* except as a time
identifier (3:7, 5:30)[24] or in an epitome (2:11, 17).[25] *(Wĕhāyâ) bayyôm hahûʾ*
is not, however, evenly distributed throughout the entire book, or even within
chaps. 1–35. In the early collections from the period of the Syrian-Ephraimite
war, it introduces expansions only at 2:20, 3:18, 4:2, and 7:18-23. In a collection originating in the Sargonic era (chaps. 10–11), it introduces expansions
at 10:20 and 11:10-11. In chaps. 28–31, the core of which dates from the time
of Sennacherib, it introduces an expansion only at 28:5. Within the foreign-
oracle bloc, chaps. 13–23, it introduces expansions to Isaianic material at 17:7,
9 and at 19:16-24, as well as an expansion at 23:15 to a block from the
preexilic Isaiah school, the Tyre oracle of vv 1-14. Except in liturgical rubrics
at 12:1, 4, the remaining occurrences are expansions to the "little apocalypse"
of chaps. 24–27 (25:9, 26:1, 27:2 — all liturgical rubrics — and 24:21, 27:12-
13). The occurrences at 17:4, 24:21, and 28:5 are in anacrusis, but the others
are in prose.

It is not to be supposed that early expansions attach only to early
collections, or late expansions only to post-Isaianic blocks. The occurrences
of transitional *(wĕhāyâ) bayyôm hahûʾ* in 2:20, 3:18, 7:18-23, 10:20, 17:4,
and 28:5 are all preexilic. The occurrence at 11:10 is exilic, and those at 4:2,
11:11, 17:7, 9, 19:16-24, 23:15, 24:21, and 27:12-13, along with those in
liturgical rubrics, are all postexilic. Thus, while only late materials may receive
late expansions, early materials may receive either early or late expansions.

1. The initial collections

We should now inspect how each block of material introduced by a futuristic formula has been placed within its context, first 2:2 par Mic 4:1's *wĕhāyâ bĕ'aḥărît hayyāmîm*. Our assessment has been that the poetic material it introduces is secondary in each context and dates from the late exilic or early postexilic period, having been composed for the purpose of providing the following collections of judgment oracles with a counterbalancing announcement of salvation, implicitly for the inhabitants of Jerusalem but explicitly for foreign nations. This formula occurs elsewhere only in Jer 49:39, in a notation from the original redactor of Jeremiah's foreign-nation collection.[26] The implied present is the time of the return from exile; the transition (in anacrusis) is to a future remote from this implied present. Marvin Sweeney has concluded that 1:1 is a superscription to the entire book (including chaps. 36–39, 40–66), that 2:1 is a superscription just to chaps. 2–4, and that 13:1 is a superscription to chaps. 13ff.[27] As an editorial unit, chaps. 2–4 date from the late sixth or early fifth century, even while containing authentic Isaianic materials at 2:6-17, 3:1-9, 12-15, and 3:16–4:1. Isa 2:18-19 and 2:20-21 are seventh-century supplements, while 2:2-4 and 4:2 are supplements that date from the late exile. The collector of this entire block was responsible for 2:1 and 2:5-6.[28]

There is no good reason to dispute this analysis. In Isa 2:2 as in Mic 4:1, the idiosyncratic formula of future time is drastically asyndetic with respect to its literary context.

It is rather evident that the late preexilic redactor responsible for Isa 2:20-21 used *bayyôm hahû'* as a connective with the intention of expounding the Isaianic day-of-Yahweh theophany poem in vv 12-17, with its epitomizing *bayyôm hahû'* at the very end.[29] In this addition, deuteronomic influence has been at work in proclaiming the futility of idols.[30] The proximate future of Isaiah's poem was to bring the humbling of proud humanity in the face of Yahweh's awesome power (vv 18-19); this new supplement explicates this humbling in the parallel events of casting away idols and hiding in caves.

Isa 3:18-23, introduced by *bayyôm hahû'*, expounds the Isaianic prophecy of vv 16-17, 24.[31] There is no sufficient reason to date it beyond the preexilic period, but it does destroy the effectiveness of the original poetry, moving from the event of judgment upon the haughty women to a pedantic enumeration of items of feminine apparel and adornment that are to be removed as well. Both are events that lie, from the redactor's point of view, within the proximate future.

Bayyôm hahû' creates a drastic time-shift in Isa 4:2 — possibly from the event of 3:16-17, 24, but more likely from the present expanded text. 4:3-6 may be seen as an independent expansion of this postexilic verse; but, as we have argued, all of vv 2-6 should be taken as a unit because late eschatological ideology as we shall analyze it in a following chapter does tend to combine diverse and even incongruent images.[32] In any event, the redactor of v 2 wishes to reverse the original image of severe decimation by means of the optimistic announcement that even for Israel's refugees *(pĕlêṭat yiśrā'ēl)* there will be pride and glory — the opposite of the thematic shame because of Yahweh's *ṣemaḥ,* the messianic ideal of postexilic eschatology. Though Israel's shaming and Israel's exaltation are connected, as it were, in a single day, there is an evident progression from the proximate future of the first to the remote future of the latter.

Within the section Isa 6:1–9:6, Isaiah's prophecies have received expansions with *(wĕhāyâ) bayyôm hahû'* only in the four attachments of 7:18-25. We have been unable to agree with those exegetes who would assign these additions to various times and different redactors.[33] A single seventh-century redactor has drawn them together from various tradition sources. In any event, it is clear that this redactor intended to explicate the dire consequences of the Assyrian invasion announced in v 17. The mention of certain *yāmîm,* "days," unprecedented "since Ephraim departed from Judah," was sufficient stimulus for using *bayyôm hahû'* (v 20) or *wĕhāyâ bayyôm hahû'* (vv 18, 21, 23) to introduce each new event. These are synchronous rather than in sequence with one another, as well as with the event of v 17, all of which are to occur in the proximate future.

The formula *wĕhāyâ bayyôm hahû'* in Isa 10:20 is temporally at opposite extremes to the additions in chap. 7.[34] The catchword *šĕ'ār* in vv 19 and 20 accounts for the attachment of vv 20-23. Wildberger has identified 10:20-23 as an addition from a "new salvation recension" dating from the period 500-450 B.C.E.[35] From the ideological situation introduced in vv 5-11 (Isaiah's proximate future) and from that of the late seventh-century expansion in vv 12-19 (remote from this proximate future), the condition of comprehensive blessedness depicted in vv 20-23 is seen as even more remote, in spite of the synchronism. It is the conditional sentence at the end of the addition, identifying this situation as God's final and definite purpose,[36] that fixes this new "day" at the very end of history. This passage is unique in that Israel's final salvation is temporally associated both with the downfall of a foreign oppressor and with Israel's foregoing condemnation as a "godless nation" (v 6). This is a pattern seen elsewhere only in Ezek 29:21 and in the apocalyptic sections, Ezekiel 38–39 and Zechariah 12–13, 14.

We have previously assigned the collocation of expansions in Isa 11:10-11 to a single redactor, who was nevertheless attaching materials from different tradition sources. The first expansion — about the root of Jesse — is postexilic and was evidently attached as further explication of the Isaianic salvation portrayal in vv 1-9 featuring the "stump" of Jesse. Somewhat later is v 11's prediction that Yahweh will reach out to recover more of the holy remnant, identifying specifically the nations from which these should be recovered and stating that this would be a second *(šēnît)* extending of Yahweh's hand. Since it is authentic Isaianic material (with or without vv 6-9) from the original collection that is here being expanded, a time-gap similar to that of 10:20 is involved. The double *wĕhāyâ bayyôm hahû'* ostensibly synchronizes the Isaianic vision of an ideal Davidide in the prophet's own time with his appointment as a *nēs 'ammîm,* "ensign to the peoples" (v 10; explicated in the further expansion with *nēs laggôyim,* "ensign for the nations," in vv 12ff.), and this second recovery (v 11). In fact, the move is from a proximate to a very remote future in each instance, and it is indeed a permanently altered condition of salvation for the nations, as well as for Israel, that is predicted.

The final passage on our list of expansions to early collections is Isa 28:5-6, a poetic pericope in which *bayyôm hahû'* stands in anacrusis. In this respect, this passage is like 17:4-6 (see below); but also in that Isaiah is the probable author of the underlying material in vv 1-4, even though the additional poetic lines are from the preexilic Isaiah school. The catchword is *'ăṭeret,* "crown," in vv 3 and 5. Either the redactor joined the two poems with use of the temporal transition, or the new poem, including *bayyôm hahû'* in anacrusis, was his fresh composition. The effect is to counterbalance a proximate judgment on "the drunkards of Ephraim" with a promise of compensating glory for the "remnant" of Yahweh's people,[37] also in the proximate future.

2. *The foreign-oracle collection*

Within Isaiah's collection of foreign oracles, chaps. 13–23, as well as in a separate collection of Isaianic materials in chaps. 28–31, further occurrences of redactional transitions appear in additions to the prophet's own oracles, the only exception being the Tyre oracle in chap. 23, which is not from Isaiah but from his early school. Wildberger is probably right in arguing that the authentic passages within chaps. 13–23 were inserted toward the end of the exile into a collection of oracles from the preexilic Isaianic school in order to endow the former with the weight of prophetic authority. In any event, it is not to them but to the inserted authentic oracles that expansions introduced by a temporal transition were usually attached. The only exception is the postexilic expansion of the Tyre oracle (23:15-16) from the time of Esarhaddon. Because the underlying material is usually authentic and the expansions are mostly very late, we find again an extreme temporal gap between original and secondary material.

There is one striking exception to this rule, and that is the occurrence of *wĕhāyâ bayyôm hahû'* in anacrusis at Isa 17:4, where Isaiah's words against Damascus and Ephraim from the time of the Syrian-Ephraimite war were immediately refocused by one of the prophet's close disciples. The temporal formula synchronizes the proximately future event(s) of military catastrophe for both nations with a resulting condition of material destitution for "the glory of Jacob," also scheduled for the proximate future. The disciple responsible for the temporal formula was almost certainly quoting here a poetic oracle that he knew from the prophet's own lips. Our observation (above, on 1:26) that Isaiah did not himself customarily employ *bayyôm hahû'* as a temporal transition makes it extremely unlikely that the formula, here in anacrusis, would have been composed by him. In any event, we do possess here the rare and precious instance of a futuristic transition being employed at a very early stage of redaction.

Although each occurrence of *bayyôm hahû'* in 17:7, 9 creates a synchronism, it is to a future remote from the proximate future of vv 1-6 that the expansions introduced by them pertain. In our previous discussions of these two additions, a postexilic date and a common redactional process have been defended. Although vv 7-8 do refer to idol worship, they are not deuteronomistic because the prediction is that all mankind, not just Israel, will forsake idols for "their Maker," that is, "the Holy One of Israel." V 9's reference to the desertion of strong cities reflects postexilic as well as exilic conditions and also seems to apply to peoples other than the Israelites. The attachment of these verses to the preceding context seems asyndetic and entirely arbitrary, making the redactor's intention in this case quite obscure.

Introductory *bā'ēt hahî'* in Isa 18:7 attaches a very late expansion to Isaianic material. As we have seen, the futuristic use of this phrase is comparatively rare elsewhere in the Old Testament, and it is unique in Isaiah. It may be that the redactor who gave Isaiah's Kush oracle universalistic dimensions in v 3 was thinking of a general situation of judgment, out of which this people should be motivated to bring worship to Yahweh. The move is from one event in the proximate future to another event in the proximate future, both belonging to a new condition or situation rather than to specific events. Thus the preexilic threat loses its historical setting altogether. The prophecy pertains now to a new age in which Yahweh's harsh judgment motivates a foreign people to share in a universal blessing.

Isaiah's lengthy judgment oracle against Egypt in 19:1-15 evidently exerted a strong influence on the imagination of Jews living during the Persian and Hellenistic periods. They could account for the Jews' comparative well-being as sojourners in this land only out of the belief that somehow divine judgment had been turned into blessing. We have argued that a succession of redactors interpreted Egypt's favorable attitude in terms of a succession of events and situations (scheduled for the remote future that is synchronized in vv 16, 18, 19, 23, and 24 to a single day of divine action), incrementally adding new interpretations of this remarkable state of bliss. Vv 18 and 19ff. seem to contain elements of *vaticinium ex eventu,* but in general this is a pure prediction of what the late guardians of the Isaianic tradition yet hoped would come to pass, leading in vv 24-25 to an astounding affirmation of Egypt's and Assyria's eventual solidarity with Israel as Yahweh's people.

Within the foreign-oracle section, chaps. 13–23, the last expansion to an inauthentic composition having an introductory futuristic transition is 23:15-16. The original Tyre oracle of vv 1-12 is late preexilic rather than Isaianic. An exilic redactor evidently thought that the construct of a seventy-year period of desolation should pertain to this foreign enemy as well as to Israel. Hence he used *wĕhāyâ bayyôm hahû'* to synchronize the beginning of this period with the event of Tyre's downfall, in spite of the fact that Tyre was not actually taken until Alexander's conquest. Perhaps this same redactor endeavored to resolve this illogic in v 13's assertion that it was the Chaldeans, not the Assyrians, who would ruin Tyre. Or perhaps he reinterpreted Tyre's judgment merely as a time of comparative forgottenness or obscurity. In vv 17-18 a postexilic redactor, aware that Tyre had not in fact been captured, refocused the prediction of vv 15-16 in terms of Yahweh's eventual intentions, which were: (1) to reestablish Tyre's reputation as a rejected harlot and (2) to devote her recovered wealth as a source of material blessings dedicated to the worship of Yahweh. This is far from claiming that Tyre, like Kush (chap. 18) and Egypt (chap. 19), should be converted to Yahweh. Nevertheless, the mention of Tyre as a source of gifts for Yahweh reveals a common redactional impulse. In spite of their intentions, foreign nations were to be led to serve Yahweh's cult in the new age of bliss. It is noteworthy that the redactors of these chapters were less concerned with the salvation of foreign nations for their own sake than for the outpouring of praise and tribute that should result from it.

3. Late postexilic expansions

Two very late expansions within chaps. 1–35, the transitional material in 11:12-16 and the rather large block of early apocalyptic material in chaps. 24–27, have received liturgical supplements at a late stage for the purpose of using these highly idealistic materials in public worship. Liturgical rubrics with *bayyôm hahû'* introduce these materials at Isa 12:2, 4, 25:9, 26:1, and 27:2. As has been argued in our study of cluster arrangements (Chapter Five), this is likely the work of a single redactor. In each instance the act of praise preceded by one of these rubrics is thought of as occurring synchronously — in the same proximate future — with the salvific situations or conditions predicted in the underlying material.

Scholars are in agreement that Isaiah 24–27, even without further expansions, is one of the very latest additions to Isaiah 1–35. The core of this unhomogeneous supplement is an expansive day-of-Yahweh poem in 24:1-20, different from the classic poem of this type, as in Isaiah 2, Ezekiel 7, Amos 5, and Zephaniah 1, in that it not only begins with, but continues and ends with, a cosmic judgment that is directed toward the foreign nations rather than toward wayward Israel. It is this feature that accounts for its attachment to the foreign-oracle collection in chaps. 13–23. *(Wĕhāyâ) bayyôm hahû'* has been seen in anacrusis to original or early poetry in 17:4 and 28:5; here in 24:21 *wĕhāyâ bayyôm hahû'* stands in anacrusis to a very late product from within the Isaianic tradition, a lyrical paean of salvation for Israel (24:21-23, 25:6-8). The already remote day of universal judgment is extended synchronically as a more remote day of salvation for those rescued from that judgment.

Finally, there are the two brief prose expansions with *wĕhāyâ bayyôm hahû'* at the very end of this long insertion. We have argued that 27:12 and 13 were added by separate redactors. Again, they expand a remote future in terms of what is also a remote future, even though the theme of ultimate return for the exiles has nothing to do with judgment on unrepentant Samaria in the immediately preceding lament.

Conclusions

1. The redaction of Isaiah 1–31

Since futuristic transitions in 31:7, 33:23, 35:5-6 are all integral, this ends our survey of the array of expansions within Isaiah 1–35 that are introduced by a temporal formula. To review: There are no authentic futuristic transitions in Isaiah with integral *bayyôm hahû';* this is therefore *eo ipso* a mark of redaction. We state this as a conclusion rather than as an assumption. Within the early collections and the foreign-oracle section, it is almost exclusively to the authentic materials, rather than to internal expansions, that redactional additions with a temporal transition have been attached. Perhaps this is not surprising, for the process of expansion with the use of an introductory temporal transition must have gone hand in hand with the direct juxtaposition of new additions not so attached. It is impossible to say whether different groups of redactors were responsible for each kind of addition. However, as has been emphasized, there is certainly a distinction in intention when either of the two kinds of expansions is made. In the case of new materials placed in direct juxtaposition to materials in the underlying text, the evident motivation is to achieve greater completeness in a comprehensive display of received revelation. But on the part of new materials connected through the use of temporal transitions, the intent is rather to draw a dramatic contrast to the underlying material, either extending the event or situation to cover additional groups or individuals — as well as different aspects — or to modify it, perhaps even counteract it, by defining Yahweh's new intention.

The general tendency in Isaiah's expansions that have temporal transitions is either to extend judgment (on the nations or on Israel) as further judgment (seen in chaps. 2, 3, 17, 23, 24) or to extend Israel's or the nations' salvation as further, more complete, salvation (seen in chaps. 11, 19, 27).[38] This places in striking relief this book's relatively few incongruent and erratic ideologies, to be more fully discussed in Chapter Thirteen, as follows: Israel's punishment transformed into Israel's salvation, 4:2; a foreign nation's punishment transformed into its salvation, 19:18; punishment on a foreign nation extended as further punishment upon it, 17:4;[39] salvation for Israel transformed into salvation for the nations, 11:10; and punishment on the nations transformed into Israel's salvation, 10:20. Although these particular patterns are infrequent and isolated, they are specially significant in Isaiah because they show that the redactors of Isaiah believed in a dialectical revelation.

As we place the list of integral transitions alongside the list of introductory transitions, an important distinction comes to light. Whether primary or redactional, the integral transitions identify a sequence from one event or situation to another (Isa 31:7 has it in reverse), while the introductory transitions place events or situations in synchronism. The integral transitions employed are, appropriately, wĕʿattâ and ʾāz but also wĕhāyâ bayyôm hahûʾ (22:20, 25, 31:7). Contrariwise, the introductory transitions are almost always bayyôm hahûʾ or wĕhāyâ bayyôm hahûʾ. The effect of this tenacious use of (wĕhāyâ) bayyôm hahûʾ as the formula of choice in introductory position is to unfold the ideological complexity of Yahweh's decisive coming day. This occurs not only where transitions appear in clusters, but everywhere in Isaiah. Isaiah's redactors explored the possibilities of the concept of the "day of Yahweh" as a comprehensive event with numerous and various effects. Logic did not always prevail as the vision moved from one event to another event within the proximate future, from a proximately future event to a remote future event, or from one remotely future event to another remotely future event. The concern was always ideological rather than chronological. The decisive day was to be Yahweh's day, and because it was to be Yahweh's day, it could include all sorts of possibilities open to his acting.

Locutions that did not belong within the vocabulary of Isaiah's redactors were bayyāmîm hahēm(mâ), hinnēh yāmîm bāʾîm,[40] and bĕʾaḥărît hayyāmîm. Another, bāʿēt hahîʾ, appears in isolation at 18:7. Though this stands out for its rarity, it does share with bayyôm hahûʾ the possibility of drawing new events or conditions into the temporal context of Yahweh's new day because — strictly translated — it refers to an event arising out of an altered situation, rather than in a sequence of future days. The plurality of future days implied in the first three formulas mentioned was apparently not entertained in the minds of these redactors.

In passing, it should also be noted that the oracle formula, *ně'um YHWH*, employed in Hosea, Amos, Zephaniah, Haggai, and Zechariah, but especially prominent in Jeremiah, is all but missing in Isaiah. A redactor from Isaiah's early school added it to the temporal transition in 22:25 for a good and special reason: to ensure that the new word about Hilkiah's downfall should be received as the expression of Yahweh's final intent within a particular sequence of events. Its absence elsewhere in Isaiah should probably be interpreted to mean that Isaiah's redactors were not especially concerned that their new vision should be received on an equal footing as an authoritative unfolding of Yahweh's intent.

Finally, it is interesting to find that our analysis allows for Barth's hypothesis of an "Assyrian recension," but only in part. Our most serious disagreement with Barth is with regard to the provenance of chaps. 7, 10, and 17–19. To be sure, he identifies the "Assyrian recension" also in a sizable number of additional passages not touched by our analysis, concerning which we have no comment except to join in Wildberger's misgivings about the peril of sacrificing far more material to this alleged recension than the evidence will strictly allow.[41]

2. The redaction of Isaiah 32–66

This brings us back, finally, to the question of the complete absence of introductory temporal transitions in Deutero- and Trito-Isaiah, as well as in a section of the book that has been strongly influenced by Deutero-Isaiah, chaps. 32–35.[42] The nonappearance of a given phenomenon where it might naturally have been expected can be significant. Most scholars agree that Deutero-Isaiah was written toward the end of the exile, and that Trito-Isaiah, along with Isaiah 32–35, dates from the late sixth century or the early part of the fifth century. However, the relatively late dating of these sections could not have been determinative in creating this sharp difference because some sections of Isaiah 1–31 were also composed after the exile; and, indeed, because some expansions to these chapters having introductory temporal transitions are much later than Deutero- and Trito-Isaiah. What is the significance, then, of the lack of introductory temporal transitions in these two major literary blocks? This question becomes even sharper when we take into account the decisive preference on the part of the redactors of Isaiah 1–31 for the locution *(wěhāyâ) bayyôm hahû'*. This becomes a distinctive mark of Isaiah's school as a whole, ranging over several centuries of time. Modern scholarship is in agreement that Deutero- and Trito-Isaiah were independent compositions; yet they also

were eventually attached to the prophecies of Isaiah, but without the employment of futuristic transitions in introductory position. Why and how did they
escape the redactional formulations that prevail elsewhere in the book?

It will be convenient to restrict our discussion of this question to the
primary block, chaps. 40–55, for this is the key to the problem. Although
various compositional levels have been seen in these chapters by a number
of scholars, the trend is currently toward the recognition of a unified authorship. Unity of authorship may be part of the answer to the question we have
posed.

If Isaiah 40–55 existed as a separate literary entity for a significant
period of time prior to being appended to Isaiah 1–31 (32–35), it is entirely
understandable that the redactors who worked on the latter would have had
no occasion to apply such expansions to the former. Although we cannot insist
that Deutero-Isaiah, eventually expanded by what is known collectively as
Trito-Isaiah, would not have been annexed to Isaiah 1–31 (32–35) until this
literary entity had virtually reached completion with all of the expansions to
it of the type under study here, it does not seem reasonable to suggest that
there was an identifiable trend or tradition of redaction at work that would
have all but completely spent itself before chaps. 40ff. were added. This entire
tradition of redactorship has shown itself to be remarkably tenacious in the
way in which it has attached new materials, and especially in its almost
exclusive preference for *(wĕhāyâ) bayyôm hahû'*.

Besides the composition of Deutero-Isaiah as a literary whole, the fact
that it contains nothing but words of salvation for exiled Israel, and the peculiar
nature of its eschatological program, may also have been factors in keeping
Deutero-Isaiah free from the type of progressive redaction that had been
operative in chaps. 1–31. A word needs to be said about each of these considerations.

Deutero-Isaiah is indeed concerned only for Israel's well-being in the
period of return from Babylonian exile. It is not surprising, therefore, that
integral futuristic transitions at 41:1 and 48:16 do expand Israel's salvation
as further salvation for Israel. This is the pattern seen also in passages directly
influenced by Deutero-Isaiah: 35:5-6, 58:9-10, 14, 60:5. However, introductory temporal transitions also expand salvation for Israel as further salvation for Israel, as in the postexilic texts, 11:11 and 27:13. There is no basis,
therefore, for arguing that there is a special ideology in Deutero-Isaiah, as
well as in texts directly influenced by it, that has not come to expression also
in the redactional additions to Isaiah 1–31.

Deutero-Isaiah does have its own distinctive eschatological program.
This has been brilliantly expounded in Hendrik Leene's recent study, *De
vroegere en de nieuwe dingen bij Deuterojesaja*.[43] Analyzing Isaiah 40–46
and 48, with special attention to chaps. 41–44, Leene identifies two special

unifying factors: (1) a performative intentionality in the entire composition and (2) a reiterated rehearsal of a succcession of divine acts along the time-line, "earlier," "later," "coming," and "new." The "earlier" events are qual-ified in terms drawn from the roots *r'š* and *qdm* ("beginning" and "previ-ous"), the "later" events by words from the root *'ḥr* ("after"), the "coming" events by the roots *bw'* and *'th* ("go, come"), and the "new" things by words from the root *ḥdš* ("new"). Leene insists that terms belonging to these seman-tic fields must not be confused with one another or substituted for one another in the interpretation of Deutero-Isaiah's eschatological program. For Deutero-Isaiah, the present moment of performative proclamation lies at the juncture between what Yahweh has already accomplished and what Yahweh is about to do. The earlier things that he performed were the saving acts of Abraham's call and Israel's safe passage through the wilderness, while the later things are those that just now have occurred in typological replication of those events, namely, the already-achieved successes of Cyrus. In them together, Yahweh's power to save has been abundantly exhibited. These are now recalled as warranty for the saving events still to come, that is, the "coming things" and the "new things," which are to consist of a new exodus and the spiritual transformation of Israel, which is to participate in this transformation as Yahweh's "servant."

Thus far Leene. It could be argued that shifts from past to present, and from present to future events are so fully realized in this schema that the type of shift effectuated in the redactional expansions that we have been studying is not to be expected. But this would be pure speculation. On what basis are we to suppose that Deutero-Isaiah's images of Yahweh's "coming" and "new" things could not have given rise to this type of redactional expansion? The only thing we do know for sure is that they did not, in fact, give rise to such expansions. The reason must lie in Deutero-Isaiah's redactional isolation and not in an assumed insusceptibility. This applies as well to materials influenced by Deutero-Isaiah in chaps. 32–35 and 56-66.

The redactional isolation of Isaiah 40–66 is an inescapable conclusion from these considerations. Of course, the canonical shape of the book — all that is directly apparent to us — does assume that eventually they were at-tached, along with chaps. 32–35 and chaps. 36–39, as an expression of a larger sense of affinity. It cannot be gainsaid that there are significant ideological and thematic links binding the respective literary blocks. A number of recent studies have brought out significant signs of interdependence among the various sections of Isaiah;[44] yet these considerations are not weighty enough in themselves to distract our attention from the fact that Isaiah 1–31 displays an involved and tenacious pattern of attaching supplements by the use of temporal transitions, while the remaining chapters of the book are without them. To all appearances, until well into the postexilic period — perhaps the late fifth or early fourth century — Isaiah 1–31 (perhaps with chaps. 32–35 already attached) remained redactionally separate from Deutero- and Trito-Isaiah.

Our analysis of redactional distinctiveness in chaps. 1–31 cannot be contravened and ought not to be ignored. Marvin Sweeney does not deny a progression of redactional stages, yet he does seem to demand a degree of redactional proximity that our evidence would appear to make impossible. Not only does he claim that Isaiah 40–66 has been drawn up out of awareness and concern for the content of the early collection, but also that the early collection was composed — at least in part — in awareness of this subsequent literary block. The five lines of evidence that he adduces in support of this conclusion are: (1) the prominence of Babylon in chaps. 1ff., chaps. 36ff., and chaps. 40ff., respectively; (2) the relative exaltation of Hezekiah in chaps. 36–39 in comparison with the Kings *Vorlage;* (3) the exodus imagery in chap. 35 in comparison with allusions to this theme in chaps. 1–31 and chaps. 40ff.; (4) dependence in chap. 1 on certain themes in chaps. 65–66; and (5) concern in chaps. 1ff. for the problems of the postexilic community. But affinities of this type need not imply direct literary derivation. They may have arisen as a tenacious, ongoing tradition accompanying this school's literary activity and in consequence of the fact that Isaiah 1–31 certainly continued to receive new additions in a process that extended on into the exilic and postexilic periods.

CHAPTER SEVEN

Jeremiah

Primary transitions	Redactional transitions
1. Integral	
4:12	*ʿattâ*[a]
7:32[b]	*lākēn hinnēh yāmîm bāʾîm něʾum YHWH*
14:10	*ʿattâ*
16:16	*wěʾaḥărê-kēn*
19:6[c]	*lākēn hinnēh yāmîm bāʾîm něʾum YHWH*
22:22	*kî ʾāz*
23:20	*běʾaḥărît hayyāmîm*[d]
30:3	*kî hinnēh yāmîm bāʾîm něʾum YHWH*
30:24	*běʾaḥărît hayyāmîm*[e]
31:1	*bāʿēt hahîʾ něʾum YHWH*
31:13	*ʾāz*
33:15	*bayyāmîm hahēm ûbāʿēt hahîʾ*[f]
33:16	*bayyāmîm hahēm*[g]
48:12	*lākēn hinnēh yāmîm bāʾîm něʾum YHWH*
49:2	*lākēn hinnēh yāmîm bāʾîm něʾum YHWH*
51:47	*lākēn hinnēh yāmîm bāʾîm*[h]
51:52	*lākēn hinnēh yāmîm bāʾîm něʾum YHWH*
2. Introductory	
3:17	*bāʿēt hahîʾ*[i] (prose addition)
3:18	*bayyāmîm hahēmmâ* (prose addition)
4:9	*wěhāyâ bayyôm hahûʾ něʾum YHWH* (anacrusis)
4:11	*bāʿēt hahîʾ něʾum YHWH*[j] (citation rubric)
5:18	[k]*wěgam bayyāmîm hahēmmâ*[k] *něʾum YHWH* (prose addition)

130

8:1	*bāʿēt hahî' nĕʾum YHWH* (prose addition)
9:24 (E 25)	*hinnēh yāmîm bāʾîm nĕʾum YHWH* (prose addition)
16:14[l]	*lākēn hinnēh yāmîm bāʾîm nĕʾum YHWH* (prose addition)
21:7	*wĕʾaḥărê-kēn nĕʾum YHWH* (prose addition)
23:5[m]	*hinnēh yāmîm bāʾîm nĕʾum YHWH* (prose addition)
23:7[n]	*lākēn hinnēh yāmîm bāʾîm nĕʾum YHWH* (prose addition)
30:8	*wĕhāyâ bayyôm hahû' nĕʾum YHWH* (anacrusis)
31:27	*hinnēh yāmîm bāʾîm nĕʾum YHWH* (prose addition)
31:29	*bayyāmîm hahēm lō' yōʾmĕrû ʿôd* (citation rubric)
31:31	*hinnēh yāmîm bāʾîm nĕʾum YHWH* (prose addition)[o]
31:38	*hinnēh yāmîm [bāʾîm]*[p] *nĕʾum YHWH* (prose addition)
33:14[q]	*hinnēh yāmîm bāʾîm nĕʾum YHWH*[r] (prose addition)
46:26	*wĕʾaḥărê-kēn*[s] (prose addition)
49:6	*wĕʾaḥărê-kēn*[s] (prose addition)
49:39	*wehayâ bĕʾaḥărît hayyāmîm*[s] (prose addition)
50:4	*bayyāmîm hahēm ûbāʿēt hahî' ᵗnĕʾum YHWH*ᵗ (prose addition)
50:20	*bayyāmîm hahēm ûbāʿēt hahî' ᵗnĕʾum YHWH*ᵗ (prose addition)

a. Cf. introductory *bāʿēt hahî' yēʾāmēr lĕ'* . . .
b. Virtual par 19:6; cf. introductory *bāʿēt hahî' nĕʾum YHWH*, 8:1
c. Virtual par 7:32
d. Par 30:24
e. Par 23:20
f. 23:5 om
g. 23:6 *bĕyāmâw*
h. Cf. *nĕʾum YHWH*, v 48 fin
i. Cf. *wĕhāyâ . . . bayyāmîm hahēmmâ* (time indicator), v 16
j. Cf. *ʾattâ* as integral transition (redactional), v 12
k-k. MT; G *wĕhāyâ bayyôm hahû'*
l. Par 23:7
m. Par 33:14
n. Par 16:14
o. Cf. *ʾaḥărê hayyāmîm hahēm* (time indicator) with *nĕʾum YHWH*, v 33
p. QMSSVss; K om

q. Par 23:5
r. Cf. integral transition *bayyāmîm hahēm,* v 16; G om vv 14-16
s. *nĕ'um YHWH* fin
t-t. MT; G om

Redaction and Ideology in Jeremiah

1. The historical setting of the book

By comparison with Isaiah, the book of Jeremiah reflects a strikingly shorter
process of composition and redaction. Its internal complexity is, however,
even greater than that of Isaiah. Various scholars argue that, in spite of 1:2
and 25:3, the man Jeremiah did not prophesy at all during the reign of Josiah
(604-609); or, if he did, that he would have uttered at that time only scattered
oracles against northern Israel, now preserved in chaps. 2–4 and 30–31.[1] In
any event, Jeremiah's career as a writing prophet is directly connected with
the events of chap. 36, dated to the fourth year of Jehoiakim (605); namely,
the reading of an early scroll followed by its immediately following burning,
and eventual redictation and expansion. As is generally accepted, that first
scroll must have contained at least the oracles concerning a menacing "foe
from the north" mentioned in chaps. 4–6. An identification of the latter with
the Scythians has now been given up; it is the Neo-Babylonians (Chaldeans)
during the last days of Nabopolassar (626-605) to whom these words pertain.
Certainly the great bulk of prophecies ascribed to Jeremiah reflect the last
two decades of the kingdom of Judah, during the reigns of Jehoiakim (609-
598), his son Jehoiachin (598-597), and his brother Zedekiah (597-586). This
was the time of a first (597) and second deportation of Jews to Babylon (586),
which Jeremiah personally escaped (chap. 40), only to become an unwilling
refugee to Egypt. The prophet's words continued to be recorded, and no doubt
redacted, in the early exile period. Scattered elements were added toward the
end of the exile and during the postexilic period, but these hardly assume the
proportions of comparable material in Isaiah.

Jeremiah is known as the "weeping prophet" not only because doom
for the nation weighs so heavily in the book as a whole, but also because the
man was personally persecuted for his unpopular message. The book is unique
in expressing deep personal concern for the nation's — and especially its
leaders' — hardness of heart, making doom inevitable. Jeremiah's career
stood in the dark shadow of the shining time of spiritual revival during Josiah's
reign. The high hopes that had been raised by the fleeting success of the
deuteronomic reform were dashed, suddenly and completely. Jeremiah wept

not so much for the looming peril upon the reigning house (chap. 22) as for the mounting evidence that the nation's covenant with Yahweh had gone thoroughly bad. Jer 5:30-31 says it all:

> An appalling and horrible thing has happened in the land;
> the prophets prophesy falsely and the priests rule at their discretion;
> my people love to have it so, but what will you do when the end
> comes?

2. The present state of research

Except in its allusions to Nebuchadrezzar's second siege and the capture of Jerusalem (588-586), the book of Jeremiah has few dates by which to fix a chronology of composition. The biographical section, chaps. 32–45, often attributed to Jeremiah's amanuensis, Baruch, is our main source of information; yet its historical reliability has been questioned, and at any rate it has proven a tantalizingly difficult task to correlate the oracular material with events mentioned in this narrative.

Robert Carroll believes that this task must be given up completely because the entire book has passed through a redactional process so complex as to put it beyond the power of critical reconstruction.[2] Other scholars are more sanguine. William L. Holladay, for instance, seems convinced that virtually all the oracular material may be correlated with septennial readings of Deuteronomy in the years 622, 615, 608, 601, 594, and 587 (cf. Deut 31:9-13).[3] This would seem far too venturesome for most scholars.

We may, at any rate, be reasonably certain that the dates given in 1:1-3, 25:2, 32:1, 36:1, and 45:1 are reliable if properly understood. They offer themselves as a chronological framework for an ongoing process of publishing and reformulating Jeremiah's message. Many scholars believe that — alongside of, or independently of, Baruch — a cohesive deuteronomistic school managed this material while adding their own preachments to it. In any event, we receive an image of an impassioned prophet speaking again and again, at first hopefully but eventually in despair, as he saw the nation's judgment looming larger and larger. As a whole, individual words of judgment from the prophet and/or his disciples were collected and brought into simple juxtaposition, but now and again expansions using some of the temporal transitions under study here were attached to underlying materials, as in Isaiah and most of the other prophetic books. By this device, judgment on Israel was extended as further judgment on Israel. When the people would not listen, or when false prophets contradicted Jeremiah's message, not only were new punishments announced, but previously announced punishments were extended and expanded.

In spite of all this, Jeremiah's book also contains messages of salvation, some of them as attachments employing temporal transitions.[4] In the light of his purchase of an ancestral field during the days of siege (32:1-25), it does not seem reasonable to maintain that salvation sayings must automatically be ascribed to Jeremiah's redactors. Nevertheless, something definitively new is in process in such a passage as 31:31-34. Holladay affirms Jeremianic authorship for this famous pericope, but virtually all critics ascribe it to the deuteronomistic school. As Siegfried Herrmann has argued,[5] there is a sophisticated theology of history in evidence here that goes well beyond the prophet's plaintive expectation of personal survival.[6]

Thus in addition to the criterion of historical reconstruction, there is the criterion of ideological differentiation. There are fewer misgivings about ascribing messages of doom to Jeremiah than about crediting him with the oracles of salvation. In assessing expansions with temporal transitions, we have allowed no facile assumptions, but each passage has been evaluated independently for data that may be useful in reconstructing the process of composition and redaction. As much as possible, we have avoided the claim of authenticity and have been content to say whether a given passage belongs within primary material — meaning material that is elemental at a specific compositional level — or redactional material — that is, clearly secondary within its specific context. Beyond that, our previous method of distinguishing between integral transitions and introductory transitions commends itself also here. It is in this connection that a third criterion, beyond those of historical reconstruction and ideological differentiation, holds out some promise. This is the question whether a given expansion is in poetry or in prose.

In spite of considerable research on this question, we are still not in a position to assume that the question of poetry *versus* prose makes no difference. Jeremiah criticism seemed to have achieved a definite consensus in the work of a number of twentieth-century scholars, the chief of whom was Sigmund Mowinckel in his monograph *Zur Komposition des Buches Jeremia.*[7] Mowinckel laid out the book in three parallel compositional strata, which he labeled A, B, and C. Stratum A consisted of original Jeremianic oracles in poetry; stratum B consisted of the book's biographical material, in prose; stratum C consisted of the deuteronomistic redaction, also in prose. Two special monographs on the redaction of Jeremiah appearing in 1973 opened up the question anew, however. These were Winfried Thiel's book *Die deuteronomistische Redaktion von Jeremia 1–25,*[8] and Helga Weippert's *Die Prosareden des Jeremiabuches.*[9] Thiel stressed the distinctiveness of style and lexicography in the D sections in contrast to those of the poetic material, identifying the D school as responsible for the definitive redaction of Jeremiah

1–25. Weippert argued for similarities between the language of the poetic and the prose sections, stressing distinctions between Jeremianic prose and the prose of Deuteronomy.

Recent major commentaries definitely show the influence of these two studies. Carroll's *Jeremiah, A Commentary* (1986)[10] agrees on the dominance of deuteronomistic redaction in the prose sections. Holladay's *Jeremiah 1* and *Jeremiah 2* in the Hermeneia series (1986, 1989),[11] buttressed by previous publications[12] and in essential agreement with Weippert, admit some influence from the deuteronomic movement but deny a special D redaction, attributing the great bulk of the book to Jeremiah and Baruch. The first volume of William McKane's *A Critical and Exegetical Commentary on Jeremiah* (1986)[13] takes a more nuanced view, seeing elements of strength and of weakness both in Thiel and in Weippert, proposing instead the notion of a "rolling corpus" in which both poetry and prose were successively expanded. The very first fascicle of Siegfried Herrmann's Jeremiah commentary for the Biblischer Kommentar series reveals what may be assumed from this scholar's earlier monograph *Die prophetische Heilserwartungen,*[14] namely, a very cautious acknowledgment of deuteronomistic redaction.

Carroll and Holladay seem to be at opposite poles. Not only does the one affirm and the other deny deuteronomistic redaction; Holladay seems overly optimistic about identifying original material while Carroll seems to be far too agnostic. Holladay has offered a detailed reconstruction of Jeremiah's ministry — something indeed that we would all like to have, were the evidence strong enough to support it. He is to be admired, if not commended, for being strongly affirmative in proposing far-reaching solutions where the evidence is sometimes lamentably weak. When all is said and done, Carroll is right in insisting that the stodgy and pious prose of the "deuteronomistic" sections could not have come directly from the author of the vibrant oracular poetry.[15]

As a guide to a discussion of temporal transitions we need something more than a division of materials into Mowinckel's strata A, B, and C. It is best to avoid the simple polarity, original *versus* deuteronomistic. Most materials with temporal transitions are in prose, but it is not clear that they display a uniform ideology or come from one particular redaction. Some are early, but others are late — even very late. Holladay's scheme of chronological sequencing is too controversial, and at the same time too complex, to be useful here.[16]

What we actually need is a structural outline that is based upon the interrelationships of various materials and various collections to one another. Perhaps we can do little better than to identify the major tradition blocks and show their relationships to the presumed original scroll. Claus Rietzschl's monograph *Das Problem der Urrolle*[17] has perhaps shown how this may be

done. Setting aside attribution to a particular school of redactors, Rietzschl
outlines an initial phase of collection, then of the collection of collections,
and finally the definitive redaction, of four major complexes: (1) judgment
oracles against Judah and Jerusalem, (2) judgment oracles against the nations,
(3) salvation prophecies for Israel, and (4) the biographical narratives. The
foreign oracles were originally attached to 25:13. Chap. 45 was placed at
20:18, which concluded the second scroll, chaps. 21–24 being a later insertion.
The redacted first scroll consisted of the original material in chaps. 1–6, with
1:1-3aα as the original superscription, dating from Jehoiakim's fourth year.
Though many scholars would differ on details, the majority would perhaps
not disagree with the essentials of this reconstruction.

The Pattern of Temporal Transitions

It is not our purpose to attempt an independent solution to these problems.
Rather, we raise these considerations to give our present study perspective
within the framework of contemporary research.[18] We have found that assumptions that may be valid for Isaiah may not directly pertain to the study
of Jeremiah. Although the book of Jeremiah has less material content than
Isaiah and covers a shorter time-period, it has in fact undergone an even more
complex process of composition, collection, and redaction.

Our list of passages with temporal transitions reveals many contrasts
between Jeremiah and Isaiah. Whereas the Isaianic redaction shows a tenacious preference for the locution *(wĕhāyâ) bayyôm hahû',* it is missing in
primary material except in biographical material at 39:17 as a time identifier;
and, except in anacrusis at 4:9 and 30:8 and in the questionable LXX reading
in 5:18, it is also missing from redactional materials. On the other hand,
redactional materials in Jeremiah show a strong preference for formulas seldom used in Isaiah, in particular *bā'ēt hahî', bayyāmîm hahēm(mâ), 'aḥărê-
ken, bĕ'aḥărît hayyāmîm,* and especially *(lākēn) hinnēh yāmîm bā'îm.*

We may now apply conclusions from our study of individual passages
in Chapters Two through Four, and of transitions in clusters in Chapter Five,
to an examination of precisely how temporal transitions fit into the text of
Jeremiah as a whole, and of their purpose. As in our study of Isaiah, this will
provide no grand solution to the overall redactional problem of this book, yet
it promises to produce insights that will need to be taken into account in future
research. In some Jeremiah passages, the presence of a specific temporal
formula will prove to have had even a larger redactional role than has been
the case in Isaiah.

There is no difficulty in agreeing upon the basic blocks in Jeremiah:

(1) the prologue in chap. 1; (2) an early block of oracular materials, 2:1–25:14; (3) a collection of foreign oracles in chaps. 46–51, originally placed, as in the LXX, after the prologue in 25:15-38; (4) a new cycle of oracles with framing narratives in chaps. 26–36; (5) an expanded collection of narratives about Jeremiah's personal fortunes during and following the final siege of Jerusalem, chaps. 37–51; and (6) an appendix in chap. 52 drawn from 2 Kings 24.

The narratives contain no futuristic transition; *bayyôm hahû'* in 39:17 is a time identifier.[19] Integral as well as introductory temporal transitions occur mainly, therefore, among the oracular collections; specifically, the early collection in chaps. 2–25, the foreign-oracle collection, and the "little book of consolation" in chaps. 30–31, expanded in chap. 33.

Without immediately adopting any particular theory of redaction, we may analyze the early block (2–25) into a series of prior collections, namely, chaps. 2–6, chaps. 7–10, chaps. 11–13, chaps. 14–17, chaps. 18–20, chaps. 21–24, and finally the summary narrative with words for the exiles to Babylon found in 25:1-14. These interior collections are fairly well marked off by introductory formulas. 7:1, 11:1, and 18:1 have the opening formula *haddābār 'ăšer hāyâ 'el-yirmĕyāhû mē'ēt YHWH lē'mōr*, "the word that happened to Jeremiah from Yahweh, as follows." 14:1 has *'ăšer hāyâ* [G(S) *wayhî*] *dĕbar-YHWH 'el-yirmĕyāhû*, "that which happened as Yahweh's word to Jeremiah." 21:1 has *haddābār 'ăšer-hāyâ 'el yirmĕyāhû mē'ēt YHWH*, "the word that happened to Jeremiah from Yahweh," followed by a temporal phrase.[20] Although a wide variety of prophetic materials are gathered in these sections, we take special note of the fact that chaps. 2–6 consist of early oracles on the themes of Judah's harlotry and the enemy from the north, chaps. 7–10 have to do mainly with cultic transgressions, and chaps. 21–24 have to do with kings and prophets.

Integral Transitions in Jeremiah

1. Primary occurrences

The display shows that integral transitions with a temporal formula are relatively more frequent in Jeremiah than in Isaiah, even though introductory occurrences prevail over integral, here as well as there. However, most of these integral transitions belong to obvious *ad hoc* redactional expansions except in the foreign-oracle section. Among primary integral occurrences, there is one of *'attâ,* two of *(kî) 'āz,* one of *wĕ'aḥărê-kēn,* one of *bĕ'aḥărît hayyāmîm,* one of *bayyôm hahû',* and four of *lākēn hinnēh yāmîm bā'îm.*

We may say the following about some of the passages on this list. Jer

14:2-10 is certainly preexilic, and that means that it must be from Jeremiah or his immediate school;[21] it is a complete doom-saying containing an accusation that summarizes the past/present situation, followed by a summary announcement concerning the present and imminent future, and the clauses introduced by ʿattâ function as the apodosis to the protasis of Yahweh's nonacceptance. Jer 16:16-18 is early exilic and possibly by Jeremiah;[22] it is in fact a *vaticinium ex eventu* in which *wĕ'aḥărê-kēn* draws a sequence from successive acts of divine judgment, ostensibly future but in fact lying in the recent past. It is difficult to date the lament in 22:20-23,[23] but if it is Jeremianic it may be one of his very first oracles against foreign nations; *kî 'āz* in v 22 draws a sequence between an act of judgment in the proximate future and the resulting condition or situation in the remote future. In contrast, the salvation announcement in 31:10-14, in which v 13's *'āz* creates a sequence between events in the proximate, or proximate and remote, future, has to be late exilic, or even early postexilic.

One occurrence on our primary list, that in 23:20, is of very special importance because it sheds definite light on the prophet's own temporal ideology. Its concern is for the immediate here and now. 23:16-20[24] has a clear apologetic aim, that of vindicating Jeremiah's dire predictions in competition with popular words of optimism ascribed to the late preexilic prophets as a group. V 16 contains a warning, and vv 17-18 a grounding for this warning in the form of an accusation with a series of rhetorical questions intended to undermine the authenticity, and hence the authority, of Jeremiah's opponents. Vv 19-20a announce Yahweh's own irresistible response to false prophecy, which is to be an imminent, completely unexpected, storm of divine wrath. The temporal formula *bĕ'aḥărît hayyāmîm* in v 20b introduces what will be the tangible result of this coming confrontation, that is, a definitive decision to the effect that the false prophets are dead wrong. As has been stated in our discussion of this passage in Chapter Four, this occurrence is a precious clue to the way in which Jeremiah himself actually associated the past/present with the imminent and the proximate future. This important item of evidence increases the unlikelihood that Jeremiah himself may have been involved in conceptualizing a remote or ideal future in the manner of his eschatologizing redactors.

We turn aside for the moment to consider a temporal formula that does not function as a transition. Jer 23:16-22 should be compared with Jeremiah's pattern of futuristic expectation as seen also in a passage with nonformulaic *bayyôm hahû'*, followed by the oracle formula, occurring in Jer 39:17. Although this expression does not function in this passage as a transition, it very likely reflects what would have been Jeremiah's own manner of speaking. The passage is part of the short biographical section 39:15-18,[25] obviously written by a disciple — Baruch or someone other — but there is no reason to think that the scribe in question was not closely reproducing the prophet's own speech pattern as well as his temporal ideology. We seem especially close here to the historical Jeremiah because the prediction of Ebed-melech's safety in the siege shares a theme found in unquestionably authentic materials elsewhere, that is, that of rescue for certain faithful individuals (himself and his potential heirs in chap. 32; of Baruch in chap. 45) out of the midst of the imminent calamities that had been made inevitable in Yahweh's emphatic restatement of his purpose. During or immediately following the frightening event of Jerusalem's ruin (*bayyôm hahû'* does not imply a sequence in this passage), Ebed-melech was to be spared. This passage is especially important because it shows that Jeremiah and his close circle of followers were indeed familiar with *bayyôm hahû'* as a current locution, even if they did not make much use of it in this book.

Within the foreign-oracles section of Jeremiah, there are three further passages having the integral temporal formula (48:11f., 49:1-5, 51:41-53), and all three have the peculiar locution *lākēn hinnēh yāmîm bā'îm,* followed in each case by the oracle formula. This particular locution occurs only in Jeremiah's book, and in Jeremiah only in such supplementary and other *ad hoc* redactional expansions.

Jeremianic authorship is virtually impossible for 48:11-12 (an interpolated Moab oracle), 49:1-5 (the book's sole Ammon oracle), and 51:41-53 (a mock lament for Babylon's fallen idols) — all for reasons previously presented.[26] If content alone were not sufficient evidence for or against Jeremianic authorship in the first two passages, the peculiar transition formula used by each of them binds them redactionally to the last-mentioned passage, where it occurs twice, at the head of successive strophes within a unitary composition. It is difficult to see how 51:41ff. could date from any time other than the late exilic or early postexilic periods. In the Moab and Ammon oracles, this formula marks a sequence from the present stance of imperturbable defiance, to Yahweh's surprising rebuff in the sequel. In 51:47 (with *nĕ'um YHWH* at the end) and 52, a more abstract and sophisticated transition is made between the remote future of the exiles' return and the downfall of Babylon's idols, creating the reverse sequences, effect to cause and after to before. The deictic particle *hinnēh,* which is normally asyndetic, is effectively neutralized by the foregoing *lākēn,* making an overall closely syndetic connection.

2. Ad hoc *redactional occurrences*

Except for the consideration that the last four occurrences are in primary material as we have defined it, they might better have been included in our list of redactional integral transitions. The reason for not having done so is that we place in the latter group only those occurrences that belong to *ad hoc* expansions. We take these up next for individual attention.

As we have interpreted it, *'attâ* in Jer 4:12b involves a logical, reverse-temporal move from the remote event of the "hot wind" back to the present/proximately future event of the prophet's speaking; this redactional element is certainly preexilic and is from Jeremiah or from his inner circle.[27]

The parallel sections, Jer 7:30-34 and 19:4-9, have each the exilic-age formula *lākēn hinnēh yāmîm bā'îm nĕ'um YHWH,* at identical transition points within their respective structures, namely, between the prophetic accusation (of present idolatry neither commanded nor imagined by Yahweh, whether the worship of the dead or Baal worship) and the dire announcement of a symbolic change of name. Although the situation may be that of the entire exilic period, the peculiar temporal formula is virtually a *per se* mark of late exilic or early postexilic redaction.[28]

The integral transitions within Jer 33:14-16 have been created by paraphrasis from 23:5-6.[29] The late exilic/early postexilic formula *bayyāmîm hahēm ûbā'ēt hahî'* explicates the introductory *hinnēh yāmîm bā'îm* of v 14, copied here from 23:5, while simple *bayyāmîm hahēm* takes the place of original *bĕyāmâw.* In the two passages, synchronisms are created between a series of divine acts of salvation within the proximate future: (1) the fulfillment of Yahweh's promise (only at 33:14), (2) justice and righteousness through David's Branch (23:5, 33:15), and (3) Judah/Jerusalem's security and renaming. Because it is missing in the LXX *Vorlage,* we have little real option but to date 33:14ff. to the late postexilic period. The addition of the first prediction (fulfillment of an older prophecy) would be meaningful only in a situation in which the promise of a righteous Davidide had been long deferred.

The remaining integral redactional transitions on our list belong to sections in Jeremiah that have an editorial function. They combine to communicate promise for Israel's future and have a bridging function within the "little book of consolation," chaps. 30–31.

As we have seen, Jer 30:1-3 is the editorial introduction to this early exilic collection;[30] v 3's formula *hinnēh yāmîm bā'îm nĕ'um YHWH,* peculiar to redactors in Jeremiah but introduced here as in Amos 4:2 by *kî,* creates a temporal move from Yahweh's command to write, with its imminently future actualization, on to the events within the proximate future that are predicted in the "book" of salvation sayings to follow.

Jer 30:23–31:1 is epexegetical to 30:22 while functioning also to create a bridge to a new collection in 31:2ff.[31] This insertion may have been present in the collection introduced by 30:1-3, but more likely it introduces a separate expansion. In any event, it is early exilic in date and is kerygmatic of Yahweh's intention for the proximate future, now that the "storm" symbolized in vv

23-24's reprise of 23:19-20 is past. The prediction is that "at that time" Yahweh will continue to be Israel's god while they will remain his people.[32]

Introductory Transitions in Jeremiah

Only relatively more numerous than Jeremianic passages with integral temporal transitions are those in which a temporal formula introduces redactional material. One striking fact is that the only occurrences with *bayyôm hahû'*, with foregoing *wĕhāyâ*, are in two passages that have it in anacrusis introducing what we have identified as poetry. The one passage, 4:9-10, is from Jeremiah's innermost circle of followers, while the other, 30:8-9, dates from the late exilic or early postexilic period. Two other passages, again one early and the other late, have a temporal formula as part of a citation rubric: *bā'ēt hahî' yē'āmēr* in 4:11 and *bayyāmîm hahēm lō' yō'mĕrû 'ôd* in 31:29.[33]

1. The initial block, chaps. 2–24

Four of the six oracular collections that we have identified in the initial block (omitting the prologue in chap. 1 and the closing summary in 25:1-14) have received redactional expansions introduced by a temporal formula. These are chaps. 2–6, chaps. 7–10, chaps. 14–17, and chaps. 21–24.

a. Chaps. 2–6

The very early collection found in Jeremiah 2–6 — parts of which probably reproduce the original scroll — has three redactional passages with introductory temporal transitions. The first is an eccentric cluster in 3:16-19, discussed in Chapter Five. Early in his ministry, the prophet made urgent complaints about the nation's harlotrous apostasy (2:1-3:10). This led to the appeals for repentance in 3:11-13, 14, 19-20, and 21-23. The restoration mentioned as contingent upon this repentance (v 14) proved to be fertile ground for the development of various expressions of what this restoration might mean. In vv 15-16 an exilic redactor predicted the return of knowledge and understanding under Yahweh's true shepherds; as a sign of this new perception, the people were to accept the final irrelevance of the ark, to be brought about by their miraculous expansion "in those days." It is not, however, to the enigmatic mention of the lost ark that a first postexilic redactor alluded (v 17), but to the promise of return to Zion in v 14, now interpreted in terms of Jerusalem's appointment as a center for international worship "at that time." To a second postexilic redactor, v 14's promise of reunification suggested the restoration of Israel and Judah as one nation and the recovery of their ancestral heritage, scheduled to occur "in those days" (v 18). These were seen as successive events in a proximate future (actually a *vaticinium ex eventu*). Thus this very first suggestion of divine leniency in chaps. 2–6 was seized upon for the attachment of late — and very late — reinterpretations, assuming that the condition of Israel/Judah's repentance would have been fully met.

The next two expansions with introductory temporal transitions are from very early levels of redaction, and, as argued in our analysis of clusters in Chapter Five, follow a very different tack. As we have urged, the announcement of imminent attack against Jerusalem in 4:5-8, 11ff. led a first redactor to add the words of vv 9-10, introduced by *wĕhāyâ bayyôm hahû' nĕ'um YHWH* in anacrusis, and a second redactor (possibly the prophet himself) to add the curious words of vv 11-12, introduced by *bā'ēt hahî'* within a citation rubric. As has been mentioned, each transition suggests the independent existence of the words being rehearsed or cited. The first is a prediction of the dismay of Jerusalem's leaders at Yahweh's apparent deception (v 10). The second is a prediction that the saying about Yahweh's hot wind is about to be realized, confirming that *'attâ,* "now," the prophet is speaking veritable words of judgment. Thus the proximate future of attack upon Jerusalem is identified as the occasion for the leaders' dismay, synchronous with a confirmation of Jeremiah's present mission as the announcer of doom as he interprets the foreign attack in the figure of a hot wind.

Jer 5:18, like 3:16, 18, has the late longer spelling *bayyāmîm hahēmmâ* (see in Chapter Four). Because such spellings group themselves in this first section of the book, it is conceivable that a copyist or editor began to correct the shorter spellings just here, then gave it up. This is at least as likely as the supposition of sheer coincidence, for there is no evidence that a single redactor or editor was at work in the three verses, 3:16, 18 and 5:18. The verses in chap. 3 are late exilic to late postexilic, while 5:18-19 has to be early exilic.

Whether or not this expansion is definitely deuteronomistic is unclear, even though the theme of punishment following transgression is in agreement with deuteronomistic ideology. An additional consideration is that the catechetical technique employed here appears also in Deuteronomy. Preceding the temporal formula is a uniquely emphatic *wĕgam,* "and indeed," the intention of which is to introduce a theological comment upon the stern words of judgment concerning the enemy from the north, the Neo-Babylonians. Just why it comes here rather than at the end of chap. 6 is not clear. In any event, the redactor in question was certainly thinking of an ongoing condition, spread out over a long period; this is the reason why he used *bayyāmîm hahēmmâ,* "in those days," rather than *bayyôm hahû'*, "on that day." He predicts that (1) in spite of the scary outlook, Yahweh's intent is not to make of Israel a *kālâ*, "wipeout," but rather to subject them to the terms of a catechetical inquiry regarding where the proper blame for foreign servitude should lie.[34] Such concern for determining who is, or are, responsible for present judgment is seen elsewhere in Jeremiah in the late passage, 31:29; both passages exhibit a high level of theological sophistication.

b. Chaps. 7–10

A second collection, chaps. 7–10, is introduced by a special redactional formula in 7:1. Deuteronomistic influence is more clearly prevalent here than anywhere else in the initial block of materials. This is true even though there can be no question but that the basis for the cultic complaints of these chapters lay in Jeremiah's own preaching, as seen most sharply in the famous temple sermon of 7:2ff. This sermon has attracted a number of prose expansions, including 7:30-34 and the poems of personal grief (the "confessions") that have contributed so much to the portrait of Jeremiah as the "weeping prophet," 8:4–9:10, 16-21, and 10:1-25. Among these prose expansions is the curious portrayal of death in 8:1-3 and the apparently loosely attached oracular threat in 9:24-25 (E 25-26). Perhaps enough has already been said about 7:30ff., with its parallel in chap. 19, but the last two mentioned passages call for additional comment.

8:1 has introductory *bā'ēt hahî'*, as in 4:11; but here it is strengthened by the oracle formula, giving vv 1-3 the added weight of explicit revelational authority. This is certainly one of Scripture's most gloomy predictions, not only accepting the image of death and desolation in 7:32-34 as the rich deserts of incorrigible idolatry, but actually recommending death as preferable to an exile that had evidently long held sway (v 3). Ideologically, it stands at opposite poles to images from recovery from death in Jer 31:40, 33:2-9; Ezek 33:10-11, 37:1-10.

Two prose sections that seem to have no connection whatever to underlying material in Jeremiah are the short passages 9:22-23 (E 23-24) and 9:24-25 (E 25-26). Nor do these two passages have anything to do with each other. The first is an isolated wisdom saying, while the second is an equally isolated foreign oracle. There is nothing to prevent the latter from being Jeremianic; this might actually be favored by consideration of the fact that Judah was included in the list of nations to be punished,[35] as well as by the observation that it was just in the period of Jerusalem's fall that prophets such as Ezekiel (35:1–36:7) and Obadiah (vv 1-14) likewise were declaiming against the closely neighboring nations who had shared Judah's guilt but had escaped her punishment. The introductory formula *hinnēh yāmîm bā'îm* (in distinction from that formula with foregoing *lākēn*) is elsewhere seen in Jeremiah in passages from the early exilic period, 23:5, 31:17, 31, 38 (see below).

c. Chaps. 14–17

Appendages introduced by a temporal formula have not been attracted to the separate collections in chaps. 11–12 and chaps. 18–20,[36] respectively. These are the sections in which most of the so-called "confessions" of Jeremiah are found (11:18-20; 12:1-4; 18:19-23; 20:7-12, 14-18). They contain additional poetic oracles of judgment on Judah — probably from Jeremiah — as well as a number of prose accounts of revelational experiences probably composed by a close disciple.

Sandwiched between these sections is the early collection in chaps. 14–17, containing similar early elements. Along with the two integral transitions at 14:10 and 16:16, this section has an early postexilic expansion in 16:14-15 with introductory *lākēn hinnēh yāmîm bā'îm nĕ'um YHWH*, a parallel to 23:7-8. 16:1-13 expands Jeremiah's grim warnings as dire preachments in the deuteronomistic mode; the background is early exilic, when death and foreign servitude had certainly become commonplace realities. The prediction that the exiles should worship other gods beside Yahweh, whose favor would be utterly withdrawn (v 13), seemed to a redactor living in a more hopeful era to need drastic revision. There was to be a new exodus, this time from the countries to the north, scheduled to occur "in coming days." The uniqueness of this transformation in Israel's future condition requires the asyndetic *hinnēh*, yet the foregoing *lākēn* connects it to the preceding word of doom, dramatizing an utter paradox in Yahweh's revealed intention.[37]

d. Chaps. 21–24

That Jeremiah 21–24 is an appendix to the initial collection is clear from the fact that it contains oracles pertaining to the kings who reigned after Jehoiakim. We have seen that this section contains two passages with integral temporal transitions (22:22, 23:20) that should be ascribed directly to Jeremiah, and elsewhere in this section authentic Jeremianic tradition is in evidence. At the same time, it is apparent that redactors from the early circle of disciples have shaped some of these materials. This is clearly the case with 21:7. On the other hand, the section on the kings (chaps. 21–22) is finished off by a hopeful oracle concerning "shepherds," that is, kings (23:1-4), much in the vein of

Ezekiel 34. It is probably early exilic; and this is the background also of its earliest expansion introduced by *hinnēh yāmîm bāʾîm*, 23:5-6. A second expansion in 23:7-8, parallel to 16:14-15, is, however, completely irrelevant here and must date from the late postexilic period. Enough has been said about 23:5-6 in our discussion of integral transitions in the parallel passage, 33:14-16, and of 23:7-8 in connection with 16:14-16.

Some special observations are appropriate with respect to Jer 21:7 (on this passage, see our discussion in Chapter Three's excursus on "revelational authority in *vaticinium ex eventu*). 21:1ff. occupies first position in this appendix in the section on the kings, and its literary core dates from a time in Zedekiah's reign when the prophet had not yet been placed in confinement.[38] Vv 8-10 must be viewed as an early expansion rather than as part of the original, because the people have already been addressed in vv 4-5.[39] As has previously been argued, v 7 is an early exilic expansion, added presumably after vv 8-10 were in place.[40] As we have seen, this is not a true prediction but a *vaticinium ex eventu*, composed in knowledge of Jerusalem's recent fall and its dire effects. The transition, *wĕʾaḥărê-kēn*, creates a temporal sequence between the proximate future of the siege and the ostensibly remote future of capture and slaughter. The oracle formula *nĕʾum YHWH* assures that death by the sword following the city's capture, rather than death by pestilence during the siege, is Yahweh's ultimate penalty.

2. The foreign-oracle collection

The arrangement of Jeremiah's foreign oracles, appearing originally after 25:13 (as in the LXX), is as follows: summary prologue, 25:15-38; against Egypt, 46:2-26; against Philistia, chap. 47; against Moab, chap. 48; against Ammon, 49:1-6; against Edom, 49:7-22; against Damascus, 49:23-27; against Kedar and Hazor, 49:28-33; against Elam, 49:34-39; against Babylon, 50:1–51:58. There is very little authentic material in this entire collection; we are inclined to limit it, with Rietzschl, to 25:15-16a, 27, 46:2-12, 13-24, 47:1-7, and 49:34-38, along with 51:59-64. Though we have identified the four occurrences of *lākēn hinnēh yāmîm bāʾîm* in 48:12, 49:2, 51:47, 52 as integral in what we call primary material, this does not suggest authenticity for these passages. Rather, the sections containing these transitions (48:11-13, 49:1-5, 51:41-53) are late exilic or early postexilic.

This means that Jeremiah's authentic foreign oracles never contained temporal transitions of the sort we are investigating, for the five introductory transitions on our list all belong within late exilic (50:4, 20) or late postexilic (46:26, 49:6, 39) materials. Jer 46:26 and 49:6 are, in fact, missing in the Septuagintal, and hence pre-Masoretic, text. They have the introductory tran-

sition *wĕ'aḥărê-kēn,* used also in a nontransitional position in 48:47 —
likewise missing in the LXX. 49:39, an appendage to the Elam oracle, shares
with late Isa 2:2 par Mic 4:2 the distinctive introductory formula *wĕhāyâ
bĕ'aḥărît hayyāmîm.* Every one of these occurrences belongs to what is in
effect a *vaticinium ex eventu,* reversing a foregoing word of doom for each
of the nations concerned in light of subsequent events. This is also the case
with the two prose additions within the Babylon section at 50:4-5 and 50:20,
which have the rare locution *bayyāmîm hahēm ûbā'ēt hahî'.* They expand the
situation of underlying material as events within the same proximate future,
which is a sham for the past/present out of which these additions have been
conceived.

3. A new cycle of oracles with framing narratives, chaps. 26–36

We have no need at this juncture to debate the merits of a complex theory of
transmission for chapters 26–36 in Jeremiah.[41] It will suffice us to observe
that the futuristic transitions that belong to this new section lack the narrative
contexting seen in chaps. 26–29, 31, 34-36.[42] This is to say that they belong
to extended oracular collections, those of chaps. 30–31 and chap. 33.

As we have seen, 30:1-3 is intended as a general introduction to the
original material in chaps. 30–31; but, in distinction from the narrative units
elsewhere in the book, it lacks a date. There are two alternative possibilities,
either that the original oracular collection of chaps. 30–31 was already extant
when the narratives were added, or that it was a later addition to the already
collected narratives. However the case may be, it looks very much as if the
original material in chap. 33 was definitely an addition to the narrative collection.[43] In v 1 a redactor has given it a nebulous chronological link, *šēnît,*
"a second time," as well as a situational setting in the enigmatic circumstantial
clause *wĕhû' 'ôdénnû 'āṣûr baḥăṣar hammaṭṭārâ,* "now he was still under
arrest in the court of the guard" (cf. 37:21). The two oracular collections of
chaps. 30–31 and chap. 33, respectively, are generally similar in ideology, in
relative provenance from the early exilic to the postexilic periods, and in that
they each include both integral and introductory futuristic transitions.

The integral transitions in this section have previously been discussed;
they are at 30:3, 24, 31:1, 13, and 33:15-16. The introductory transitions are
at 30:8, 31:27, 29, 31, 38, and 33:14. Every one of them extends Israel's
punishment or salvation as Israel's further salvation, and all except 30:8
move from a situation or event in the proximate future to another event in
the proximate future. In 30:8 the move is from a proximate to a remote
future.

a. Derivative oracular materials

We first take up the introductory transitions at 30:8, 31:29, and 33:14, for the reason that each introduces what we may believe to be previously existing materials. 30:8 has the transition in anacrusis; 31:29 has a citation rubric; 33:14-16 is a paraphrase of 23:5-6.

Jer 30:8 shares with 4:9 the distinction of using the familiar temporal formula (rare in Jeremiah) *wĕhāyâ bayyôm hahû',* followed by *nĕ'um YHWH,* in anacrusis. The late exilic or early postexilic text offered in vv 8-9 is definitely poetic in structure. The foregoing lament (vv 5-7), culminating in a poignant reference to *hayyôm hahû',* "that day" (apparently stimulated by the phrase *'ēt ṣārâ,* "a time of distress"), led one of the exiles — or a redactor speaking for the exiles — to insert a current saying about a remotely future bursting of foreign bonds, freeing the exiles to serve Yahweh and David anew.

The original tight bond between 31:27-28 and 31:31-34 has been inter-rupted by a late exilic insertion at vv 29-30 introduced by *bayyāmîm hahēm,* extending the proximately future "coming days" of vv 27-28 to include a situation that is to pertain throughout that period ("in those days"). It is very likely that this passage stands under the influence of Ezek 18:2, where negation of the popular saying about eating sour grapes has an integral position. In any event, the proverb had independent status for Jeremiah's redactor. It has been introduced here under a theological impulse similar to that manifested in 5:18-19, itself a relatively late passage, exhibiting a peculiar theological ra-tionale concerning moral concerns about the bearing of divine judgment upon Israel. Here the proverb is cited as a rationale of moral responsibility for the exiles' current predicament: those who die for their sins are specifically those who will have eaten the sour grapes, not their fathers.

Our previous comparison of Jer 33:14-16 with 23:5-6 made it clear that this pericope is a late — even very late — paraphrase. Because 23:5-6 dates from just before or soon after Jerusalem's fall, the temporal formula that introduces 33:14-16, *hinnēh yāmîm bā'îm,* is definitely a locution that belongs to the early rather than late Jeremianic redaction. Within chap. 33, separate oracles in vv 1-9, vv 10-11, and vv 12-13 are ideologically compatible with 31:27-28, 31-34, 38-40, reflecting the situation of the early exilic period, and expressive of the modest hope that apparently derived from Jeremiah's pur-chase of the ancestral field reported in chap. 32. The next following verses in chap. 33, however, contain promises concerning Yahweh's purpose for the Davidides (17-18, 19-22, 23-26). These verses are not germane to anything in chap. 33 except our citation of an older promise in vv 14-16. Although scholars are in general agreement that this highly ideological material ex-presses an anticipation of Davidic restoration that is also seen in early postexilic passages such as Hag 2:23, Zech 4:6-9, and Isa 53:3, the fact that it is missing in the LXX argues for later rather than earlier composition.

Thus we have seen that three of the six pericopes introduced by temporal transitions in Jeremiah 30, 31, and 33 show dependence on preexisting materials or traditions, now reinterpreted as applicatory to the end of the exile. Each is an independent and relatively late attachment to the original writings contained in these chapters coming from Jeremiah's close circle at the beginning of the exile.

b. A concluding cluster, 31:27-28, 31-34, 38-40

All that remains for our consideration, then, is the three short pericopes in Jeremiah 31 that are introduced by *hinnēh yāmîm bā'îm* followed by *nĕ'um YHWH*. In our foregoing study of cluster occurrences, we argued that a single redactor, someone from the prophet's close circle, drew these three pericopes together from tradition sources at hand to be used as an appropriate synopsis of the new hope that Jeremiah's "little book of consolation" was to contain. There is every reason to believe that the redactor in question was the same as he who employed the introductory formula *kî hinnēh yāmîm bā'îm*, with *nĕ'um YHWH*, in the redactional introduction at 30:3. In 31:27, 31, and 38 the formula without *kî* introduces these three units of nonderivative prose material (in distinction from temporal formulas with derivative material in 30:8, 31:29, and 33:14, just discussed). These successively articulated the three major elements of concern for those who were now experiencing — or had but lately experienced — the cataclysmic ruin of 586: (1) revival of the life of the community, (2) a new and perfect covenant to take the place of the one that had been shattered, and (3) the rebuilding and resanctifying of Jerusalem. These were not announced as new events in themselves, but as altered situations or conditions, scheduled for the same proximate future as that predicted in 30:3.[44]

With the elimination of 30:8-9 and 31:29-30 (along with 33:14-16) from consideration at this early level of redaction, the relative homogeneity of 31:27-28, 31-34, 38-40 stands out, especially in view of the fact that the introductory formula in all three is identical. Two particular phenomena are crucially important here: (1) that *lākēn hinnēh yāmîm bā'îm nĕ'um YHWH* is elsewhere in Jeremiah the peculiar formula of a late exilic or early postexilic redaction, and (2) that the formula without *lākēn* never occurs as an integral transition in Jeremiah except with *kî* in 30:3. It appears as an introductory transition only in our three pericopes, along with 9:24 (E 25) and 23:5 par 33:14. As we have seen, 9:24 is possibly Jeremianic, and so is 23:5; in any event, they are both early exilic in date (33:14ff. being a late paraphrase of

23:5f.), the same time period that we claim for the three pericopes we are discussing.

It is at this point that we may draw upon our previous analysis of temporal transitions in clusters. It has been shown that there are four distinct possibilities for close arrangements: (1) that a cluster may mark a systematic redaction within an array of passages; (2) that a cluster may result from the collection of diverse materials from a variety of sources on the part of a single redactor; (3) that a cluster may mark an incremental process of epexegesis on a similar theme by a succession of redactors; and (4) that a cluster may mark thematically similar materials that have been added atomistically by separate redactors. The collocation in Jer 31:27f., 31ff., 38ff. is best explained as a realization of the second possibility.

This counters Holladay's claim that vv 31-34 is a Jeremianic original, added to previously collected Jeremianic words in vv 27-28 (vv 38-40 being added late in the postexilic period). But a compelling objection to assigning these three units to separate redactional processes is their diverse *topoi*. Clusters that have been atomistically created by separate redactors are elsewhere thematically similar (cf. Isa 27:12-13; Ezek 38:10, 14, 18, 39:11; Amos 9:11, 13; Zeph 3:9-10; Zech 12:3–13:4, 14:6-20). Those that have been created in incremental epexegesis by a succession of redactors are also thematically similar (Isa 19:16-24; Jer 3:16-18, 4:9-11, 46:26, 48:47, 49:6, 39; Amos 8:9, 11, 13). In contrast, clusters of thematically diverse materials, drawn from a variety of sources, are elsewhere seen to be the creation of a single redactor (Isa 7:18-23, 11:10-11, 17:7-9; Hos 2:18, 23 [E 16, 21]). This makes it at least probable that the three units we are discussing belong to a single redactor, for if the cluster of these three units had been created atomistically by different redactors, this must then be an exception — an outstanding and glaring exception. While this does not make Holladay's view impossible, it does make it unlikely.

To be sure, this line of reasoning might be rendered invalid if it could actually be demonstrated that any one of these three pericopes demands a date significantly later than either, or both, of the others. There is no problem with vv 27-28 *vis-à-vis* vv 31-34, each of which contains the locution "the house of Israel and the house of Judah," seen elsewhere in Jer 5:11, 11:10, 17, 13:11, and 33:14. But Holladay, with others, claims that vv 38-40 have to be late postexilic. This is because they refer to a certain "tower of Hananel," mentioned elsewhere only in Zech 14:10 and Neh 3:1, 12:30. Nevertheless, the tower in question had not been identified. To claim that its mention is a token of lateness because it is not mentioned elsewhere in Jeremiah is purely an *argumentum e silentio*. The reference in v 40 to a valley filled with dead bodies may very well be seen as a parallel to Jer 7:33, 19:7, and 33:5. Furthermore, the holiness referred to in this verse applies only to specified portions of Jerusalem, not to the entire city, and certainly it does not consist of a comprehensive state of sacredness within the temple precincts as a whole, as in Ezekiel 40ff. (cf. the Qumran Temple scroll). Finally, the absolute way of speaking about "the city *(hā'îr)*" is paralleled in Jer 30:18 (cf. Ezek 4:1, 33:21). The conclusion is that there is no compelling reason to give vv 38-40 a postexilic date. Our dating for the cluster as a whole demands that it must have been available to Jeremiah's early exilic redactor.

The fact that vv 38-40 cannot definitely be identified as deuteronomistic will weaken the widely held claim that the other two pericopes must be deuteronomistic. Herrmann's book, *Die prophetische Heilserwartungen,* claims this both for vv 28f. and for vv 31-34;[45] so also Thiel, *Die deuteronomistische Redaktion von Jeremia 1–25,*[46] and Carroll, *From Chaos to Covenant.*[47] Holladay, to the contrary, argues that 31:27-28 was composed by Jeremiah to close off the prophet's scroll of hope for Judah in chaps. 30–31, dating from the second siege period, and that vv 31-34 is the prophet's somewhat later expansion, also made during the second siege.[48]

We ask, Are Jeremianic provenance and deuteronomistic redaction in these verses altogether incompatible with each other? Holladay seeks to explain elements of deuteronomistic affinity with the claim that Jeremiah was incorporating deuteronomistic language and imagery in vv 31ff., but composition was by the prophet himself. He intended it for use in the presumptive ceremony of the recitation of the Torah held at the Feast of Booths in the fall of 587, just after the fall of Jerusalem. Carroll claims, to the contrary, that the new covenant concept in these verses is emphatically non-Jeremianic. He attributes other references to the covenant in Jeremiah (1:1-11, 34:8-22) to a deuteronomistic redaction, arguing that if 31:31-34 were indeed composed by Jeremiah, it would have to constitute a counsel of despair on his part and a surrender of his strongly held moral principles. Jeremiah, having conceded defeat and withdrawn from the moral struggle, could not have been true to what he stood for while advocating reliance on something that was already done and finished. Therefore, says Carroll, these verses could have come only from the deuteronomistic school, reaching out for a new theological principle based on the hope of Israel's complete spiritual transformation.

In our view, Holladay is wrong in breaking up the cluster, and he stands on shaky ground in attributing this kind of prose directly to the prophet. Also, his argument for a precise date and ritual occasion (itself altogether unlikely just following the fall of the city) remains speculative. Though his suggestion in itself may have some plausibility, it remains entirely conjectural. Furthermore, evidence for deuteronomistic influence in Jeremiah may just as readily be interpreted as evidence for a general deuteronomistic reworking of received Jeremianic materials. No doubt the influence was mutual, not just in one direction. We are not willing to go so far as to say that the redaction in these verses was specifically deuteronomistic, but we do insist that the work of an early redactor close to the prophet, reshaping the prophet's message under his influence or direction, is all but certain.

Carroll on his part is to be criticized for allowing an extraneous moral judgment to influence his claim that Jeremiah could not have been true to himself while composing such verses as these. Who is in a position to refuse to Jeremiah the same readiness for drastic change that characterized, for instance, Ezekiel, his equally rigid and moralistic contemporary (see especially Ezek 33:8-20, 37:7-10). Jeremiah continued to call for the people's repentance, and it is clear especially from chap. 32 that he did cling at least to a fragment of hope. The redactor-disciple who composed 31:31-34 in Jeremiah's name may have gone further than the prophet himself would have been willing to go, but who can prove that Jeremiah would necessarily have repudiated what this person had written?

Carroll's judgment has no doubt been affected by his notion, expressed elsewhere, that drastic eschatological changes must result from serious disillusionment. As we have seen in Chapter One, Carroll's book, *When Prophecy Failed,* argues that it is regularly the nonrealization of prediction that triggers a rationalization within a group that has heretofore clung to that prediction. Our observation is that this process was only minimally present within Old Testament prophecy, and that there were factors other than sociological disillusionment and cognitive readjustment at work in producing new predictions. We shall argue this question again in Chapter Thirteen, where we expect to demonstrate that there were a multiplicity of possible factors for revision.

It seems that Carroll has held Jeremiah high on a pillar, while ascribing to weakling epigones the kind of drastic changes that a man of his high moral stature would never had allowed. Not only has Carroll's sociological analysis been pressed too far. It is sheer romantic rationalizing in his thinking that raises a prophet like Jeremiah to such a level of high-principled superiority that refuses to tolerate revision.

We are arguing for the position that Jeremiah did not himself compose 31:31-34, anymore than he was directly responsible for vv 27-28 and vv 38-40, and that a redactor from his inner circle of followers created this. Nevertheless, this redactor was conscientiously drawing on his own hearing of the prophet's message, revising Jeremiah's ideas in a direction that was responsive to the new situation of ruin and exile.[49] Thus these three pericopes express what someone among Jeremiah's early followers believed the prophet's message to be for a new day. The redactor who composed 30:1-3 as a preface to the "little book of consolation" very probably drew these three units together as a synopsis and conclusion to it. The three identical temporal transitions in vv 27, 31, and 38 may either be original to each separate pericope or have been supplied by the redactor who brought them together.

c. The interpretation of Jer 31:31-34

Although 31:31-34, along with vv 27-28 and vv 38-40, has been identified as
prose, this should be modified to make allowance for probable poetic fragments in vv 33aβb and 34bβ.[50] We mention this because it may have some
bearing on the question of composition and redaction. Departing from the
prose styling of the pericope as a unitary composition, the short sections in
question display a tight and measured parallelism. They each come at the end
of a prose prediction concluding with the oracle formula *ně'um YHWH,* and
their evident purpose is explication or illustration. In v 33 two three-foot bicola
with a chiastic structure explicate the entity indicated by the demonstrative
pronoun *zō't,* the noun *habběrît,* and the circumstantial clause introduced by
'ăšer:

> *nātatî 'et-tôrātî běqirbām*   I will put my law within them,
> *wě'al libbām 'ektăbénnāh*   and on their heart I will write it;
> *wěhāyîtî lāhem lē'lōhîm*   and I will be for them a god,
> *wěhēmmâ yihyû-lî lě'ām*   and they will be for me a people.

In v 34 a two-foot bicolon grounds the absence of any need for exhortation
or catechesis in the reassurance given to the recent objects of divine wrath
that they are now in a state of complete forgivenness. Again the structure is
chiastic:

> *kî 'eslaḥ la'ăwōnām*   For I will dismiss their iniquity,
> *ûlěḥaṭṭā'tām lō' 'ezkōr-'ôd*   and their sin I will no more
>   remember.

When snatches of poetry like these are preserved within a prose framework, there must be a reason. The probable cause in this passage is that they
are especially memorial; and they are memorial because they probably derive
directly from the author to whom the pericope as a whole is attributed. In
other words, there is a strong reason to believe that precisely these words
derive from Jeremiah, while the surrounding prose material is from his fol-
lower.

One remaining question is whether, as held by some critics, vv 33-34
in themselves constitute a later addition. Is the covenant of vv 33f. the concept
of still another redactor? Two considerations make this extremely unlikely:
(1) that the momentous announcement of a new covenant in v 31 requires
explication beyond the negation of v 32; and (2) that in vv 27-28 there is a
similar dual structure in which the opening announcement ("I will sow") is
explicated in a separate clause beginning with *wěhāyâ,* specifying how
Yahweh will watch over "the house of Israel and the house of Judah" in the
future, in contrast to the way in which he watched over them in the past. The

structural element of future-past is crucial in both pericopes. That of vv 31ff. requires a positive explication of the future new covenant, set in starkest contrast to the now-nullified covenant made with the forefathers "on the day" of the exodus from Egypt. Thus the suggestion that vv 31-32 might be isolated from the two verses that follow should be resisted. Nothing ought to be made of the change from "the house of Israel and the house of Judah" in v 31 to "the house of Israel" alone in v 33 because Jeremiah's redactors regularly cherish the prospect of the reunification of a single Israel out of what were formerly two separate political entities.

Nevertheless, it is natural to query whether the phrase *'aḥărê hayyāmîm hahēm*, "after those days," does not create a new temporal sequence from the "coming days" of v 31. Part of the answer lies in the observations that (1) the expression *'aḥărê hayyāmîm hahēm* is found only here, and (2) that it serves here as a mere time identifier, not as a transition. In other words, it is not parallel structurally to the pericope's introductory temporal formula, *hinnēh yāmîm bā'îm*. Since it makes no sense to argue that the covenant of vv 33f. is somehow entirely new and different from that of v 31, the counter-referent of *'aḥărê hayyāmîm hahēm* has to be the negative condition or situation of v 32b, espressed in the circumstantial clause *'ăšer hēmmâ hēpērû 'et-bĕrîtî wĕ'ānōkî ba'altî bām*, "in which circumstances they broke my covenant, even while I was their husband (master)." This means that the events, actions, or conditions of vv 33f., namely, the covenant making, the internalizing of the law, the intuitive knowing of Yahweh in contrast to the non-teaching of this knowledge, and, most of all, the forgiveness and the nonremembrance of sins, are placed in direct sequence from the situation of covenant breaking, rather than from the new covenant that is predicted for the "coming days."

The early exile is the "now" of this text's promulgation. Both the making of Yahweh's new covenant (v 31) and the specific events or conditions that explicate the making of this covenant (vv 33-34) lie in the proximate future with respect to this present. The promise comes, and the anticipated fulfillment will come, as the astounding reversal of a lamentable past in which God's design has been continually frustrated by an ungrateful people.

Conclusions

1. The integral transitions

We may now summarize our findings regarding temporal transitions in Jeremiah. We go back to recall the outcome regarding Jeremiah's integral transitions, both primary and redactional.

First the primary. Four are preexilic and derive from the prophet or his immediate school: those of 14:10, 16:16, 22:22, and 23:20. Five others are late exilic or early postexilic: 31:13, 48:12, 49:2, 51:47, 52. Thus there is an approximate balance between early and late.

In contrast, integral transitions that occur within redactional additions tend to be late: one is from a preexilic redactor (4:2), three are early exilic (30:3, 24, 31:1), and four are from the end of the exile or early Persian era, occurring in two doublets, one in which the original formula is maintained (7:32 par 19:6) and one in which new formulas are supplied (33:15-16).

Altogether there are eighteen integral occurrences, nearly as many as the twenty-two introductory occurrences. The theme of judgment against Israel, and occasionally against the nations, dominates in the primary integral passages. On the contrary, among the redactional integral occurrences, those that are early (4:12) or late (7:32, 19:6) are directed against Israel; those that come from the early exilic period (30:3, 24, 31:1) or from long after the exile (33:15-16) promise salvation for Israel.

2. The introductory transitions

Turning to the list of introductory transitions in Jeremiah (as elsewhere, all are redactional), we ascertain that the time-range is strikingly shorter in comparison with the parallel list for Isaiah. From the preexilic redaction, all within a cluster, three announce judgment on Israel (4:9, 11, 12). From the early exile two texts announce Israel's punishment (5:18-19, 21:7), one announces the nations' punishment (9:24 [E 25]), and our famous three announce Israel's salvation after punishment (31:27f., 31-34, 38-40). All the remaining passages on this list are late exilic or early postexilic (3:17, 18, 8:1-3, 16:14-15 par 23:7-8, 30:8-9, 31:13-14, 33:14-16, 50:4-5, 20); all except 8:1-3 promise Israel's salvation. In addition, three late postexilic passages (46:26, 49:6, 39) proclaim salvation for foreign nations.

Introductory transitions often occur in groupings, some of which also contain time identifiers or integral transitions (3:16-18; 4:9-12; 7:32–8:1; 16:14-16; 23:5-7; 30:3–31:11; 31:27-40; 33:14-16; 46:26, 49:6, 39; 48:12, 49:2; 50:4, 20; 51:47-52). It may be well to keep this in mind as we observe that several sections in the initial Jeremiah collection contain neither integral nor introductory futuristic transitions; these are the oracular collections in chaps. 1–2, chap. 10, chaps. 11–13, and chaps. 18–20. Transition formulas are also entirely absent from the narrative pericopes, chaps. 24–29, 32, and 34–45.

3. Distinctive and nondistinctive usages

We repeat the previous remark about the virtual absence of *bayyôm hahû'* as a futuristic transition in Jeremiah. With foregoing *wĕhāyâ* this locution occurs as a transition in only one early (4:9) and one late (30:8) passage. Both are in redactional additions,[51] and both are integral occurrences with a following *nĕ'um YHWH*.[52] Other integral temporal formulas used as transitions in Jeremiah are the following: *kî 'āz* (2x), *'attî* (2x), *bā'ēt hahî'* (1x), *bayyāmîm hahēm* (2x), *bĕ'aḥărît hayyāmîm* (2x), *wĕ'aḥărê-kēn* (1x), *kî hinnēh yāmîm bā'îm* (1x), and *lākēn hinnēh yāmîm bā'îm* (6x). Introductory occurrences include the two with *wĕhāyâ bayyôm hahû'*, along with *bā'ēt hahî'* (3x), *bayyāmîm hahēmmâ* (2x), *bayyāmîm hahēm* (1x), *bayyāmîm hahēm ûbā'ēt hahî'* (2x), *hinnēh yāmîm bā'îm* (6x), *lākēn hinnēh yāmîm bā'îm* (2x), *wĕ'aḥărê-kēn* (3x), and *wĕhāyâ bĕ'aḥărît hayyāmîm* (1x).

Formulas that Jeremiah himself probably or certainly employed are *'attî, 'āz, 'aḥărê-ken, bĕ'aḥărît hayyāmîm,* and (but not as a transition) *bayyôm hahû';* all are used as integral rather than introductory transitions. Formulas that Jeremiah himself definitely did not use are *bā'ēt hahî'* and *bayyāmîm hahēm(mâ).*

The temporal formulas that were preferred by Jeremianic redactors as transitions varied from period to period, as follows:

Preexilic: *'attî,* 4:12; *wĕhāyâ bayyôm hahû',* 4:9; *bā'ēt hahî',* 4:11; early exilic: *bā'ēt hahî',* 31:1; *bayyāmîm hahēmmâ,* 5:18; *(kî) hinnēh yāmîm bā'îm,* 9:24 (E 25); 23:5, 30:3, 31:27, 31, 38; *wĕ'aḥărê-kēn,* 21:7; *bĕ'aḥărît hayyāmîm,* 30:24 (par 23:20);

Late exilic/early postexilic: *wĕhāyâ bayyôm hahû',* 30:8; *bā'ēt hahî',* 3:17, 8:1; *bayyāmîm hahēmmâ,* 3:18; *bayyāmîm hahēm,* 31:19; *bayyāmîm hahēm ûbā'ēt hahî',* 33:15, 50:4, 20; *hinnēh yāmîm bā'îm,* 33:14 (from 23:5); *lākēn hinnēh yāmîm bā'îm,* 7:32, 16:14, 19:6, 23:7, 48:12, 49:2, 51:47, 52;

Late postexilic: *wĕ'aḥărê-kēn,* 46:26, 49:6; *wĕhāyâ bĕ'aḥărît hayyāmîm,* 49:39.

Three formulas that are definitely distinctive of the Jeremianic redaction as a whole are *(lākēn) hinnēh yāmîm bā'îm, bayyāmîm hahēm ûbā'ēt hahî',* and *nĕ'um YHWH* following the temporal formula. A word of summary may be useful here concerning each of these three formulas.

4. Lākēn hinnēh yāmîm bā'îm

A check of the concordance shows that, among the prophetic books, Isaiah and Jeremiah are the most prolific in the use of the deictic particle *hinnēh,* but Jeremiah is special in producing the locution *hinnēh yāmîm bāʾîm*. As we have seen, outside Jeremiah the only occurrences of this formula are at 1 Sam 2:31; 2 Kgs 20:17 par Isa 39:6; Amos 4:12, 8:11, 9:13. In Jeremiah it is a formulation from the late preexilic or early exilic periods, the occurrences being at 9:24 (E 25), 23:5, 30:3, 31:27, 31, 38, 33:14. It is certain that this is a relatively early locution, therefore, in distinction from other formulas under study here, including the peculiar *lākēn hinnēh yāmîm bāʾîm*.

All occurrences of the latter formula without *lākēn* except those in Jer 31:38 and Amos 4:2 belong to passages in which Yahweh himself speaks, although in these two exceptions other special formulations in the passage ensure that it is Yahweh who is speaking. Apart from Jer 9:24 (E 25), which announces punishment on Judah and the neighboring nations, the prediction pertains to individual transgressors or to Israel/Judah/Jerusalem. In the non-Jeremianic passages, doom is announced, but in Amos 9:13 and the remaining Jeremianic passages, it is salvation that is announced. Unlike the formula with preceding *lākēn, hinnēh yāmîm bāʾîm* does not have a structural position at the point of transition from accusation to announcement, even though foregoing sections within the Samuel and Kings passages do take pains to specify guilt. We mention, finally, that the oracle formula directly follows this temporal formula in every passage except 1 Sam 2:31.

Lākēn hinnēh yāmîm bāʾîm is also a locution special to the redaction of Jeremiah (7:31, 16:14, 19:6, 23:7, 48:12, 49:2, 51:47, 51), but all the passages are late, dating from the late exilic or early postexilic periods. This peculiar formulation stands between the accusation and the announcement in 7:31 and its virtual parallel in 19:6, condemning idol worshipers in Jerusalem. It also stands between the accusation and the announcement in 48:12 and 49:2, providing the main structural transition in separate oracles against the nations. In the remaining passages it introduces a prose expansion (16:14, 23:7) or provides a transition to a new poetic strophe (51:47, 52) that announces Israel's salvation.

Observations of the distinction between *hinnēh yāmîm bāʾîm* and this formula with *lākēn* have proven useful in our foregoing redactional analysis. The intended effect, as we have noted, is to draw together what otherwise, with the formula without *lākēn*, stands in asyndetic discontinuity with respect to the underlying material.

5. *Bayyāmîm hahēm ûbāʿēt hahîʾ*

The apparent pleonasm *bayyāmîm hahēm ûbāʿēt hahîʾ* appears only in Jer 33:15, 50:4, 20, and Joel 4:1 (E 3:1). In the first passage, where it is integral, it is introduced as a transition from v 14b, interpolated into an interpretive paraphrase from 23:5. In the other Jeremiah passages, as in Joel, it introduces prose expansions. Each passage announces salvation for Israel. Definitely in the three Jeremiah passages, though not in the late Joel passage, which has *kî hinnēh* before it, it represents an ideological redaction that has touched only the fringes in the growth of the book as a whole. It reveals a pedantic concern that what it announces shall occur not only at a particular time but also in a special situation.

6. Nĕ'um YHWH[53]

More revealing of redactional ideology in Jeremiah is the penchant of adding *nĕ'um YHWH* directly to the transition formula. This is seen only in redactional elements, either with integral or with introductory transitions. This means that it is not found with *'attâ, 'āz*, or, in Jeremiah, *bayyôm hahû'*; but in addition it does not appear with *bayyāmîm hahēm(mâ)* or with *(wĕhāyâ) bĕ'aḥărît hayyāmîm*.

On the other hand, it does follow *wĕhāyâ bayyôm hahû'* in 4:9 and 30:8, both times in anacrusis. It follows *bā'ēt hahî'* in two out of four passages (8:1, 31:1), *wĕ'aḥărê-kēn* in 21:7, and *bayyāmîm hahēm ûbā'ēt hahî'* in the MT of 50:4, 20. Most remarkably, it always follows *(lākēn) hinnēh yāmîm bā'îm* (7:32 par 19:6, 9:24 [E 25], 16:14 par 23:7, 23:5 par 33:14, 31:27, 31, 38, 48:12, 49:2, 51:52), the only exception being 51:47.

The significance of the frequency with which the oracle formula occurs in Jeremiah may be seen when comparing this book with other books. In Jeremiah it accompanies a temporal transition in twenty-two out of thirty-nine passages. In contrast, it occurs in Isaiah only once (22:25); in Ezekiel never; in Hosea in two of nine passages (2:18, 23 [E 16, 21]); in Amos in three of eight passages (8:9, 11, 9:13); in Micah in two of nine passages (4:6, 5:9 [E 10]); never in Habakkuk or Nahum; once in the single Haggai passage (2:23); and in Zechariah in three of seventeen passages (3:10, 12:4, 13:2). Furthermore, in virtually every passage on this list where it does occur, it is redactional.

In our earlier discussion of this formula we took note of an apparent intention in affixing it to one of the temporal formulas under study, and this becomes especially important when we realize how frequent it actually is in Jeremiah.

The expression *nĕ'um YHWH* has been widely discussed and intensively analyzed. In three hundred sixty-five Old Testament passages where the divine name accompanies *nĕ'um*, "utterance of," the preponderant place for it is at the end of an oracle, and its function there is to identify and legitimize the foregoing as an authentic word of revelation. Occurrences within the body of an oracle are almost always to be suspected as intrusions in which a redactor is attempting to extend revelational authority to include his addition or expansion.

Clearly this is the case also in the vast preponderance of passages where it is attached to a temporal formula of transition. In passages where the temporal formula introduces a redactional expansion, the affixing of *nĕ'um YHWH* has the evident purpose of assuring that the shift to a new event or situation is guaranteed by the divine intention. This is the case with virtually every occurrence, whether in Jeremiah or in one of the other prophetic books. The same is true in the few instances in which *nĕ'um YHWH* follows an integral transition formula, that is, one that provides a transition between a before and an after (Isa 22:25; Jer 7:31, 19:6, 30:3, 31:1, 48:12, 49:2, 51:52; Hag 2:23; Zech 12:4). This virtually never happens in original materials, and certainly not in Jeremiah. (The single original passage is Hag 2:23, which is especially notable for this remarkable difference.)

It is interesting also to observe that, while *nĕ'um YHWH* does follow *wĕhāyâ bayyôm hahû'* in the two Jeremiah passages where this temporal formula occurs (4:9 and 30:8), outside Jeremiah it may be either *bayyôm hahû'* (Isa 22:25; Mic 4:6; Hag 2:23; Zech 3:10, 12:4) or *wĕhāyâ bayyôm hahû'* (Hos 2:18, 23 [E 16, 21]; Amos 8:9; Mic 5:9 [E 10]; Zeph 1:10; Zech 13:2) that draws *nĕ'um YHWH* to itself. On the contrary, the only other temporal formula that draws *nĕ'um YHWH* to itself outside Jeremiah is *hinnēh yāmîm bā'îm,* vastly preponderant in Jeremiah. Thus we are more than justified in claiming that the addition of the oracle formula to an introductory temporal formula is distinctive for the redaction of the book of Jeremiah.

The combination of temporal formulas with the oracle formula appears, furthermore, at various redactional stages. Most occurrences are from the time just before, and just after, the beginning of the exile; but the end of the exile, with the return, is also an important period. The beginning and the end of the exile were viewed, as we know, as markers for entire new epochs for Yahweh's people; the new word of a redactor speaking as Jeremiah amidst these momentous events often required that he add this special formula of assurance, claiming that his new prediction was Yahweh's more ultimate and more decisive word.

Thus Jeremiah stands out among the prophetic books also in the dramatic way in which its redactors announce a decisive reinterpretation of Yahweh's will. At the beginning of the exile, the preferred temporal formula was *hinnēh yāmîm bā'îm,* pointing to a proximately future event that would dramatically amend, extend, or counteract the revelation already given. Later, the connective word *lākēn* was added to this formula, perhaps to show that somehow a new event in the proximate or remote future was organically connected to the old event, even while it was decisively distinct from it. *Nĕ'um YHWH* was almost always added to the temporal transition to support the claim that this new event was the more ultimate, equally authoritative revelation of Yahweh's purpose.

Listed according to the various periods to which they pertain, the passages in Jeremiah with futuristic transitions that are strengthened by the oracle formula *ně'um YHWH* are the following:

1) Preexilic:

4:9: The appearance (reappearance?) of the Chaldeans will put Jerusalem's leaders in panic and confusion as they witness the nonfulfillment of hopeful predictions that they should experience peace.

2) At the beginning of the exile:

5:18: Destruction and exile are not intended as annihilation but as a demonstration of moral responsibility;

9:24 (E 25): Death (v 21 [E 22]) or similar menaces for Judah will reach out to include all the conspirators against Babylon, including Judah;

23:5: Assurance of Israel's restoration under new and worthy "shepherds" stimulates a specific promise regarding the ideal Davidide, the bringer of absolute righteousness;

30:3: At a time when grim prophecy had come true, the prophet is instructed to write Yahweh's new book, validated by the assurance of restoration;

31:1: The execution of fierce wrath to the limit of Yahweh's intention does not alter his relationship with his covenant people;

31:27: The former menace of plucking up and breaking down (cf. 1:10) under Yahweh's watchful eye will be superseded by his watchful building and planting;

31:31: The covenant that has been broken will be superseded by Yahweh's sovereign and creative act of giving a new covenant undergirded by the thorough internalization of religion;

31:38: The city that was destroyed will be rebuilt, encompassing the graveyard of the dead within its sacred precincts.

3) During the exile:

7:32 par 19:6: Topheth and Hinnom, sites of gross idolatry, will be renamed "the valley of slaughter" because of the numerous dead that will be in them;

8:1: The bones of Jerusalem's idolatrous leaders will be unburied and scattered as an image of the exiles' true condition.

4) At the end of the exile:

48:12: Moab, which has remained at ease, will be overturned and shattered;

49:2: The Ammonites who have dispossessed the Gadites will be destroyed in battle;

50:4: When Babylon is destroyed, repentant Israelites and Judahites will come back to their city, joined in an everlasting covenant;

50:20: When Babylon is destroyed, the exiles will be restored to their land and cleansed of sin;

51:47, 52: When the exiles think once more of Jerusalem, Babylon will have been destroyed.

5) Late in the postexilic period:

33:14: The prediction of a righteous Branch (23:5-6) will yet be fulfilled.

These were the special items of ideology that Jeremiah's redactors underscored by the method of adding the oracle formula to a formula of transition. They were reacting to a series of crises, either to counter false hope and false religion, or to restore a true hope when it had been abandoned. They not only believed that they were speaking as and for the prophet (Jeremiah was possibly his own redactor in 4:9), but they believed that in announcing a new revelatory event, they were speaking for Yahweh.

CHAPTER EIGHT

Ezekiel

Primary transitions		Redactional transitions
1. Integral		
7:3	*ʿattâ*[a]	
19:13	*weʿattâ*	
24:27		*bayyôm hahûʾ*[b]
26:18	*ʿattâ*	
27:34	LXX *ʿattâ*	
32:14	*ʾāz*	
38:8	*miyyāmîm rabbîm . . . bĕʾaḥărît haššānîm*	
38:14		*hălōʾ bayyôm hahûʾ*
38:16		*bĕʾaḥărît hayyāmîm*
38:19		*ʾim lōʾ bayyôm hahûʾ*
39:25		*ʿattâ*
2. Introductory		
29:21		*bayyôm hahûʾ* (prose addition)
30:9		*bayyôm hahûʾ* (prose addition)
38:10		*wĕhāyâ bayyôm hahûʾ*[c] (prose addition)
38:18		*wĕhāyâ bayyôm hahûʾ* (prose addition)
39:11		*wĕhāyâ bayyôm hahûʾ* (prose addition)

a. Cf. situational *ʿattâ* (v 8).
b. Cf. *bayyôm hahûʾ* as gloss (v 26).
c. The messenger formula precedes.

Redaction and Ideology in Ezekiel

1. Ezekiel's linguistic tradition

In comparison with Isaiah and Jeremiah, the book of Ezekiel shows little tendency toward the expansion or correction of underlying materials with use of the formulas under study here. The probable explanation is that the main period of redactional activity for the book of Ezekiel was drastically compressed in comparison with that of the other "major prophets." As we have seen, the redaction of Isaiah continued over several centuries, while the redaction of Jeremiah was essentially complete within a single century. Setting aside the late exilic and early postexilic apocalyptic block in Ezekiel, chaps. 38–39, with the expansive vision of the new temple in chaps. 40–48, also late exilic in its initial formation, we may date both the work of the prophet himself and the work of his close school of disciples, which together produced the entire text of chaps. 1–36 (that is, apart from numerous, mainly non-Septuagintal glosses) during the period after 592 and during the first few decades of the exilic period.

Ezekiel belongs within the same linguistic tradition with Isaiah in its choice of futuristic transitions, for here as there *(wĕ)ʿattâ* and *ʾāz* are the preferred integral transitions, while *(wĕhāyâ) bayyôm hahûʾ* serves as the main formula for introducing redactional expansions. There is no similarity, however in the scope and relative frequency with which the two sets of formulas appear in Isaiah.

On the other hand, Ezekiel shows hardly any similarity at all with Jeremiah in regard to its choice of temporal formulas of transition; Ezekiel is far more sporadic and restricted in its use of such formulas. Much has been made of the linguistic and ideological resemblances between Ezekiel and Jeremiah,[1] but this has in no way affected the way in which they each choose and employ futuristic transitions. We observe also that Ezekiel does not emulate Jeremiah's frequent habit of attaching *nĕʾum YHWH*.

It is clear that the schools of Jeremiah and of Ezekiel were, and remained, quite separate from each other with regard to the ways in which each engaged in eschatological speculation.[2] It is also clear that the school of Isaiah and the school of Ezekiel were quite independent of each other in this regard. Although they both drew from a narrow stock of formulaic possibilities, the ways in which they sought to realize these possibilities were quite different.

Here are some of the specific differences that mark the use of futuristic transitions in Ezekiel in comparison with Isaiah and Jeremiah: (1) There are scattered occurrences of integral *(we)ʿattâ,* twice in oracles against Israel (7:3, 19:13) and once in an oracle against a foreign nation (26:18), in each instance in poetic oracles of judgment from Ezekiel himself. (2) *ʾāz* is an integral transition in another poetic passage (32:14) coming from Ezekiel's school, curiously modifying the theme of Egypt's downfall. (3) Elsewhere in Ezekiel 1–32 there are no further futuristic transitions except in an *ad hoc* integral redactional prose expansion at 24:27 and in introductory redactional prose expansions at 29:21 and 30:9 (all with foremost *bayyôm hahû'*), announcing Israel's salvation, Jerusalem's doom and Egypt/Ethiopia's doom, respectively. (4) This completes the list for the prophet Ezekiel and his immediate school, for the remaining integral (38:8, 14, 16, 19, 39:25) and introductory (38:10, 18, 39:11) futuristic transitions belong to the complex Gog pericope (except in 38:8 and 16, always with a construction with *bayyôm hahû'*). (5) The oracle formula *nĕ'um YHWH* is completely lacking in this book.

Because of the sporadic appearance of futuristic transitions in Ezekiel, one would scarcely be justified in attempting a detailed redaction-historical analysis of this book solely on the basis of this phenomenon — or lack of it. From a preliminary survey it is already clear, however, that in attempting to evaluate the occurrences that are found, we must be sensitive to the current state of research on this dynamic book.

Several things may be said to set the matter in order. First, since Cooke's (1936), Eichrodt's (1965-66), and especially Zimmerli's (1968-69) commentaries it is no longer arguable that the prophet carried out his ministry anywhere else than in Babylonia, where he was among the exiles from Jerusalem of 597 B.C.E.[3] Second, it is no longer the fashion to deny prophecies of salvation to the dour prophet who enunciated the grim denunciations of the first part of this book. Third, Zimmerli's patient labors have succeeded in identifying to most scholars' satisfaction the basic compositional strata within this book. Zimmerli has not posited *a priori* ideological boundaries between these stages as a basis for source criticism, but has rather applied a painstaking text-critical, source-critical, and form-critical analysis in order to gain an overall profile of the prophet, with his special ideology, and of his school of disciples, with their eager adaptations of their master's preaching.

2. Ezekiel as a preacher of judgment

We can now see quite clearly why Ezekiel was so severe and intense in his oracles of judgment against his own people. He was speaking about the Jews remaining in Jerusalem as well as about his fellow exiles, but he was speaking for and to the latter. He was deeply offended by, first, the violence they were doing against the holy majesty of their god, and second, by their persistent stubbornness in refusing to acknowledge that they had indeed come under a judgment that threatened their very existence as a nation and as a people. The exiles of 597 were being held hostage in Tel-abib to guarantee that the kingdom of Judah under Zedekiah would remain true to the treaty (*běrît;* RSV at 17:18, "covenant") with Nebuchadrezzar of Babylon.

As we know from Kings and Jeremiah, a spirit of reckless ultra-patriotism was at that moment gaining the upper hand in Judahite politics, in spite of the severe measures imposed by Nebuchadrezzar in 597. Apparently, the exiles who had been taken away with Jehoiachin, to whom Ezekiel had been called to prophesy, were moved by the same spirit of self-assertion as prevailed in Jerusalem. In Chaldea as in Jerusalem, there were prophets who spoke as patriots (cf. Jeremiah 23, 27–28, Ezekiel 13), encouraging their countrymen to think that the great king's power would soon be broken and that the exiles should then be recovered. Ezekiel had to stand firm against his fellow exiles who were indulging in this wishful thinking because he rightly saw it as a self-deceiving effort to coerce Yahweh; but he also perceived that this was the way to certain ruin, for if Nebuchadrezzar were finally forced to take drastic measures to put down an insurgency in Jerusalem, it would be the exiles who were already in Chaldea who would end up suffering the most. Their exile had been at least implicitly provisional, allowing the hope that Nebuchadrezzar might relent if he were assured of faithful and loyal behavior on the part of the Jews who had been left behind in the homeland. But this hope would be lost irretrievably for "the house of Israel" who were already in Chaldea if Jerusalem should be so irresponsible as to bring upon itself the ultimate punishment.

Thus Ezekiel's bitterness has to be understood first of all in the light of his personal predicament and that of the exile community. Not only were the exiles being held hostage by the Neo-Babylonians; they were being held hostage even more firmly by the erratic behavior of their fellow Jews at home. The prophecies in chaps. 1–24 of Ezekiel's book, which are arranged in approximate chronological order, reveal an intensifying sense of doom in the mind and heart of Ezekiel. His refusal to bring an oracle from Yahweh when he was visited by the community's elders (8:1, 14:1, 20:1), his (perhaps symbolic) inability to speak (3:24-27, 24:27, 33:22), but especially his inability to show grief over his wife's demise (24:15-24), were ominous signals that the bitter, bitter end was very near, and that nothing whatever could now be done to avert it.

The book of Ezekiel is notable for several special innovations. This book has a remarkably wide range of genres and special formulas.[4] It draws upon an unusual variety of ancient traditions. It also shows a remarkable fecundity in employing visual and symbolic images. Thus this book gives extensive development to the vision genre (1:1–3:15, chaps. 8–11, 37:1-10; cf. chaps. 40–48) and to that of the symbolic-act oracle (3:22–5:17, 12:1-16, 17-20, 21:18-32, 24:15-27, 33:22, 37:15-28). It bases oracles on extended (chaps. 16, 17, 19, 23, 27, 31, 34, 28:11-19, 29:1-16, 32:1-16, 17-32, 33:1-9) and limited (3:16-21, chaps. 6 and 15, 20:45–21:7, 21:8-17, 22:17-22, 24:1-14,

28:1-10, 29:17-21, 30:20-26, 33:30-33) metaphors. It develops the diatribe form based on a rejected and offensive citation (12:21-25, 26-28, chaps. 18 and 26, 33:10-20, 23-29, chap. 35, 36:1-15, 16-38, 37:11-14). This variety shows that Ezekiel possessed not only a keen mind but also an unusually vivid imagination. Oracles that are based on a special theme (chaps. 7 and 13, 14:1-11, 12-23, chap. 20, 22:1-16, 23-31, 28:20-26, 30:1-19) display a rare tenacity and power of penetration. Some of these special features appear in salvation oracles, but the great majority have been employed to sharpen the image of impending doom.

Another remarkable feature of the book is Ezekiel's extensive recording of precise dates. Not only do these provide an approximate chronology for the successive visions and oracles; they also reveal this prophet's strong sense of the passage of time in Judah/Jerusalem's ineluctable march to its end. Four pericopes that seem to tighten the noose of doom for Yahweh's people and city (1:2ff., 8:1ff., 20:1ff., 24:1ff.) range in date from the fifth to the ninth year of Jehoiachin's captivity. The fourth of these dates is that of the second siege of Jerusalem commencing in January of 588.[5] During the eleventh and twelfth years of Jehoachin's captivity (588-586),[6] Ezekiel also composed[7] an oracle against Tyre (26:1ff.) and five oracles against Egypt (29:1ff., 30:20ff., 31:1ff., 32:1ff., 17ff.) under the conviction that these major powers shared Judah's culpability for the ill-fated conspiracy against Nebuchadrezzar.[8]

In the tradition of Amos 5:18-20, Isa 2:6-21, and Zeph 1:7-18, Ezekiel believed that the last great day, "Yahweh's day," was imminent, and that this would bring the end of history for Judah, the last surviving section of the erstwhile Israelite nation (see chap. 7, 12:21-25, 26-28, 33:33). This was Yahweh's ultimate day for his people — not necessarily the end of time, but ultimate in the sense that on this awesome day every issue between Yahweh and his people would come to final adjudication.[9] Though he was now living far away from Jerusalem, Ezekiel recorded the day (not the date, which was supplied by a redactor; see above) when Nebuchadrezzar put this city under final siege (24:1-2), and thereafter he fell silent until the day when the exiles received word from *happĕlîṭ mîrûšālaim,* one of those who had survived Jerusalem's destruction but who had been brought now to join the exiles, that *hukĕtâ hā'îr,* "the city has fallen" (33:21). The date of the messenger's arrival has been dutifully recorded by Ezekiel as the "twelfth[10] year of our exile, in the tenth month, on the fifth day of the month." According to our reckoning, this should be January 8, 585. In 24:25-27[11] a redactor wrongly equated it with "the day when I [Yahweh] take from them their stronghold (etc.)," that is, the day of Jerusalem's actual fall on the seventh of Ab in the year 586.

3. Ezekiel as a preacher of salvation

It is this event that ended Ezekiel's alalia, enabling him to speak once more (33:22; cf. 24:27). But now the judgment was final; in other words, now that the "day of Yahweh" had arrived, Ezekiel's new speaking would not be — could not be — a new word of doom. If it was to be a word of revelation from Yahweh, it would have to be, therefore, a prophecy of salvation. And that is what Ezekiel thenceforth proceeded to preach. There was still doom to preach for the nations, especially for those that had shared Judah's guilt, for the "day of Yahweh" had not yet arrived for them.

That the "day of Yahweh," though ultimate and final, may come to be referred to as an event of the past is illustrated by Ezekiel's allusion to the exile as a past event in his metaphor of the shepherds and sheep in chap. 34. V 12 in that chapter is structured as a comparative sentence: "As a shepherd seeks . . . so will I seek." The verb in the second clause is a futuristic imperfect, and syntactically dependent on it is the *wāw*-consecutive perfect with its objective pronoun, *wehiṣṣaltî 'ethem,* "and I will rescue them"; this is explicated by a prepositional phrase, *mikkol-hamměqômōt 'ăšer nāpōṣû šām,* "from all the places where they have been scattered"; and this is in turn explicated by a second prepositional phrase, *běyôm 'ānān wa'ărāpel,* "on a day of cloud and doom" (cf. Zeph 1:15). This is metaphorical language that unmistakably belongs to the imagery of the day of Yahweh. It is now over and past, though its evil effects, from which Yahweh promises to rescue his "sheep," remain.

The question of why Ezekiel made such a dramatic about-face, once Jerusalem had been destroyed, has been widely discussed. Gerhard von Rad follows the wrong tack in his treatment of Ezekiel in his *Old Testament Theology*[12]; he offers a psychological explanation, crediting Ezekiel's independence of spirit for the change. But the solution is theological rather than psychological. There are two especially crucial concepts in Ezekiel's earlier preaching that explain this change. The first is the complete vindication of his bitter reproof, directed to the exiles; the second is what may be called his sense of existential standing before Yahweh's judgment.

As has been said, Ezekiel was alarmed that the exiles were in double jeopardy, held hostage both to Nebuchadrezzar and to interim politics in Jerusalem. He did not blame Nebuchadrezzar for the discomfiture of the exile community or for the sword that continued to dangle over Jerusalem; rather, like Jeremiah, he recognized the Babylonians as Yahweh's ordained instrument of judgment. Certainly, he did not blame Yahweh, whose condescension and patience had long since been worn out (cf. chaps. 16, 20, 23). He did blame the Jerusalemites, and he blamed the exiles for encouraging them — or at least for clinging to an idle hope and refusing to learn the lesson of Yahweh's judgment in history. The event of 586 completely vindicated Ezekiel; but he was in no mood to gloat. Rather, he shared his people's grief (see especially 24:15-24). But he knew that Yahweh had a further, more final word for them and that he was to continue as Yahweh's spokesman.

A particular image that he seized upon was that of the watchman in 33:1-9. This was certainly not a special office for Ezekiel to assume, as H. Graf von Reventlow has maintained,[13] but a strong metaphor for his crucial role in warning the "wicked" man to turn from his evil way. Now that Jerusalem's fall had effectuated Yahweh's purpose, those who had survived the four sore acts of judgment, sword, famine, evil beasts, and pestilence (14:21), scattered now to distant nations or maintaining a precarious existence in a ruined land, were under the juridical category of "wicked." The only remaining question was whether they would retain the "hard forehead and the stubborn heart" (3:7) that had caused their disaster, and thereby further confirm that they indeed deserved this label.

This is part of the explanation for Ezekiel's change. The other part is his belief that "righteousness" and "wickedness" are relational, existential concepts that may be changed by attitudes and circumstances. It has been said that Ezekiel 18 preaches "individual responsibility." It does more than that. Two related purposes are accomplished in this chapter: (1) a thorough refutation of the notion that the punishment merited by sin can be inherited from generation to generation; and (2) a rebuttal of the claim that a sinner's eventual repentance cannot avert further punishment. This thoroughly motivates Ezekiel's urgent call to repentance at the end of the pericope, vv 30-32, for no one is locked either into generational coresponsibility or into the syndrome of sin, guilt, and punishment.

In Ezek 33:10-20, this is further explicated. It is said there that "righteous" and "wicked" pertain only to how a person stands before God at each particular moment. These are not therefore badges of honor or brands of shame, indelibly marking each man in perpetuity. But Ezekiel is not engaging here in theoretical speculation; he is carrying out his duty as a "watchman." The "house of Israel" to whom these words are directed were like the unheeding city in that they were fatalistically accepting the label of "wicked" and assuming the state of spiritual death appropriate to that label (cf. Jer 8:1-3), showing by this that they had learned nothing whatever from their calamity. Ezekiel repeats a ditty that they were reciting (v 10):

kî-pĕššā'ēnû wĕḥaṭṭ'ōtênû	But our transgressions and our sins
'alênû	are upon us,
ûbām 'ănaḥnû nĕmaqqîm	and we waste away in them;
wĕ'ēk niḥyeh	so how shall we live?

This was in actuality an insidious way of blaming God, so that the one who had put the blame on them is made responsible for their spiritual death. But Ezekiel will have none of that. In impassioned words this most "evangelical" of all prophets repeats Yahweh's oath that his purpose (RSV "pleasure") is not the death of the wicked but their repentance, by which they may live. Thus it all comes to the point where the beleaguered city of the watchman allegory will accept the responsibility of heeding a warning of death, so that this may in fact become the way of life for them. Following an impassioned plea to turn back, Yahweh states that if Israel is to die as a people, it will be by their own act, by their own refusal to accept responsibility. "Why will you die, O house of Israel?" (v 11).

This is, in truth, the essence of Ezekiel's eschatology. Very similar to 33:1-20 is the more famous passage, that of the revived bones in 37:1-14, where Ezekiel repeats a similar ditty (v 11) speaking of bones being dried up, hope being lost, and the exiles being hacked away like fallen branches. There the wonderful secret is revealed that Yahweh can nevertheless send — and will send — his life-creating spirit, the same as in Gen 2:7. Yahweh does not promise here an individual physical resurrection, but these three gifts for disconsolate Israel: the divine spirit within them, their restoration to life as God's people, and their return to their own land (v 14a), that they may finally know that Yahweh has predicted and performed all that has happened to them (the recognition formula; Ger. *Erweisformel*) (v 14b).

If we accept 37:1-14 as authentic, there is no sufficient reason to deny to the prophet the promise of a new heart and a new spirit in 11:19, 36:26-27. But to claim more for Ezekiel soon encounters the phenomenon of an intensive redaction carried on by the school of Ezekiel. As Zimmerli has shown, virtually every chapter within Ezekiel 1-37 has been interpolated and expanded by this school, and it is therefore hazardous to say what Ezekiel himself may have predicted. One thing is for certain, and that is that Ezekiel's followers seized upon both his oracles of judgment and his promises of salvation as anchors for a widely developed eschatology, mainly of salvation for Israel, and very much in the tradition of Deuteronomy and Jeremiah, no doubt giving inspiration for the eventual preaching of Deutero-Isaiah.

Siegfried Herrmann has devoted fifty pages in his book *Die prophetische Heilserwartungen* (pp. 241-91) to an analysis of the Ezekiel school's prolific ideology of restoration (see the displays on pp. 286-87). He does not find it useful to separate Ezekiel's original ideas from those of his school; and certainly we should be ready to admit that the prophet's own thought may lie at the basis of most of the expansions that were carried out by his school. Herrmann places special emphasis on the distinction between Jeremiah's eschatology, which has to do with Yahweh's freedom to act in sovereign grace in a future yet to come, and what he calls the theocratic, torah- and temple-based eschatology of Ezekiel and his school. We should be cautious, however, in directly associating chaps. 40ff. with the massive early redaction that was carried on while Ezekiel was still alive. While some scholars, including

Zimmerli, are hesitant to deny chaps. 40–48 to Ezekiel, it is certain that they constitute in any case a literary block quite apart from the rest of the book, and that they embody an ideology that stands at far remove from that of the prophet and his immediate school. And definitely this is true, as Zimmerli emphasizes, of the Gog apocalypse in chaps. 38–39, which was brought to a formal conclusion by the addition in 39:23-29 of words that clearly refer to the end of the exile.

4. The growth of the book

Though one might not in every instance agree with Zimmerli, he does certainly offer a useful and generally trustworthy guide to the three distinct compositional-redactional strata that make up Ezekiel 1–37. These are (1) the prophet's own oracles; (2) expansions by his immediate school of disciples; and (3) late, mainly scribal, alterations. The expansions from Ezekiel's school are fairly uniform in their technique and ideology, their main aim being to elucidate and contemporize Ezekiel's words for a new generation. The scribal alterations are sporadic and atomistic, and are of no direct relevance in our study.

It is possible to distinguish various levels of collection. Pericopes among the oracles against Israel that are dated and/or provided with a circumstantial setting (chaps. 1–3; 8–11; 20; 24) are likely to have been the first collected, and the remaining pericopes were subsequently inserted in an approximate chronological sequence into this collection. The same procedure was carried out in the foreign-oracles section.

We are able to observe how individual oracles were drawn to each other. For example, individual *Erweisworte* in 13:10-16 and 22-23 were connected to the separate woe-oracles of vv 3-9 and 18-21; then each twin-oracle, that against the prophets and that against the "prophetesses," was joined together to create a unified pericope on the subject of false and idolatrous prophecy. A political allegory about an eagle in chap. 17 was originally joined to another political allegory about a lioness in chap. 19 through use of the formula "And you, son of man, take up a lamentation . . ." (19:1). Two dissimilar pericopes in 33:23-29 and 30-33 were twinned, that is, joined by the connective formula "and you, son of man" (v 30).

There is no use in giving further examples, for primitively discrete pericopes must certainly be exegeted as complete units within themselves before being interpreted in terms of new structures created by their combination. It is possible to point out some of the larger units, but they do not concern us for the moment. Eventually, chaps. 1–37 were separated into the three major sections of the book: (1) oracles of judgment against Israel; (2) oracles of judgment against the nations; and (3) oracles of salvation. This is the arrangement that one sees also in Zephaniah and that was eventually super-imposed upon Isaiah and Jeremiah.

As has been mentioned, an analysis of individual occurrences of futur-istic transitions in Ezekiel has little potentiality for shedding light on the growth of the book as a whole, and certainly it will add little to our under-standing of this book's varied and extensive inventory of eschatological im-ages. This information, on the other hand, is important for our thorough understanding of these transitions.

Integral Transitions in Ezekiel

1. In primary materials

Integral futuristic transitions that belong to primary materials in Ezekiel are rare. The passages where they do occur involve a move from one event to another in temporal sequence or in logical consequence from one to the other. Except for the unique formula in 38:8, which is in prose, they are part of the poetic structure of the pericopes to which they belong, and may be attributed directly to the prophet or his immediate circle. The four occurrences of *(wĕ)ʿattâ* are definitely in authentic oracles, twice in the collection against Israel (7:3, 19:13) and twice in the foreign-oracle collection (26:18, 27:34 LXX). The single occurrence of *ʾāz* (32:14) belongs within the foreign-oracle collection and may be from Ezekiel.

Each of these passages has been previously discussed, but there are additional remarks to be made. First, concerning 7:3. Three separate literary complexes, 3:16–5:17, 6:1-14, and 7:1-27, have been placed between the call vision, 1:2–3:15, dated in the fifth year of Jehoiachin's exile, and the great temple vision, chaps. 8–11, dated in the sixth year of this exile. Each of these interpolated complexes contains Ezekielian material that has been expansively redacted by Ezekiel's disciples, beginning perhaps very soon after the proph-et's own words were recorded. The first two complexes are structured as symbolic-act oracles; the third is based on the motto *qēṣ,* "end."[14] It consists of two originally distinct poems, the first of which appears in parallel recen-sions. The essential problem of chap. 7 is the seriously disordered text; the LXX lacks parts of the MT or presents them in a different sequence. Thus the primary step in exegeting this pericope has to be text-critical,[15] but attention to form and structure is also essential.[16] Zimmerli's seminal study on the so-called recognition formula *(Erkenntnisformel),*[17] "Then shall you know that I am Yahweh," is the clue to dividing the pericope into three independent poems (vv 2-4, vv 5-9, and vv 10-27), for it concludes each separate poem as elsewhere in authentic Ezekielian materials. Each poem is structured as a prophetic proof saying. Vv 2-4 and vv 5-9, parallels of each other, are announcements of punishment addressed to "the land of Israel" along with an apostrophized "inhabitant of the land." Following introductory formulas, each contains an impersonal description of an imminent calamity that is tantamount to the dreaded day of Yahweh, then a declaration of Yahweh's intervention in wrath and judgment, and finally one of Ezekiel's stock formulas, the "no pity" formula, ending with a recapitulation and then the recognition formula.

It is only in the first parallel that the temporal formula *'attâ*[18] appears, and there its position is between the impersonal description, "An end has come upon the four corners of the land," and the announcement of divine intervention. Yahweh's outpouring of wrath in judgment is equivalent to the coming of the end; yet a logical, if not a temporal, sequence leads from the one to the other. In other words, the end is the announced event, the wrath and judgment are its consequences. This expresses very well Ezekiel's own eschatology of judgment: though it be yet future, it is seen as already present in essence, with inevitable and imminently future consequences to follow.

The remaining occurrences of *wě'attâ* (19:13) or *'attâ* (17:34 LXX, 26:18) are each in allegories belonging to the genre dirge. The passages to which they belong all exhibit the then-now pattern, contrasting former glory and well-being with present ruin.

In an early process of collecting Ezekiel's oracles, the eagle and cedar allegory of chap. 17 was attached to the lioness and the vine allegories in chap. 19. Because the formula *wě'attâ (ben-'ādām),* "and you, (son of man)," elsewhere links stages or episodes within a larger pericope (cf. 2:8, 4:1, 9, 5:1, 33:7, 10), the prophet himself may have made this arrangement. However, 19:10-14a was composed in an historical situation different from that of vv 2-9, where the lioness has to be Josiah or the royal establishment as an institution, and the young lion who is brought to the king of Babylon has to be Jehoiachin, taken captive in 597. Vv 10-14a allude to a mother-vine that may be Israel or the surviving remnant of the dynasty, represented by Zedekiah and perhaps others of royal blood. Although the text is somewhat uncertain, the feminine verb in v 13 makes it probable that the "mother" as vine, rather than Zedekiah specifically, is the subject of the transplanting in the wilderness, and probably also of the verbs in v 13. In any event, transitional *'attâ* in v 13 signalizes a significant new move; namely, a transplanting to barren ground symbolic of the Babylonian exile, for the vine itself. The logic is faulty, for a vine that has been plucked up, cast down, dried up, stripped of fruit, withered, and consumed by fire could hardly have survived in any form. This is meant as a paradox similar to that of life out of death that dramatizes Ezekiel's eschatology in 33:10f. and 37:1ff. It is precisely this element of paradox, together with the then-now pattern that these verses share with 26:17-18 and

27:32-34, that makes Ezekielian authorship probable in this rather vapid expansion to the more vigorous poem of 19:2-9.

The initial oracle against Tyre, found in 26:1-6, like the initial oracle against Egypt in 29:1ff., has been dated. It has been successively expanded by further oracles against Tyre; then by a further Tyre collection in 27:1ff., with its accretions; and eventually by a Sidon oracle in 28:20ff. One of the attachments to 26:1-6 is a dirge in 26:17-18 that moves from the theme of Tyre's former glory to the present (ʿattâ) dismay among Tyre's dependencies, dated "on the day of your fall (yôm mĕpaltāk), parallel to ʿattâ (LXX; MT ʿēt) bridging the gap between the "then" of Tyre's wealth and glory to the "now" of her wreck at sea.

It is all but certain that Ezekiel himself composed these dirges. Although on the surface a past event is being contrasted to a present event, we know from historical sources that Tyre had not yet fallen, and would not fall during Ezekiel's lifetime.[19] The glory of Tyre continued at Ezekiel's time as a present reality, so that its ruin as a more distantly future event has to be extrapolated from the certainty of divine judgment. This dirge over a fallen foe functions thus as the futuristic prediction of a fate yet to come. Unlike 19:2ff., 10ff., which are genuine laments, these dirges for Tyre are mock laments, the equivalent of taunts or invectives similar to that of 26:1-6. Because Ezekiel believed that Tyre stood under the judgment of God as surely as Judah and Jerusalem, the "now" of 26:18 and 27:34 introduces a sequence from iniquity to ruin as certain as that which was soon to be experienced, or had already been experienced, by Judah.

2. In redactional materials

This book's sole integral futuristic transition within redactional material is at 24:27. Ezekiel's prophecies in chaps. 1–37 have been extensively expanded by such redactional material, attached in the middle or at the end of primary literary blocks. Some expansions may actually be from Ezekiel himself (as in Jeremiah), but virtually all of them must have been done by his school, either as explications of his meaning or as new applications of his predictions.

An example of the latter occurs in the climactic chapter, chap. 24, postdated at v 1 by a redactor-disciple to the ninth year (of Jehoiachin's captivity) in order to coincide with the beginning of Nebuchadrezzar's siege in 588. The command to record this specific occasion (v 2) is followed by the allegory of a pot on the fire (vv 3-14) and the report of a symbolic act, with its accompanying interpretation, concerning the prophet's behavior upon the imminent death of his wife (vv 15-24). As Zimmerli has shown, both these pericopes have been heavily interpolated. The original symbolic-act oracle is based on the correspondence between the taking away of Ezekiel's wife and the taking away of Israel's sanctuary, involving the murder of her young people; but a disciple in vv 22-23 alters the correspondence to match Ezekiel's refusal to mourn in public with a prediction of Israel's lack of opportunity for ritual mourning, to become a reality in the imminent deportation. Thus the emphasis shifts from Yahweh's act to the consequences of this act in terms of the experience of the exiles-to-be.

By the same or another redactor, a similar move has been made in vv 25-27. Though these verses are introduced by the accustomed formula of internal transition, *wěʿattâ ben-'ādām*, it cannot be Ezekiel who wrote these verses, for they appear to make a serious error that he surely would never have been capable of making: synchronizing the day of Jerusalem's fall in August 586 with the day when its report reached faraway Chaldea in January of 585 (cf. 33:21).

There is neither need nor opportunity at this point to enter into the extended discussion that would be required if we were to deal fully with the problems of Ezekiel's chronology. It must suffice for the present to say that we date the years of captivity from Nisan to Nisan (the month of the Babylonian new year) commencing soon after the surrender of Jerusalem on the second of Adar in Nebuchadrezzar's seventh year (cf. B.M. 21946), equal to March 16, 597 in our chronology. This would allow for the arrival of news of Jerusalem's fall in Chaldea on 5 Tebeth of the twelfth year of Jehoiachin's captivity (33:21), a reasonable and understandable six months later.[20]

But the interpretation of 24:25-27 does not depend on establishing precise dates for these two events. Because of the dating, 33:21-22 probably belongs to the earliest collection (that is, of dated judgment oracles against Israel; see above). It records the very most crucial date in Ezekiel's eschatology, that of the day when anguished waiting, symbolized by the prophet's dumbness, gave way to numbing certainty. In Chaldea, Ezekiel did not know, and perhaps never found out, the precise date of Jerusalem's fall. The historical event in itself was not revelatory for him, but the shock of hearing the news received from one of the new exiles, a survivor (RSV fugitive) of Jerusalem's destruction. This meant the end of everything that Ezekiel had ever cherished; but it was also the beginning of a new phase of ministry for him, symbolized by the opening of his mouth.

This is what the redactor in 24:25-27 attempts to reconstruct in his reinterpretation of the symbolic-act oracle of vv 15-24. He continues to represent Yahweh as speaking. He repeats the recognition formula in v 24 that concluded the original pericope. Yahweh's speaking, however, continues in the second person, rather than in the third person as in v 24, identifying Ezekiel as a "sign" to Israel. The redactor paraphrases the dramatic language of v 21, altering at the same time a second-person address to Israel to a third-person reference. "My sanctuary *(miqdāšî)*" becomes "their stronghold *(māʿûzām),*" while "what you have compassion for *(maḥmal napšĕkem)*" becomes "what concerns them *(maśśāʾ napšām).*" The redactor's intent is to equate the day when Yahweh took away everything worth living for with the day when Ezekiel's mouth was opened. Thus he goes beyond the convergence of events as reported in 33:21-22. The day when Ezekiel's mouth was opened is not synchronized with the report "The city has fallen," but with the event of Yahweh's final, drastic deed. Although *bayyôm hahû'* in v 27[21] creates this synchronism, there is also significant progression in a cause-and-effect sequence from the taking away of captives to the opening of the prophet's mouth. Though he fails to understand the sequence of events in 33:21-22, this redactor is as certain as Ezekiel himself that the day when everything ended for Israel was also the day of something decisively new for the prophet and for his people.

Introductory Transitions in Ezekiel

In Ezekiel, futuristic transitions do not appear in poetic anacrusis or in any kind of formal rubric, as in Isaiah and Jeremiah. Outside chaps. 38–39 there are only two occurrences, and both of these introduce prose additions to foreign oracles. In each instance, the temporal formula is foremost *wĕhāyâ bayyôm hahû'*. As in a number of Isaiah passages with this particular formula, these seem random and atomistic, having been added in all probability by separate redactors during the early exilic years.

To all appearances, each of the redactional verses in question has been added to a primary text already attached within its context, even though they do not directly explicate these respective pericopes. Just as words of salvation for Israel in 28:24, 25-26 close off the collection of oracles against Tyre (26:1–28:19) and Sidon (28:20-23), the word of salvation for Israel in 29:21 originally closed off Ezekiel's original collection against Egypt. 29:17-20 is this book's latest dated pericope, and, though put in its present position in the final redaction, it initially stood at the end of chap. 32. According to the redactor who attached 29:21 to vv 17-20, the day when Yahweh will give Egypt to Nebuchadrezzar as wages for his fruitless labor before Tyre is also to be a day when three great good things will happen: (1) a horn will sprout for the house of Israel, (2) Yahweh will open Ezekiel's mouth among them, and (3) they will know who Yahweh truly is (a modified recognition formula).

As Zimmerli and other commentators believe, the "horn" is not to be associated with special aspirations concerning the Davidides; it is rather a widely used symbol of strength and success, while the "sprouting" is to be understood in the light of such texts as Jer 31:27-28.[22] The "opening of the mouth (*pithôn peh;* cf. 16:63)"[23] is to be experienced by an unidentified audience, undoubtedly a revived Israel. This is by no means typical Ezekielian language but belongs to a redactor who changed the standard "then shall you (2ms) know that I am Yahweh" to "then shall they know . . . ," in spite of the second-personal address in the preceding clause. According to this redactor, this was to happen in the same proximate future as the predicted success of Nebuchadrezzar.

A somewhat similar process produced the prose prediction introduced by *bayyôm hahû'* in 30:9. As a fragment of epexegetical interpretation added to the day-of-Yahweh poem in 30:2-8, it has more relevance within its own context than has 29:21 within its context. It extends the mention of Kush's anguish in v 4 and the mention of the breaking of Egypt's helpers in v 8 as a prediction that messengers should bring anguish to the Kushites "on the day of Egypt's doom" (cf. Isa 18:1-2). This would be an event more remote than that of Egypt's ruin — scheduled for the proximate future — even though the two events are synchronized for "the day of Yahweh" in vv 22-24. Although 30:1-19 is an insertion that breaks the original chronological framework, the poetic sections may be authentic. This epexegetical gloss is unmistakably from the prophet's early exilic school. Prior to the insertion of this little collection between 29:16 and 30:20, it had been already attached to vv 2-8 along with vv 10-12 and vv 13-19.

Temporal Transitions in the Gog Apocalypse

1. The original pericope, 38:2-9, 39:1-5, 17-20

In our discussion of clusters in Chapter Five, we described the succession of futuristic formulas in Ezekiel 38–39 as the work of individual redactors who used these as a device for expressing proto-apocalyptic ideals of various kinds. Although there is a thematic association among the expansions marked by these transitions, there is little evidence of the type of incremental epexegesis that one finds in Isa 19:16-25. The additions are mainly eccentric and atomistic, like those found in Zech 12:3–13:4 and 14:6-20. Nevertheless, it is important to distinguish between the transitions that are integral and those that are introductory within this context, as well as between primary materials having them and those that belong to expansions.

Zimmerli's compositional analysis of this material seems entirely successful, and may well be our guide in identifying, first of all, the original pericope as such. The style is borrowed from that of authentic materials elsewhere. Following the prophetic-word formula at the very beginning, there are three distinct announcements of coming calamity, all notably succinct, in 38:2-9, 39:1-5, and 39:17-20. The first features the hostile assembly and its aggressive advance toward the "mountains of Israel"; the second concerns Gog's defeat on the same "mountains of Israel"; and the third concerns a sacrificial feast for the birds and beasts, also on the "mountains of Israel."[24] The first two sections contain addresses to Gog that follow the formula for a challenge to a duel, "Behold, I am against you." The third section has a command to address the birds and beasts, who are also assembled at Yahweh's direction and are to come as the instruments of his purpose. Though the form of the prophetic oracle is used in each new section of this composition, it hangs together as a striking tableau, creating a dramatic staging of history's climactic moment, with its aftermath.

2. The expansions

The thematic and structural unity that is evident in this composition has been all but destroyed, to a degree unusual even for the much-redacted book of Ezekiel, by the heaping up of unrelated redactional digressions. Although no final date can be found for this process, it stands to reason that none of these expansions can be earlier than that of the main composition in its original form. Both the original composition and its expansions contain temporal formulas that must be analyzed for their ideology and for the role they play within the redactional process.

The secondary expansions to the Gog apocalypse have arisen as a series of comments pertaining to the respective sections of the original composition. These may be briefly characterized as follows:

(1) 38:10-13, speculation about Gog's motivation based on v 8's mention of the inoffensiveness of restoration Israel, leading to an attribution of envy and greed to Gog and his allies as the reason for their aggression;

(2) 38:14-16, identifying awareness of Israel's secure dwelling (v 8) as the motivation for Gog's attack, while affirming that this was nevertheless brought about according to Yahweh's greater purpose, that of vindicating his own holiness in the sight of many nations;

(3) 38:17, an editorial "aside," probably with Isaiah 14 and Jeremiah 2–6 in mind, wondering whether the mythical enemy was actually the same as the one predicted by the prophets;

(4) 38:18-23, a baroque scene of the day of Yahweh, articulating the content of an angry oath to the effect that the God who had summoned the

enemy horde would also be ready for them, with all the forces of the cosmos as his weapons;

(5) 39:6-8, epexegesis to 38:1ff., 39:1ff., extending Gog's judgment to Magog and the enemy coastlands, scourging them with fire; also affirming the divine purpose of making both the nations and Israel aware who Yahweh is, while firmly identifying this event as the fulfillment of prophecy ("This is the day of which I have spoken," v 8);

(6) 39:9-10, a new tableau showing what is to happen to all the weapons of war that will be left on the field after the battle is over (cf. v 3), stating that they will suffice for fuel for seven years for "those who dwell in the cities of Israel," and concluding with the oracle formula;

(7) 39:11-16, still another tableau reflecting speculation about what will have to be done with all the dead bodies in order to keep the land from ritual impurity "on the day when I show my glory" (v 13, with another oracle formula);

(8) 39:21-22, a statement that the effect will be Yahweh's glorification and self-revelation; the nations will witness his judgment while "the house of Israel" will be confirmed in perpetuity in their knowledge of who Yahweh is;

(9) 39:23-29, theological reflection regarding Yahweh's purpose in subjecting his people to a well-deserved punishment and announcing (v 25, with the messenger formula and temporal *'attâ* as an integral transition) the spiritual blessings that will be experienced by a people restored to their land; this too ends in an oracle formula.

We must now evaluate the effect of the temporal transitions that appear within this elaborately enlarged composition. There are integral transitions in 38:8, 14, 16, 19 and 39:25, as well as introductory transitions in 38:10, 18 and 39:11. All three of the introductory transitions are a stereotyped *wĕhāyâ bayyôm hahû'*. Among the integral transitions, *bayyôm hahû'* follows *hălō'* in 38:14 and *'im lō'* in 38:19, but the remaining three are different altogether.

Because the transitions in 38:8 and 39:25 are crucial for dating this composition, we set them aside temporarily, taking up first in order the temporal formula in 38:14. It belongs to an expansion introduced by *lākēn*, next the commissioning formula, then the messenger formula. It is in the form of a rhetorical question with the interrogative particle and the negative particle, immediately preceding the temporal formula. There is no good reason to follow the LXX here in amending the verb *tēda'*, "you shall know," to *tē'îr*, "you shall be stirred up" (cf. *BHS*mg, RSV) because the rhetorical question has the intent of synchronizing Gog's earliest awareness that Israel is dwelling securely in its own land (cf. v 8) with his departure *(bw')* prior to his attack *('lh)* (v 16).

Within the expansion, at v 16, there is a further integral transition, *bĕ'aḥărît hayyāmîm,* which, though rare in the Old Testament, is certainly not to be equated with the unparalleled *bĕ'aḥărît haššānîm* in v 8. It seems too facile to explain it merely as a reflex of the idiosyncratic formula in v 8, for one would expect, if that were the case, that the latter expression should have been retained. It is better to explain it as performing a role as in Jer 23:20, where it simply means, "at the time of fulfillment"; that is, at the end of the process of waiting for the prediction in question to come true. As in Jeremiah, it has to do with convincing those who have chosen to believe otherwise; only, here it is "the nations" that need convincing rather than the optimistic Israelite prophets. The temporal formula, dating the ultimate consequence of Gog's "knowing" mentioned in v 14, refers to a final event or situation within the remote future.

At 38:19 an elliptical oath formula, *'im lō',* is followed by synchronizing *bayyôm hahû',* another integral transition formula. Its effect is to draw an equation between the day of Gog's invasion, which arouses Yahweh's wrath (v 18), and all manner of frightful events following in fulfillment of Yahweh's oath. All this lies in the same remote future to which the composition as a whole alludes. Although the day-of-Yahweh calamities are actually consequences of the oath, the effect of this formula is to make them simultaneous with Gog's attack.

We come now to the three stereotyped occurrences of *wĕhāyâ bayyôm hahû'* appearing in 38:10, 18 and 39:11 (including the first as an introductory formula because the preceding messenger formula does no more than mark the following expansions as revelation). All that needs to be said about these occurrences is that they synchronize the events that they introduce with Gog's invasion in general and specifically with various aspects of that invasion. In 38:10, it is the initial moment of getting ready for the attack that is referred to; the temporal transition synchronizes Gog's scheming with his getting ready, reflected in the further scheming on the part of notorious slave merchants to seize the many captives that will be taken in the coming invasion (v 13). In 38:18, the day in question is, rather, that of Gog's actual onslaught, leading to Yahweh's oath and its direct fulfillment. In 39:11, the formula relates to what is a consequence of the attack and Yahweh's victory, namely, the beginning of a seven-month project of burying all the dead, rather illogically equated in v 13 with "the day when I reveal my glory."

Along with 38:14-16, these three passages are different from the remaining expansions in that they aim to synchronize certain events or conditions with the last, climactic day. In other words, the coincidence in time is of paramount interest for them. It can be no more than a guess whether they may have been all composed by the same redactor.

In our previous discussion of *'attâ* in Ezek 39:25 (see in Chapter Two), we reached the conclusion that 39:23-29 is the work of the initial redactor of the apocalypse, someone working shortly after the return from exile, as v 28 makes sufficiently clear. In this expansion a then-now pattern is dominant: the "then" of the exile is to be replaced by the "now" of restoration and return, assured by the messenger formula in v 25aα and by the oracle formula in v 29.

In spite of the fact that this expansion begins with a reference to "knowing," it is unlikely that it is a compositional extension of vv 21-22, or that it was written with those verses already in the text. The reason is that those verses make a distinction between the nations' "seeing" and Israel's "knowing"; also because the reference in vv 23ff. is to the events of Israel's exile and return, rather than to the event of Gog's defeat. On the other hand it is clear that the original Gog apocalypse must certainly have lain before the eyes of this redactor, for vv 23ff. do not in themselves constitute a significant composition in their own right.

Nevertheless, it is also clear that this redactor's interest has shifted entirely away from the dominant theme of the apocalypse, which is Yahweh's victory following Gog's attack on those who will have already returned from exile. He calls attention away from the question of restoration to Israel's eventual peril before the looming cosmic forces and back to the question of Israel's well-deserved suffering in the exile. This had indeed been the main problem of the prophet Ezekiel and of the exiles who were with him in Chaldea, but the memory and the shame of it certainly would have remained vivid after the return, motivating this first redactor's grandiose theological apologia for the divine purpose in the midst of it all. The reason why this expansion must have been the first is that it does not indulge in cosmic speculations as the other expansions do but interprets the initial apocalypse in terms of the kerygmatic purpose of Ezekiel's original ministry to the unrepentant and the disconsolate. Thus this earliest redactional expansion provides a *terminus ad quem* for the original apocalypse, which must date to the (late) exile because the expansion reflects an initial phase of the return from that exile. (For further remarks about this pericope's place within the overall redaction of the book, see in Chapter Eleven.)

3. The integral transition at 38:8

One may now appreciate why we have reserved for final discussion the very first temporal transition to be encountered within the pericope, Ezekiel 38–39. This is the unparalleled *bĕ'aḥărît haššānîm* in 38:8. Although the content of this verse is not poetic in form, there is a vestige of parallelism in the opening clause: *miyyāmîm rabbîm tiqqāpēd bĕ'aḥărît haššānîm tābō' 'el 'ereṣ mĕqub-*

beṣet mēʿammîm rabbîm, "After many days/years, you will be mustered; at the end of years you will come against a/the land collected out of many peoples." There is designed chiasmus and alliteration in the counterpoised phrases *miyyāmîm rabbîm* and *mēʿammîm rabbîm.* Elsewhere in the Old Testament *miyyāmîm rabbîm* refers to the past only, designating a significantly large, but undetermined or unspecified, number of days (= years); cf. Josh 23:1l; Judg 11:4, 14:8, 15:1; 2 Chr 21:19. This solitary futurist occurrence of the phrase has to be at least a partial parallel to the following *bĕʾaḥărît haššānîm,* which is certainly not the equivalent of *bĕʾaḥărît hayyāmîm* in v 16. As has been suggested, the latter term refers to the time when a given prediction comes true, as in Jer 23:20. The formulation with *haššānîm* in 38:8, on the contrary, reflects the apocalyptic speculation that arises when many "days" of waiting become many long years (cf. *šānâ* in parallel with *yôm* in Isa 61:2). Fully developed apocalypticism, as in Daniel 9, readily speaks of years, or even "weeks" of years, to come. A rationale for this lies perhaps in the statement of Jub 4:30, "One thousand years are as one day in the testimony of the heavens" (cf. Ps 90:4; Ep. Barn 15; 2 En 33; 2 Pet 3:8).

In any event, it is certain that Ezek 38:8 is speaking of an indefinitely long period, ostensibly separating Yahweh's preparing of Gog from the actual invasion, but in actuality creating a temporal separation from that event on the part of the quasi-prophet who repeats these words as words from Yahweh. We should pay special attention not only to the parallel phrases "many days" and "many peoples," but also to the distinction between Gog's mustering (*pqd* niph.) and Israel's regathering (*qbṣ,* ptcp).

We have identified the passages where a futuristic formula marks the transition from one event to another event within the remote future, but here a futuristic integral transition involves a move from the remote future of the regathering of the exiles (already dwelling securely once again in the land of Israel) to the still more remote future of Gog's invasion.

It is significant that this transition has been made in the original apocalypse. It is not the contrivance of a subsequent redactor wishing to extend the future event of the primary material. What is involved is an entirely new and distinct way of thinking about future time. The event announced in this passage presupposes that a remotely future event, the return from the exile, is already past. This contrived conception is very far removed from the imminentistic eschatology of the prophet Ezekiel. His own futuristic preaching had an immediately pragmatic concern: either to warn sinners to repent, or to comfort those already under judgment and in danger of giving way to despair. But Ezek 38:8 places future events into distinct eons separate from each other, thus charting out Yahweh's plan for an end-time beyond exile and return.

This is what has made Zimmerli quite certain that the Gog apocalypse could not have come from Ezekiel or his immediate school. In his discussion of this passage he remarks (BKAT XIII/2, p. 945):

> Ist es im Rahmen der Verkündigung Ezechiels, die in ihren übrigen Worten sehr deutlich immer auf ein Nächstes weist, denkbar, dass der Prophet nun auch einmal auf ein Nachnächstes, d.h., einen zweiten Schritt göttlichen Handelns über den zunächts zu erwartenden ersten (die Sammlung der Zerstreuten) hinaus deutet. Es geschiet darin ohne Zweifel etwas Neuartiges. Ein erster Schritt auf dem wege zur Apokalyptik, die es unternimmt, eine Folgeordnung kommender Ereignisse aufzustellen, ist darin getan.[25]

4. Conclusion

Most scholars share the opinion that the Gog apocalypse is non-Ezekielian. The earliest expansion in 39:23-29 creates an early postexilic *terminus ad quem*, but what can be said about a *terminus a quo?* Theoretically, the date of the original composition could be late exilic or early postexilic, but its self-conscious replication of traditional prophetic formulations leads one to conclude that it must have been composed at a time when the strong influence of Ezekiel still held sway, and this certainly would have been more dominant among those who were yet in exile than it would have been among those who eventually returned.

The Gog apocalypse is not at all similar in conception to the temple vision of chaps. 40ff. It certainly is not dominated by temple ideology or by ritual concerns, but rather by the authentically prophetic themes of an inviolable Zion, the holy war, and the day of Yahweh. It shares these with other proto-apocalypses, such as those in Isaiah 24–27, Joel 4, and Zechariah 12–14. It is the priestly side of Ezekiel that has been developed in chaps. 40–48, but here in chaps. 38–39 it is his truly prophetic side that has been given further expression. The fact that these two opposing interests appear together in apocalyptic additions to the same prophetic book is clear indication that apocalypticism as an ideology proved to be useful, if not entirely congenial, to each of them.[26]

CHAPTER NINE

The Preexilic Minor Prophets

Primary transitions	Redactional transitions
1. Integral	
Hos 2:12 (E 10)	*wĕʿattâ*
3:5	*ʾaḥar*
5:7	*ʿattâ*
7:2	*ʿattâ*
13:2	*wĕʿattâ*
Amos 4:2	*kî hinnēh yāmîm bāʾîm*
6:7	*lākēn ʿattâ*
7:16	*wĕʿattâ šĕma dĕbar YHWH*
Mic 3:4	*ʾāz*
4:9	*ʿattâ*
4:10	*kî ʿattâ*
4:11	*wĕʿattâ*
4:14 (E 5:1)	*ʿattâ*
Hab 1:11	*ʾāz*
Nah 1:13	*wĕʿattâ*
Zeph 3:11	*kî ʾāz*[a]
2. Introductory	
Hos 1:5	*wĕhāyâ bayyôm hahûʾ* (prose addition)
2:18 (E 16)	*wĕhāyâ bayyôm hahûʾ nĕʾum YHWH* (anacrusis)
2:23 (E 21)	*wĕhāyâ bayyôm hahûʾ nĕʾum YHWH*[b] (anacrusis)
Joel 3:1 (E 2:28)	*wĕhāyâ ʾaḥărê-kēn* (anacrusis)
4:1 (E 3:1)	*kî hinnēh bayyāmîm hahēm ûbāʿēt hahîʾ* (prose addition)
4:18 (E 3:18)	*wĕhāyâ bayyôm hahûʾ* (anacrusis)

Amos 8:9	*wĕhāyâ bayyôm hahû' nĕ'um YHWH*[c] (anacrusis)
8:11	*hinnēh yāmîm bā'îm nĕ'um YHWH*[c] (anacrusis)
8:13	*bayyôm hahû'* (anacrusis)
9:11	*bayyôm hahû'* (anacrusis)
9:13	*hinnēh yāmîm bā'îm nĕ'um YHWH* (anacrusis)
Mic 2:4	*bayyôm hahû' yiśśā' 'ălêkem māšāl* . . . (liturgical rubric)
4:1[d]	*wĕhāyâ bĕ'ahărît hayyāmîm* (anacrusis)
4:6	*bayyôm hahû' nĕ'um YHWH* (anacrusis)
5:9 (E 10)	*wĕhāyâ bayyôm hahû' nĕ'um YHWH* (anacrusis)
Zeph 1:10	*wĕhāyâ bayyôm hahû' nĕ'um YHWH* (anacrusis)
1:12	*wĕhāyâ*[e] *bayyôm hahû'*[e] (anacrusis)
3:9	*kî 'āz* (anacrusis)[f]
3:11	*bayyôm hahû'* (anacrusis)
3:16	*bayyôm hahû' yē'āmēr lĕ'* . . . (liturgical rubric)
3:20	*bā'ēt hahî'* (prose addition)

a. Cf. introductory *kî 'āz* (v 9)
b. MT inserts gloss *'e'ĕneh;* GSyr om.
c. GSyr; MT *'ădōnāy YHWH*
d. Par Isa 2:2
e-e. G; MT *bā'ēt hahî'*
f. Cf. integral *kî 'āz,* v 11 (redactional)

Hosea

1. Redaction and ideology in Hosea

Although Amos is earlier than Hosea, we take up Hosea first because of its position in the canonical sequence. Within the prophetic collection, Hosea is very special in that it represents our sole surviving prophetic document from northern Israel. This makes it especially precious in that it is one of our few sparse witnesses to the dialect, political ideology, and theology of the northern realm. That it derives from northern Israel accounts for the relatively poor state of preservation of the original text. After the collapse of the northern kingdom, which Hosea forecast, an earlier form of his book must have been brought to the temple in Jerusalem and been put in the hands of the Judean scribes, who made minor alterations and added glosses of their own. During the century and a half from 722 to 586, this served as a sourcebook of early Yahwistic prophecy, which was now seen as a warning concerning the apostasy of the Judahites and a forecast of the looming menace of the Neo-Babylonians.

The instrument of judgment for Hosea was to be triumphant Assyria, whose kings made a series of incursions into Palestine during the last twenty years of the existence of the kingdom of Israel (742-722). As Hosea saw it, political irresponsibility on the part of a succession of inept kings went hand in hand with the nation's spiritual bankruptcy as a cause for imminent doom. The bond between Yahweh and this people had been shattered, for they would not withdraw from their infatuation with the emblems and rites of Baalism. It was Hosea who first developed the theme of Israel as a wayward wife (cf. also Jeremiah 2–3, Ezekiel 16 and 23), and this theme dominates his book.[1]

Apart from evidences of minor mishandling and ideological alteration on the part of Judean scribes, the book of Hosea as we have it is essentially from the prophet himself,[2] but it shows also a pre-Jerusalemite redaction in at least three stages, dating from the closing decades of the eighth century B.C.E. We must distinguish between the disciple who composed the biographical account in 1:2-9 and an early redactor who composed 2:1-3, 18-25 (E 1:10–2:1, 16-23) in an effort to balance words of doom with words of salvation. It is probable that the poem about the wayward wife in 2:4-17 (E 2:2-15) and the prose report of 3:1-5 (without the glosses, *wĕ'ēt dāwîd malkām* and *bĕ'aḥărît hayyāmîm*) refer to the same woman and were composed by Hosea himself. 1:5 is the work of still another pre-Jerusalemite redactor, probably from the late eighth century.

Our foregoing analysis has attributed the temporal transitions in 2:12 (E 10), 3:5, 5:7, 7:2, and 13:2 to Hosea, and those of 2:18, 23 (E 16, 21) to the earliest levels of redaction. All of Hosea's own transitions are integral, while all the redactional transitions, including that of 1:5, are introductory.

2. Integral transitions

We see that *(wĕ)'attâ* is Hosea's own main choice as a temporal formula for providing a transition to his predictions of present and imminent judgment. As elsewhere, it is always integral. The styling found in the oracular collection (chaps. 4–14) is the same as that of 2:12 (E 10).

In 2:12 the move is from the past (with consequences in the present) to the present time of Gomer's waywardness, described in vv 7-10 (E 5-8), then on to the present and imminent future of her punishment (vv 12-15 [E 10-13]); this leads eventually to the proximately future restoration promised in vv 16-17 (E 14-15).

In 5:7 the move is from the past-present of Ephraim/Israel's apostasy (vv 3-7a) to an imminent scourge, scheduled to occur at an appearance of the new moon (the event of v 6 precedes, coincides with, or follows this scourge).

In 7:2, all action is within an ongoing present that includes Yahweh's past, present, and potentially future acts, as identified in the circumstantial clauses (6:11b–7:1aα), "when I would restore the fortunes of my people Israel," and "when I would heal Israel." Yahweh makes an investigation (7:1aβ-2) and finds the deplorable fact that "now their deeds encompass them, they are before my face" — which is to say that Ephraim is overwhelmed by a guilt that brings it directly into judgment before Yahweh.

In 13:2 there is movement from a past of honor and guilt for Ephraim (v 1) to the present of continual idolatry (v 2); then to an imminent future of characterless insubstantiality (mist, dew, chaff, and smoke).

Judging from the regularity with which Hosea uses *(wĕ)ʿattâ* to mark the transition from a past of divine forbearance and human guilt to a present of divine judgment, the prophet's own "eschatology" (if we may call it that) consisted of the prognostication of ineluctable calamity for the chosen people. The only modification to this pattern is seen in the hopeful prediction of 3:5, employing the unparalleled futuristic transition *ʾaḥar*. Though many scholars have been suspicious of the authenticity of 3:1-5, there is no persuasive reason for denying the original words in this passage to the prophet. He certainly did write parallel words of hope in 2:16-17 (E 14-15). But, as has previously been argued, v 4 must reflect a time in Hosea's life when he had already witnessed the beginnings of political and spiritual devastation, to be followed, according to his own expectation, by a future repentance and restoration (v 5). Hence an actual present masquerading as future is transmuted into a true future; which is to say that v 4 is an isolated instance of a *vaticinium ex eventu,* on which an actual prediction is subsequently based.

3. Introductory transitions

The inauthentic passages that expand authentic materials in Hosea are all found within the Gomer complex. They are all introduced by the transition formula *wĕhāyâ bayyôm hahûʾ,* but they are not all by the same redactor. In 2:18, 23 (E 16, 21) this formula stands in poetic anacrusis, while in 1:5 it is part of a prose expansion. This accords with the fact that a close disciple must have written the expansions in chap. 2 — possibly paraphrasing later utterances of Hosea himself — while 1:5 is the work of a more remote redactor. Poetry has thus been expanded as poetry, and prose as prose. Although each passage creates a move from one event to another within the proximate future, the transitions in chap. 2 extend the imagery of the underlying material, adding salvation themes that are implicit in this material, while 1:5 ignores the underlying family imagery and simply adds one historical allusion to another; that is, it exchanges a geographical reference to "Jezreel" for one that is political and military.

4. The oracle formula

We note, finally, that the oracle formula *ně'um YHWH* appears in 2:18 and 23, but not in 1:5. As an historical note, added for completeness, 1:5 did not require revelational validation, but this was absolutely essential in 2:18-23 and 23-25 as equally authoritative revelations of Yahweh's beneficent purpose. It seems reasonable to suggest that Hosea's own sentiment lay behind each of these affirmations.

5. Conclusion

This brief scrutiny of the work of one of the very first writing prophets already brings to light some of the distinctions that will become important in our further inquiry. The man Hosea occasionally introduced temporal transitions for the purpose of connecting Israel's sinful act to its consequent judgment (2:12 [E 10], 5:7, 7:2, 13:2) or of predicting an act of divine grace following judgment (3:5). The work of three redactors employing introductory rather than integral temporal transitions may be seen in the "biographical' section, chaps. 1–3. There was first a disciple who composed the prose account of 1:2-9. He did not employ temporal transitions, but a redactor from late in the seventh century did interject his own special interpretation of the Jezreel naming at 1:5, employing a synchronizing *wěhāyâ bayyom hahû'*. Chronologically in between these two additions, very probably in close temporal proximity with the first, is the work of the disciple-redactor who expanded the faithless wife poem of chap. 2 in terms of Yahweh's eventual intention, employing the transition *wěhāyâ bayyom hahû'* (2:18, 23 [E 16, 21]) to introduce scenes of bliss following on Gomer's eventual restoration. It cannot be gainsaid that the expansion in 1:5 is trivial while those of chap. 2 are momentous in their respective reinterpretations of Yahweh's purpose. Nevertheless, they all assume that the Deity may change his attitude toward Israel. For the redactor of chap. 2, this is posited on a prior repentance on the part of the guilty — an authentic biblical theme. For the later redactor of 1:5, on the contrary, the shift is arbitrary and unmotivated.

Amos

1. Redaction and ideology in Amos

Although Amos is like Hosea in addressing the northern kingdom, the two differ in several important respects. One difference is that Amos is a few decades earlier and makes no direct reference to the looming Assyrian menace.[3] Another difference is that, while Amos did the prophesying recorded in his book in northern Israel, his words were put in writing, either by himself or by disciples, after he had been expelled by Amaziah (7:10-17) and had returned to his native Judah, which means that Amos is in actuality a Judahite book.

This accounts for the well-preserved condition of this book, as compared with the book of Hosea. It is certain, all the same, that Amos's book was composed in stages from several early collections of material. The very earliest element must have been the Amaziah narrative in 7:10ff. There was also a very early collection of vision reports (7:1-9, 8:1-3, 9:1), an early (chaps. 3–6) and a later (8:4-8, 9:2-9) collection of disconnected oracles, and in addition the subsequently expanded collection of foreign oracles in 1:3–2:5 leading into the oracle against (northern) Israel in 2:6-16. Added to these early collections are a number of comparatively late expansions in 8:9-14 and 9:11-15, each having introductory temporal transitions to independent predictions.

A much-discussed problem is that of the causes leading to the earliest recording of Israelite prophecy with the appearance of this book. One idea has been that the actual occurrence of an earthquake, as predicted in 9:1, confirmed Amos as a true spokesman from Yahweh (cf. Zech 14:5), making all his words worth preserving.

A more probable explanation is based upon the prophet's experience of rejection, recorded in 7:10-15 along with the grim oracle that he spoke against the agent of that rejection (vv 16-17), which, once written down, would have stimulated an effort to record all of Amos's words. The four (7:1-3, 4-6, 7-9, 8:1-3) or five (including 9:1) vision oracles were then put in writing, perhaps by Amos himself. A disciple who evidently misunderstood the term "house of Jeroboam" in 7:9 (which, judging from poetic parallelism, actually referred to the Bethel sanctuary) inserted the Amaziah report at 7:10-17. Soon thereafter the authentic oracular collections were added, and eventually also the redactional collections at the end. Because no authentic Amos oracle has been preserved from the time of his return to Judah, we would assume that the original material in chaps. 8–9 was soon added to this corpus. The remaining material in these chapters was gradually appended during the latter decades of the eighth century and down to the early exilic period. (On the redactional procedures involved, see further in Chapter Eleven.)

We have reason to view the bulk of Amos's book, accordingly, as the work of the prophet in close collaboration with his early disciples, whoever they may have been. Amos's preaching was focused sharply on those offenses that caused him great alarm regarding the eventual survival of the northern kingdom, most particularly the social wrongs and symptoms of spiritual indifference that he encountered on his foray into the territories of that kingdom. Although he still saw the possibility of escape from the disasters he foretold (cf. 5:4-6, 14-15, 24), this was posited on the apparently unlikely reforms that he demanded. Certainly Amos never witnessed any such reforms, but only the political and military calamities that brought the end of the northern kingdom. His own immediate disciples could not influence him to utter additional predictions of salvation to offset the despair, similar to those added by the early disciples of Hosea.

Discussions of Amos's eschatology[4] have naturally concentrated on his famous woe-oracle in 5:18-20 concerning the frightening *yôm-YHWH,* "day of Yahweh." It is all but certain that this passage has inspired other day-of-Yahweh oracles in Isa 2:12-17, Zeph 1:7-18, and elsewhere. It is important that we should recognize not only that the Amos passage has had a profound influence, but also that its theme is central to Amos's preaching; and furthermore that the concept was already well established within his own tradition. He felt compelled to challenge a popular misconception of what Yahweh's coming "day" would be. It had apparently been widely believed, at least in the northern realm, that the events of history were tending toward one special day when Yahweh would act finally and decisively, but this notion was cherished because its effect would be to comfort and vindicate the abused Israelites, suffering from foreign aggression. But for Amos, Yahweh would not consent to serve solely as the instrument of Israel's pious hopes because they had ceased being submissive to him, bringing upon themselves the same wrath that they imagined only the nations outside Israel deserved.

Thus the day of Yahweh was to bring darkness for the wayward Israelites and not light (cf. 8:9-10). It would frighten them, surprise them with its ferocity and unpredictability, and destroy them. This is what gave all of Amos's preaching such urgency and marked him as a prophet of relentless and unrelieved calamity. Amos was so appalled by the breakdown of religion and morality among the chosen people that he was certain that even Israel's special status with Yahweh would not protect them on this looming day of retribution (cf. 3:1-2, 9:7-8).

We should consider the futuristic transitions in Amos against this ideological background. From our awareness of the inventory of temporal formulas used in the prophetic literature in general, we are able to weigh the significance of the ways they are used in this, the earliest book in the entire collection. Once again we find a striking difference between those transitions that are integral and those that are introductory. Although Amos uses *bayyôm hahû'* in epitomes at 2:16 and 8:3,[5] he never uses this expression as an integral transition. The expressions that he does employ, however, are anything but formulaic or stereotyped. As he uses them, they are fresh and natural, organically embedded in the pericopes to which they belong. On the contrary, the introductory transitions, which are redactional here as elsewhere, are markedly stereotyped, both in form and in function.

2. Integral transitions

4:1-3 is a pithy and vivid judgment oracle typical of Amos. He is generally fond of the element of surprise — the dimension of the transcendent, interjected where it is the least expected — and so it is here. In a summons to hear, the addressees are given a mocking and ironic title, "cows of Bashan," and are then accused of specific sins in parallel with circumstantial clauses (v 1). The announcement or threat that follows is introduced as an oath sworn by Yahweh against them, defining an altogether unexpected future looming just over the horizon of their present. This imminent future is to bring a drastic reversal of fortunes in the form of the shocking and humiliating experience of being put in bonds and then taken into exile. The syntax here has the deictic declarative *hinnēh yāmîm bā'îm*, followed by verbs of action. As we have seen, this is a formula that Amos shares exclusively with the deuteronomistic historian and the redactors of Jeremiah, with the remarkable difference that this passage lacks the following oracle formula *ně'um YHWH* that appears in the redactional expansions to Amos at 8:11 and 9:13 and regularly in Jeremiah. As in Jer 30:3, it follows the particle *kî*. Amos is more fresh and natural than are his redactors and the redactors of Jeremiah in the use of this transition.

Amos 6:4-7 is closely parallel, thematically as well as terminologically, to 4:1-3. In this case those addressed are masculine; they are held to be guilty of idleness and indifference rather than of the intentional oppressiveness that is mentioned in 4:1-3. The integral transition is a combination of *lākēn* with *'attâ*, found only here. Elsewhere in Amos *lākēn* functions as a common transition between the element of the accusation (invective) and the announcement (threat), but it seems strange that *'attâ* should directly follow it. With *lākēn* standing before it, this formula certainly has to be temporal rather than situational; and this means that the going into exile that results from the past/present sin of easeful indifference also lies in the present, stretching into the imminent future.[6] This rather strange way of speaking well expresses a sense of compelling urgency. As the past slips into the present, and the present into the future, sin leads directly to guilt, and guilt leads imperceptibly into punishment.

The third integral temporal transition in Amos, at 7:16, shares with 4:2 and 6:7 a rare power and freshness, for *wě'attâ* combined with the summons to hear, *šěma děbar-YHWH*, is like the formulation in 1 Sam 15:1 in connecting a foregoing identification of the source of prophetic authority with a particular exercise of that authority. The command to hear his words of denunciation follows sequentially from Amos's apologia, which means that as he begins to speak, he speaks not his own words, but Yahweh's. (See our concluding interpretation of this pericope in Chapter Thirteen.)

These three passages bring Amos's own "eschatology" to expression. In 4:2-3 and 6:7, the event that is imminent is punishment on Israel, and in 7:16-17abα it is the punishment on Amaziah and his household, implying as well punishment upon Israel (17bβ). The first two transitions belong to woe-oracles against the oppressive upper classes, while the third is in a private oracle directed against an errant representative of institutional power, as in 1 Sam 15:1ff. Upon each group, Yahweh's judgment will be sudden and soon.

3. Introductory transitions

This brings us to Amos's introductory transitions. Elsewhere these belong to secondary additions, and so here. They appear in two clusters toward (8:9-10, 11-12, and 13-14) and at the end (9:11-12, 13-15) of the book. Having given special attention to Amos's original, integral temporal transitions, we are in a position to witness an important difference in the fact that 4:2f., 6:7, and 7:16f. all predict an imminent deportation for errant groups or individuals within Israel, while these secondary materials all predict a state of being affecting all Israel, or representative groups within Israel, that is to result from (8:9f., 11f., 13f.) or modify (9:11f., 13ff.) Yahweh's bitter day of judgment. In 8:9f., this is a state of cosmic darkness and universal mourning; in 8:11f., it is a famine of Yahweh's word and a frantic search for it; in 8:13f., it is thirst for those who have trusted false gods. On the contrary, in 9:11f. it is a raising up of "David's booth," leading to Israel's domination over Edom and other nations, while in 9:13-15 it is a paradisaical fruitfulness similar to that predicted in Joel 4:18 (E 3:18).

Three passages within these two series have a transitional *(wĕhāyâ) bayyôm hahû'*, while the other two have transitional *hinnēh yāmîm bāʾîm* followed by the oracle formula. It could be argued that the predictions of a single day place emphasis upon an initiatory event that leads to a new condition (darkness, thirst, raising up), while those that announce a period of days contemplate an enduring state or condition as such (famine, fruitfulness, restoration, rebuilding, replanting). But the point about entering into a decisive new state of being is quite relevant. To Amos's redactors, it is the lasting consequences of judgment rather than the judgment itself, as experienced in historic events, that are predicted.

In our foregoing discussion we arrived at some clarity with regard to the literary relationships between these five additions and their respective contexts and among one another.[7] Although the theme of famine in 8:1ff. may have been suggested by the cessation of feasting mentioned in vv 9f., there is no direct dependence of the one image upon the other. The famine theme may have suggested that of thirst in vv 13-14, but again there is no clear dependence. Thus we cannot speak of a cumulative epexegesis here similar to that in Isa 19:16-25. All the same, they all speak of the direct effects of divine judgment (chap. 8) or salvation (chap. 9), and must be attributed, with some differentiation, to the school of Amos as it existed in the preexilic period. The reference to Beer-sheba in 8:14 shows a Judahite refocusing, yet it is clear from the parallel mention of Samaria and Dan that the fate of northern Israel is still the main concern. That the three pericopes of chap. 8 are grouped together is also significant. Precisely why they have been inserted just here in the middle of original material is not clear, unless the reason be that 9:1-10 (probably without the doxology in vv 5-6), collected together because of the theme of shaking, was added after 8:9-14 had already been attached. On the other hand, it is entirely certain that the two early exilic salvation sections, 9:11-12 and 13-15, were placed where they are because 9:10 represented the end of Amos's book at the conclusion of the preexilic period.

Although the redactional process by which these five additions became part of the text was essentially atomistic, it is important to see that, on the one hand, those with a judgment theme have been kept separate from those with a salvation theme, while, on the other hand, these two groupings have influenced each other in the choice of temporal formulas. Thus *bayyôm hahû'* in anacrusis introduces both a judgment pericope (8:13-14) and a salvation pericope (9:11-12). *Hinnēh yāmîm bā'îm,* in both instances with a stereotyped *nĕ'um YHWH,* introduces both a judgment pericope (8:11-12) and a salvation pericope (9:13-15). Such set expressions do not directly date a given pericope, yet this adherence to distinct speech patterns does suggest the existence of a late "Amos school" with at least some linguistic cohesion.

More than anything else, the choice of the temporal formula *hinnēh yāmîm bā'îm,* followed by the oracle formula, suggests an influence on Jeremiah, or from Jeremiah, because this occurs so often in that book and nowhere else in the prophetic literature (cf. Jer 9:24 [E 25], 23:5 par 33:14, 30:3, 31:27, 31, 38; preceded by *lākēn,* 7:31 par 19:6, 16:14 par 23:7, 48:12, 49:2, 51:47, 52). Everywhere in Jeremiah but in 51:47 this temporal formula is followed by *nĕ'um YHWH.*

It is generally possible to show some special purpose for adding this formula; and it is conceivable that Amos's redactors intended some special stress on revelational authority in 8:11 and 9:13, as well as in 8:9, where the oracle formula follows *wĕhāyâ bayyôm hahû'.* On the other hand, we recall that *hinnēh yāmîm bā'îm* occurs without *nĕ'um YHWH* in deuteronomistic materials at 1 Sam 2:31 and 2 Kgs 20:17 par Isa 39:6. These are in prophetic discourse within the structures of individual narratives, having in these instances no apparent intent to emphasize the speakers' authority. In contrast, it does seem that the occurrences in Amos and in Jeremiah are approaching a stereotype.

In any event, a triangular influence between the redaction of Amos, the deuteronomistic redaction, and the Jeremianic redaction is made quite certain by these linguistic affinities. In Amos, deuteronomic/deuteronomistic influence may also be seen in the theme of a vain search for Yahweh's word (8:11f.; cf. Deut 30:11-14), in the polemic against idol worship (8:14; cf. Deut 4:25-28), and in the reference to the land of Israel as a gift of Yahweh (9:15; cf. Deut 12:1). On the other hand, the ideology of the early Jeremianic redaction is reflected in Amos 9:15's mention of the replanting of Israel after it will have been plucked up (cf. Jer 31:28).

A final word may be added regarding the fact that in these additions to the earliest prophetic book, Amos, the temporal formula occurs regularly in anacrusis to poetry and not as part of a prose addition, which is general in the later books.[8] We have recorded 8:11f. as poetic, but the identification is uncertain; it has parallelism, but the meter is irregular. The remaining four pericopes are definitely poetic. In Isaiah and Jeremiah, poetic additions with temporal formulas in anacrusis were either composed relatively early or they existed in preceding oral tradition. In these examples from Amos it is by no means clear that preexisting poetic structures are being reproduced. Since 8:9f. does replicate a major theme of Amos's authentic prophecies, it is conceivable that an early redactor reproduced in metrical parallelism what he remembered from the prophet's preaching; but it is equally possible that this person felt very much akin to the prophet and was endeavoring to reproduce the form of Amos's preaching as well as its ideational content.

In any event, it is important to note that Amos's redactors preferred the poetic form, which makes them distinctive in comparison with the redactors of most other prophetic books. Every book that has a temporal formula in anacrusis except Joel[9] is preexilic, whereas postexilic additions introduced by a temporal formula are almost always in prose.[10]

4. Conclusion

Certain important features of the composition and redaction of Amos have been illuminated by our study of temporal transitions. Those found in the prophet's own oracles (at 4:2, 6:7, 6:17) are integral to their context and are fresh and natural in their styling. Each passage predicts imminent calamities for the unrepentant. The addressees are certain wayward groups or individuals within Israel whose doom foreshadows that of the entire nation.

On the contrary, the employment of temporal formulas in the two redactional series at 8:9ff. and 9:11ff. approaches a stereotype of form paralleling a notable monotony of theme. Here it is the nation, without distinction, that is consigned to judgment or promised a paradisaical bliss. Still, the three pericopes of 8:9-10, 11-12, and 13-14 refurbish recognizable themes from the authentic preaching of the prophet. It is 9:11-12 and 9:13-15 that introduce themes for which there is no direct parallel in the authentic sections of the book, the first being the rebuilding of Jerusalem and the conversion of foreign nations, the second being the motif of prolific nature. The appendages in chap. 8 served a disciple of Amos, possibly during the prophet's lifetime, to round off the preserved records of Amos's preaching in the form of a permanent record. Those of chap. 9 bear witness to the fact that soon after the destruction of the "booth of David" there were others who gave the book a one hundred-eighty degree spin, reinterpreting Amos's grim prophecies in terms of Yahweh's more ultimate purpose to save, now in application to Jerusalem rather than to Samaria.

Both in the employment of *hinnēh yāmim bā'îm* and in that of *nĕ'um YHWH,* we have discovered a close formulaic connection between the deuteronomistic redaction, the redaction of Jeremiah, and the redaction of Amos. The affinity with the deuteronomistic school should come as no surprise, but that with the Jeremian redaction is rather striking. The fact that the occurrence of introductory temporal transitions in Amos stand in anacrusis to poetry and introduce poetry, whereas such transitions in Jeremiah introduce prose, may be a decisive clue that the direction of influence was from Amos toward the deuteronomistic history and then to the redaction of Jeremiah.

Micah

1. Redaction and ideology in Micah

The book of Micah has a variety of secondary expansions, but virtually all of these appear in a second, clearly demarcated section comprising chaps. 4–7. In this book as in most others, several of such expansions have been introduced redactionally by a temporal transition, the most noteworthy being the distinctive *wĕhāyâ bĕ'ahărît hayyāmîm* in 4:1. As we have seen, Mic 4:1-4 is a virtual word-for-word parallel to Isa 2:2-4. These two passages are poetic in form and have the transition formula in anacrusis, which strongly suggests that it was an editorial element already attached to the poetic material in the *Vorlage* for both versions. The two passages are definitely postexilic, in spite of some disclaimers. The final Micah redactor who juxtaposed chaps. 4–7 with chaps. 1–3 certainly considered 4:1-4, with attachments already present in vv 5 and 6-7, an appropriate vehicle for extending chaps. 1–3, making the temporal formula a transition not only to 4:1-7 but to the entire section, chaps. 4–7.

From a redactional point of view, Micah is different from Amos and similar to Hosea in inserting expansions with temporal transitions into the body of the book, rather than at the very end. It differs from Hosea in inserting some of these expansions into a section of the book that is itself an expansion.

Scholars are in general agreement about the historical background of Micah 1–3, but not about that of chaps. 4–7. The original material in chaps. 1–3 constitutes an initial collection of oracles, with incidental glosses, from the prophet, Micah of Moresheth. These oracles were occasioned mainly by the presence of Sennacherib's troops in the Shephelah region during the Assyrian invasion of 701 B.C.E. In 3:9-12 Micah extended his gloomy predictions to the fate of Jerusalem itself. Although this city did not at that precise time become a "heap of ruins" and a "wooded height," as Micah said (for Jerusalem was not destroyed by Sennacherib), Micah's boldness in predicting calamity even on the holy city was remembered well enough later on to be cited in Jer 26:18-19 as a premier example of prophetic authority and inviolability.

2. Transitions within the initial collection, chaps. 1–3

Micah 1–3 has two passages with a futuristic formula of transition, one secondary and the other original, at 2:4 and 3:4, respectively. Most scholars take 2:4-5 as an authentic continuation of the woe-oracle in vv 1-3, and assume that initial *bayyôm hahû'* in 2:4 is nothing but a stylistic alternative to the *'ēt rā'â* mentioned in the final clause of the judgment announcement at v 3. Although v 4 may express Micah's sentiments, two considerations make the assumption of originality highly unlikely. The first is that Micah's prophecies of judgment are elsewhere tightly structured, with *lākēn* as a stereotyped linking element between the accusation (invective) and announcement (threat); cf. in 1:13-14, 3:5-7, 9-12.[11] Elsewhere in the prophetic literature where this genre is found, *lākēn* is used in a similar way.[12] Where there are additional elements beginning with *lākēn,* these must be suspected of being secondary, and this is almost certainly the case with Mic 2:5. This verse, introduced by a second *lākēn* within the same context, is not an *ad hoc* gloss as has been suggested; but, on the other hand, it cannot be taken as an original part of the woe-oracle. The only remaining alternative is that it belongs with v 4.

A second consideration arises out of our present study. One has to be suspicious when *bayyôm hahû'* appears to explicate another expression of time, for in the few passages where it is brought into direct proximity in this fashion, it has either proven to be part of a secondary expansion, or it represents an element of a special redactional device.

The first is true in Jer 30:8, where it interprets *hayyôm hahû'* and *'et ṣārâ* in the preceding verse; in Zeph 3:11, where it explicates an event introduced by *kî 'āz* in v 9; and in Zech 3:10, where it explicates *yôm 'eḥād* in the verse before it. In each of these passages, independent considerations have confirmed redactional supplementation.

The second situation is true in Zeph 1:7-12, where a redactor (possibly Zephaniah himself) has supplied *wĕhāyâ bĕyôm zebaḥ YHWH* in v 8, *wĕhāyâ bayyôm hahû'* in v 10, and another *wĕhāyâ bayyôm hahû'* in v 12 (LXX). All three temporal phrases are in positions of anacrusis before independent poetic Yahweh sayings.[13] In addition, there are the introductory cluster appearances that were previously studied, but these are, of course, all in redactional material.

Accordingly, Mic 2:4 would be quite without parallel if it actually did represent an original continuation from vv 1-3. Some explanation would have to be offered for the apparently deliberate substitution of one temporal expression for another. As we have seen, *bayyôm hahû'* and *bā'ēt hahî'* are far from being synonymous with each other, and we have never observed variation between them solely for stylistic effect in all the literature that we have examined.

We are confident in concluding that Mic 2:4-5 is redactionally separate from vv 1-3. This allows us to recognize that the phrase *kî 'ēt rā'â hî'*, in an appraising summary at v 3bβ, signalizes the intent not only of v 3 but of the entire woe-oracle (cf. the thematic *rā'* in v 1 and *rā'â* in v 3aβ).

Something else that has come out of our foregoing study may be of help at this point. We have established the existence of a form of liturgical rubric that includes the temporal expression *bayyôm hahû'*, virtually every example of which occurs in Isaiah (12:1, 4, 25:9, 26:1, 27:2; cf. Zeph 3:16). Although it is an act of praise and thanksgiving that is usually called for, the person who wrote Mic 2:5 may have been attempting something equally formal in his use of a form calling for a liturgical act of lamentation. This may have been meant to be taken metaphorically rather than as a formal directive (as may indeed have been the true intent with regard to the songs of thanksgiving in the prior list), but in any event it is a scene of liturgical response that is being imaged.[14] V 5 with its introductory *lākēn* may be seen then as introducing the private interpretation of the redactor, which he also wished his addressee(s)[15] to make with regard to the subject of the lamentation.

We shall refrain from entering into a discussion of the severely damaged text in v 4 except to remark that the question of the function and derivation of the temporal expression is not affected by problems of reading.[16] Imaginary wailers are being depicted in the act of reciting a liturgical lament that would

be at least somewhat germane to the situation of those who are addressed in
v 3. It was, however, the ones oppressed who lost their hereditary lands, and
not the oppressors, as in v 2. Because v 4 speaks to a social-economic practice[17] that almost certainly would no longer have been followed in the postexilic period, it is best to ascribe Mic 2:4-5 to a preexilic (that is, seventh-
century) redactor who felt strong kinship with the prophet Micah. *Bayyôm
hahû'* synchronizes the proximately future event of the threatened "evil time"
with the proximately future event of the lament. It is not at all certain that the
lament was mock, that is, intended as a taunt.

The time word *'āz* functions as an integral transition in Mic 3:4. Although
it serves as the virtual equivalent of *lākēn* in joining the accusation of vv 1-3
to the announcement of v 4, there must be some special reason why *lākēn*
was not chosen. Since *'āz* is not situational, it must be temporal; and this
means that there is a temporal sequence from the present oppressing to a
proximately future non-answering. This does not involve a shift from one
event to another, but from one condition or situation to another within one
temporally contiguous event.[18]

3. Transitions within the secondary collection, chaps. 4–7

Scholars generally agree that authentic Mican material is also contained in
chaps. 4–7 even though, because of the necessary late dating of 4:1ff., this
collection has to have been made in the postexilic period. It is remarkable, to
say the least, that a school loyal to the memory of the prophet Micah should
have remained intact for at least two hundred years. Jer 26:18f. serves as a
reminder that Micah's words were held in high esteem for a long time. We
have a parallel example to such long-term tenacity in Isaiah. Furthermore,
there was certainly a close collaboration between Isaiah's tradents and those
of Micah, as Isa 2:2-4's parallelism with Mic 4:1-4 reminds us.

In any event, there is authentic material in one of the passages introduced
by a temporal transition within chaps. 4–7: that in 4:8–5:3 (E 4), possibly
extending to include the clause *wĕhāyâ zeh šālôm,* "and this shall be peace,"
in 5:4 (E 5). The other passages in this section with such transitions are either
from the seventh-century redaction or from that of the postexilic period.

We have discussed Mic 4:1ff. in connection with its parallel in Isa 2:2-4,
arriving at the conclusion that both passages date from the postexilic period.
We observed that the unique transition formula *wĕhāyâ bĕ'ahărît hayyāmîm,*
previously attached in a common *Vorlage,* brings the action from the implied
present when the *Vorlage* was composed down to a remotely distant future.
What is predicted is highly idealistic and permanently ongoing: the elevating
of the temple mount above the height of every other mountain; the pilgrimage

of "many nations" for the purpose of receiving *torah* and "the word of Yahweh," going forth only here; Yahweh's universal judgeship; the re-use of weapons of war as instruments of peaceful productivity; and the resulting peaceable hospitality among all mankind. All this represents a radical and permanent change within the elemental conditions of human existence, not only for Israel but for the entire world. We observe that Mic 4:4b has a grounding clause that is absent in the Isaiah parallel: *kî pî YHWH ṣĕbā'ôt dibber,* "for the mouth of Yahweh has spoken."[19] The attachment of v 5, a variant to the exhortation of Isa 2:5, is an apologia for loyalty to Yahweh in the face of the unavoidable recalcitrance of foreigners to being converted to Yahweh in the stead of native gods.

Mic 4:6-7 is an expansion later than the material to which it is attached (vv 1-5). The reference to Yahweh's unending rule (*mē'attâ wĕ'ad-'ôlam,* "from this time hence forevermore") in v 5 explains why these additional verses were attached after the major editorial move within the book had already been completed. Besides the reference to Yahweh's kingship, elements that certainly date vv 6-7 as late postexilic are the metaphor of the exiles as "the lame" (*haṣṣolē'â;* cf. Zeph 3:19) and the technical use of *šĕ'ērît* as a stereotyped designation for the exiles as a group. *Bayyôm hahû'* is the redactional formula of transition here, as in 2:4 and 5:9 (E 10). The remote future of vv 1-4 (5) is the ostensible temporal setting of this late expansion, and it constitutes a permanent new condition or situation, as in the preceding verses, even though it is an initiatory event (the regathering) that leads into it. It is probable that this is not a true *vaticinium ex eventu,* but an idealistic prediction of renewed, more perfect restorations following upon the first.

Having put this block of postexilic materials in position at the beginning of his new collection, the redactor-editor next began to introduce Mican and non-Mican oracles from various times and on various themes. First in order was a preexilic collection comprising 4:8–5:4a (E 5a), 5:4b-8 (E 5b-9), and 5:9-14 (E 10-15). We are directly concerned with this section and not at all with the further expansions in chaps. 6–7, because those chapters contain no temporal transitions.[20] The mention of Zion in 4:7 seemed a natural place for attaching 4:9ff., commencing with another reference to Zion/Jerusalem.

Over against those scholars who give 4:8–5:4a a postexilic date, we are convinced that the reference to a Babylonian exile in 4:10 calls for a preexilic date and makes authenticity possible and even probable. Attention to the Isaiah legend in 2 Kgs 20:12-19 par Isaiah 39 concerning a visit to Hezekiah's court on the part of emissaries from what was then the dependent kingdom of Babylon helps us see what the writer may have had in mind. We previously gave that passage some attention with regard to the opening transition, *hinnēh yāmîm bā'îm,* in v 17 (6). There is no compelling reason to view that account as unhistorical, and there is no reason to claim that no one else but the author of the prophet legend (eventually also the deuteronomistic redactor) may have felt misgivings about the danger of an eventual exile to Babylon, possibly resulting from this visit. This prediction of an exile to Babylon, even while the Assyrians were dominant, occurred during Isaiah's ministry, which was also the time of Micah; and since the pericope as a whole fits best into this period, we have justification for assigning it to Micah himself.[21]

The expectation cherished in this remarkable pericope must be understood in the light of Micah's prediction of ruin for the city of Jerusalem in 3:12. Micah fully expected that the Hezekiah who had not been strong enough to prevent Sennacherib from desolating the Judean countryside would be unable to defend Jerusalem. His view was, evidently, that the Davidic dynasty was somehow at fault; hence he predicted the rise of a collateral branch, either from the Davidic house or from another lineage from the ancestral family of Jesse.

Crucial to the structure of 4:8–5:3 are the two 2ms personal pronouns (*wĕʾattâ*, "and/but as for you . . .") at 4:8 and 5:1 (E 2)[22] in address to Jerusalem and Bethlehem, respectively. Also structurally significant are the integral temporal occurrences of *ʿattâ*, "now," in 4:9, 10, 11, 14 (E 5:1), defining successive stages or aspects of the calamities that Micah foresees for the time of Sennacherib's invasion (including for a reason unknown to us an exile to Babylon, though it was governed at the time by Assyria). The stages or aspects in question are marked by the recurrent "nows" of particular perils (ineffective rule, exile, foreign attack, siege), interspersed with intimations of Yahweh's greater and counteracting design (4:10, 12).

The mention of the ruler's cheek being struck (v 14) is climactic in this section; it leads to the more ultimately climactic promise found in 5:1-3 (E 2-4). Here, too, temporal expressions, though not functioning as transitions, are crucial. An imminent future in which Bethlehem becomes a "mother" (*ʿad-ʿēt yôlēdâ yālādâ*, "until the time when she who bears will give birth")[23] is to terminate the time of Yahweh's giving the nation up to its enemies (v 2a). Once this has occurred, exiles from Israel and from Judah shall return (v 2b), while this new, true "shepherd" makes his flock secure; and through this he (either the Bethlehemite ruler or Yahweh) becomes great among the nations in the new "now" (v 3) of salvation that cancels out the old "nows" of imminent peril. Through the emergence of this rival Bethlehemite ruler, "whose origin is from of old, from ancient days" (4:14), the "former" dominion, that is, the true kingship of the daughter of Jerusalem (4:8), shall be restored, and "this shall be peace" (5:4a [E 5a]).

Unless this promise is to be seen as one grand *vaticinium ex eventu* — which it is not — this remarkable pericope (so crucial in eventual Christian ideology) is effectively illumined only by the supposition of Mican authorship. It would hardly fit any circumstance later on in the seventh or in the sixth century known to us. By it we may gain a more complete conception of Micah's "eschatology" than would otherwise be possible.[24]

It would appear that Micah changed from predicting Jerusalem's ruin (3:12) to predicting the emergence of a more worthy kingship in Jerusalem. Not only was he mistaken about his first expectation but also about the second. Nevertheless, Micah may have been validated as a canonical prophet precisely because 3:12 was eventually fulfilled in the event of 586. On the other hand, his promise for one out of Bethlehem Ephrathah was not literally fulfilled, except as it was transformed into a messianic text of prime importance both for Judaism and for Christianity.

The pericope introduced by *wĕhāyâ bayyôm hahû'* in Mic 5:9 (E 10) shows strong influence from the deuteronomic/deuteronomistic program against intrusive idolatry, and must accordingly reflect, on its part, the work of a late seventh-century redactor. It is later than 5:4b-8 (E 5b-9), promising effective action against the Assyrians and the reinvigoration of "Jacob." Probably with the Judahites in mind, vv 9-14 provides epexegesis to vv 4b-8. To counteract the triumphalist note of v 8, it introduces a Yahweh-saying threatening the destruction of the baalistic images that continued to exist in the land throughout the Assyrian period, along with the destruction of the cities and strongholds that supported them (and presumably were supported by them). Not only does this pericope offer a theme that is strange to the book as a whole; it also involves an entirely unique ideology for modifying the foregoing prediction of salvation for Israel in terms of a threat against Judah. The proximate future of this threat, guaranteed by the oracle formula after the temporal introduction, is synchronized with the proximate future of Assyria's defeat.

4. Conclusion

The book of Micah is certainly unique as a relatively short composition showing many levels of redaction. If it does anything, this again testifies to the especially high regard in which the man Micah was held over two centuries and more. His own "eschatology" as coming to expression in the integral use of transitions in 3:4 *('āz)* and in 4:9, 10, 11, 14 (variations of *'attâ*) was limited to matters of imminent concern, first Yahweh's refusal to be available to the oppressing class, and second the emergence of a new ruler in a new "now," terminating the perils of Assyrian siege. The futuristic ideology of his early redactors (2:4, 5:9) was rooted in present deficiencies and involved judgment for wayward groups or for Israel/Judah as a whole. That of his late and very late redactors (4:1, 6), on the other hand, assumed a return from exile already past and envisaged an ideal bliss for and through Jerusalem.

As has been said, Micah himself used only *'attâ* and *'āz* as temporal transitions. Like the redactors of Isaiah, the redactors of Micah employed *(wĕhāyâ) bayyôm hahû'*, like *wĕhāyâ bĕ'aḥărît hayyāmîm* in 4:1, either in anacrusis or in a formal rubric. In view of the fact that Isaiah's redactors used the same two formulas, and the first rather frequently — but almost always in prose expansions — it is noteworthy that Micah's redactors also stuck to poetry, with the temporal formula in anacrusis, for introducing such expansions. This is further evidence of a remarkable linguistic and formulaic tenacity among Micah's redactors.

In light of the fact that the prophet did not use the oracle formula, its addition to temporal formulas in the redactional verses, Mic 4:6 and 5:9 (E 10), is especially important. The seventh-century redactor who added 5:9-14 (E 10-15) was calling attention to Yahweh's anger toward the continuing idolatry of hypocritical Judahites gloating because the menacing Assyrian empire had fallen. On the contrary, the late postexilic redactor who was responsible for inserting 4:6-7 was intent on counteracting the grand universalism of 4:1-4, identifying Jerusalem as a haven for returning Jewish exiles rather than as the goal of universal pilgrimage.

It seems ironic that these two impulses run directly counter to each other. Both aspirations are emphatically claimed, by addition of the oracle formula, as God's more ultimate revelation. Nevertheless, they seem to reach out in opposite directions while expressing ideas that were of no special concern to the prophet Micah. The first expansion resists a chauvinism that misinterprets divine justice when brought to bear on foreign nations, excusing oneself of blame for unrepented sin, while the other qualifies the notion that God may intend the well-being of all mankind by re-emphasizing his special purpose with regard to his much-injured people, Israel. Each is asserted as a more ultimate expression of the divine intention. Depending on one's vantage point, each is indeed true. This only points up the need for ongoing revelation and the continuous reapplication of that revelation.

Nahum and Habakkuk

By the end of the seventh century, the Assyrian empire had been destroyed. In his great triumph at Carchemish (605), Nebuchadrezzar dealt with the Egyptians under Necho, who were attempting to come to the aid of the last Assyrian resistance. Nebuchadrezzar quickly imposed his rule over Judah, still rejoicing over its liberation from the Assyrians. The two prophets Nahum and Habakkuk carried out their respective ministries just at this crucial moment of history, the one claiming the defeat of Assyria as divine revelation, the second claiming the defeat of Judah's new masters, the Neo-Babylonians, as divine revelation. Nahum is essentially a celebration of Nineveh's downfall in 612, while Habakkuk serves as an apologia for the rise of the Neo-Babylonian empire as Yahweh's instrument for punishing the wayward Judahites under Jehoiakim (609-598), while pointing to an ensuing judgment upon those same Neo-Babylonians in an imminent future, for which the prophet was urged to wait in patient assurance (2:2-4).

Neither Nahum nor Habakkuk has been expanded literarily through the use of the kind of redactional transitions under study here. They may not have enjoyed sufficient stature within the exilic and postexilic communities to have attracted significant redactional expansions of this sort. In other words, these two prophets probably did not have personal schools of close adherents surviving over decades or centuries, as was the case with the three "Major Prophets" and the minor prophets already discussed.

Each book does contain a single integral temporal transition, however. Integral *wĕ'attâ* in Nah 1:13 moves the action from past/present affliction to a present/imminent future of the breaking of bonds. Vv 12-13 is a salvation saying placed in Yahweh's mouth and apparently (because of the 2fs address) spoken to Jerusalem; very likely it was used as a liturgical response in the temple service, celebrating the end of Assyrian domination.[25] This interpretation accords very well with this book's conception of Judah's place in history at this time of drastic change. Nahum did not foresee the looming menace of a new threat to the nation's independence and well-being in the form of the Neo-Babylonian empire; he saw only the end of Judah's affliction and rejoiced at a fleeting moment of liberation. It is understandable that this kind of "eschatology" did not invite redactional readjustment to a situation of new and far more severe affliction.

Integral *'āz* in Hab 1:11 moves the action from the present and the imminent future to a proximate future, that is, from the events of the Chaldeans' (Neo-Babylonians') ever-expanding aggressions, occurring in historical events but presented to Habakkuk in the form of a vision, on to the grim reality of their sweeping everything before them, threatening Judah's newly-won independence. The time is the reign of Jehoiakim, who has paid scant regard to obligations imposed by covenantal morality. Habakkuk's complaint is of a general perversion of justice under his misrule (1:2-4), to which Yahweh responds by calling his attention to the Chaldeans, who are to serve Yahweh in bringing punishment on Judah for these wrongs (vv 5-11). 1:11 is climactic in this vision and points to what lies directly ahead in the proximate future.[26] The Chaldeans are just now attacking their near neighbors; soon ("now") they will get around to attacking Judah. This is the proximate future that looms in the vision; nevertheless, Yahweh has his more ultimate purpose in a future that lies immediately beyond.[27]

Zephaniah

Although Zephaniah, too, is short, it differs from Nahum and Habakkuk in containing several temporal transitions that are indications of major redactional expansion. There are no primary integral temporal transitions and only one redactional transition that is integral. All other temporal transitions are introductory. Zephaniah did have a school of close disciples, some of whom remained active during the early postexilic period.

1. Temporal transitions in the original collection, 1:1–3:8

The question of Zephaniah's date is complex, but several indications seem to point to the early years of Josiah's reign (641-609) as the most likely time for the prophet's ministry. The main evidence for an early date is the references to rampant idolatry (1:4b-5) and the unruliness of Jerusalem's officials and the nobility (1:8-9). These would seem to require a time before Josiah began his sweeping reforms or established firm authority within the royal household. But alternatively, the period could be some decades later, during the time of the rise of the Neo-Babylonian empire. The book could be more confidently dated if the Scythians, rather than the Neo-Babylonians, could be identified as the foreign foe threatening Judah and giving occasion for the call to repentance in 2:1-4.[28]

Certainly the threat of invasion, whether by the Scythians or the Neo-Babylonians, was sufficiently frightening to cause Zephaniah to invoke the vivid day-of-Yahweh imagery seen in the entire first chapter, which the prophet presented as Yahweh's punishment on the leading classes in Jerusalem (1:4ff.; cf. 3:1-5). Either that the menacing Scythians had not yet appeared before Jerusalem, or that the Neo-Babylonians had not yet made their decisive move, is implied in Yahweh's command in 3:8 for the guilty in Jerusalem to wait for his action (cf. Hab 2:3).

This occurs at the very end of the original Zephaniah collection. We cannot learn from this book what did in fact happen next — the Babylonian exile. Zephaniah's postexilic school did not refer to it, but rather to spiritual transformation and material prosperity within the returned community.

In our analysis of Zeph 1:10, 12 in Chapter Three we observed that there are three temporal phrases in vv 7-13 that provide redactional links to elements of preexistent Yahweh speeches, now preserved in vv 8aβb-9,[29] vv 10-11, and vv 12-13. These phrases are *wěhāyâ běyôm zebaḥ YHWH* in v 8, *wěhāyâ bayyôm hahû'* with following *ně'um YHWH* in v 10, and an original *wěhāyâ bayyôm hahû'* (MT *wěhāyâ bā'ēt hahî'*) in v 12. These mark the earliest stage of redaction, that of collection and arrangement with proper linkage, and may have been by Zephaniah or, more probably, by a close disciple. The same person, the prophet or his disciple, was responsible also for v 7. It is important to see that these phrases stand in anacrusis, introducing poetic material already at hand. The two transitions at vv 10 and 12 create synchronisms with the temporal phrase in v 8, in effect identifying the terrifying day of Yahweh as a day of sacrificial feasting in which the addressees would represent the victims. The divine punishment on the unruly upper classes, the noise of destruction within the city, and Yahweh's search for the self-satisfied are each depicted as events in the same proximate future.

Along with other oracles against Judah-Jerusalem in 1:2-6, 14-16, 3:1-4, 6-8, Zephaniah delivered the foreign-nation oracles in 2:5-7, 8-9, 12-14. As the menacing foe approached Jerusalem, bringing near the grim day of Yahweh described in 1:14-18, Zephaniah summoned those who were humble and righteous in Judah/Jerusalem to a solemn fast in the hope that "perhaps you may be hidden on the day of the wrath of Yahweh" (2:1-4). After the danger had passed (assuming either that the invaders were the Scythians or the Neo-Babylonians after Carchemish), he may have led the people in the liturgy of thanksgiving now preserved in 3:14-15, and he may also have spoken the promise of victory found in 3:16-18aα.

During the early exile period the Moab-Ammon oracle (2:10-11) was expanded and a taunt concerning Nineveh (2:15) was composed, probably by an early disciple. At the end of the exile or during the early postexilic period, redactors expanded 3:1-4, 6-8 by adding 3:9-10, 11-13. The same redactors added Zephaniah's liturgy (3:14-15) and promise of victory (3:16ff.), and they composed 3:20 as a conclusion to the expanded book. Eventually a final editor provided a superscription and rearranged all this material into three separate sections: (1) judgment oracles against Jerusalem, (2) judgment oracles against the nations, and (3) salvation oracles and related materials. This editor kept 3:1-4, 6-8 directly attached to 2:15 because of the striking structural similarity between the taunt against Nineveh and the woe-oracle against Jerusalem.[30]

2. Temporal transitions in the secondary collection, 3:9-20

Our reconstruction of the redactional process that produced the book of Zephaniah must distinguish sharply between salvation sayings that are preexilic and those that are postexilic, even though they were apparently all added as part of the postexilic expansion. Most of this material is in poetic form. *Bayyôm hahû' yē'āmēr lîrûšālayim* is a liturgical rubric similar to those in Isaiah, introducing the victory promise of vv 16-18aα,[31] while both *kî 'āz* in v 9 and *bayyôm hahû'* in v 11 stand in anacrusis. V 20, introduced by *bā'ēt hahî'*, is in prose.[32]

We must examine more closely the redactional processes involved in chap. 3. It may be seen, first of all, that vv 9-10, vv 11-13, vv 18aα-19, and v 20 are all Yahweh speeches. Zephaniah's original collection had ended with a Yahweh speech in 3:6-8, containing a complaint that certain unnamed Jerusalemites have refused to heed the lesson of Yahweh's work against the nations (v 7). Unidentified addressees are there commanded (v 8) to wait for a future day that will bear witness to Yahweh's authority in bringing his hot anger upon nations and kingdoms, ostensibly including recalcitrant Jerusalem.

This is where Zephaniah's own expectation broke off; the coming judgment is not further specified. During his own lifetime Zephaniah would have seen many disturbing signs that the kingdom of Judah was fated to share in a richly deserved universal judgment, but beyond this he could not see.

Zephaniah's late redactor, however, lived to see the ultimate effects of what Zephaniah predicted, both in the altered conditions of the exile and in those of the return from exile. Turning entirely around the threat of universal judgment, this redactor added the promise of a marvelous change of speech, leading to a universal conversion (v 9), which in turn would result in "my dispersed ones," that is, the Jewish exiles, returning from lands far away to worship in Jerusalem (v 10). As has been said, *kî 'āz* in v 9 stands in anacrusis; it should be translated "but then" because the redactor is not making an independent asseveration but is drastically reversing the very judgment that Yahweh threatens in v 8. Now salvation, both for the nations and for Israel, substitutes for judgment, both for the nations and for Israel. Although ostensibly the "then" of v 9 is contemporaneous with the "day" of v 8, in effect it extends this day into something entirely new.

A second Yahweh speech in vv 11-13 is put in the form of direct address to the city (implied in the 2fs forms in vv 11-12a). It is introduced by *bayyôm hahû'* in anacrusis, with a new *kî 'āz,* probably the sign of the same redactor, in integral position within it (the only occurrence in the book). Here *kî* should be translated "for" because it explains the removal of shame in v 11a by the promise of vv 11b-13. The redactor remembers what he failed to mention in vv 9-10: the reason why the inhabitants of Jerusalem had come under judgment in the first place ("the deeds by which you have rebelled against me"), and he realizes that they must now experience a radical change in their spiritual condition, one that will produce a strict separation between "your proudly exultant ones" and "those who are left in Israel," described also as "a people humble and lowly."

The rest of chap. 3 may be the work of a second late redactor. Initial *bayyôm hahû'* appears in the liturgical rubric that introduces what we have previously identified as Zephaniah's victory promise, vv 16-18aα. It was attached to the probably authentic thanksgiving hymn in vv 14-15 before the two together were connected to vv 11-13. Previous to or following this attachment, the same redactor added a new Yahweh speech in vv 18aβ-19. He may also be responsible for the promise of restoration in v 20, introduced by *bāʿēt hahî'*. The temporal transitions appear to synchronize the rejoicing of vv 14f., the victory promise in vv 16ff. (with the rescue of vv 18aβ-19), and the gathering and restoration of v 20. However, the substitution of *bāʿēt hahî'* in v 20 for predominant *bayyôm hahû'* allows for an ongoing process, perhaps even a distinct new era, rather than a unique and unitive event.[33]

3. Conclusion

In summary we may say that the temporal transitions in Zephaniah 1 differ from those in chap. 3 in two respects: (1) they predict judgment for Israel/Judah (in the form of the awesome "day of Yahweh") rather than their salvation; and (2) they pertain to the proximate rather than remote future. With regard to futuristic ideology, Zephaniah himself stood with Jeremiah and Ezekiel. Like them, he could see only the imminent and ineluctable end. He placed the foreign peoples under a parallel judgment, yet his oracles against them did not produce ideological expansions introduced by temporal formulas. The temporal formulas in 1:10, 12 LXX, along with that in 1:8, authentically communicate Zephaniah's own expectation; they were composed either by him or by a close disciple. Any other disciples that he may have had during his own lifetime made no effort to amend his predictions. Nevertheless, his postexilic redactors believed that they were entitled to expand, even reverse, his prophecies. For them, the same Yahweh who had brought the exile intended the restoration.

Finally, it may be noted that the oracle formula *nĕ'um YHWH* is attached to a temporal formula only in 1:10. As in the Yahweh speeches at 1:2, 3 and 2:9, it invokes a special level of revelational authority. Apparently because they were not at all anxious about the question of authority, the redactors who employed the temporal formulas in chap. 3 made no use of the oracle formula.

Eschatology and Redaction among the Preexilic Minor Prophets as a Group

Among the preexilic minor prophets, we have noted the virtual absence of the kind of prose expansions that use an introductory temporal formula, seen regularly in Jeremiah and Ezekiel, but especially in Isaiah. We may summarize our findings as follows:

1) Original materials in the preexilic minor prophets have integral formulas and are always poetic; secondary materials having temporal formulas of transition are also in poetry, but they have their temporal transitions either in anacrusis or in a liturgical rubric (Zeph 3:16).
2) Original and early redactional materials tend to announce judgment, while exilic and postexilic materials always announce salvation.
3) The expansions introduced in Hos 2:18, 23 (E 16, 21) alter Israel's judgment as Israel's salvation; this is also the case in Micah's composition in 4:9ff., in exilic Amos 9:11, and in postexilic Mic 4:1 and Zeph 3:9.
4) Mic 5:9 (E 10) has a remarkable reversal of Israel's victory into Israel's (and the nations') punishment.
5) The extension of Israel's salvation as further salvation is always postexilic (Amos 9:13; Mic 4:6; Zeph 3:11, 16, 20).
6) *(Wĕ)'attâ* and *'āz* are the temporal formulas that are preferred as transitions (all integral) within the authentic passages, whereas *bayyôm hahû'* (usually with preceding *wĕhāyâ*) is the formula employed in virtually all the secondary expansions.

We are able to observe very little change in futuristic ideology from one preexilic minor prophet to another. They are steady in their prediction of looming calamity. Sometimes it is their early redactors, but mainly it is their late redactors, who have modified their grim prophecies in terms of the salvific events that will emerge from Israel's ordeal of purging.

In this respect the preexilic minor prophets take their stand with the three "great" prophets, Isaiah, Jeremiah, and Ezekiel. Micah and his redactors show especially strong affinities with the Isaiah school. The redactors of Amos show direct influence from, or have exerted influence upon, the Jeremianic redaction. Otherwise this early group of minor prophets speak with their own peculiar voice, giving witness out of their own special situations to Yahweh's sovereign work in history.

CHAPTER TEN

The Postexilic Minor Prophets

Primary transitions	Redactional transitions
1. Integral	
Hag 2:23	*bayyôm hahû᾽ nĕ᾽um YHWH . . .*
Zech 8:11	*wĕ῾attâ*
12:4	*bayyôm hahû᾽ nĕ᾽um YHWH*
2. Introductory	
Joel 3:1 (E 2:28)	*wĕhāya ᾽aḥărê-kēn* (anacrusis)
4:1 (E 3:1)	*kî hinnēh bayyāmîm hahēmmâ ûbā῾ēt hahî᾽* (prose addition)
4:18 (E 3:18)	*wĕhāyâ bayyôm hahû᾽* (anacrusis)
Zech 3:10	*bayyôm hahû᾽ nĕ᾽um YHWH . . .* (prose addition)
8:23	*bayyāmîm hahēmmâ*[a] (prose addition)
12:3	*wĕhāyâ bayyôm hahû᾽* (prose addition)
12:6	*bayyôm hahû᾽* (prose addition)
12:8(1)[b]	*bayyôm hahû᾽* (prose addition)
12:9	*wĕhāyâ bayyôm hahû᾽* (prose addition)
12:11	*bayyôm hahû᾽* (prose addition)
13:1	*bayyôm hahû᾽* (prose addition)
13:2	*wĕhāyâ bayyôm hahû᾽ nĕ᾽um YHWH* (prose addition)
13:4	*wĕhāyâ bayyôm hahû᾽* (prose addition)
14:6[c]	*wĕhāyâ bayyôm hahû᾽* (prose addition)
14:8	*wĕhāyâ bayyôm hahû᾽* (prose addition)
14:9	*bayyôm hahû᾽* (prose addition)
14:13	*wĕhāyâ bayyôm hahû᾽* (prose addition)
14:20[d]	*bayyôm hahû᾽* (prose addition)

a. The messenger formula precedes.
b. The second *bayyôm hahû'* in this verse is a time identifier.
c. *Bayyôm hahû'* in v 4 is a time identifier.
d. Cf. epitomizing *bayyôm hahû'* in v 21.

Joel

1. The authentic materials, chaps. 1–2

Since the books of the postexilic minor prophets lack editorial superscriptions with historical information, their respective dates must be determined mainly from internal data. The general period to which Joel belongs is between the time of Malachi,[1] which is mid-fifth century, and the time of well-developed apocalyptic as seen in the additions to Zechariah, and especially Daniel. Even though Joel displays much of the spirit as well as the technique of the classical prophets, the mention of the "elders" as community leaders (1:14, 2:16) and of the priests as cultic ministrants (1:9, 13, 2:17)[2] clearly shows that the book belongs to the time when Judah no longer had kings. Also, imagery for the "day of Yahweh" no longer points to a foreign invader but to a locust plague of vast proportions. The book could well be placed in the time of 1-2 Chronicles, therefore, but it contains materials in 3:1–4:21 (E 2:28–3:21) that belong in a somewhat later period when apocalyptic speculation was coming to prominence in Judaism. It is this additional material that contains a few futuristic formulas of the type under study here, and we shall turn to it following a few comments regarding original Joel.

There are no original or integral temporal transitions anywhere in Joel, only the formulas that introduce redactional expansions in chaps. 3–4. *Wĕgam-'attâ* in 2:12 might be listed as an integral occurrence, were it not for the fact that this instance of *'attâ* is certainly situational[3] rather than temporal. Within the present and imminent future lies the dreadful "day of Yahweh" described in vivid detail in 2:1-11. The summons to show repentance that follows is synchronous with, and integral to, the experience of this calamity or the immediate prospect of it. Thus the "eschatology" of Joel himself consists of no more than the spiritual attitude of repentance on this specific occasion, leading to the assembly for public fasting mentioned in 2:15-17. The original book ends with a narrative report (2:18) of Yahweh's favorable response, which includes divine promises of renewed prosperity and happiness (vv 19-27).

2. The secondary materials, chaps. 3–4

Nothing should be more apparent than that the last two chapters of Joel are concerned with problems far removed from those of an isolated and impoverished postexilic community during a time of famine. Joel 3:1-2 (E 2:28-29) extends the imagery of Ezek 11:19 and 36:26-27 to the point of affirming the outpouring of the divine spirit upon every age-group and social class. 3:3-5 (E 2:30-32) introduces the concept of an assembly for Yahweh's final judgment upon those who exiled and enslaved Yahweh's people (cf. 4:19-22 [E 3:19-22]). These elements attracted a variety of impassioned sayings that have to do with a battle against the nations and their final judgment (4:9-16a [E 3:9-16a]), as well as epexegesis on 4:1-3 (E 3:1-3) threatening specific reprisals on Tyre, Sidon, and Philistia (4:4-8 [E 3:4-8]).[4]

One thing to be noted is that those who are said in 3:5 to have been delivered (*mlṭ* niph.) and are designated as a *pĕlēṭâ*, "that which survives," and *śĕrîdîm*, "refugees," represent the same group that will finally adhere to Yahweh on the "great and terrible day of Yahweh," but these are not specifically the survivors of the Babylonian exile. Their coming to Zion mentioned in 3:5 is other, therefore, than the return of Jewish captives to the land of Israel following the deportation to Babylon, as is the rule elsewhere in the prophetic books (cf. Isa 27:13; Ezek 39:25-29; Mic 4:6-7, among passages with temporal transitions). The coming to Mount Zion mentioned here is ideologically unique; it is an event in the final state of the whole world, when a distinction that has long held historical Israel in Yahweh's care will be turned into an irreversible cosmic separation. The "great and terrible day" of Joel 3–4 is more therefore than the repeatedly threatened "day of Yahweh," experienced in calamities within history: it is the ultimate day of cosmic judging (cf. Mal 3:9 [E 4:1]).

Except in that 4:4-8 (E 3:4-8) is a probable late insertion within this section, these two chapters were likely added to chaps. 1–2 in the sequence of their present order within the text. Due to the variety of ideologies that underlie the various pericopes, there is no strict logical sense in the manner in which they have been joined to one another. Nevertheless, the distinctive temporal formulas that occur in 3:1 and 4:1 were certainly designed to make an emphatic temporal connection of new materials to that which precedes them.

Like *wĕhāyâ bayyôm hahû'* in 4:18 (E 3:18), *wĕhāyâ 'aḥărê-kēn* in 3:1 (E 2:28) stands in poetic anacrusis. This may or may not mean that the contents of the two pericopes preexisted in oral form, being reduced here to written form; but it can be seen that the pericopes that they introduce do deal with themes that are more familiar than those of most other pericopes in this section.

The following may be noted about the formula in 3:1: (1) it is only here that *'aḥărê-kēn* is preceded by *wĕhāyâ,* and it is only here that the formula stands in anacrusis; (2) this is one of only two occasions in which the time-shift does not actually involve a *vaticinium ex eventu.*

Most other occurrences of predictive *'aḥărê-kēn* are based on specific historical events (cf. Jer 16:16, 21:7, 46:26, 49:6), but Joel 3:1, like Isa 1:26, is a genuine prediction. The latter two passages forecast profound spiritual changes in highly ideological language (Isaiah: Jerusalem renamed the faithful city; Joel: a universal outpouring of the divine spirit). We should also keep in mind that whenever *wĕhāyâ* precedes a futuristic formula, an abrupt but lasting change is implied; this is the case, for instance, with regard to the single integral occurrence of *wĕhāyâ bayyôm hahû'* occurring at Isa 22:20, creating a drastic shift from Shebna's deposition to Eliakim's investiture.

With these facts in mind, one should be very cautious about suggesting that Joel 3:1 might be the prophet's own expansion to his climactic and highly idealistic prediction in 2:27. That passage is specifically pro-Israel, while 3:1-3 has neither ethnic nor nationalistic restrictions of any kind. This prediction is as innovative in its Joelian context as it later became in New Testament theology (Acts 2).

We have previously given special attention to Joel 4:1, particularly with respect to its relationship to the immediately preceding context (see in Chapter Four). The initial conjunction *kî* implies that the redactor of 4:1-3 intends to comment on 3:1-6 (E 2:28-32). The temporal transition that he creates here is unique. Not only does he make the temporal reference as broad as possible by employing the combinational form *bayyāmîm hahēm ûbā'ēt hahî',* indicating a changed situation as well as an extended temporal duration (cf. Jer 33:15, 50:4, 20), but he adds a preceding *hinnēh,* seen elsewhere in the familiar locution *hinnēh yamîm bā'îm.* The artificial temporal transition that results apparently intends to refer back to the series of events in the entirety of Joel 3:1-6 (E 2:28-32) (the outpouring of the spirit; the cosmic wonders; perhaps also the deliverance of the survivors) that are to precede or accompany the world's final day, "the great and terrible day of Yahweh." These are therefore penultimate events of history; and this redactor intends to include among them the resolution of the matter of greatest concern to him and his fellow Jews of the late postexilic period: reprisal on foreign nations for exiling and enslaving "my people and my heritage" (4:2). This is to occur just after, or simultaneously with, the restoration of Judah and Jerusalem, mentioned in a circumstantial clause in v 1.

Thus does this redactor refocus cosmic judgment as final vindication for Yahweh's people. In addition, he or another redactor expanded further predictions of Jerusalem's/Israel's restoration (vv 16-17) with the idyllic imagery of 4:18, which is conventional both in ideology and in the way in which the familiar formula *wĕhāyâ bayyôm hahû'* is employed.

We are able to see, therefore, that futuristic transitions are used in Joel only in the redactional additions, and then always as introductory formulas. The transition in 3:1 and the one in 4:18 expand Israel's salvation as further salvation, and they both refer to a future that is remote from that of the original Joel. The peculiar formulation in 4:1 introduces an ideological sequence that is found elsewhere only in apocalyptic texts, namely, a move from a general scene of judgment to the vindication of Israel occurring in and through judgment of Israel's enemies. Both the general judgment and this special judgment take place in the penultimate future, without differentiation. There will be nothing beyond this except "the great and terrible day of Yahweh."

3. Conclusion

In summary it may be said that the authentic material in Joel involves a "here and now" futurism that stands in stark relief over against the highly developed cosmic eschatology of this book's redactors. Each of the temporal transitions created by these redactors points to conditions or situations of ultimate finality: the universal presence of the divine spirit, a calling of wrongdoers to retribution, and an idyllic transformation of nature, with Jerusalem at the center of all (cf. Ezekiel 47; Rev 22:1-2).

The original book of Joel (chaps. 1–2) reflects an "eschatology" of imminent catastrophe, occasioning a public religious act to elicit Yahweh's beneficent response. Ideological as this may be, it remains within the realm of the historically possible and the traditionally appropriate.

Perhaps the most profound difference between chaps. 1–2 and chaps. 3–4 is that those concerned with Yahweh's irruptive act in these redactional supplements are not a famine-ridden community of postexilic Jews nor those first returning from Babylonian exile; rather, they are the ultimately faithful pious adherents of the one true religion, separated decisively from the wicked. Their coming to Zion is cosmologically final rather than another "day" in the series of "days of Yahweh" that are equivalent to calamitous historical events.

Although all the materials in Joel 3–4 were added incrementally and indicate significant nuances in ideology, they show the clear marks of emerging apocalypticism. It is important to observe how drastically innovative 3:1-3 (E 2:28-29) is in comparison with the context to which it is attached. It shifts the scene from "my people" and "Israel" in 2:26-27 to "all flesh"; in other words, from the context of the biblical covenant to that of religious anthropology. Even if the redactor's intent went no further than to universalize prophetic inspiration only within Judaism, it had a universalistic dimension in this laicizing of spiritual empowerment.

Finally, it is important to call attention to the innovative ideology of

4:1-3 (E 3:1-3), which interprets cosmic judgment as instrumental to the salvation of Yahweh's covenant people. As a motif that is seen elsewhere only in the early apocalyptic literature, it serves to reverse the incipient universalism of 3:1-3. This fact reminds us that we should not assume that the apocalypticists held to identical visions of the future.

Haggai

1. Redaction and ideology in Haggai

Corresponding to the contrast between the historically orientated prognostication of the authentic materials in Joel and the cosmically and dualistically orientated ideology of the additions to that book is a striking contrast between the respective expectations for the future in Haggai and in Zechariah. Though Haggai's "eschatology" is emphatically idealistic, it is concretely this-worldly, whereas Zechariah, both in its authentic and in its secondary sections, projects a schematically ultimate state of being.

Although there is evidence of secondary expansion within the two short chapters of Haggai, the book hangs together as a series of dated oracles, all from the second year of Darius I, 520 B.C.E.[5] These concern, respectively, the poverty of the restoration community, the devastated condition of the temple, the problem of ritual uncleanness,[6] and the rumors concerning instability in the Persian empire during the transition from Cambyses to Darius. There is nothing here that speaks of a remote future. Rather, Haggai's oracles either urge the community to take measures that will lead directly to a solution (1:1-14, 2:15-20) or they point to Yahweh's sovereign intention in the current upheaval (2:6-8, 21-23).

There can be no mistaking the crucial significance of sequences and durations in this small book. What one would infer from the fact that all the oracles are dated is confirmed by the special emphasis that is placed on the immediate future in 2:15, 18. Here is a twice-repeated command to take stock of the opportunities of the present moment, *śîmû-nā' lĕbabkem min-hayyôm hazzeh wāmā'ĕlâ*, "put your attention on what is to happen from this day forward."[7] This corresponds to a similar, past-orientated command in 1:5 (repeated redactionally in v 7), *śîmû lĕbabkem 'al darkêkem*, "put your attention on (what have been) your ways." Both at 2:15 and at 1:5 — as well as in 2:4 — situational *wĕ'attâ* connects a negative consideration with a divine call for faith and action.

The immediate future of Yahweh's effectual action that will justify the people's faith and reward their obedience is forecast in 2:6-7 and 2:19b.

Following the messenger formula in v 6aα is a peculiar expression that defines a short duration in the immediate future, '*ôd 'aḥat mĕ'āt hî'*, "it is yet for one short moment" (6aβ). At the end of this brief moment Yahweh will agitate the whole world ("the heavens and the earth," etc.) in order also to agitate the nations, in effect shaking loose their treasures for the benefit of the temple. This is the assurance that nullifies the past and present devastation of the temple. A corresponding assurance nullifies the persistent evidence of poverty (*'ôd . . . ['ôd]*); this is Yahweh's promise (2:19b) that *min-hayyôm hazzeh*, "from this day onward," he will indeed bless them.

2. The concluding oracle, 2:20-23

On the very day of receiving this second assurance, Haggai received his fourth and climactic oracle, 2:20-23. The first two oracles had been addressed to Zerubbabel and Joshua together, while the third had been for the priests and the people. This final oracle is for Zerubbabel alone. This descendant of David is designated as *paḥat*, "governor," but he is now addressed as a soon-to-be-king. Yahweh repeats the announcement of v 6 that he is shaking the heavens and the earth (2:21),[8] but the purpose is no longer the provision of treasures for the temple, as in 2:7. Now it is for the specific purpose of undermining any and all political or military forces that might threaten to prevent Zerubbabel's investiture.[9]

It is just here, in the last verse of Haggai, that we find this book's only futuristic transition, a familiar *bayyôm hahû'*, followed by a resounding *nĕ'um YHWH ṣĕbā'ôt*. It is not only integral and authentic; it is climactic within the pericope and within the book. I previously thought that this verse was a futuristic epitome,[10] but the foremost position of the temporal formula argues against it. This formula is, instead, an emphatic synchronizer between the imminently future events of vv 21-22 and the intended effect of those events, Zerubbabel's investiture (v 23).[11] Yahweh's intention is revealed in the announcement of two actions in sequence, both of which are confirmed by further occurrences of the oracle formula. Yahweh announces that he will take (impf.) Zerubbabel, that is, separate him out from all potential candidates; this is affirmed by the immediately following *nĕ'um YHWH*. The purpose of this, expressed by a perfect consecutive verb, is to effectuate the second action, that is, make him "like a signet ring" (the comparative designates a symbolic action or typological function that may be distinct from an actual, public ceremony);[12] this is followed by a grounding clause indicating Zerubbabel's special election, confirmed by a final *nĕ'um YHWH ṣĕbā'ôt*.

Haggai's expectation was sharply focused upon the immediate future: the removal of ritual uncleanness; the end of the famine; the arrival of treasures for beautifying the restored temple; and the symbolic, if not actual, placing of a royal ring upon the finger of Zerubbabel.[13] The last expectation is far from messianic in the traditional sense. It is not predicted for a remote and ideal future, but for the situation of the very moment.

Thus this book ends with a sharply focused private oracle, whose prediction is underscored by the thrice-occurring oracle formula. It should be noted that Haggai's futuristic ideology conceives of Yahweh's action in the world at large, as instrumental to salvific events on behalf of Israel, here as in 2:7-8 (cf. Isa 45:1ff.). Haggai insinuates, but does not directly state, that the nations who are thus involved in Israel's restoration are at the same time being punished. This is what distinguishes Haggai's "eschatology" from the apocalyptic ideology that was emerging at this same period, which places special emphasis on the judgment of the nations as the precondition for Israel's full enjoyment of Yahweh's favor (cf. Isa 24:21-23; Ezekiel 38–39; Joel 4; and Zechariah 12–14).

Zechariah

The question of redactional continuity is especially acute in the book of Zechariah. It can scarcely be argued, as might be possible with respect to Isaiah, that late expansions significantly articulate the essential ideology of the earlier part of the book. In matter of fact, the futuristic expectation of Zechariah 1–8 and that of chaps. 9–14 are worlds apart. It must have been a purely editorial convention that added the latter chapters, containing two extended series of predictions with introductory *(wĕhāyâ) bayyôm hahû'*.

1. First Zechariah, chaps. 1–8

a. The authentic materials

Not only do the dating formulas in chaps. 1–8 place Zechariah's activity in the same historical situation as Haggai; their frequency of occurrence indicates that here, too, sequences and durations play a major role in defining the intention of individual pericopes, as also of the composition as a whole.[14] Unfortunately, the insertion of epexegetical comments, as well as some rearranging, has created confusion. 1:1-6 may be seen as a preface to the "night visions," with the oracular command at the end (6:9-15) as an epilogue.

Kurt Galling has suggested that the date given in 1:7 originally belonged at 6:9. He places 1:8-15, 2:1-4, 2:5-9, and 6:1-8 at the time when the first returnees were about to depart for the land of Israel, 1:16-17 and 6:15a at the time when the rebuilding of the temple was about to commence, and 2:14-16, 3:1-9, 4:1-5, 4:6-10a, 5:1-5, and 5:5-11 at a time when the work of rebuilding was in progress.[15] 7:1-14 is somewhat later (the fourth year of Darius), while 8:1-23 appears to be a late précis or synopsis of still other oracles by Zechariah or his epigones.

Most scholars agree that Zech 6:9-14 has been reworked to eliminate an original reference to Zerubbabel. If the date found in 1:7 does indeed belong here, it is very tempting to interpret this remarkable pericope in the light of Hag 2:21-23. The Haggai passage, which predicts an imminent investiture for that person, using *bayyôm hahû'* as a climactic integral transition, is dated to 24/IX in Darius's second year (cf. 2:10), while the original text of Zech 6:9ff. would be dated to 24/XI, precisely two months later,[16] in the same year. The crowning with gold required here of the prophet Zechariah may be intended as an actualization of Hag 2:21ff.

Bayyôm hahû' in v 10 is a synchronizing time-identifier that is certainly not to be removed from the text as a gloss.[17] The prophet was immediately to take from certain newly arrived repatriates a quantity of silver and gold that they had brought, and on the very same day bring it to the "house" of Josiah in the form of a kingly crown for the investiture of a person other than the "Joshua son of Jehozadak" mentioned in the present text.[18] *Bayyôm hahû'* may be more than a synchronizer: it may be fraught with eschatological significance in terms of Haggai's announcement. This is, to be sure, speculative, and the point should not be pressed. In any event, we may be certain that Zechariah's own "eschatology" was also "here-and-now" oriented. His futuristic ideology included no more than the return from the exile, the rebuilding of the temple, and probably an expectation of the special recognition of Zerubbabel as the secular leader of the community.[19]

The only other integral temporal transition in these chapters is in the probably authentic material at 8:9-13, an oracular exhortation closely similar to those of Haggai. As has been noted in Chapter Two, emphatic *wĕʿattâ* at the beginning of v 11 provides the major turning point in this pericope, and it is set in contrast to three expressions of time occurring in the preceding context, and to yet another in v 11, each of which functions as a time identifier rather than as a transition. The pericope is in poetic meter except for the messenger formula at the beginning, the expression *kî lipnê hayyāmîm hahēm,* "for before those days," at the beginning of v 10, and the entirety of v 11, introduced by transitional *wĕʿattâ* and concluded by an emphatic *nĕʾum YHWH ṣĕbāʾôt.* "In these days" in v 9 marks an ongoing present, beginning with the event ("since the foundation of the temple of Yahweh Sebaoth") that introduced the present situation. In order to give special prominence to this momentous present, another duration ("before those days")[20] is also mentioned, a time of wagelessness, insecurity, and strife (v 10). In contrast to all of this, Yahweh announces his new intention (v 11), then this new and decisive present and imminent future are defined (vv 12-13). Negatively stated, this is not to be like the earlier days *(kayyāmîm hārî'šōnîm)*. Positively stated, this will bring peace, increase, honor, and salvation — reasons enough for the concluding exhortation, "Fear not, but let your hands be strong."

This striking interplay of temporal durations and sequences is precisely what also characterizes Haggai. These two prophets, with certain unidentified others (8:9), believed that they stood at the very climax of Yahweh's work in the history of Israel.

b. The secondary materials

Coming to redactional expansions with a temporal transition in First Zechariah, we take note first of all that each of the two passages in question, 3:10 and 8:23, is in prose. Virtually all minor-prophet occurrences place the temporal formula in poetic anacrusis (exceptions are Joel 4:1 [E 3:1], which is in prose but is even later than original Zechariah, and Hos 1:5, which is an *ad hoc* remark from a relatively remote redactor). This means that the prose expansions of first Zechariah (along with Joel 4:1) depart from the practice of the minor prophets as a group, associating themselves with the great-prophet tradition of Isaiah and Jeremiah. This will also hold true, as we shall see, of the serial expansions in Deutero-Zechariah.

There is little thematic or ideological affinity between 3:10 and 8:26, or between them and the original preaching of the prophet Zechariah, or between them and the apocalyptic expansions of chaps. 12–14. These two verses show no concern at all for the prophet's own imminentistic expectations, namely, the return of the exiles, the rebuilding of the temple, and the investiture of Zerubbabel.

Zech 3:10, introduced by *bayyôm hahû'* and the oracle formula, interprets the foregoing private oracle to Joshua, concerning his and the community's proximate future,[21] in terms of its general effect in the remote future. It is like Mic 4:4 in repeating an ancient saying about universal prosperity and hospitality (cf. 1 Kgs 4:25).

8:23, with *bayyāmîm hahēmmâ* as its introductory formula, interprets the intra-Israelite universalism of vv 20-22, expressed in an authentic Yahweh saying, in terms of a multinational universalism identifying the Jewish people as the mediators of salvation to all mankind. Here the move is from a situation in the remote future to another activity in the remote future, in which the ultimate implications of Israel's salvation are to be brought to effect.

c. Conclusion to Haggai and First Zechariah

The original books of the contemporary prophets Haggai and Zechariah employ only two futuristic transitions, both of which are integral to the pericopes where they are found. *Bayyôm hahû'* with the oracle formula introduces Yahweh's imminent purpose in the concluding verse of Haggai, 2:23, interpreting the contemporary cosmic and political upheaval as the immediate preparation for Zerubbabel's investiture, which was to be an act of Yahweh rather than the expression of human authority. *Wĕ'attâ* in Zech 8:11 introduces the new conditions of peace, prosperity, and security that are just at this moment beginning to emerge in strong contrast to the destitution and insecurity of the immediate past. On the contrary, *bayyôm hahû'* in Zech 3:10 and *bayyāmîm hahēmmâ* in Zech 8:23 serve only to expand the eschatological images of the materials to which they are attached, in each instance extending a proximately future state of bliss.

2. Second Zechariah, chaps. 9–14

a. The relationship between First Zechariah and Second Zechariah

We turn now to an extended list of integral (12:4) and introductory (12:3, 6, 8, 9, 11, 13:1, 2, 4, 14:6, 8, 9, 13, 20) temporal transitions within what has been called Deutero- or Second Zechariah,[22] all of which utilize the formula *(wĕhāyâ) bayyôm hahû'*. The influence of the late additions to Isaiah may be seen in a concentration on the theme of Yahweh's kingship in Jerusalem, as well as in this specific choice of temporal formulas.

In my book *Yesterday, Today and Tomorrow,* I was able to identify *hayyôm* in 9:12 as a time identifier within an identifying characterization, *bayyôm hahû'* in 9:16 as part of a futuristic epitome, *bayyôm hahû'* in 11:11 as part of a past epitome, and *bayyôm hahû'* in 14:21 as part of another futuristic epitome.[23] These conclusions are important for the exegesis of the passages where each of these temporal expressions is found.

The transitional occurrences of these temporal formulas within chaps. 12–14 were also discussed in my book, as well as in Chapter Three in the present study. They require, however, a more extensive analysis. The compositional history of Zech 12:1–13:6 and of chap. 14 is exceedingly complex, and no consensus has emerged concerning the function of the clusters of temporal transitions within them.

Although there are certain linguistic and ideological links between First and Second Zechariah, it is now all but universally agreed among critical scholars that the two were quite separate compositions in their origin. Another critical conclusion that has been widely if not universally accepted is that Second Zechariah comes from one or more centuries later than First Zechariah. These conclusions give special urgency to the questions of how and why these two separate compositions became a single book. A widely held opinion has been that it was an editorial contrivance that joined them: Zechariah 9–11, then Zechariah 12–14, and finally Malachi, were put in sequence at the end of the "Twelve Prophets" collection because of the word *maśśā'*, "burden," that is, "oracle," at the head of each of them. This explanation may indeed be correct with respect to the attachment of Malachi (though relative dating may also have been a factor), but it cannot answer the question whether Zechariah 9–11 and Zechariah 12–14 were originally separate compositions. This depends on an internal analysis of each section and in particular on an observation of the syntactical position of the word *maśśā'* within each context.

There may be some validity in the claim that redactional ideology in chaps. 9–14, and particularly in chaps. 12–14, is a natural extension of redactional ideology from chaps. 1–8, as Brevard S. Childs urges in the following explanation:

> What then is the effect of linking chs. 9–14 with 1–8? In my judgment, the effect is to expand, develop, and sharpen the theological pattern of the end time which had begun to emerge in Proto-Zechariah. The redaction of chs. 1–8 had reworked the older language of the second exodus in the light of the historical deliverance from Babylon in order to make it bear witness to an eschatology which had envisioned the coming of the new age falling together with the return from Babylon. Now a new prophetic pattern emerges which distinguishes between the return from the exile and the coming of the end time. Israel had returned to the land, but the promise of redemption still lay in the future.[24]

What Childs is in effect saying is that the futuristic idealism of First Zechariah's redactors — which we have observed in 3:10 and 8:26 — reaches beyond the imminentistic, historically oriented expectation of the prophet Zechariah (and Haggai); but also that there is a shift from mild idealism (as in the just-mentioned passages) to the prediction of what he calls "the end time," as in chaps. 12–14.

Properly considered, we ought not to be speaking of an "end time" until we encounter the full-blown apocalyptic of such a book as Daniel, expressed especially in his use of *qēṣ*, "end," at 9:26 and 12:13, of *'ēt qēṣ*, "the end time," at 11:35, 40, 12:4, 9, and of *lĕqēṣ hayyāmîm*, "until the end of the days/years," in 12:13,[25] and in the extracanonical apocalyptic writings. The development that is truly central in the ideology of Zechariah 12–14 is its radically altered interpretation of the theological significance of the return from exile. This is no longer depicted as an event bringing blessing to the Jewish survivors, but the cause of continuing — indeed, increasing — hazards and alarms.[26]

b. The present state of research

The important difference between the "eschatology" of Zechariah 9–11 and that of chaps. 12–14 is that the former still refers to events of the historical present and imminent future (such as the returning king of 9:9-10 and the annulled covenant of 11:4-16), while the latter refers to a remote — not specifically final — future.

Yet there is evidence that chaps. 9–11 and chaps. 12–14 are redactionally connected to each other. In his monograph *Sacharja 9–14, Untersuchungen von Text und Form*,[27] Magne Saebø has made a strong case for identifying the "shepherd" of chaps. 9–11.[28] As he explains it, Zechariah 9–10 is the result of a process of continuous accretion, apart from which 11:4-16 and 12:1b–13:6 independently arose, until they were joined to it with 11:1-3, 17, 12:1a, and 13:7-9 as linking elements. Saebø's view is that these last-mentioned verses provide the definitive redactional perspective of the section as a whole. Chap. 14 is seen then as a later addition that disturbs the unity of viewpoint achieved in this redactional combination.

Saebø has by far the better of it in treating 13:7-9 as an element deriving from the definitive redaction of chaps. 9–13. Most interpreters are comfortable with accepting 12:1–13:6 and 14:1ff. as two quite independent pericopes, but this leaves them with the question of how 13:7-9 got between them. The solution generally accepted by older scholars has been that it does not belong here, but has probably been displaced from its original position following 11:17. However, this solution is both arbitrary and capricious, for why should it have been placed just here? Otto Plöger[29] wants to go to the other extreme in insisting that 13:7-9 is an integral part of a single composition embracing both 12:1–13:6 and chap. 14, but careful examination of the text reveals that this is completely unjustified. Benedikt Otzen,[30] influenced by Elliger's commentary in the Alte Testament Deutsch series,[31] claims that it belongs here as an ideological parallel to 12:2-7, accentuating a rivalry between Judah and Jerusalem; but the discrepancy between the form and spirit of this poetic Yahweh speech and the discursive, ambling style of 12:1–13:6 only obscures whatever parallel there may be.

Saebø's success in defining the real role of 13:7-9 has carried over, on the one hand, to his larger treatment of 12:1–13:6 and, on the other hand, to that of 14:1ff. He is the only scholar who has realized the compositional and redactional significance of the two parallel series of temporal transitions within the latter two passages.

Five scholarly monographs on Zechariah 9–14 were published during the sixties and seventies, as follows: P. Lamarche, *Zecharie IX–XIV, structure litteraire et messianisme* (1961); B. Otzen, *Studien über Deutero-sacharje* (1964); H.-M. Lutz, *Jahwe, Jerusalem und die Völker* (1968); M. Saebø's monograph, mentioned above (1969); and Ina Willi-Plein, *Prophetie am Ende, Untersuchungen zu Sacharja 9–14* (1974).[32] Since the first three titles appeared before Saebø's book, they could not have shown acquaintance with his work; Saebø does discuss them. Willi-Plein certainly should have been aware of Saebø's book, however, but makes no mention of it. Whatever the special values of these four studies may be, their individual efforts at unravelling Zech 12:1–13:6 and 14:1ff. fall far short in comparison with Saebø's study, and this is precisely because only Saebø knows what to do with the plethora of *bayyôm hahû'*s.

In addition to nontransitional *bayyôm hahû'* in 12:8(2) and 14:3, and to epitomizing *bayyôm hahû'* in 14:21, *bayyôm hahû'* is an introductory transition formula in 12:6, 8(1), 11, 13:1, 14:9, 20, while *wĕhāyâ bayyôm hahû'* appears as an introductory transition formula in 12:3, 9, 13:2, 4, 14:6, 8, 13. All these occurrences are literarily independent of one another and introduce successive new prose additions. Alongside these introductory occurrences, *bayyôm hahû'* with following *nĕ'um YHWH* is to be identified as an integral transition in 12:4. Is there any sense or order in this perplexing array? The only thing that is very much like it is the series of *bayyôm hahû'*s in Isa 19:16-24 and the series of *bayyôm hahû'*s and *wĕhāyâ bayyôm hahû'*s in Ezek 38:10–39:11. But the Isaiah list is shorter and fairly homogeneous, while the list in Ezekiel is shorter, less variegated, and more disjointed than here.

It is little wonder that the commentaries and most of the monographs are able to do little with this phenomenon. They may take notice of the presence of one of these formulas in a passage under discussion, but rarely endeavor to explain it. Here as elsewhere, they are inclined to mark them as glosses whenever they seem intrusive. For example, the apparatus in *BHS*[mg], edited for Zechariah by Karl Elliger, registers the occurrences in 12:8(2) and 14:4 as probable glosses (but cf. Elliger's ATD commentary); they are, in fact, the two nontransitional time identifiers that we have identified and surely belong to the putative proto-Masoretic text.[33] On the other hand, Elliger is like other critics in his willingness to divide up Zech 12:1ff. and 14:1ff. into original and secondary materials in complete disregard of the temporal transitions within them. In his ATD commentary, he marks the following as original: 12:1-21, 3a, 4a, bβ, 5, 6b, 9-14; 13:1-6; 14:1-4aα, b, 5b-6, 7aα[1]-9, 11aβ, 13, 14b, 16-17, 19; the remainder is secondary. This simply means that

Elliger sees no literary-critical significance whatever in the occurrence of the temporal transitions.

The opposite extreme is seen in the treatment of Lamarche. He views all the occurrences of *bayyôm hahû'* and *wĕhāyâ bayyôm hahû'* not only as original, but as specially designed catchwords within an elaborate chiastic structure.[34]

Those who have followed our foregoing discussion will immediately sense that there is something basically wrong with each of these approaches. We have found no passage anywhere in the Old Testament in which either (1) temporal formulas occur in close succession as integral transitions or (2) series of original, integral transitions are interleaved with series of secondary, introductory, or integral transitions. On the one hand, it is wrong to chop up a passage the way Elliger does in complete disregard for the occurrence of temporal transitions. On the other hand, it must be objected against Lamarche that we have nowhere observed a series of temporal transitions, especially in long and complex sequences, designed expressly as compositional elements in the interior design of complete, unredacted passages.[35]

How then must we proceed? There certainly is ample evidence of literary supplementation. There is also such a wide variety of *topoi* that we know we must look for elements that seem similar, yet indicate divergence. Among these are a number of key words or expressions, such as *'ammîm* over against *goyyim,* which the RSV, for example, renders as "peoples" and "nations," respectively. But these must be examined with caution because expressions that one writer may prefer, and are therefore signs of that writer's activity, may also serve as triggers for the same expressions on the part of a redactor.

Our discussion of *wĕhāyâ bayyôm hahû'* as a variant of *bayyôm hahû'* in Chapter Three should warn us that it should not automatically be taken as the sign of distinctive authorship. Yet we have noted that the *wĕhāyâ* variant certainly does have a notably disjunctive effect, especially when it is followed by an imperfect or a participle, and that this may tend to give greater weight and solemnity to the new prediction. Either variant may have been chosen in a given passage, therefore, for stylistic reasons.

Without careful scrutiny, it is impossible to judge whether this greater weight or solemnity attaches to any particular occurrence of *wĕhāyâ bayyôm hahû'* in Zech 12:1ff. and 14:1ff. We take note of the fact, however, that both variants introduce special new *topoi,* marking each of them off from one another while producing an impressively incremental image of what "that day," that is, "the day of Yahweh" (14:1), will be. In addition, there is significance in the fact that it is the Yahweh speeches in 12:1–13:6, occurring at 12:2-4, 6, 9-10 and 13:2, that tend to employ the *wĕhāyâ* form. But the *wĕhāyâ* variant may also introduce third-person description, regularly so in chap. 14 (at vv 4, 6, 8, 13; cf. 13:4). We take note furthermore that *ně'um YHWH* follows *bayyôm hahû'* in 12:4 and *wěhāyâ bayyôm hahû'* in 13:2.

c. Magne Saebø's analysis of Zech 12:1ff. and 14:1ff.

We turn to Saebø's book to observe in detail what he has accomplished, and perhaps to improve upon it in the light of what we have discovered.[36] Saebø has identified an important clue in that *wěhāyâ bayyôm hahû'* introduces Yahweh speeches three out of four times in 12:1–13:6. Because of this, his analysis may confidently be taken over as the first step in our own reconstruction.

For Saebø, the Yahweh speeches with this variant introduce three different *Kernworte,* from which two or three stages of redactional enlargement have developed, as the case may be.[37] The resulting sections may be placed in parallel columns, as follows:

Unit A	Unit B	Unit C
Introduction, 12:1b		
Kernwort, 3-4a	*Kernwort,* 9-10	*Kernwort,* 13:2
2nd stage, 2a, 4bα, 6	2nd stage, 11-14, 13:1	2nd stage, 3-6
3rd stage, 2b, 4bβ, 5	3rd stage, 12:8	
	Binding element, 12:7	

As we see it, there are three minor faults with this reconstruction: (1) it relegates 12:2's opening clause, with *hinnēh 'ānōkî* plus participle, to the secondary level; (2) it fails to connect the integral temporal formula in 12:4 with v 2a; and (3) it wrongly gives integral status to *bayyôm hahû'* in 12:6 and to *wěhāyâ bayyôm hahû'* in 13:4. Saebø does not distinguish between integral and introductory formulas of transition, but we on our part would have no excuse for failing at this point to use this distinction to our advantage.

Saebø is even more insightful in his analysis of Zechariah 14. He has taken an independent approach to the enigma of how the three sections in this chapter that begin with *wěhāyâ bayyôm hahû'* (vv 6-7, v 8, vv 13-14) relate to one another. As he sees it, they each mark the beginning of units of traditional material that are epexegetical to the core unit of chap. 14 in vv 1-3. The first and the third are units that elaborate on the day-of-Yahweh theme of those opening verses, while the second, together with vv 4-5, is an elaboration upon the theophany theme of those same verses.[38]

Gratefully acknowledging Saebø's impressive contribution to the solution of these problems, we would venture to put forward a refined proposal that takes advantage of the new information that has developed from our present study. A cardinal rule in our reconstruction will be that the respective temporal formulas, with the demarcations that they imply, must receive their full due. Because the composition of Zech 12:1ff. and of 14:1ff. has been inordinately complex, our reconstruction must likewise be complex; but above all we must seek a reasonable explanation for the plethora of temporal transitions.

d. Temporal transitions in Zech 12:1–13:6

Taking up first 12:1–13:6, we offer a new structural outline that identifies all the formulas of transition, including others of significance alongside the special temporal transitions that we have been studying:

Redactional Units	**Transitions**
I. Introductory, 12:1	
A. Editorial title, 1a	
B. Doxological introduction, 1b	
II. Original oracle, 2, 3b-4a	*hinnēh 'ānōkî*, 2a (introductory)
	bayyôm hahû' ně'um YHWH, 4a (integral)
[glosses, 2a, 4b]	
III. Redactional expansions	
A. Jerusalem's/Judah's victory	
1. Yahweh speech, 3a	*wĕhāyâ bayyôm hahû'* (introductory)
2. 3rd-person development, 5, 7, 8bᵃ	
3. Epexegesis:	
a) Judah's fervor, 6	*bayyôm hahû'* (introductory)
b) Jerusalem's shield, 8a	*bayyôm hahû'* (introductory)
B. Internal renewal	
1. Yahweh speech, 9-10	*wĕhāyâ bayyôm hahû'*, 9 (introductory)
2. 3rd-person development, 12-14	
3. Epexegesis:	
a) Mourning, 12:11	*bayyôm hahû'* (introductory)
b) Cleansing, 13:1	*bayyôm hahû'* (introductory)

C. Religious purging
   1. Yahweh speech, 2   *wĕhāyâ bayyôm hahû' nĕ'um*
                                        YHWH (introductory)
   2. 3rd-person development, 3 *wĕhāyâ kî* (integral)
   3. Epexegesis, 4-6   *wĕhāyâ bayyôm hahû'*, 4
                                         (introductory)

a. Time-identifying *bayyôm hahû'* is in v 8aβ.

(1) The original day-of-Yahweh oracle

Saebø is on safe ground when he assigns 12:1a to the penultimate redactor-editor who drew chaps. 9–13 together with use of the shepherd pericopes 11:1-3, 7, 13:7-9, at the same time identifying chap. 14 as a final addition to the completed corpus.

The word *maśśā'* must be taken as part of a word-chain that includes *dĕbar-YHWH,* creating a title for the section, "Burden of Yahweh's word." The following prepositional phrase, *'al-yiśrā'ēl,* must be translated "against Israel," not "concerning Israel." As indicated by the *athnach,* the oracle formula *nĕ'um YHWH* serves then with the following doxological phrases as a distinctive way of introducing the initial oracle in which Yahweh announces what he is about to do (*hinnēh 'ānōkî* plus the participle, v 2) in making Israel a *sap-ra'al,* "stumbling block," to its near neighbors (*lĕkol-hā'ammîm sābîb,* "to all the surrounding peoples"). And how that is to come about is introduced in v 4a by an integral *bayyôm hahû'* with phrases borrowed from the holy-war tradition concerning a *timmāhôn,* "panic," that will fall on every warhorse and a *šiggā'ôn,* "madness," that will affect every rider.

This appears to be the sum and substance of the original oracle, with the probable exception of a transition clause in v 3b, which broadens the reference to all the surrounding peoples to "all the nations *(gôyê)* of the earth."[39] A glossator — probably not one of the pro-Judahite redactors responsible for vv 5-8 — added v 2b and v 4b, extending the reference to Jerusalem to include Judah.[40]

This may seem brief and lapidary, but in fact many of the primitive holy-war passages in the Old Testament are similarly short.[41] It contains the prediction of an event that must have loomed threateningly throughout the postexilic period: a universal alliance for the purpose of destroying Jerusalem. But this gnawing *Angst* also provided a fresh occasion for the response of faith. Even in the face of such extreme peril, a panic from Yahweh would throw the enemy forces into confusion and Jerusalem would prove to be a beaker of intoxicating drink.

(2) The initial expansions

This assurance, confirmed as Yahweh's true revelation *(nĕ'um YHWH),* either immediately or very soon stimulated three expansions marked by the expanded formula of introduction, *wĕhāyâ bayyôm hahû'*. These had to do, respectively, with the problem of Judah's relationship to Jerusalem (12:3a, 5, 7, 8b), with the problem of ritual uncleanness (12:9-10, 12-14), and with the persistent presence of idols (13:2-3). Because these three expansions display much the same internal structure, it is all but certain that they emanate from a single redactor. Yet, because they each address different problems, they are probably to be seen as independent compositions on the part of this redactor, which he drew together here.

The new Yahweh.speech beginning in 12:9 recapitulates the substance of the foregoing verses, but this verse serves also as an introduction to the matters of mourning and cleansing, rather than continuing the thought of vv 2-8. Also, the oracle formula that strengthens the transition formula in 13:2 is clear indication that the matter it introduces constitutes a new move on this redactor's part.

The style of each successive expansion is similar: a new Yahweh speech leads into a third-person exposition, after which each section receives an item or items of epexegesis (12:6, 8a, 11, 13:1, 4-6). Although each new Yahweh speech has introductory *wĕhāyâ bayyôm hahû'*, each following section of third-person development lacks the temporal transition (13:3 has integral *wĕhāyâ kî*), while each separate section of concluding epexegesis has introductory *bayyôm hahû'* or *wĕhāyâ bayyôm hahû'* (13:4).

Despite the possibility that our arrangement may be considered unjustifiably schematic, we insist that the text does embody this arrangement. The separate events of the Yahweh speeches are designedly set for "that day," that is, the day of Yahweh's victory (12:2a, 4a). What Yahweh declares in each new section is in the third-person expostulation, with no new temporal move; then a new redactor (or redactors) uses a new temporal transition to introduce his prediction of synchronous (not sequential) new activities, seen as ongoing conditions or practices rather than as unitive events.

(3) 12:3a, 5, 7, 8b

Something further should be said about the third-person expansions, introduced between the Yahweh speeches and the concluding epexegesis. First of all, concerning the section on Jerusalem's and Judah's victory (vv 3a, 5, 7, 8b): we do not see the sharp antagonism here that many interpreters have found. The concern is not to advance Judah's claim in opposition, or even contradiction, to that of the city (a notion that one may mistakenly infer from 14:14a), but rather to assert a right to an equal share in Jerusalem's victory on the part of the surrounding countryside.

Yahweh is still speaking in v 3a, but the new image of Jerusalem as *'eben ma'ămāsâ,* "a heavy stone," represents a drastic shift from that of a

"cup of reeling" in v 2a. (The redactor placed it here, before the conclusion
of the underlying oracle, because it was for him a continuation of Yahweh's
initial announcement.) The third-person development begins in v 5 with attention to what the *'allupê yĕhûdâ*, "Judahite chieftains,"[42] will say to themselves, acknowledging that the *yōšĕbê yĕrûšālaim*, "inhabitants of Jerusalem,"
are indeed strong, but only "through Yahweh Sebaoth their god." In v 7 it
goes on to claim that victory is or will be with the "tents" of Judah first in
order that the renown *(tip'eret)* of "the house of David" and of the "inhabitants
of Jerusalem" should not exceed that of Judah. V 8b concludes this expansion,
acknowledging that the "house of David" shall be "like God," that is, "like
the angel of Yahweh before them."

(4) 12:6, 8a

We may believe that it was very soon that still another redactor or redactors
expanded this prediction with two separate words of epexegesis beginning
with *bayyôm hahû'*. V 6 picks up the reference to the princes of Judah,
emphasizing their ferocity in "devouring" *'et-kol-ha'ammîm sābîb*, "all the
surrounding peoples" (cf. v 2) so that (*wāw*-consecutive perfect) Jerusalem
may remain in existence where it belongs.[43] V 8a explains that Yahweh's
shield will protect the "inhabitants of Jerusalem," while the feeblest shall
have the strength of David. The effect of the temporal transitions is to synchronize these two events with the event of v 3 and v 4a.

(5) 12:9–13:1

There is a more ample Yahweh speech at the beginning of the second prime
expansion at vv 9-10.[44] This includes a retrospect reference in v 9 to the great
battle, claiming that it will be Yahweh's intent *(bqš)* to destroy the attackers.
It goes on to announce Yahweh's action with respect to a mysterious person
who has been pierced *(dqr)*.[45] It is a "spirit of compassion and supplication"
that this one will "pour out," leading to bitter mourning on the part of those
who have committed this crime — if that is what it is. Here the tandem
expression seen in v 7, "house of David and inhabitants of Jerusalem," is part
of the Yahweh speech rather than of the third-person development.

The third-person development in vv 12-14 extends this action. Though
it is in Jerusalem that this mourning shall begin, it will be extended throughout
the land (or countryside, *hā'āreṣ;* cf. 13:2) and be carried out by four distinct
groups: the Davidides, the Nathanites, the Levites, and the Shimeites, with
separation of the male members of each group from their wives.

To this second section of combined Yahweh speech and third-person
development, a later redactor or redactors appended the words of epexegesis
in 12:11 and 13:1, again employing introductory *bayyôm hahû'* in each verse.
12:11 cryptically compares Jerusalem's weeping to the notorious ritual weep-

ing for the fertility god Hadad-rimmon. 13:1 specifies the means (a marvelous fountain) by which "the house of David" and the "inhabitants of Jerusalem" shall purge themselves of uncleanness.

(6) 13:2-6

The oracle formula in 13:2 points to the climactic nature of a third expansion with its introductory *wĕhāyâ bayyôm hahû'*. The Yahweh speech of v 2 announces two specific acts of religious purging. Yahweh declares that he will drive out the memory of the idols that remain in the land by cutting off *(krt)* their very names, then he adds that he will also remove (*'br* hiph.) both the prophets and the "spirit of defilement."[46]

The third-person development in v 3, introduced by *wĕhāyâ kî,* is an illustrative, casuistically styled conditional clause, to the effect that even if anyone should venture to act as a prophet, his very own parents shall denounce him as a liar and pierce *(dqr)* him through while in the very act of prophesying.

Vv 4-6 is epexegetical to this announcement, explaining that in such an act "every prophet" shall (echoing Amos) renounce professional prophecy and go back to the livelihood of agriculture, explaining certain wounds on his back as inflicted in the very "house (temple?) of his friends." Here at the very end of the entire pericope, the more weighty *wĕhāyâ bayyôm hahû'* synchronizes these admissions on the part of putative prophets with Yahweh's act of removing "the prophets and the unclean spirit" from the land (cf. v 2), as well as with the day of Yahweh's great battle (12:2a, 3b-4a).

(7) Thematic shifts within this pericope

Throughout this remarkable pericope the emphasis is continually on the theme of separation or division; but this is not identical with that of the other material in chaps. 9ff. In the original oracle of 12:2, 3b-4a, it is that between the nations and Jerusalem, or between Yahweh and the nations — a theme of increasing transcendence and particularism typical of the postexilic period as a whole. In the first expansion it is that between the city and the Judahite enclave; but, as we understand it, this is based on the claim of fairness and not on outright hostility. In the second expansion it is that between the mourners in Jerusalem and the mourners in the land, the latter being subdivided by families and sexes. In the third expansion it is that between a putative prophet and his parents and friends. But each variety of distinction or separation is dissimilar to that between Judah and Israel (Samaria) reflected in 11:14; also to that between the shepherds and the sheep, that is, the leaders and the people, in 11:17, 13:7; also to that between the two-thirds that shall perish and the one-third that shall survive in 13:7-9.

It becomes abundantly clear that there were strong tensions within the community of Zechariah's redactors, and that their "eschatology" addressed the resolution of these tensions rather than the usual postexilic problems of returning and rebuilding, coming to expression in Zechariah 1–8. In the main, the resolution would have to come mainly as the result of Yahweh's act (12:10, 13:2), yet the community itself would be called upon to participate in bringing Yahweh's action to its fullest potential. What needed to take place on their part would take place synchronously with Yahweh's primary deed of defeating Jerusalem's enemies. Thus the day of Yahweh's victory is to be filled with new actions and a new situation bringing that victory to its fullest purpose and effect.

e. Temporal transitions in Zechariah 14

Little of this emphasis on distinction and separation comes to expression in Zechariah 14. Such distinction is, rather, the premise from which it begins, that is, that in v 2 between the Jerusalemites who will be lost in the nations' attack and those who survive it. The actual (vv 3, 12-15) or potential (vv 18-19) animosity of the nations is, of course, thematic; but this is eventually resolved to make way for the theme of unity and universality. We agree with Saebø that this chapter is a very late attachment to "Second Zechariah," with no literary connection at all to chaps. 12–13. What is most striking is that it develops even further the tendencies of proto-apocalypticism, proliferating the use of the two variants of *bayyôm hahû'* with as much apparent abandon as in 12:1–13:6.

Although thematic Yahweh speeches do not function here as in 12:1ff., new beginnings with introductory *wĕhāyâ bayyôm hahû'* do fall into meaningful positions, just as in 12:1ff. Saebø identifies an original day-of-Yahweh saying in vv 1-3, and from this traces the work of three different redactors — or perhaps of three different streams of tradition.[47] The first of these develops holy-war imagery implicit in vv 1-3, the second develops the theophany theme of vv 1-3, and the third develops an unmotivated sacerdotal interest.

We generally adopt this line of analysis, but it is necessary to make some modifications in it in the light of the present study. We offer the following structural outline to show the position and function of transitional elements, including the familiar *(wĕhāyâ) bayyôm hahû':*

Redactional Units	**Transitions**
I. Original day-of-Yahweh saying, 1-3, 9a	*hinnēh yôm-bā'*, 1 (introductory)
(oracular extract, 2)	*wĕhāyâ*, 9a (integral)
[gloss, 9b	*bayyôm hahû'*, 9b (introductory)]

II. Expansions
   A. Elaborations of the
   theophany motif
      1. Divine appearance at Mt.
      of Olives, 4-5a[a]

2. A restoring river, 8, 10aα, 11	*wĕhāyâ bayyôm hahû'*, 8 (introductory)
[gloss, 10aβ-b]	
B. Elaborations of the holy-war motif	
1. Endless day, 6, 7b	*wĕhāyâ bayyôm hahû'*, 6 (introductory) *wĕhāyâ*, 7b (integral)
[gloss, 7a	*wĕhāyâ*, 7a (integral)]
2. Panic and spoils, 13, 14b	*wĕhāyâ bayyôm hahû'*, 13 (introductory)
[gloss, 14a	*wĕgam* (introductory)]
3. Epexegesis: the plague, 12, 15b	
C. Cult-ideological expansions	
1. Universal feast of booths, 16-19	*wĕhāyâ*, 16 (introductory) *wĕhāyâ*, 17; *wĕ'im*, 18 (both integral)
2. Comprehensive holiness, 20-21c	*bayyôm hahû'*, 20a (introductory) *wĕhāyâ*, 20b, 21 (integral)

a. One should note time-identifying *bayyôm hahû'* in v 4.
b. Inclusio: *wĕzō't . . . hazzō't*
c. Cf. epitomizing *bayyôm hahû'*, 21 fin.

(1) The original day-of-Yahweh oracle, 14:1-3, 9a
Because of its second-person feminine pronouns, v 1 must be understood as an address to the city or populace of Jerusalem. The original oracle was not composed with 12:1–13:6 in mind, which concerns Jerusalem but does not address it.

    Despite this initial stance of making an address to Jerusalem, the city is mentioned in the third person elsewhere in chap. 14. Introductory *hinnēh yôm-bā laYHWH* is followed by a series of *wāw*-consecutive perfects, here and throughout vv 2-5, but there is no proper sequencing of events, as is normal to this syntactical construction. Because *wĕḥullaq*, "and shall be taken," in v 1 already presupposes the event that is described in v 2, the clause it introduces relates directly to the "day" announced. Saebø's suggestion that v 2 constitutes an implicit citation may explain this unnatural sequential shift.[48] This is attractive because v 2 is styled as a Yahweh speech (the only one in this pericope), while v 3 reverts to a third-person description of Yahweh's action. We are to interpret the attack, plundering, ravishing, and exile as a reflection of the event of 586, functioning as a typological image and serving as a model for every new situation of comparable imperilment in which Jerusalem might eventually find itself in future history.

It is especially this feature that so sharply distinguishes the ideology of chap. 14 from that of chap. 12, which contains no intimation of Jerusalem's jeopardy. It would seem reasonable to argue that this is a ploy motivated by the themes of separation and survival in 13:7-9, just preceding this chapter in the completed text of Zechariah 9–13 as it apparently lay at this redactor's disposal.

The fact is that the emphasis here lies not, as in 13:7-9, on a process of internal distinction and separation, but on Yahweh's battle against the attacking nations (14:3)[49] and upon the universal kingship of Yahweh that is to result from his victory (v 9a).

Though we agree with Saebø that the original day-of-Yahweh saying reaches its climax in v 3 and that vv 4-5 are secondary, we view v 9a as its proper conclusion rather than as an isolated cult-ritualistic fragment associated with vv 16ff. This interpretation would account for its inclusion within the passage while taking note of the fact that v 16 constitutes an entirely new move based upon the combination of the theme of the surviving nations with that of Yahweh's kingship.

(2) 14:4-5, 8

Saebø is quite persuasive with respect to the secondary nature of vv 4-5, which introduces the fantastic image of a rearranged topography for the mountains and valleys surrounding Jerusalem.[50] Vv 4-5, artificially connected to vv 1-3 by the time-identifying *bayyôm hahû'* in v 4, reaches a climax in the coming of Yahweh as "my God," rather than as universal king, as in v 9a.

A further secondary attempt at elaborating the theophany theme is introduced in v 8 by the temporal phrase *wĕhāyâ bayyôm hahû'*. This verse describes a stream of "living waters" that will issue from Jerusalem, then flow east and west to encircle the entire land *(yissôb kol-hā'āreṣ);* it is similar to the Arabah mentioned in Ezek 47:1-8 although its westward branch enters the region of Geba and Rimmon (v 10aα). This second topographical rearrangement unmistakably reflects the mythological imagery of Gen 2:10-14, but it is obvious nonetheless that Ezekiel 47 is its direct source of inspiration (cf. also, from Ezekiel, the motif of the return of Yahweh's glory from the east in 43:2).[51]

(3) 14:6-7, 13-14
Parallel materials were soon introduced in vv 6, 7b, and vv 13-14 with successive occurrences of *wĕhāyâ bayyôm hahû'*. The first attachment is a development of the unending-day motif from Josh 10:12-13, while the second is a replication of the parallel themes of a supernaturally produced panic (*mĕhûmat-YHWH*, not *maggēpâ*, "plague," as in vv 12 and 15) and of booty taken from the conquered. Both are normative to the ancient holy-war tradition. These expansions have been intertwined with the theophany expansions in such a way as to suggest that more than a single redactor was involved. They are not successive extensions by the same redactor, as in 12:1–13:6.

(4) 14:12, 15
Saebø's analysis assigns vv 12 and 15 to the redactor or redactors who produced the cultic images of vv 16-19 and vv 20-21, but there is in fact nothing specifically cultic here. The penchant for creating extensive lists, such as the specification of body parts in v 12b and that of affected animals in v 15, may reflect a priestly habit of mind; but the main thing to pay attention to is the inclusio created by *wĕzō't* at the head of v 12 and final *hazzō't* in v 15. Vv 12 and 15 envelop vv 13-14[52] and must be seen as a designed refocusing of those verses with the imagery of 2 Kgs 19:35 in mind. Adding the *maggēpâ* image to that of the *mĕhûmâ*, this element of epexegesis seems to take cruel delight at the plight of the victims, whether human or animal.

(5) 14:16-19, 20-21
Definitely cult-ideological are the expansions in vv 16-19 and vv 20-21. *Bayyôm hahû' yihyeh* introduces an image of comprehensive holiness in 20f, which concludes with a remarkable epitome with transitional *yihyeh* and final *bayyôm hahû'* in v 21b. It hardly seems that vv 20-21 were designed as a comment on, or alteration of, vv 16-19; hence this should be seen as a parallel expansion within this tradition rather than as a further element of epexegesis.

As for vv 16-19, the following may be said: the reference to the plague in v 18 is certainly drawn from vv 12, 15; the intent is to extend the image of Yahweh's universal kingship, drawn from v 9a, in terms of the nations'[53] inclusion in the invitation to participate in the Feast of Booths. The only problem appears to be whether they will actually accept this generous invitation.

These verses communicate the ideal of universality while allowing for a self-created separation, ideologically paralleling the separation of Jerusalemite victims and survivors in v 2. The inclination toward comprehensiveness takes quite a different direction in vv 20-21, where it applies only to "Jerusalem and Judah," making the intrusive *kĕna'ănî* ("merchant," with possible innuendo of the gentilic "Canaanaite") superfluous and unwelcome.[54]

(6) 14:7a, 9b, 10-11, 14a

In this explanation it has been possible to account cogently for virtually every occurrence of *(wĕhāyâ) bayyôm hahû'*. The occurrence of either variant is the indicator of a special interpretive move. This also pertains, finally, to one of the four glosses, that in v 9b, with an introductory *bayyôm hahû'*. In affirming theoretical monotheism it means to insist on cultic exclusivity. It was added naturally to the solemn declaration in v 9a affirming Yahweh's universal kingship.

Other glosses do without a temporal introduction, though similar transitional forms are used. *Wĕhāyâ* in v 7a, alongside *wĕhāyâ* in v 7b,[55] introduces an item of cosmic reflection regarding "that day" mentioned in v 6. An extended gloss in vv 10aβ-11 draws interest from the well-watered land back to Jerusalem, ideally arranged and safely situated.[56] Someone more acrimonious than the reactors and glossators of chap. 12 ventured in 14:14a to suggest that Judah might itself have a part in the attack upon Jerusalem.[57]

(7) Thematic shifts within this pericope

Every one of the predictions introduced by *(wĕhāyâ) bayyôm hahû'* except the one in vv 13-14 has to do with a new and permanent state of ideal being, and the event of a holy-war panic in vv 13f. is not imaged in terms of a unique historical future so much as in terms of a typological transition to a state of being in which the wealth of all the nations will continually be brought to Jerusalem. It is a strikingly baroque imagination that contemplates the synchronizing of all this with the coming day of Yahweh mentioned in v 1.

Many of the idealistic images that were employed in the writings of the earlier prophets have been brought together here in one comprehensive panorama. This expresses a tendency that had been only partially brought to realization in the Gog apocalypse, as well as in Zechariah 12–13. The logic of this type of forecast assumes that nothing truly significant can occur following "Yahweh's day" or apart from it, so that any actual history under which the Jewish people must continue to live becomes ideologically irrelevant.

It is this above all that should warn us against the attempt to identify historical allusions in Zechariah 14; it is an abstraction from history rather than a reflection of it. We should also pay close attention to the previously mentioned fact that the decimation of Jerusalem's population in v 2 is assumed rather than predicted.

The typological model of Jerusalem's siege, capture, and plunder, along with the ravishing of its women and the exile of half its population, is based of course on the calamitous event of 586; but this is intended as a paradigm of any and every past and future attack upon Yahweh's people and city. Although we know very little of Jerusalem's actual circumstances prior to the time of Antiochus IV, we may be quite sure that "all the nations" were never united in any such attack. Every potential menace is therefore combined within this image. This is a peril that constantly confronts the city; and once it is removed, perfect and comprehensive bliss will result.

Implied in 12:2ff., but here clearly spelled out, is a strong sense of vulnerability. So long as Yahweh's land and people exist on this earth, they will be threatened by forces beyond their control, and therefore it must be Yahweh's final and decisive intervention that alone brings relief. Clearly, the persons who composed this material saw little relevance in the meager resources available to the postexilic Jews, inside or outside Palestine. Historical involvement could no longer be counted upon to bring relief and restore Israel's primeval bliss, as in the expectation of Proto-Zechariah and the other canonical prophets. History was now (once again) the problem, rather than the solution.

f. Social ideology in Zechariah 12:1ff. and 14:1ff.

Disillusionment with the return from exile is what motivates the escapist solution of emerging apocalyptic. This can be seen with special clarity in the book of Daniel, particularly in chap. 9.[58] Some of this disillusionment is also to be recognized in such a "theocratic" book as that of the Chronicler, whose constant admonitions and exhortations for "Israel" to actually be what Yahweh intended it to be imply that the return under Cyrus's edict did not, after all, result in a perfect state of bliss.[59] The big difference, so strikingly outlined by Otto Plöger in his book *Theocracy and Eschatology,* is that 1-2 Chronicles still expects Israel's ideal to be realized within the parameters of historical existence, whereas apocalyptic looks for this beyond history.

Plöger is certainly right in calling attention to the similarity of Deutero-Zechariah's intensifying separatism and escapism, on the one hand, and, on the other hand, the eschatological extremism of the second-century *hasidim,* leading — as most scholars interpret it — to the separatism and escapism of the Qumran movement. Plöger should not have been so sure, however, that these *hasidim* were the group responsible for Zechariah 12–14. There is no unambiguous evidence of a confrontation between rival parties in this section. Furthermore, Plöger is certainly wrong in claiming that chaps. 12–14 are a unified composition and that such a composition reflects precisely the parlous situation of the *hasidim* in conflict with the priestly party that controlled Jerusalem before and after the time of Antiochus IV.[60]

Lutz's monograph has shown the acute divergence between Zech 12:1ff.'s tradition of an attack on Jerusalem and that of Yahweh's attack on the nations in chap. 14.[61] Even more importantly, 12:1ff. looks for a solution that pertains solely to Jerusalem while 14:1ff. expects the nations who were once enemies to participate alongside the surviving portion of Yahweh's people in a final and absolute state of bliss.

We must accordingly be hesitant about Plöger's claim, endorsed by Paul Hanson,[62] that proto-apocalypticism is endemically at variance with priestly and cultic ideology. I have argued elsewhere that priestly, wisdom, and apocalyptic thinking share a distinctive way of looking at time and history.[63] Here I would simply call attention to the fact that the proto-apocalypticists who were responsible for Zech 12:1ff. and 14:1ff. were unable to think of a final solution outside the parameters of priestly and cultic idealism. Public mourning and ritual purification (12:11–13:2) lead to the ideal state of bliss without which the victory of 12:2ff. would be meaningless, and the effect of the victory of 14:1ff. is, according to this chapter's redactors, both to bring the survivors of the nations into Jerusalem's cultic orbit (vv 16ff.) and to turn all that is profane into a state of perfect and comprehensive holiness (vv 20-21).[64]

g. The function of these passages within the book

Nothing could be more certain than that Zechariah 9–14 originated in an era quite different from that of chaps. 1–8. Since there is no redactional link between these two sections of the book, there is nothing but a tenuous connection between the eschatological ideology of Second Zechariah and that of First Zechariah. The former has certainly been more strongly influenced by themes from the great prophets Isaiah, Jeremiah and Ezekiel than by themes from First Zechariah.[65] The gap between the two sections of the book is wider, therefore, than that within the book of Isaiah, where at least the main thematic source for Deutero-Isaiah has been proto-Isaiah.

Very little can be said with assurance about the historical background of Second Zechariah, and it is best to refrain from unwarranted speculation.[66] It does seem likely that Alexander's conquest lies behind chap. 9, and a permanent divorce between Judah and Israel (11:14) possibly reflects the Samaritan schism, whenever that occurred. But who the sheep and the shepherds were remains obscure, as well as the identification of the saved remnant of chap. 11.[67]

Those for whom Zechariah 9–14 were written were confronted by three unwelcome realities: (1) that the imperial powers that held them in subjugation were more of a threat than a source of help and relief; (2) that the return from exile had not resulted in an ideal reunification of all Israel, and what unity did exist was constantly threatened by strife and estrangement within; and (3) that the temple cult had not cleansed the people of sin or given them spiritual renewal. The effect of these tenacious problems was, for the proto-

apocalypticists of Second Zechariah, to cause them to despair about the possibilities of history and encourage them to look beyond the events they were
experiencing to an ideal state of being in which all external perils would be
removed, all that was truly Israel would be united, and Yahwistic religion
would finally be fully purged.

The scenario of such a future is certainly more sharply focused in
Zechariah 14 than in chaps. 9ff., including 12:1ff. Saebø explains that the
redactor of chaps. 9–13 bound 12:2ff. into these chapters under the motif of
a severe coming judgment that would at last lead to Israel's purging and
reconversion, restoring a new sense of distinctive peoplehood within the
covenant with Yahweh (13:8-9). Thus the great battle of 12:2ff. is not, in fact,
the last event of history, but a battle that leads to the restoration of covenant
living.

This is the answer that the redactor of chaps. 9–13 gives to the apocalypticist of 12:2ff. Nothing can be more final in an existential sense than a
state of being in which Yahweh declares, "They are my people," and in which
they respond, "Yahweh is my God" (13:9). This is in fact a reaffirmation of
the eschatology of Hos 2:18-25 (E 16-23) as well as a prolepsis of 1 Pet 2:10.

Thus Zechariah 9–13 defines what is ultimate in a spiritual sense, not
in terms of chronological sequence. Chap. 14, on the other hand, reconstructs
the entire cosmos, making future attacks on Israel impossible by bringing the
nations under allegiance to Yahweh as universal king, rearranging the land
and the city, and removing the distinction between what is holy and what is
profane.

It should also be observed that Zechariah 14 goes beyond Ezekiel 38–39
in focusing futuristic expectation on Jerusalem and the temple rather than on
the land of Israel. Both in the sections belonging to its original core (38:8,
39:2, 4, 17) and in the redactional additions (38:11, 16, 18-19, 39:9, 12-15,
28), the Gog apocalyse is concerned with the imperilment of the land following
Israel's return, while Jerusalem remains unmentioned.[68]

The Gog apocalypse remains within the patriarchal tradition of the
promise of land and peoplehood. That changes in Ezekiel 40–48, which is the
major source for the imagery of Zechariah 14. With reminiscences of the
Isaianic tradition of an inviolable Zion, the menace to Jerusalem rather than
to the land of Israel becomes thematic in this chapter, as it has been in
Zechariah 12:1–13:6. Hope for the land as such has been given up and
everything has been concentrated in Jerusalem, less as a political entity than
as a cultic center.

The apocalypticists of Zech 12:1ff., but especially those of chap. 14,
have relativized all that is secular and historical within Israel's futuristic
expectations, substituting an image that is at the same time narrowly partic-
ularistic and ideologically transhistorical.

Conclusions concerning the Postexilic Minor Prophets as a Group

We may briefly summarize our observations concerning the postexilic *versus* the preexilic use of futuristic transitions within the Book of the Twelve Prophets.

The integral transitions that appear frequently in the preexilic minor prophets have become rare in the postexilic minor prophets. Of the passages that do contain them, two that have them give strong expression to an imminentistic expectation (Hag 2:20-23, Zech 8:9-13), while the one that remains (Zech 12:2a, 3b-4a) employs the temporal formula to introduce the climax of a divine act that is scheduled for the present crisis to which it speaks.

Occurrences that introduce redactional expansions are even more strongly in the ascendancy in the postexilic minor prophets than in the preexilic passages that we have examined, and the variants *bayyôm hahû'* and *wĕhāyâ bayyôm hahû'* hold almost complete sway. The peculiar eschatological program of the late additions to Joel occasioned the choice of transition formulas not found elsewhere (*wĕhāyâ 'ahărê-kēn*, 3:1; *wĕhinnēh bayyāmîm hahēm ûbā'ēt hahî'*, 4:1) while *bayyāmîm hahēmmâ* in Zech 8:23 relates a naively idealistic expectation (ten gentiles seizing a Jew's robe) to a whole series of sanguinary expectations within the preceding context.

Within the book of Zechariah the formula *(wĕhāyâ) bayyôm hahû'* has come to special prominence. The influence of the additions to Isaiah and of the Gog apocalypse in Ezekiel is evident; but, as we have seen, these are found only in the proto-apocalyptic sections, 12:1ff. and 14:1ff. The word *wĕhāyâ*, used in these pericopes also without a following *bayyôm hahû'*, seems especially appropriate for introducing drastically different and permanent conditions or states of being. This is to say that the eschatology of these sections is not concerned with unitary events, except when an event introduces a permanent change, as in 12:3.

Initial levels of redaction in Zech 12:1ff. and 14:1ff. are marked by *wĕhāyâ bayyôm hahû'*, while the formula without *wĕhāyâ* usually introduces late levels of redaction. It is especially remarkable that the epitome in 14:21b and several of the expansions introduced by a temporal transition (13:1, 14:9b, 20; also 14:6, 13 with foregoing *wĕhāyâ*) have a form of *hyh*, "be" or "become," as the main verb. Here the expectation has already moved beyond what historical event may produce — or even beyond what Yahweh's direct action in historical event may produce — to a transcendental state that has virtually independent existence.

It is significant that only Joel (3:1, 4:18) has a temporal formula in anacrusis — a construction prevalent among the preexilic minor prophets. This is the form best suited for attaching traditional materials, but Zechariah does entirely without it. The new material in Zechariah that is introduced by a temporal transition is exclusively in prose.

As elsewhere in the prophetic collection, this is also the form best suited to the communication of speculative concepts. Though motifs from the past may be recalled in some of these prose expansions, they tend to be bold and innovative in imaging the future. This is one among several items of evidence that traditional prophecy is surely coming to an end and that oracular revelation is being supplanted by reflective interpretation and speculation.

Finally, it is worth pointing out that a predominant theme of the post-exilic minor prophets is the punishment of the nations as a prerequisite to Israel's full salvation (Joel 4:1; Zech 12:1ff., 14:1ff.; cf. Hag 2:20-23). In this, too, the influence of Ezekiel 38–39 is evident — that is, the original Gog apocalypse with its early expansions, apart from 39:23-29, the original redactional conclusion. The assumption is that the return has already occurred, but restored Israel is still in peril. In the additions to Joel this problem is solved in terms of a final judgment upon the nations. In Second Zechariah it is solved in terms of Yahweh's victory over enemies attacking Jerusalem, leading to stringent reforms in 12:1ff., and in 14:1ff. to Yahweh's universal kingship and comprehensive holiness in his land and among his people.

PART THREE

Futuristic Transitions
in the Traditioning Process

CHAPTER ELEVEN

Distribution according to Redactional Levels

Introduction

We have examined each of the biblical books containing futuristic transitions with sufficient detail to allow us to draw some significant conclusions with regard to the process in which such transitions have been put to service in the composition and redaction of the various books. Upon initial review, it may seem that no distinction may be made about how they came individually into the scriptural text, except for the rather obvious conclusion that most of the integral occurrences are in primary materials as we have defined them and, equally obviously, that the introductory occurrences are redactional. However, we are now prepared to go beyond this in suggesting how each occurrence may have come into the expanding text.

In recent years, much has been made of the technique or discipline of "redaction criticism," which is generally distinguished from the study of literary composition as such — known as "source criticism."[1] Taken in the broadest sense, redaction criticism is an analysis of the entire compositional and editorial process — oral and literary — that transforms elemental units into larger complexes through combination, restructuring, and amplification.

In this definition, redaction will not be directly equated with editing, which is a strictly literary and organizational procedure within the redactional process. It is the main task of editing to arrange compositional blocks into a document — a book or other type of publication — providing transitions and introductory items of various kinds. On the other hand, redaction taken in the broad sense in which we are using the term begins virtually where literary composition begins. It includes the entire creative and developmental process. At the earliest level, it is in practice virtually impossible to distinguish the original words of an author from his own or his immediate disciples' initial

241

recording and reshaping of these words. Redaction in this sense may start even at the oral stage, perpetuating and perhaps recasting a linguistic unit that has been preserved in memory or tradition, now put into suitable form for a more advantageous and public presentation.

While no special effort has been exerted in the present study to argue for the authorship or originality of particular passages, we have paid attention to this question as a point of departure for all subsequent redaction. That is to say, the concept of originality has been maintained mainly for gaining a perspective from which to evaluate the various levels or stages within this extended process of redaction.

It has been convenient to group occurrences of futuristic transitions first of all formally and structurally; that is, as to whether they appear integrally within pericopes or as introductions to literary supplements. It has furthermore been important to locate integral transitions in terms of whether they belong to primary materials — which may already include blocks of inauthentic materials (added of course by redactors) — or whether they belong to *ad hoc* comments or elaborations (always redactional). An impressive fact emerging from our analysis has been that every passage with an introductory temporal transition constitutes such an *ad hoc* attachment.

It is crucial for the ensuing discussion that we should make a special effort to define precisely where within the redactional process — extending from initial shaping through preliminary collocations or revisions, to and beyond every subsequent level of redaction up to the definitive editing — individual passages with integral or introductory temporal transitions should be located. In almost every instance, we now have in hand sufficient data for the assignment of these passages to distinct redactional levels. This may not always be absolutely certain, given the paucity of external information, but it will be seen to have a high degree of probability in its favor, sufficient to allow us to draw some significant conclusions.

Although these conclusions apply only to the special group of predictive passages that have temporal transitions, there are important implications for the entire process of secondary expansion within Scripture, including that which produced redactional attachments without such transitions.

In theory, any or all of the following levels of redaction may have been involved in the development of any given text: (1) initial shaping and recording; (2) preliminary collocation and reshaping; (3) the establishment of major tradition complexes; (4) pre-editorial supplementation; (5) definitive editing; and (6) post-editorial supplementation. In certain instances, a particular text may have actually repeated some of these levels. Within passages with futuristic transitions as a special group, we accept the responsibility of attempting to unravel these levels from one another. For this task, the techniques of textual criticism, source analysis, and form criticism are essential.

Beyond the scope of redactional expansion and alteration lie the stages of (1) scribal glossation and (2) canonical ordering. Neither of these stages has, in fact, produced any of our temporal transitions. The rare instances in which a temporal formula, particularly *bayyôm hahû'*, has been identified as a scribal gloss, or as part of such a gloss, do not involve its use as a temporal transition.[2]

Taking the predictive passages with temporal transitions as a special group, we may assign each passage to one of the levels mentioned, supporting our assignments in many instances with special arguments beyond what has been offered in the foregoing analysis of the individual formulas and individual books.

It will be helpful to display these passages in a generally chronological order: that is, preexilic, exilic, and postexilic, with early and late occurrences within each category. However, it is less temporal order as such that defines these assignments than the situational background of each passage.

The early preexilic passages reflect the background of the eighth- and seventh-century Assyrian menace, while the late preexilic passages are concerned with the emerging Neo-Babylonian empire; in both sets of passages it is Israel/Judah's sinfulness that creates a problem. The early exilic passages directly reflect the catastrophe of 586 and are concerned with the theological problem of the destruction of temple and city, the deportation of the people, and the apparent end of the covenant and of other essential elements of biblical religion. The late exilic passages, on the other hand, have to do with the imminent conclusion of the exile and the opportunity for return and restoration. The early postexilic passages reflect the initial return but are concerned for the immediate problems of the restoration community, while the late postexilic passages confront the continuing problems of late Judaism, in particular the ambiguities of life under foreign rule.

Level I: Initial Shaping and Recording

The first redactional level, that of initial shaping and recording, involves either the author himself or an amanuensis — more probably a close disciple than a professional scribe. The fore-given material may be a block of oral tradition familiar to the author, or it may be his own fresh creation. In his own mind he may have already reshaped it to a more appropriate form as he now seeks, from one motive or another, to preserve it in writing.[3] To use a convenient example: it seems probable that Micah himself was recording one or more of his previous utterances as he joined them with the use of the initial word in 3:1, *wā'ōmar*, "and I said." Furthermore, although each of the major call-vision complexes, those in Isa 6:1-11, Jer 1:1-14, and Ezek 1:1–3:15, has undergone nonauthentic expansion, they each go back to more schematic originals, spoken by and/or recorded by the prophet in question. The purpose of Level I redaction in these passages is to preserve authoritative words and deeds for those not present at the initial hearing and/or viewing of them, and at the same time to present them in the most effective and authoritative form. These are random examples, but they illustrate the general situation that pertains to this redactional level, and they illumine the situation into which our present examples fall.

We have assigned all primary integral passages on our list — and only them — to this first level of redaction. In narrative discourse outside the prophetic corpus, in Isaiah, in Jeremiah, in Ezekiel, in the Twelve Prophets, and in Daniel, the integral transition formulas that come into use at this level are mainly *(wĕ)ʿattâ,* "(and) now," and *ʾāz,* "then," creating a temporal move to the present or imminent future; also *hinnēh yamîm ba îm,* "behold, days are coming," involving a future beyond the present scene. At this level the favorite "eschatological" locution, *(wĕhāyâ) bayyôm hahûʾ,* of all secondary strata within the prophetic corpus is virtually absent as an integral transition, occurring only in Hag 2:23 and Zech 12:4.

We note also that integral occurrences within narrative discourse are all early and appear only in private oracles. Most of these integral occurrences are either in authentic preexilic oracular materials or in supplementary materials in late-exilic or early postexilic writings, such as Deutero- and Trito-Isaiah.

The passages belonging to Level I may be arranged in a list according to their respective periods of origin, with an indication of the temporal formulas employed in each of them, as follows:

1) Preprophetic

    1 Sam 2:27-36 (*wĕʿattâ nĕʾum YHWH,* 30; *hinnēh yāmîm bāʾîm,* 31)
    1 Sam 15:1-35 (*wĕʿattâ šĕmaʿ-lĕqōl dibrê YHWH,* 1b)
    2 Sam 7:1-29 (par 1 Chr 17:1-27) (*wĕʿattâ,* 8 [7])
    2 Sam 12:1-25 (*wĕʿattâ,* 10)
    2 Kgs 20:12-19 (par Isa 39:1-8) (*hinnēh yāmîm bāʾîm,* 17 [6])

2) Preexilic
  a) Early
    Isa 1:21-28 (*ʾaḥărê-kēn,* 26)
    Hos 2:4-17 (E 2-15) (*wĕʿattâ,* 12 [10])
    Hos 3:1-5 (*ʾaḥar,* 5)
    Hos 5:5-7 (*ʿattâ,* 5)
    Hos 7:1-7 (*ʿattâ,* 2)

Hos 13:1-3 (*'attâ*, 2)
Amos 4:1-3 (*kî hinnēh yāmîm bā'îm 'ălêkem*, 2aβ)
Amos 6:4-7 (*lākēn 'attâ*, 7)
Amos 7:12-17 (*wĕ'attâ šĕma' dĕbar YHWH*, 16)
Mic 3:1-4 (*'āz*, 4)
Mic 4:8–5:3 (E 4) (*'attâ*, 9; *kî 'attâ*, 10; *wĕ'attâ*, 11; *'attâ*, 14 [E 5:1])
b) Late
Jer 14:1-10 (*'attâ*, 10bβ)
Jer 22:20-23 (*kî az*, 22b)
Jer 23:16-22 (par 30:23-24) (*bĕ'aḥărît hayyāmîm*, 20b [24b])
Ezek 7:1-4 (*'attâ*, 3)
Ezek 19:10-14 (*wĕ'attâ*, 13)
Ezek 26:17-21 (*'attâ*, 18)
Ezek 27:1-9, 25b-36 (*'attâ*, 34 LXX)
Nah 1:12-13 (*wĕ'attâ*, 13)
Hab 1:5-17 (*'āz*, 11)

3) Exilic
a) Early
Jer 16:16-18 (*wĕ'aḥărê-kēn*, 16b)
Ezek 32:9-15 (*'āz*, 14)
b) Late
Isa 34:1–35:10 (*'āz*, 35:5, 6)
Isa 41:1-20 (*'āz*, 1b)
Isa 48:1-16 (*wĕ'attâ*, 16)
Isa 60:1-7 (*'āz*, 5)
Jer 31:10-14 (*'āz*, 13)
Jer 48:11-13 (*lākēn hinnēh yāmîm bā'îm nĕ'um YHWH*, 12)
Jer 49:1-5 (*lākēn hinnēh yāmîm bā'îm nĕ'um YHWH*, 2)
Jer 51:41-53 (*lākēn hinnēh yāmîm bā'îm*, 47; *lākēn hinnēh yāmîm bā'îm nĕ'um YHWH*, 52)
Ezek 38:1-9 (*miyyāmîm rabbîm . . . bĕ'aḥărît haššānîm*, 8)

4) Postexilic
a) Early
Isa 58:1-14 (*'āz*, 8, 9, 14)
Hag 2:20-23 (*bayyôm hahû' nĕ'um YHWH . . .* , 23)
Zech 8:9-13 (*wĕ'attâ*, 11)
b) Late
Zech 12:1-2a, 3b-4a (*bayyôm hahû' nĕ'um YHWH*, 4)
Dan 10:18–11:1 (*wĕ'attâ*, 10:20)
Dan 11:2–12:4 (*ûbā'ēt hahî'*, 12:1 *bis*)

No good purpose would be served by extending the discussion of individual passages on this list beyond what has already been said in analyzing the various formulas and their appearance within the respective biblical books. We should emphasize that the passages listed are all in primary materials. There are no *ad hoc* redactional occurrences, whether the temporal formula be integral or introductory. We shall return to examine the imagery of these materials after we have concluded our discussion of further redactional levels (see Chapter Twelve).

Level II: Preliminary Collocation and Reshaping

The second level of redaction is that of preliminary collocation and reshaping, that is, the bringing together, with alterations and appropriate transitions, of related or similar materials, almost always from the original author. In many instances, this has proceeded by stages. As an example of a primitive stage of collocation, we may cite the drawing together of Amos's early ("call") visions in 7:1-3, 4-6, 7-9, 8:1-3, done more likely, as we have said, by a disciple than by the prophet himself. Many other examples might be cited; one from Ezekiel could be the "twinning" of oracles against the prophets in 13:1-16 and of oracles concerning the "prophetesses" in 13:17-23. As an example of a more sophisticated type of redaction at this level, we may mention that which lies at the earliest compositional level in the book of Ezekiel, a collection of oracles that are either dated or prefaced by circumstantial descriptions, or by both, in 1:1ff., 8:1ff., 14:1ff., 20:1ff., 26:1ff., 29:1ff., 31:1ff., 32:1ff., 33:21-22. Here dating and historical situationing are the prime organizing principles.

Elsewhere in the prophetic corpus, thematic similarities and catchwords or phrases have been as important as chronological sequencing in ordering the particular collocations. The intent in each redactional procedure at this level is to offer a more complete and balanced presentation of the prophet's message than what might be provided by a random and atomistic recording of individual proclamations.

The following is a list of the passages that probably came into the text at this level:

1) Preexilic
   a) Integral (none)
   b) Introductory
      (1) Early: Isa 7:18-19, 20, 21-22, 23-25; 17:4-6; Hos 2:18-22 (E 16-20), 23-25 (E 21-23); Mic 2:4-5

(2) Late: Zeph 1:10-11, 12-13

2) Exilic
   a) Integral redactional
      (1) Early: Jer 30:1-3 (*kî hinnēh yāmîm bā'îm,* 3); 30:23–31:1 (*bĕ'aḥărît hayyāmîm,* 30:24; *bā'ēt hahî',* 31:1); Ezek 24:27
      (2) Late (none)
   b) Introductory
      (1) Early: Jer 31:27-28, 31-34, 38-40
      (2) Late (none)

3) Postexilic (none)
    In assigning specific occurrences to appropriate slots on this list, we are again able to draw upon the details of our foregoing analysis, and it would be superfluous to rehearse the arguments here. We have again sorted out the passages belonging to this level according to general periods — preexilic, exilic, and postexilic. Comment is required on the various passages on this list in order to give our classification clarity.

1. The preexilic passages

We offer first some comments regarding the preexilic occurrences, those found in Isaiah, Hosea, Micah, and Zephaniah. Of course, there are no passages here with integral transitions because all such passages belong to Level I, that of initial shaping and recording. Thus we have only to do with introductory occurrences.

    As we have argued, Isa 7:18-25 and 17:4-6 came into the initial Isaianic collocation at a comparatively early period. Close disciples of the prophet were certainly involved. Isa 7:1-17 is the report of a prophetic word delivered during the Syro-Ephraimite war; probably a single redactor among Isaiah's disciples collected the prose sayings of vv 18f., 20, 21f., and 23-25, redirecting the threat to the subsequent Assyrian invasion. A close disciple was also responsible for 17:4-6, with *wĕhāyâ bayyôm hahû'* in anacrusis at v 4. This draws together related but separate oracles, each of which is authentic, once again refocusing the Syro-Ephraimite threat in terms of the larger Assyrian menace.

    A similar process produced the preexilic passages at this redactional level belonging to Hosea, Micah, and Zephaniah. It is tempting to explain Hos 2:18ff. and 23ff. as paraphrases on the part of a close disciple of strong sentiments — if not public utterances — of Hosea himself, very much in the spirit of 2:1-3 (E 1:10–2:1). The last-mentioned passage, with the other two, draws together the independent third-person narrative of 1:2-9 and the Hoseanic poem of 2:4-17 (E 2-15), constructing a redactional framework for an initial collection of Hoseanic materials.

Although we have established Mic 2:4-5, with its quasi-liturgical intro-duction, as secondary within its context, the disciple who composed it almost certainly intended it as an expression of Micah's own sentiment.

Finally, the three temporal phrases in Zeph 1:8aα, 10aα, and 12aα create an initial redactional framework, integrating separate Yahweh sayings into the unit comprising vv 7-13. It is impossible to surmise whether the prophet acting as redactor or a disciple-redactor created this larger unit, but the material is unquestionably authentic.

2. The exilic passages

This brings us to the exilic passages. Those that contain integral formulas of transition within redactional passages appear only in the two major prophetic books, Jeremiah and Ezekiel.

As we have argued, Jer 30:1-3 is the redactional introduction to the supplementary oracle collection promising salvation following judgment, 30:1–31:40. This is material with strong Jeremianic traditions, showing also the influence of Deuteronomy. The transition formula in 30:3, underscored by the oracle formula, introduces a citation of what the prophet is commanded to write. The temporal formula points to a drastic change of fortunes in the very near future and, like its occurrences in 31:27, 31, and 38, is a special marker of Jeremiah's early redactors.

The same or an earlier redactor was responsible for the bridging section, 30:23–31:1, in which the last portion of the prophet's own words in 23:16-20, including a now-functionless *bě'aḥărît hayyāmîm*, depicts the past, and a new formula *bā'ēt hahî'*, again with the oracle formula, points to the permanent basis for Israel's salvation in the midst of judgment, namely, the promise of Yahweh's continuing covenant.

Also belonging to the early years of the exilic period are three Jeremiah passages with the distinctive formula *hinnēh yāmîm bā'îm* and the oracle formula. In each of these the temporal formula is introductory. It has been feasible to assign Jer 31:27f., 31ff., and 38ff. to the redactor who was re-sponsible for the collection of oracular materials in chaps. 30–31, the same as the one who composed the first three verses of chap. 30. He was saving these materials in order to give them a new impact. As we have argued, these three short pericopes round off the entire unit, and the function that they now share with one another is to draw a composite picture of an idealized future for those who had experienced Yahweh's final wrath. To be sure, the Jeremiah who had so long predicted judgment could hardly have spoken these words unless it should have been through one of his disciples. The redactor-disciple in question was perhaps bold to speak what Jeremiah himself could not bring himself to speak.

The early exilic redactor who was responsible for the annotation in Ezek 24:25-27 intended to draw together the redacted symbolic-act oracle of 24:19-24 (and possibly the entire cycle of dated oracles) and the notice at 33:21-22 of how the news of Jerusalem's fall came to Ezekiel in exile. Although the latter is dated some months after Jerusalem's actual fall, the redactor telescopes the two events chronologically while treating them together as the final act of Yahweh's judgment on Jerusalem.

Level III: The Shaping of Major Tradition Complexes

The third level of redaction is that of establishing major tradition complexes, in which a variety of more primitive collocations, transmitted together, are placed into a normative association with one another. Claus Rietzschl has done this for Jeremiah. He has identified six distinct tradition complexes in Jeremiah 1–14, as follows: chaps. 1–6, chaps. 7–10, chaps. 11–13, chaps. 14–17, chaps. 18–20, and chaps. 21–24.[4] Examples from Ezekiel might be the collection of oracles against Judah's near neighbors in chap. 25, the collection of oracles against Tyre-Sidon in chaps. 26–28, and the collection of oracles against Egypt in chaps. 29–32.

It need hardly be said that in this process other secondary materials may also have been included — those that arose within earlier redactional expansion. Certain of them may, indeed, have come into the text as elements of the same Level III process, helping shape these major tradition complexes.

By assigning certain passages to this level, we intend to explain them in terms of what each of them does toward shaping such units. Without claiming certainty, we affirm a high degree of probability for our assignments at this level. In every instance it may at the very least be affirmed that their entry into the text at this level has more in its favor than a possible entry at any of the other levels.

The purpose of redactional supplementation at this level is to provide an interpretive perspective upon more extended blocks of traditional material. The following is a list of the passages that we would associate with this third redactional level:

1) Preexilic
   a) Integral redactional
      (1) Early (none)
      (2) Late: Jer 4:11-12 (ʿattâ, 12b)
   b) Introductory
      (1) Early (none)
      (2) Late: Jer 4:9-10, 11-12

2) Exilic
   a) Integral redactional (none)
   b) Introductory
      (1) Early: Jer 9:24-25 (E 25-26); 21:7; 23:5-6; Ezek 29:31
      (2) Late (none)

3) Postexilic
   a) Integral redactional
      (1) Early: Ezek 39:23-29 (ʿattâ, 25)
      (2) Late (none)
   b) Introductory
      (1) Early: Isa 2:2-5
      (2) Late (none)

1. Jer 4:9-12

At various points in the foregoing study we have discussed the intrusive verses, Jer 4:9-12, taking them not as a unity but as the product of two closely related interpretive moves on the part of Jeremiah's early redactors. We should not follow those exegetes who take 4:9-12 as a compositional unity for three good reasons: (1) the respective temporal transitions are never used together within the same original pericope;[5] (2) if vv 9-10 and vv 11-12 did actually belong together, *bāʿēt hahîʾ* would be integral without establishing a sequence, making instead a given situation or period of time synchronous with the "day" of a specific historical event; and (3) vv 9-10 is a Yahweh speech that both predicts and interprets an event, while the literary unit comprising vv 11-12 is in the form of an impersonal report that cites a traditional saying while noting the prophet's personal response to it. This is why we have so insistently argued that vv 9f. is a redactional insertion, and that vv 11f. is a subsequent comment upon it, perhaps by Jeremiah himself.

Although Jeremiah 2-6 is in a redictated — not original — form (cf. 36:32), these chapters together form a major tradition complex of the sort under consideration here. The unifying theme is that of the threat from the north, very probably that of the Neo-Babylonians. First-person Yahweh speech is dominant throughout these chapters; it is addressed either to a 2fs "thou" — implying the city, or possibly the land, for which the Hebrew words are feminine — or to a 2mp "you" — implying the people. But "I," "me," and "my" do not always refer to Yahweh in this section. In 2:1, 3:6, 11, 4:19, 21, 22(?), 23-26, 31, 5:4-5, 6:10-11a, 26, as well as in 4:12, they refer to the prophetic spokesman.[6] Also, the first-person plural refers to the community in 3:22b, 24-25, 4:8, and 6:24, 26. This is not generally to be taken as a mark of secondary accretion; rather, it shows that Jeremiah felt deeply and personally involved in what he was commissioned to proclaim.

All this material originated at what we would identify as redactional Level I, but 4:9f., 11f. (the latter with first-personal pronouns) belong neither at this level nor at the level of the postexilic intrusions with temporal transitions in 3:16-18, which is Level IV (see below). It is best to explain them as an effort on the part of Jeremiah and his early redactors, applied when chaps. 2–6 were being brought together in the redictated scroll, to reflect on the psychological effect of this redirected revelation, first on the community leaders (v 10) and then on Jeremiah himself (v 12).

2. Jer 9:24-25 (E 25-26)

It did not prove possible in our foregoing discussion to identify a reason for the insertion of Jer 9:24-25 (E 25-26) into its literary context, but its attachment just here may become meaningful upon the assumption that it came into the text as part of the redactional process that drew together chapters 7 through 10. In this major tradition complex there is much attention to cultic abuses, but this is limited mainly to 7:1–8:3, and in general the oracles gathered here have a broader scope.

The materials in this complex that originated between 605 and 586 were concerned with the nation's continuing unrepentance and the unavoidable calamity that threatened because of it. Some materials indicate that the calamity was already in progress or had already occurred. This means that the tradition complex, without secondary intrusions, was brought together redactionally very soon after Jerusalem's fall, and this is the time that must be assigned also for the insertion of 9:24-25 into it.

One special problem for the prophet at this moment of crisis was the failure of those who claimed to be wise to provide saving counsel (cf. 8:8-9, 9:11-15 [E 12-16], 22-23 [E 23-24]), and another problem was the fact that Judah's collaborators in conspiracy against Nebuchadrezzar might actually escape punishment while Judah suffered. To conclude this section, therefore, Jeremiah calls in 10:23-25 for Yahweh to do two things: (1) gently correct him for his trust in prideful wisdom and (2) punish the nations that have attacked — or abetted the attack upon — "Jacob." It would certainly seem plausible to suggest that the wisdom reflection in 9:22f., along with the prediction in vv 24f., came into the text along with these concluding reports. It is unclear why they were placed just where they are, unless 10:1-22 was subsequently added; nevertheless, assignment of 9:24-25 to this redactional level has more to commend it than assignment to any other level.

3. Jer 21:7, 23:5-6

The prophetic-word formula *haddābār 'ǎšer hāyâ 'el-yirmĕyāhû mē'ēt YHWH*, "the word that happened to Jeremiah from Yahweh," serves in Jer 21:1 not only as the introduction to the ensuing report of an oracular inquiry, but also as a redactional introduction to a separate tradition complex comprising chaps. 21 to 24, attached as an addendum to chaps. 1–20.

Though the contents are variegated and certainly include secondary materials,[7] this complex has mainly to do with the fate of Josiah's offspring on the throne of Judah, especially Zedekiah. Probably before the section on the false prophets (23:9-40) and Jeremiah's first-person vision report in chap. 24 were attached, an early exilic redactor, one of Jeremiah's close disciples, composed two special oracles concerning Zedekiah, 21:7 and 23:5-6 (the latter probably in immediate connection to 23:1-4). In these two oracles the oracle formula *nĕ'um YHWH* underscores that these constitute Yahweh's ultimate revelation concerning what had happened to Zedekiah, and this shows this redactor's intent in bringing the entire collection together. The first expansion is a *vaticinium ex eventu* of Yahweh's eventual purpose in Zedekiah's and Jerusalem's overthrow, while the second expansion predicts a compensating future scion of David who will faithfully image the implication of the king's name, *ṣidqiyyāhû*, "Yahweh (is) my righteousness."

4. Ezek 29:21

Also from the beginning of the exile and accompanying the redactional formation of a distinct tradition complex is Ezek 29:21, introduced by the transition formula *bayyôm hahû'*. We may believe that it was attached to 29:17-20 when this pericope stood at the conclusion of the foreign-oracle collection.[8] As such, it interprets the entire series — not just the Nebuchadrezzar pericope — as an expression of Yahweh's ultimate benign purpose for his people in subjecting the foreign nations to the same judgment that had fallen on Judah/Jerusalem.

5. Ezek 39:23-29

Already in our discussion in Chapter Two we identified Ezek 39:23-29, with integral 'attâ at v 25, as the initial redactional expansion to an original, late-exilic Gog apocalypse (38:2-9, 39:1-5, 17-20). This material came into the text as a redactional device for combining the apocalypse with the preliminary collocation of salvation texts that now appears in Ezekiel 33–37, thus creating one of the major tradition complexes within this book. The redactor who composed 39:23ff. may indeed have been responsible for shaping the entire inventory of salvation texts into a literary unit. Working just after the end of the exile, during the early years of the return, he refocused the Gog material — without its later expansions — in terms of Yahweh's plan for Israel's restoration. His apologia in 39:23-29 for the divine purpose in permitting the exile of Yahweh's people was intended as epexegesis not only to the Gog material, but to the entire salvation collection.

6. Isa 2:2-4(5)

We have reserved Isa 2:2-4(5) for final treatment in this section because it is also from the early postexilic period.[9] In our previous discussion we dated the composition of this pericope, including its opening formula wĕhāyâ bĕ'aḥărît hayyāmîm, to this period, and this unquestionably demands that the formation of the literary unit comprising chaps. 2–4, including its opening rubric in 2:1, must also have occurred as late as that.[10] Here too, then, the presence of an introductory temporal formula marks the formation of a distinct tradition complex.

Level IV: Pre-Editorial Supplementation

A fourth level of redaction, which may in many instances have occurred prior to that of Level III — that of the production of major tradition complexes — is that of ideological expansion and/or alteration prior to the level of definitive editing (Level V). Here we place all new oracular materials within the prophetic books that were recorded expressly for the purpose of supplementing preexistent units and complexes. The new units as such may have been drawn from primary materials or from earlier redactional units, as the case may be.

One random example may suggest the redactional activity at this level that was widespread throughout the growth of the prophetic collection. The account of divine judgment on Jaazaniah and Pelatiah in Ezek 11:1-13 expands the description of Yahweh's glory departing from the temple in the original verses of Ezekiel 8–11. This occurred prior to the formation of the collection of oracles against Israel in chaps. 1–24 and certainly before the definitive editing of the book as a whole.

Redactional activity at this level appears to have been unusually creative in the production of appendages that are introduced by one of the temporal transitions under study here. The essential aim of redaction at this level is apologetic. The purpose of using a temporal formula for introducing additional materials is to create a definite temporal move, sequential or synchronic, to a new event, a new situation, or even a new epoch. The added materials may have been drawn from published or unpublished sources, authentic or inauthentic. Others were the free composition of someone endeavoring to contemporize the prophetic message for a new generation. In some instances, the underlying text is contradicted or otherwise nullified in the light of its apparent nonfulfillment; or the purpose may simply have been to make room for additional, superseding revelatory insights.

Far more of the passages under study belong to this level than to any other level, and they come from every period, preexilic, exilic, and postexilic. We may list them according to periods of origin, again distinguishing early from late, as follows:

1) Preexilic
   a) Integral redactional
      (1) Early: Isa 22:19-23 (*wĕhāyâ bayyôm hahû'*, 20); 22:24-25 (*bayyôm hahû'*, 25)
      (2) Late (none)
   b) Introductory
      (1) Early: Isa 2:20-21; 3:18-23; 28:5-6; Hos 1:5; Mic 5:9-14 (E 10-15)
      (2) Late (none)

2) Exilic
   a) Integral redactional
      (1) Early: Jer 7:30-34 (*lākēn hinnēh yāmîm bā'îm*, 32); 19:4-9 (*idem*, 6)
      (2) Late (none)
   b) Introductory
      (1) Early: Isa 23:15-16; Jer 5:18-19; 8:1-3; Ezek 30:9
      (2) Late: Jer 30:8-9; 31:29-30; 50:4-5, 20

3) Postexilic
   a) Integral redactional
      (1) Early: Isa 16:13-14 (*wĕʿattâ dibber YHWH lēʾmōr*, 14); 31:6-7 (*kî bayyôm hahû'*, 7); 33:23 (*ʾāz*, 23b); Ezek 38:14-16 (*hălōʾ bayyôm*

hahû', 14b; *bĕ'aḥărît hayyāmîm,* 16b); 38:18-23 (*'im-lō' bayyôm hahû',* 19b); Zeph 3:11-13 (*kî 'āz,* 11b)

    (2) Late (none)

  b) Introductory

    (1) Early: Isa 10:20-23; 11:10, 11; 17:7-8, 9; 18:7; Jer 3:17, 18; 16:14-15; 49:39; Ezek 38:10-13, 18-23; 39:11-16; Zeph 3:9-10, 11-13, 16-17, 20; Zech 3:10; 8:23

    (2) Late: Isa 19:16-17, 18, 19-22, 23, 24-25; 24:21-23; Joel 3:1-3 (E 2:28-29); 4:1-3 (E 3:1-3), 18 (E 4:18); Zech 12:3a, 5, 6, 7, 8a, 9-10, 11, 12-14; 13:1, 2-3, 4-6

It should not be surprising that by far the largest proportion of passages under study came into the text at this fourth level of redaction; also that they are predominantly postexilic. All the prophetic books with redactional temporal transitions, except Amos, are represented. Isaiah has five early preexilic passages, one early exilic passage, nine early postexilic passages, and six late postexilic passages. Jeremiah has four early exilic passages, four late exilic passages, and four early postexilic passages. In Ezekiel there is one early exilic passage, along with the early postexilic expansions to the Gog apocalypse. Hosea has a single early preexilic passage. Joel has three late postexilic passages. In Micah there is a single early preexilic passage. The Zephaniah expansions in 3:9-20 are all early postexilic. Proto-Zechariah has two early postexilic passages, while Deutero-Zechariah has a sizable list of late postexilic expansions in 12:1ff., 14:1ff.

In distinction from the passages with redactional transitions that belong to Level II (preliminary collocation and reshaping) and to Level III (shaping of major tradition complexes), the passages on this new list are always directly concerned with the explication of the materials to which they are attached.[11] As has been mentioned, the purpose is essentially apologetic. By extension or refocusing, these new redactional elements aim to add a larger perspective to the divine intention regarding the event in question. In only four passages, Jer 5:18-19, 8:1-3; Ezek 30:9; and Mic 5:9-14, does an expansion deny or otherwise counteract the affirmation of the underlying material; and even in the last-mentioned passages the intent is to perfect the focusing of the terms of an inherently paradoxical situation.

Although the passages in question are too numerous and varied to allow facile categorization, certain distinctions may be made that will be useful for understanding their respective functions. Redactional activity at Level IV may in some instances precede Level II and Level III activity, as well as following Level III activity. This is to say that explicative and apologetic additions may enter the text before certain stages of preliminary collocation and reshaping, or before the shaping of certain tradition complexes, as well as prior to Level V activity, that of definitive editing. These are generally applicable distinctions that apply also to the passages under study here, those with futuristic transitions, whether integral or introductory.

It is rather striking also that a significant number of passages on this list have temporal transitions in clusters. Refining our analysis of such clusters in Chapter Five, we would point out that they came into the text in a variety of ways.

From single redactors come the clusters in Isa 11:10-11, 17:7-8, 9; Jer 50:4-5, 20, all postexilic. From different redactors, but added incrementally, are those in Isa 22:19-25, which are preexilic with the transitions in integral position, and Isa 19:16ff. and Joel 3:1-3, 4:1-3 (E 2:28-29, 3:1-3), which are postexilic with the transition formulas in introductory position.

In addition, there are two postexilic clusters in which a more complex pattern is evident. The first of these is Ezekiel 38–39, within which three distinct postexilic expansions have introductory *wĕhāyâ bayyôm hahû'*. These came into the text later than the initial, early postexilic, redaction seen in 39:23ff. They were followed by a variety of further expansions, most of which were introduced by a temporal formula. All the redactional material within Ezekiel 38–39 is essentially atomistic rather than incremental.

The second complex passage is Zechariah 12:1–13:6 with its three redactional expansions with introductory *wĕhāyâ bayyôm hahû'*; namely, 12:3aff., 9ff., 13:2f. These represent an initial redaction within this particular passage, atomistically expanding the original core in 12:1b-2a, 3b-4a. The remaining expansions within this pericope, several of which have introductory *bayyôm hahû'* or *wĕhāyâ bayyôm hahû'*, are from subsequent levels of redaction within the same school of interpreters.

Our further discussion of materials at this fourth level of redaction will be facilitated by grouping the passages into separate stages: stage A for those that were inserted prior to Level II; stage B for those that were inserted between Level II and Level III; and stage C for those that were inserted between Level III and Level V. Although we cannot in every case claim certainty, we should suggest what is at least probable concerning these various ways in which Level IV materials may have been inserted into the text.

1. Stage A: Additions made prior to Level II

The following are passages with futuristic transitions that were probably added following the initial recording (Level II) and prior to a preliminary collocation (Level III):

Isa 2:20-21. Probably before the formation of the redactional unit chaps. 2–4, the Isaianic day-of-Yahweh poem of vv 12-17 (concluding with epitomizing *bayyôm hahû'*) received two redactional supplements that are actually variants of each other, vv 18f. and vv 20f. Introductory *bayyôm hahû'* in v 20 makes explicit the synchronism between the humbling of human pride (v 17) and humankind's terror-stricken throwing away of idols.[12]

Isa 3:18-23. Although this insertion might have been made at various levels within the redactional process, the probability is that it was made fairly soon after the primary material in 3:16-17, 24-26, 4:1 was composed. The strong metaphor of the debasing of Zion's proud daughters would have provoked this list of confiscated finery at this very early stage, rather than after early collocations and complexes were already formed.

Isa 22:19-23; 24-25. These were successive expansions made by two different redactors soon after the private oracle concerning Shebna in vv 15-18 was recorded, certainly prior to the erratic placement of the revised pericope within its present context.

Isa 23:15-16. Isa 23:1-12 is a preexilic oracle against Tyre. In the early exilic period the redactor who identified the Chaldeans in the place of the Assyrians in v 13 used a reprise of v 1 appearing in v 14 as a point at which to attach a prediction that Tyre, like Judah, should suffer a seventy-year exile. The prediction did not, in fact, come true, giving rise in vv 17-18 to a postexilic reinterpretation, to the effect that (surviving) Tyre should instead provide treasures for Yahweh's sanctuary in spite of her continuing harlotries.

Isa 24:21-23. Bahar hazzeh and *YHWH şĕbā'ôt* in 25:6 indicate that 25:6-8 was the original continuation of 24:21ff., added to the day-of-Yahweh poem in 24:1-20 before the poem of declarative praise in 25:1-5 severed the connection between these two segments.

Isa 28:5-6. Since 28:7ff., part of a later attached, but original, cycle of Isaianic materials in chaps. 28–31, is a new pericope, it is probable that these verses were connected to vv 1-4 before such a collection was made.

Jer 50:4-5, 20. Two redactional expansions share here the peculiarity of having the same unusual formula *bayyāmîm hahēm ûbā'ēt hahî'*, making ascription to a single redactor highly probable. They are similar to each other in predicting restoration for Israel and Judah jointly, but the fact that they each expand predictions of Babylon's downfall (vv 2-3, 18-19, respectively), but not the similar prediction against Babylon in vv 9-16, makes it probable that they were attached in their respective positions prior to the initial collocation of anti-Babylon materials in chaps. 50–51.

Zech 12:3a, 5-14, 13:1-6. The original core of this section is 12:1b-2a, 3b-4a. Before 12:1a was added as a redactional link between chaps. 9–11 and 13:7-9, and certainly prior to the editorial attachment of chaps. 9–13 to chaps. 1–8, two stages of redaction added the remaining materials within 12:1–13:6 (see the extended discussion in Chapter Ten).

2. Stage B: Additions made between Level II and Level III

The following few passages with futuristic transitions came into the text at this juncture:

Isa 31:6-7. An early redactor — possibly Isaiah himself — used the introductory formula *kî kōh 'āmar-YHWH 'ēlāy,* "for thus Yahweh spoke to me," in v 4, to join the woe oracle of vv 1-3 and the poem in vv 4-5, 8-9 on the inviolability of Zion. Probably before the tradition complex of chaps. 28–31 was formed, a postexilic redactor added the call for repentance with motive clause that has been inserted at vv 6-7, with its integral *kî bayyôm hahû',* in the belief that the prediction of 2:20-22 concerning the day of Yahweh would soon be fulfilled.

Jer 49:39. Within the original collocation of Jeremianic foreign oracles, consisting of 25:15-16a, 46:2-12, 13-14, 47:1-7, 49:34-38, 51:59-64, there is no occurrence of any futuristic transition. However, the annotation concerning Elam's ultimate reversal of fortune, introduced by the formula *wĕhāyâ bĕ'aḥărît hayyāmîm* in 49:39, came into the text before this collocation was expanded by the remaining materials and shaped into one of Jeremiah's major tradition complexes.

Ezek 30:9. Individual undated oracles concerning Egypt (vv 1-4, 6-8, 10-12, 13-19) were inserted together into the collocation of dated oracles concerning Egypt that, together with similar collocations concerning the near neighbors of Judah and Tyre, creates Ezekiel's separate section of judgment oracles against foreign nations. Like several other expansions throughout this complex, 30:9 was added as a comment on 30:1-4,[13] and possibly on 30:6-8 as well, but very probably before the unit 30:1-19 was juxtaposed with the dated collection and prior to the transfer of 29:17-20, 21 to its present position.

Mic 5:9-14 (E 10-15). In our foregoing discussion we assigned Mic 4:8–5:3 (E 4) to the prophet Micah. The oracle promising deliverance from Assyria in 5:4-8 (E 5-9) may be from Micah or an early disciple. Before this material was combined with a preexisting collocation of judgment oracles in chaps. 6–7, the warning words of 5:9-14 were attached to the two salvation oracles.

Zech 3:10. After the quasi-symbolic act oracle of 3:1-9 was added to Zechariah's "night vision" collection (1:8-15; 2:1-4 [E 1:18-21]; 2:5-9 [E 1-5]; 4:1-6aα, 10b-14; 5:1-4, 5-11; 6:1-8), but before the initial summons to obedience in 1:1-6 was prefixed to this collection and chaps. 7–8 were attached to it, Zechariah's early redactor added 3:10 in a glowing mood of optimism respecting the ideal consequences of Joshua's cleansing and the removal of the land's guilt *bĕyôm 'eḥād,* "on a single day."[14]

Zech 8:23. This ingenuously idealistic expansion came into the text with the completion of a collection of oracular summaries in chap. 8, probably before this chapter was combined with chaps. 1–6 (7).

3. Stage C: Additions made between Level III and Level V

This leaves a lengthy list of Level IV expansions that were certainly or very probably inserted following the formation of the major tradition complexes:

Isa 10:20-23. Hans Wildberger is probably correct in dating the authentic material within Isaiah 10–11 to the Sargonic period, 705-701 B.C.E. Since 10:20-23 is clearly postexilic, it is probable that it came into the text after the formation of the literary block in 5:1–11:9, perhaps even after this had already been expanded with the addition of chaps. 2–4 and chap. 1.

Isa 11:10, 11. Perhaps at the same time that 10:20ff. was added, the same redactor added these verses to the literary block of 5:1–11:9.

Isa 16:13-14. V 12 looks like an early gloss to the collection of Moab oracles in 15:1–16:11. The reflective insertion in 16:13-14, with integral *wĕʿattâ,* may have been added after the foreign-oracle collection had already been formed. Although this redactor had a limited future in his purview ("in three years"), we have no means of identifying the historical event that he anticipated.

Isa 17:7-8, 9. These are random predictions that were probably added to the Isaianic material in 17:1-6 as much as two centuries later, also after the foreign-oracle collection had been made.

Isa 18:7. This postexilic expansion was made later than the foreign-oracle collection and long after the original oracle against Egypt.

Isa 19:16-17, 18, 19-22, 23, 24-25. These are incremental expansions dating from early to late in the postexilic period, also after the foreign-oracle collection had already been made.

Isa 33:23. Probably before chaps. 36–39 and chaps. 40ff. were attached, the diverse materials in Isaiah 32–35 came into the text. To a liturgy making subtle innuendoes against Egypt, the taunting words of 33:23, with integral *ʾāz,* were attached.

Jer 3:17, 18. To the authentic exhortation in 3:14, 19-20, a late exilic redactor added vv 15-16, long after the major complex representing the re-written scroll was formed. In the early postexilic period separate redactors added expansions in vv 17 and 18 with different introductory transition formulas, v 18 using the formula of v 16's time identifier, *bayyāmîm hahēmmâ,* while alluding to the land and heritage mentioned in v 19.

Jer 5:18-19. These verses contain an exilic reflection upon v 10's mention of an unthinkable *kālâ* for Israel and Judah. This piece of deuteronomistically influenced theologizing — much in the spirit of Jer 31:29-30 — was added after the formation of chaps. 2–25 and long after the promulgation of Jeremiah's rewritten scroll, preserved in chaps. 2–6.

Jer 7:30-34, 19:4-9. Comparison with other Jeremianic occurrences of the peculiar locution *lākēn hinnēh yāmîm bāʾîm* followed by the oracle formula dates these two passages no earlier than the early exilic period. Comparison with each other suggests that in each passage both the "because" clause and the "therefore" clause are firmly rooted in Jeremianic tradition, even though the separate passages have been redactionally adjusted as relevant expansions of the separate tradition complexes to which they belong, that is, chaps. 7–10 and chaps. 18–20, respectively.

Jer 8:1-3. These deeply pessimistic verses further expand the redactional expansion in 7:30-34, predicting that the bones of the numerous dead mentioned there would be exhumed after burial for the express purpose of being exposed to the heavenly luminaries, and adding that death would be preferable to a life of foreign exile.

Jer 16:14-15. The Jeremiah school remained sufficiently intact throughout the exilic period to employ the same distinctive temporal formula as in 7:32 and 19:6, *lākēn hinnēh yāmîm bāʾîm nĕʾum YHWH,* as a formula of transition to an oracle of salvation, inserting this just following a preexilic, Jeremianic judgment oracle in 16:1-13 and just before a further judgment oracle (a *vaticinium ex eventu*) from the redactor who had been responsible for the early collection of Jeremiah's oracles that constitutes chaps. 2–25.

Jer 30:8-9. After the complex of oracles and narratives in chaps. 26–36 had been formed, this prediction about serving Yahweh in the place of foreign oppressors was attached to explicate the day-of-Yahweh poem in vv 5-7.

Jer 31:29-30. A citation rubric with *bayyāmîm hahēm* serves to insert a late exilic reflection concerning the applicability of the sour-grapes aphorism into an already completed complex constituting chaps. 30–31, probably after the unit chaps. 26–36 had been formed.

Ezek 38:10-13, 14-16, 18-23, 39:11-16. After the redactional supplement in Ezek 39:23-29 had linked the primitive Gog apocalypse of 38:2-9, 39:1-5, 17-20 to the collection of salvation oracles in chaps. 33–37, other apocalypticists from within the Ezekiel school attached 38:10ff., 18ff., 39:11ff. (all with introductory *wĕhāyâ bayyôm hahûʾ*) in epexegesis upon the original material; among still later expansions was 38:14-16.

Hos 1:5. Following the formation of chaps. 1–3 as a unit and probably before this unit was connected editorially with chaps. 4–14, a preexilic redactor added 1:5, shifting the typology of the name Jezreel from an historical to a geographical reference.

Joel 3:1-3, 4:1-3, 18 (E 2:28-29, 3:1-3, 18). To the finished-off, original book in chaps. 1–2, apocalypticists of the Joel school added the prediction of a universal gift of the prophetic spirit (3:1-3 [E 2:28-29]). This was soon expanded by predictions about the penultimate and the final day (3:4-6, 4:1-3 [E 2:20-32, 3:1-3]). Random additions on the theme of universal judgment made room for a description of nature's marvelous transformation (4:18 [E 3:18]). The redactors in question employed distinctive transition formulas in distancing these still future events from the imminently future crisis of the authentic book.

Zeph 3:9-10, 11-13, 16-17, 20. Zephaniah's original book in 1:1–3:8 was focused on the crisis of a foreign invasion during the late preexilic decades. A series of postexilic redactors, working atomistically, completely refocused the book with regard to Yahweh's ultimate purpose for his people, which now would be to purify, humble, and restore them.

Level V: Definitive Editing

The fifth level of redaction is that of definitive editing, consisting primarily of topical arrangement and appropriate prefacing. We clearly see the results in the superscriptions[15] and in the gathering of three special types of oracular material, namely, judgment oracles against Israel, judgment oracles against the nations, and salvation oracles for Israel, to establish the main contours of the books Jeremiah (LXX), Ezekiel, and Zephaniah.

In some instances this type of editing occurred in stages. For example, Isaiah 1–35 must have once received normative editorial shaping prior to the second editing that was designed to include the new blocks of material found in chaps. 36–39 and chaps. 40–66.[16] In the case of Jeremiah, some editorial reshaping occurred late enough to allow Jeremiah's collection of foreign oracles to be moved from the normative intermediate location, as seen in the LXX arrangement, to a final position in the proto-Masoretic text.

The intent of redaction at this level is to present a complete and ordered corpus of materials ascribable to a given prophet. Though this redactional level is of little direct interest for the present study because it has generally been unproductive of our special kind of new materials with futuristic transitions, a very few passages have most probably been generated in connection with this process of editorial shaping.

Otherwise than at Levels I through IV, there are no integral temporal transitions in passages entering at this fifth level. Arranged according to periods of origin, the passages assigned to this level are the following:

1) Preprophetic: 1 Sam 3:12-13abα[1]
2) Preexilic prophetic: Amos 8:9-10, 11-12, 13-14
3) Exilic (none)

4) Late postexilic: Isa 12:1-3, 4-6, 25:9-10a, 26:1-6, 27:2-6, Mic 4:1-4.

It is striking that the passages on this short list are either fairly early or fairly late. One of the occurrences outside the prophetic collection is in prophetic discourse within narrative at 1 Sam 3:12f. In our foregoing discussions concerning *wĕ'attâ* in 1 Sam 2:30, *hinnēh yāmîm bā'îm* in 2:32, and *bayyôm hahû'* in 3:12, we took the position that the first two are integral transitions within the predeuteronomistic structure of 2:17-36. The third introduces a redactional insertion that is almost certainly to be credited to the deuteronomistic editor of the deuteronomistic history, which extends from the historical framework of the book of Deuteronomy to the end of 2 Kings. "All that I have spoken concerning his [Eli's] house from beginning to end" refers back to 2:27ff., already in its deuteronomistic form. The special expansion in 3:12-13abα[1] is of programmatic importance within the Deuteronomist's overall redaction.[17]

The other early occurrences belong together following Amos 8:8, which is the end of this earliest prophetic book in its initial form. It is more plausible to associate the collocation Amos 8:9f., 11f., 13f. with an early book-making process than to explain them as atomistic expansions of the kind found at redactional Level IV.

These three short poetic oracles with temporal transitions in anacrusis almost certainly derive from separate redactors rather than from a single redactor, because otherwise they would probably have used the same — or virtually the same — formula, as in Isa 7:18f., 20, 21f., 23ff. Yet they must all be associated with the definitive editing of Amos, which probably occurred sometime in the seventh century. An oracular collection in chaps. 1–6 had previously expanded the collection of call-visions (including the narrative report of 7:10-17). In the late eighth century or the early seventh century, an editor added a random selection of additional oracles (8:4-8) and concluded the work with his adaptation (8:9-10) of the book's dominant day-of-Yahweh theme, affirming this by the use of the oracle formula, "utterance of Yahweh [   ]" (v 8). Very soon, two incremental additions were made, namely, those of vv 11f. and 13f. This redactional activity produced the initial book of Amos. Eventually other authentic oracles, those of 9:1-10, were added to it, and finally two exilic oracles with introductory temporal formulas, those of 9:11f. and 9:13ff., were attached, representing redactional Level VI.

The editing of the lengthy book of Isaiah also occurred in stages, one of which produced chaps. 1–31 and still others (or another) of which produced the combination that included chaps. 32–35, 36-39, 40-66.

The five curious liturgical responses introduced by special rubrics with *bayyôm hahû'* at Isa 12:1-3, 4-6, 25:9-10a, 26:1-6, and 27:2-6 were probably added as part of the book-making process at the same time when very late insertions were being made at 11:12-16, 24:1–25:8, and 26:7-21.[18] It is reasonable to suggest that Isaiah as a book may have been drawn together at this stage for the specific purpose of use in liturgical reading and recitation.[19]

The debate over priority for either Isa 2:2-5 or Mic 4:1-5 may perhaps be resolved now in favor of the Isaiah passage through consideration of where each belongs within the redactional process. As we have seen, the Isaiah passage belongs at Level III, that of the shaping of major tradition complexes, but the Micah passage belongs to Level V because it is the editorial hinge on which the entire book is constructed. Scholars agree that chaps. 1–3 and chaps. 4–7 developed independently of each other, and that chaps. 4–7 function as an appendix to the first three chapters within the edited book. We have argued that two separate sections within this appendix, that of the remarkable salvation saying in 4:8–5:3 and that of the oracular collection in chaps. 6–7, had already been joined together during the late preexilic period by the insertion of 5:9-14 (E 10-15). Without 4:6-7, which belongs to Level VI, a postexilic editor joined this collocation to chaps. 1–3 to form what is substantially the canonical book of Micah.

Level VI: Post-Editorial Supplementation

A sixth level of redactional activity is similar in technique to that of Level IV. We must reckon with it because definitive editing did not preclude the possible addition of still more new material. There can be little expectation of discovering authentic material at this late level. As in Level V, at this level there is no example of an integral temporal transition. Examples of this very late type of redactional expansion may readily be identified in the considerable number of non-Septuagintal expansions within the prophetic collection, particularly in Jeremiah and Ezekiel. The intent of this very late supplementation would have been to reinterpret still further the divine nature and purpose in the light of altered conditions in late postexilic Judaism.

Passages with futuristic transitions belonging to this redactional level are the following:

1) Preexilic (none)
2) Exilic: Amos 9:11-12, 13-15
3) Late postexilic: Isa 4:2-6, 27:12, 13; Jer 23:7-8, 33:14-16, 46:26b, 49:7; Mic 4:6-7; Zech 14:6-7, 8, 9, 13-14, 20-21.

Each of these assignments invites a brief word of explanation. Previously we established three facts about the Amos passages on this list: (1) they are certainly both exilic; (2) they were composed by separate redactors; and (3) the temporal formula in the latter passage, as also in 8:11, has strong affinities with the deuteronomistic school and the early Jeremianic redaction. What is important here is that Amos's book had certainly received its normative editing before 9:11f. and 13ff. were added. They stand thus as a true appendix to the edited book of Amos, correcting that prophet's bitter words for a new age but in no way altering or adding to its essential message.

The remaining passages on this final list date from the late postexilic period, as we would expect from the nature of the material.

Isa 4:2-6 is well developed in its ideology, but one should notice particularly the comprehensiveness of its imagery, that of cleansing in detail, of the cloud of glory over all of Zion (not just over the temple, as in Ezekiel), and of the transformation of cosmic forces, going beyond Zech 12:10–13:6 in the direction of Zech 14:1-11, 16-21. This addition to the book of Isaiah is so late that it must certainly have come into the text after the formation of chaps. 1–31 and probably after the definitive editing of the entire book. In any event, it is very loosely attached within its context, adding nothing whatever to its meaning. Its only internal connection is the temporal formula *bayyôm hahû'* in 3:18 and 4:1; but its repetition of that formula is completely stereotyped and artificial.

Perhaps not quite so late, but after the editing that introduced the liturgical rubrics at Isa 25:9, 26:1, and 27:2, random attachments on the diaspora theme, with *wĕhāyâ bayyôm hahû'* as transitions, were made at Isa 27:12 and 13.[20] Apart from the phrase *hinnēh yāmîm bā'îm nĕ'um YHWH* at the beginning, Jer 23:7-8 has nothing in common with immediately preceding vv 5-6; in fact, it originally appeared following v 40 (cf. LXX). Jer 23:7-8 is not even thematically related to 23:5-6. It prefixes *lākēn* to the temporal formula in the fashion of the late Jeremianic redaction. In our foregoing discussion we determined that vv 5-6 came into the text as part of the process that shaped chaps. 21–23 as a major tradition complex, but vv 7-8 are a paraphrase of 16:14-16 (a Level IV insertion), from which it has borrowed the *lākēn hinnēh yāmîm bā'îm nĕ'um YHWH* formula of introduction. Since it is not to be explained as an element in the definitive editing of Jeremiah (Level V), it has to be a post-editing expansion.

Jer 23:5-6 has its doublet in 33:14-16, which is lacking in the LXX. This means that the latter passage is also post-editorial. Like 23:7-8, it makes no impact whatever on the interpretation of its immediate context. Both these passages represent an erudite interest in finding a suitable, if casual, place within the prophetic text.[21]

Inserted after the book of Jeremiah was formed were two further non-Septuagintal expansions, each with introductory *wĕ'aḥărê-kēn*, those of 46:26b and 49:6. They are structurally similar to Jer 48:47a, also a non-

Septuagintal expansion, which has the same formula in nontransitional position. Each of these three very late additions creates a *vaticinium ex eventu* modeled after 49:39.

Although it might be possible that Mic 4:6-7 was attached to vv 1-5 before those verses became the major editorial link within the book, it is equally likely that these verses were added after the book was formed.

This is probably the case, finally, with regard to the five expansions in Zechariah 14 that are introduced by *(wĕhāyâ) bayyôm hahû'*. In our extended discussion of this chapter, vv 1-3 and v 9a were identified as the literary core. The entire chapter is to be viewed as a final, post-editorial attachment, not only to the immediately preceding redactional unit that was created when chaps. 12–13 were attached to chaps. 9–11, but probably as well to the complete, edited book that includes chaps. 1–8. In any event, it is clear that chap. 14 modifies the edited book's message in a way that is hardly suggested by the book as the product of a long and complex redactional process. Certainly it adds nothing of significance to the interpretation either of Deutero-Zechariah or of the entire book.

Beyond Redaction

Having defined and described six distinct levels of redaction that pertain generally to all types of biblical material, we have assigned to these respective levels every instance of futuristic refocusing with the use of temporal transitions, in and outside the prophetic corpus. The complex redactional activity that we have illustrated from this material was the motor by which tradition development was driven. As we have seen, this activity was regularly motivated by internal forces, that is, from within the spiritual fellowship (a prophetic school, an historically determined political-social group, or an ideological movement) that had accepted the responsibility of preserving and interpreting units of traditional material passed down from a particular prophet or from the prophets as a group. This was a dynamic — if not to say, irrepressible — process of incremental expansion. From the first level of redaction to the last, the eschatological hope of Israel was constantly being broadened. This did not end when the individual books received their final expansion, but only when the concept of canonization had put a stop to the possibility of further growth. After this the *traditum* of biblical revelation became subject to one or another *traditio* of exegetical interpretation.

It is understandable that there could be no further occurrence of redactional expansion, with or without the employment of explicit temporal connectives, once canonization had occurred. We need to be very self-conscious in defining what canonization actually was, carefully avoiding several recent attempts to blur the distinction between inner-scriptural and extra-scriptural interpretation. On the one hand, we are not to think of a formal declaration or determination, such as those made by the Pharisees at Jamnia or the credal formulations of the early church. These were actually no more than the ratification and clarification of something long before determined, with a strongly apologetic aim. On the other hand, we are not willing to speak of redactionally expanding tradition as a process contiguous with the process of canonization, or to blur the essential discontinuity between precanonical refocusing and postcanonical exegesis.

Among contemporary scholars, Brevard S. Childs has been the most effective champion of the view that the ultimate "canonical" message of a particular biblical book might possess greater importance than the ideas coming to expression at individual stages in the growth of the book.[22] He has offered, to be sure, an admirable and necessary corrective to the once-dominant scholarly ideology that saw value and authority only in the "authentic" words of the biblical writers. As a skilled practitioner of historical and literary criticism, Childs is able to identify and appreciate the biblical word at every stage and for every circumstance. Yet he does refer to "canonization" as implicit throughout the process of tradition development, that is, as a goal or ideal toward which all preliminary literary development was progressing, up to the final stage when nothing more was — or could be — added.

We must insist, however, that nothing was implicit or in any way predetermined in the way Scripture developed toward its final, canonical form — historical or theological. Having arrived at this insight from a close study of the special passages presently under consideration, we generalize by suggesting that this is true not only within the prophetic corpus, but for all of Scripture. We would take the adventitiousness of the historical process far more radically than Childs seems to do. There was no historical necessity whatever in what the traditionists of our material have created. The new images of the future that inspired them were in intuitive response to the pressures of the specific circumstances of their special times. If history had been otherwise, they would have written otherwise than they did.

This is not to deny that they were themselves mentally and spiritually conditioned by the very traditions they were expanding, or that they were anything but ingenuous in their attempt to write as they believed the original prophet in whose name they wrote would have written, given their circumstances and responsibilities. But it was above all the historical particularities of their times and situations that were forcing — and enabling — them to write as they wrote.

To be sure, canonization might have been inevitable in the sense that what is dynamically expanding will, in the end, need to be closed off, once the forces empowering it have faded away. Many scholars are of the opinion that the drying up of prophetic inspiration is what brought prophetic tradition-development to its end, but this is to state the obvious. The question remains, What made prophetic inspiration dry up? There must have been historical forces at work, known or unknown, to have caused this. The point is that prophecy did not have to end where it ended, except only through the exigencies of particular historical forces. Our surmise is that prophecy ceased in Israel when it had become more a threat than a help to the increasingly institutionalized, that is, nomistic, community.

A group of contemporary scholars that includes James A. Sanders occupy different ground than Childs in their virtual equation of precanonical tradition development with canonization, and it is to this that we object even more than to Childs's minimalizing of historical adventitiousness. To equate inner-scriptural and extra-scriptural development confuses a process of unrestrained creativity with a subsequent process of institutionally bound rationalizing.

Sanders has developed what he calls a method of "comparative midrash," in which he places inner-scriptural and extra-scriptural tradition development on essentially the same basis.[23] Certain other scholars, such as Isaac Seeligmann, have compounded this confusion by identifying inner-scriptural expansion as "midrash," refusing to distinguish it from the rabbinical method usually referred to by the name "midrash."[24] It is to be noted that in his influential book *Biblical Interpretation in Ancient Israel*, Michael Fishbane shows commendable caution over against this blurring of distinctions by speaking of distinct types or tendencies of inner-biblical "exegesis" ("legal," "aggadic," and "mantic"), expressly rejecting the term "midrash" as a term to be applied to inner-biblical expansion.[25]

There is little opportunity within the compass of this study to enter more fully into the debate about canon and midrash, but one should pay attention to Magne Saebø's helpful analysis of canonization in his recent study "Vom 'Zusammen-Denken' zum Kanon."[26] Saebø explains canonization as the end-stage of a process in which the late postexilic Jewish community's consensus ("Zusammen-Denken"), based on essential heuristic principles that were then dominant in that community, came to be superimposed upon the individual books that had been drawn together as sacrosanct and authoritative holy Scripture. At this stage no further free expansion was allowed; on the contrary, the application of this type of normalizing pressure began to narrow and refine the stock of acceptable Jewish viewpoints. Elements that were now disparate with the community's most essential beliefs were not directly censored or removed from Scripture; they were simply brought into a condition of relative innocuousness through rearrangement and occasional corrective comment.

Though further examples could have been cited, Saebø offers two that are especially illuminating: (1) the "second epilogue" to Qoheleth (Eccl 12:12-14), which places all the rather alarming statements of the book (especially 11:9's espousal of a belief that is actually forbidden in Num 15:39) under its concluding nomistic ban; and (2) the prepositioning of the nomistic first Psalm as a guide to understanding the already completed Psalter. He emphasizes that normalizing expansions and tendentious rearrangements of this type did not develop naturally in the traditioning process, but were superimposed from without.

As Saebø explains, Scripture was now being compared with Scripture. Viewpoints that had become offensive, or at least suspect, to the community were deprived of their appeal by the assertion of the viewpoint that had now become normative and essential. As has been said, this occurred at a juncture beyond all the redactional levels that we have been studying. It assumes not only that each book had now reached its "final" form and had been subjected to definitive editing, but that certain books, groups of books, or sections within books were relativized by the superior authority that had been given to certain other books, in particular the Torah.[27]

Saebø is justified in his insistence that canonization did not come about mysteriously or arbitrarily, as some scholars have suggested, but entirely as a result of community consensus. This is precisely what made canonization so radically different from free tradition development through redactional expansion. No longer were individuals or groups allowed the liberty to add to what had already been laid down. It was a matter of closing off the tradition, of subjecting the deposit of a dynamic inspirational process to the final verdict of community opinion.

There were three distinct elements within the canonization process: (1) restricting the content of Scripture and establishing the arrangement of the individual books; (2) establishing a standard text by weeding out variant readings; and (3) superimposing a normalizing viewpoint by the techniques that Saebø has described.

These three factors effectively brought the dynamic expansion of Scripture to an end. Interpretation and reinterpretation could henceforth come about only through one or another form of exegesis, including the midrashic method of the rabbis and the apologetic method of the early church.[28]

We understand, then, why there could have been no redactional level beyond the six that we have described. We may recall the intentions of the six levels that we have defined in order to compare them with that of canonization:

Level I: to record the authoritative "words" of an individual prophet for a wider audience, as well as for posterity (cf. Isa 8:16; Jer 36:32);

Level II: to offer a more complete and balanced presentation of the prophet's message;

Level III: to provide interpretive perspectives for extended blocks of material ascribed to the prophet;

Level IV: to contemporize individual prophetic messages for a new generation by the introduction of additional revelatory insights, thereby extending, reinterpreting, or superseding traditional images;

Level V: to present a relatively complete and ordered corpus of materials ascribable to a given prophet;

Level VI: to reinterpret the prophetic message still further for a new age.

At all these levels there was an irrepressible dynamic development toward more pertinent appropriations of revelation, the tendency being to include as much as possible. On the contrary, the intent of canonization was to neutralize troublesome variants by establishing the form and content of a completed Scripture.

We do not forget to mention the long, drawn-out process of scribal emendation that was applied to the text of Scripture. Some of this occurred along with the redactional process, but most of it was applied to the already canonized scriptural text. This was not merely a matter of erudition applied to a close study of the scriptural text, for it too had an apologetic purpose. This is especially clear with regard to such elements as the *tiqune sopherim*, the pre-Masoretic emendations of the scribes, whose general aim is to remove scandalous readings like the statement that Job's wife urged him to "curse" God (Job 2:9). The scribes also made casual, nontendential emendations in order to rectify real and imaginery mistakes in the text out of a misguided impulse to correct one text through comparison with others, often compounding errors in the process. This, too, was an essentially apologetic procedure because the scribes were not merely acting in their capacity as learned scholars, but were self-consciously engaged in a pious enterprise to preserve what they thought to be a more "perfect" form of Scripture.

It should not be surprising that neither canonization nor scribal emendation produced any of the temporal transitions that we have been studying. The few random glosses involving one of our formulas (especially *bayyôm hahû'*) that were noted early on in the present study fail to create transitions.[29]

CHAPTER TWELVE

Themes in Futuristic Imaging

Introduction

We come now to the task of analyzing images or *topoi,* with the particular aim of determining where and how these may fit into patterns of tradition development. It is necessary at this point to separate once for all those passages that have integral temporal formulas from those with introductory formulas; and, further, to distinguish among the first group between those that are in primary materials and those that are in *ad hoc* redactional insertions.

These separations will produce the three main subheadings of this chapter. In each main section we shall offer a display of interrelationships between the various components, that is, negative images over against positive, respective addressees, and the four kinds of images. For those passages that have more than one type of image, we shall list the one that is dominant. As will be argued, only those images that express spiritual ideals or have cosmic themes may properly be spoken of as eschatological; therefore the distinctions that we are making here must be carefully observed.

Primary Predictions with Integral Transitions

1. Patterns

Negative images
  1) Historical
    a) For individuals:

Positive images
  1) Historical
    a) For individuals:

1 Sam 2:1-36; 15:1b-4;   2 Sam 7:8-16 par; Hag 2:23
12:10-12; 2 Kgs 20:17-18
par; Amos 7:16-17

b) For Israel: b) For Israel:
   Amos 4:2b-3; 6:7; Mic 4:9,   Hos 3:5; Nah 1:13
   10, 11, 14
c) For the nations:
   Jer 48:12-13; 49:2;
   51:47-48, 52-53; Ezek
   26:18; 27:34

2) Symbolic   2) Symbolic
  a) For Israel: a) For Israel:
    Jer 16:16b; Ezek 19:13-14;   Isa 1:26b; 35:5, 6; 58:8; 60:5
    Hos 2:12-15; 5:7b

                                      b) For the nations:
                                      Ezek 32:14-15

  b) Lament: Hab 1:11
3) Spiritual   3) Spiritual
  a) For Israel: a) For Israel:
    Jer 14:10bβ; 23:20b; Hos   Isa 48:16; 58:9a, 14; Jer
    7:2b; 13:2; Mic 3:4   31:13; Zech 8:11-13
  b) For the nations:
    Jer 22:22b
4) Cosmic   4) Cosmic
  a) For Israel: Ezek 7:3-4   a) For Israel: Isa 41:1
        b) For Israel and against the nations:
           Ezek 38:8-9; Zech 12:4a; Dan 10:20; 12:1

We take note of the presence on this list of virtually all our preprophetic
passages, each of which is directed to individual addressees serving as
eponyms for a family or dynasty. Each passage of this type predicts a specific
historical event that would decisively affect the addressee and those associated
with him.

We observe also the strong preponderance of negative over positive
images, particularly among those that predict historical events. We note also
that Israel is most often the addressee. Apart from the apocalyptic occurrences,
which are comprehensive in including both Israel and the nations, only six
passages concern only the nations.

2. Imagery

It will be useful at this juncture to examine precisely what the types of images are among these predictions, and to inquire about the place of the respective images within the onflowing current of prophetic tradition. The function of each of these occurrences within specific books and passages has already been examined. Almost never is it necessary to search elsewhere in order to understand the images that the respective passages develop, but additional comments may be in order.

We call attention once again to the concentration in these passages on realistic historical expectations. This is obvious in the passages with historical images, but it will also be seen in several passages with symbolic images standing for historical realities. All passages with integral temporal transitions belong, of course, to the Level I redaction.

a. Historical images

(1) In private oracles

1 Sam 2:31-36	Deposition of the Elides
1 Sam 15:1b-4	A *herem* on Amalek
2 Sam 7:8-16 par	A "house" for David
2 Sam 12:10-12	A sword on David's house
2 Kgs 20:17-18 par	Plunder and exile for Hezekiah's dynasty
Amos 7:16-17	Exile for Amaziah's family
Hag 2:20-23	Zerubbabel's investiture

We must take the passage about Zerubbabel's investiture as a realistic forecast of an at-least symbolic crowning. The tradition-historical background for this certainly includes the high-flown idealistic images of a Davidic ruler that had been developed already in the preexilic period (e.g., in Isa 9:1-6 [E 2-7]) and refined during the exile (as, e.g., in Jer 23:5-6). It is striking that absolutely nothing in the book of Haggai prepares for it; it is not even inevitable from the immediately preceding context (vv 20-22) predicting the imminent overthrow of foreign nations. This was to be, therefore, a drastically irruptive event, an action of sheer transcendence on Yahweh's part, in the prophet's present and imminent future.

The precise model for this is to be seen in the two preprophetic passages on our list that are marked as examples of *vaticinium ex eventu*, namely, 1 Sam 2:32ff. and 2 Kgs 20:17f. par. Although they betray the fact that the predicted events have in fact already occurred, they like the other preprophetic passages point to historical events as realistically conceived.

(2) Calamities for Israel/Judah/Jerusalem

Amos 4:2b-3	Dispossession and exile
Amos 6:7	Exile for revelers
Mic 4:9	Absence of a king/counselor
Mic 4:10	Exile to Babylon
Mic 4:11	Attack of the nations
Mic 4:14 (E 5:1)	Siege, violence on the king

Themes bound to the holy-war tradition appear in the early preexilic verses, Mic 4:11 and 14, which refer to an imminently expected foreign onslaught against Jerusalem, that is, the Assyrian invasion under Sennacherib. Themes from the holy-war tradition may be given a cosmic dimension, but this does not occur here; it occurs only in apocalyptic materials from late periods (Ezek 38:8f.; Zech 12:4; Dan 10:20). It is not surprising that each Amos passage, 4:2f., 6:7, and 7:16f., predicts exile to a foreign country; but Mic 4:10 has a similar prediction, although with reference to Babylon rather than Assyria as the place of exile (see in Chapters Two and Nine).

(3) Punishment for the nations

Jer 48:12-13	Calamity on Moab
Jer 49:2	Calamity on Ammon
Jer 51:47-49, 52-53	Babylon's destruction
Ezek 26:18	Mock dismay at Tyre's fall

(4) Israel/Judah's restoration

Hos 3:5	Return and conversion

The theme of Israel's return appears for the first time in Hos 3:5. Although the temporal transition *'aḥar* points to a time beyond the immediate future of v 4, during which the Israelites were to be without the monarchical and cultic establishments (the two prime sources of Israelite apostasy), Hosea announces his realistic expectation that an historical return, posited on the people's true conversion, would follow soon upon this condition of deprivation. It is interesting to note that a disillusioned glossator amended Hos 3:5 by adding a future-pointing time identifier, *bĕ'aḥărît hayyāmîm,* at the end of this verse.

b. Symbolic images

Symbolic and metaphorical speech had always been commonplace in ancient

Israel. We cannot therefore be surprised at the range and variety of symbolic images that are enlisted in our passages as potent vehicles for expressing expectations for the future. Among our primary passages with integral temporal transitions, some symbolic images directly point to historical events, while others suggest spiritual realities. Thus the symbolic passages provide a bridge between the preceding historical group and the spiritual group to follow.

(1) Historical realities

Jer 16:16b	The Babylonians as hunters
Ezek 19:13-14	Jehoiachin as a withering vine
Ezek 27:34	Tyre as a wrecked ship
Nah 1:13	Breaking of Assyrian yoke/bonds
Hab 1:11	The Chaldeans as a destroying wind

One of the five symbolic passages pointing to historical events is directed against an unfortunate Judahite king; the others concern foreign nations. Three of these passages draw upon mythological allusions employed elsewhere in Scripture. The reference in Jer 16:16b to the Neo-Babylonians as *ṣayyādîm*, "hunters," unmistakably recalls the description of Nimrod in Gen 10:9 as a *gibbôr ṣayid*, "heroic hunter." The favoring image in Ezek 32:14 of abundant waters for Egypt draws upon familiar Nilotic mythology, prominent throughout Ezekiel's collection of Egypt oracles in chaps. 29–32.[1] The image of Tyre as a wrecked ship in Ezek 27:34 draws on the theme of Ezekiel's Tyre oracles that is dominant throughout chaps. 26 and 27. The vine/vineyard image in Ezek 19:13-14 is not in itself mythological in origin; it is a familiar metaphor for Israel (cf. Isa 5:1-7; Jer 2:21; Ezek 15:1-8; Hos 10:1; Ps 80:8-13); here the withering of the vine is a symbol for Jehoiachin's untimely exile.

The remaining symbolic image on this list having historical allusions is that of the destroying wind in Hab 1:11, but it too has mythological innuendoes in its use as a symbol of theophanous power (cf. 2 Sam 22:11; Ezek 1:4), especially when it comes from the east (Exod 10:13, 14:21; Hos 13:15).

(2) Spiritual realities

Isa 1:26b	Renaming of Jerusalem
Isa 35:5-6	Healing of blind, deaf, lame, and dumb
Isa 58:8a	Light and healing
Isa 60:5	Delight and enrichment
Ezek 32:14	Abundant waters in Egypt
Hos 2:12-15 (E 10-13)	Uncovering of Gomer's lewdness
Hos 5:7b	A destructive new moon

The symbolic images on this list standing for positive spiritual realities are those that are commonly employed in Deutero- and Trito-Isaiah and in the Psalter: healing, light, happiness, and enrichment. Jerusalem's renaming in Isa 1:26 is a powerful metaphor for complete and drastic transformation (cf. Ezek 48:35). The negative symbol of acute embarrassment in Hos 2:13-15 (E 11-13) stands for Israel's apostasy. It has striking parallels in Ezek 16:35ff. and 23:22ff.

(3) Material and spiritual realities

Zech 8:11-13	A sowing of peace

Although Zech 8:9-13 is historically oriented (cf. its references to past poverty and vulnerability), its main theme of spiritual retribution and restoration is symbolized by the core promise of *zera' haššālôm*, "a sowing of peace."[2]

c. Spiritual images

(1) Subjective states

Isa 58:8b	Delightful confidence
Jer 31:13	Joy and merriment
Hos 13:2	Persistence of idolatrous worship

(2) Objective conditions

Isa 48:16	New revelation
Isa 58:9a	Yahweh's responsiveness
Jer 14:10bβ	Yahweh's remembrance of guilt
Jer 22:22b	Lebanon's confoundment
Jer 23:20b	Fulfillment of prophecy
Hos 7:2b	Yahweh's remembrance of sins
Mic 3:4	Withdrawal of revelation

Among the nonsymbolic predictions of spiritual realities, we must distinguish subjective from objective images. In the first category, Hos 13:2 predicts Israel's persistence in idolatry, while Isa 58:14 and Jer 31:13 predict happiness, joy, and confidence for those who are to be saved.

More objectively, Yahweh's calling of sinners to account (Jer 14:10b; Hos 7:2b) and his withholding of revelation (Mic 3:4) are images of Israel's lostness, while his new revelation (Isa 48:16) and responsiveness to prayer (Isa 58:9) stand for Israel's saved condition. The important passage Jer 23:16-20 (see our analysis in Chapter Four) affirms an objective reality in which

Jeremiah's audience becomes able to understand clearly the full bearing of negative prophecy delivered against them.

d. Cosmic images

(1) Nonapocalyptic

Isa 41:1	The nations' witness regarding Israel
Ezek 7:3-4	Unrelenting wrath on the day of Yahweh

(2) Apocalyptic

Ezek 38:8-9	Gog's invasion
Zech 12:4a	Panic on horses and riders
Dan 10:20	Michael's war against the nations
Dan 12:1	Deliverance from extreme peril

It is a universalistic concept approaching cosmic dimensions in Isa 41:1 that enlists the nations to stand in Yahweh's court of judgment to bear witness to what he is about to do on behalf of his people Israel. This proves in fact to be the basic metaphor of Deutero-Isaiah as a whole. In Isa 41:1 it remains a metaphor. Here lies, however, the germ of all the apocalyptic speculation that was to develop in late Old Testament and intertestamental literature. The world is a court and history is an arena in which Yahweh's sorely tried people will be rescued from enemies of every sort and Yahweh's honor will be elaborately displayed.

Another potent universalistic image assuming eventual cosmic dimensions is that of the day of Yahweh. Ezek 7:3-4, like Isa 2:9-21, Amos 5:18-20, and Zeph 1:2-18, employs a metaphor that approaches theological reification. In these preexilic passages the day of Yahweh comes as an unwelcome surprise for Israel, apparently imagining that Yahweh's final judgment would bear only on her enemies. In postexilic ideology in general, and specifically in the apocalyptic passages on this list, day-of-Yawheh imagery combines with holy-war imagery to serve instead as threats against Israel's enemies, a reversion to the discredited expectations of the preexilic period. Now Amos's dramatic query, "Why would you have the day of Yahweh" (5:18) would no longer be understood, for this image had been turned to Israel's comfort.

e. Conclusion

It would be superfluous to carry further the analysis of this primary integral material, for its eschatological repertoire is not significantly different from that of prophetic prediction in general. The variety of images that these primary passages employ ranges from the literally historical to the suprahistorically ideal. In any event, these predictions were mainly suited to the immediate situation of the individual prophets (or quasi-prophets) and their audiences.

This is clear, first of all, from the images themselves, but it is especially apparent from the specific temporal formulas that are employed. The great preponderance of passages on this list have either *(wĕ)ʿattâ* or *ʾāz* as temporal formulas and make predictions for the present, for the imminent future, or for the proximate future (that which lies just beyond the imminent). Other temporal formulas used as transitions are less frequent, but it is certain in any case that all these passages were shaped by the speaker/writer's own immediate situation and point to the ongoing flow of historical event. Thus forecasts of this type are in direct continuity from the present moment, even involving in many instances the immediate past out of which the present has emerged. The employment of futuristic transitions in these primary passages implies only that there are definite steps or sequences in God's way of working with humankind, each of which is designed to bring a decisive change in humankind's relationship with God.

3. *Historical futurism* versus *eschatology*

It is at this point that I would like to insert the following from my study of "The Day Future" in my book *Yesterday, Today and Tomorrow:*

> It must be significant that, among ancient peoples, those who were the most acutely aware of historic time, past and present — namely, the Hebrews of the Bible — were also the people who actually had the most to say about the future. . . . For them the future depended solely on two factors: God's will and man's response to it. Somehow, even nature and historical event were unable to interfere with the interaction of these two factors because both were manifestations of the divine will and were therefore under God's control. . . . The Hebrews were so intensely interested in the future because they knew they had a share in shaping it; also because they believed their God was waiting on their action. Actually, it was not until the prophets had made them aware of God's will and purpose in the ominous historical movements threatening their late nationhood that they began to think very much about what the future would bring, and then it was in terms of what God was about to do in response to man's doing, and what man would consequently do in response to God's doing — never in terms of bare "historical" occurrence. Always the future day that awaited them was predicted in terms that were calculated to influence their present behavior.

If it was to be a day of woe, it was designed to move them to repentance and conversion; if it was to be a day of bliss, it was designed to move them out of despair. . . . Israel's prophets were predicting the future only as a proximate projection of the present. They were immediately deducing the future out of the present, less by way of political astuteness than out of faith in the being and nature of Israel's covenant God.[3]

This dictum definitely applies to the function of those integral futuristic transitions that are found in primary materials. It is important to see that each new moment was crucial and decisive in its peculiar way for what was to follow. History consists of an interminable sequence of decisive moments, turning points along the way of life. Any particular event may be as existentially crucial as any of the others.

This is not to suggest that deliberate choices made at one moment may not be modified, canceled, or reversed at subsequent moments of crisis and decision. The changes reflected in the list of passages we are studying are seldom linked in direct sequence from the one to the other (but cf. the unique series of events mentioned in Mic 4:8–5:3), yet each was critical for the situation in which the prediction was made.

It is this that nullifies the rather pretentious attempt of Georg Fohrer in an article called "Die Struktur der alttestamentlichen Eschatologie."[4] Fohrer adopts the widely held position that "eschatological" prediction is unabashedly optimistic, that it derives specifically from the discredited cultic prophecy of the preexilic period, and that it amounts to a betrayal of the radically principled antiestablishment preaching of the great classical prophets. This "eschatological" prophecy results from an attempt to correct for what Robert Carroll calls "cognitive dissonance."[5] What Fohrer emphasizes is that it assumes the inauguration of an entirely new era that is sharply separate from the mainstream of biblical history. He professes to find a textual basis for this in the drastic reversal of fortunes promised by Haggai *min-hayyôm hazzeh wāmā'ĕlâ,* "from this day and onward" (2:15, 18), decisively introducing an era of perfect bliss.[6]

Fohrer wants to make this the model for "eschatological" prophecy in general, but no less suitable example could have been chosen. As has been argued in the foregoing discussion of this passage, Haggai is in fact engaged in what we have called "imminentistic futurism." Marvelous as the promise might be (ample provision in the midst of drought and poverty), it was neither schematic nor ideological, but concerned for the returnees' urgent physical needs. There was nothing idealistic here; it did not issue from adherence to establishment optimism but from a challenge to the returnees' faith at one existentially crucial moment in their pragmatic experience.

It is amazing not only that Fohrer should so grossly misinterpret this particular passage, but especially that he dares use it to bolster his notion of two asymmetrical eras in history. When we look at apocalyptic, we do see the notion of two separate eras. But there is far less evidence of this in the Old Testament than what many scholars claim. It is not clearly present even in Daniel, which places the decisive eschatological event at the very end of history, not between two separate eras. Where we will definitely find it is in the pseudepigraphal apocalypses, and most especially in the writings of the Qumran community. For an elucidation of two-era eschatology as it was conceived within this community, one might consult the persuasive analysis offered by Shemaryahu Talmon in his article "Waiting for the Messiah: The Spiritual Universe of the Qumran Covenanters" (1988).[7] But there is nothing of this in the canonical Old Testament, and there is certainly no hint of it among the passages under study here.

It is well to take this opportunity to settle at last on a definition of the terms "eschatology" and "eschatological." As studies on this problem proliferate, confusion seems to grow with regard to the proper meaning and application of these terms. Setting aside ill-tempered logomachies, we should adopt a pragmatic working definition once and for all.[8] It is not essential that we adhere to strict etymology (Gk. *eschatos,* "last," "final"), but we should certainly look for an inner-biblical criterion. The cumulative results of the present study, observed but not yet defined, offer just such a criterion.

It would seem reasonable to reserve the term "eschatological" for predictions that drastically reduce the realistic historical element in futuristic expectation[9] and, on the contrary, to adopt a term such as "historical futurism" for those predictions that view the future as a realistically expected (though often marvelous) extension of the past and present.[10] Certainly the most decisive theological distinction in all futuristic prediction is that between an immediately ensuing history (indeed, *Heilsgeschichte!*) in which mankind will fully and freely participate and a new condition or state of being that has been radically transformed from above, apart from human potentiality as it was once created and as it has continually been experienced in the historical events of the past.

As we may apply this distinction to the passages under study here, the boundaries may often seem blurred because one type of futurism may tend to merge with the other. Yet the distinction must be maintained. This is why we have taken the trouble to distinguish between the four kinds of images: historical, symbolic, spiritual, and cosmic.

Among the examples belonging to our first list, symbols from nature and human culture may be nothing more than metaphors for historical realities; but they may also be metaphors for certain spiritual conditions. In the realization that spiritual conditions or states of being may also result from certain historical events, we are cautious of labeling any of our passages predicting such conditions or states of being as "eschatological" in the strict sense. Examples of images that we do identify as strictly eschatological will emerge in our examination of the passages remaining to be studied.

"The nations' witness" in Isa 41:1 is eschatological because it involves a fantasy that is quite impossible upon the scene of realistic history, possible only in the mind of God. Apocalyptic passages on this first list and in the lists remaining to be studied are clear representations of the eschatological, not only because of their cosmic dimensions, but because of the way they schematize the world and future event. Although they employ images drawn from historical entities (often those of the traditional, highly idealized holy war), they have unmistakably crossed the barrier between the historical and the theological.

In studying our next two lists of passages, those for integral redactional transitions and for introductory redactional transitions, it will be well to keep in mind two determinative characteristics of biblical apocalyptic, which are its radical dualism and its radical futurism.[11] Radical dualism makes an absolute moral and spiritual separation between the "righteous" and the "wicked" within human society. Radical futurism is an ideology that sharply separates the era of human history as we know it (including the period of *Heilsgeschichte* (cf. Dan 9:25) from a state of perfect bliss at the end, promised only to the righteous and purged of all the ambiguities of history.

It may be said that, to the extent that certain nonapocalyptic predictions on our list erase the imperfections of human nature, reach beyond moral striving, and reconstruct the cosmos, they are tending strongly toward the same radical process of dualistic and futuristic ahistoricizing. These are the predictions, along with the distinctly apocalyptic predictions, that should be defined as "eschatological"; the others should be kept distinct from them and given a name such as that which we have proposed. In the ideologically fuzzy predictions that we call eschatological, a facile idealism has gone entirely beyond metaphor and symbol, and historical event has given way to theological fantasy.

Secondary Predictions with Integral Transitions

The passages that fall into a second category, those of predictions with integral transitions appearing in secondary rather than primary material, need to be listed separately. Since they share with the previously treated primary passages in employing integral transitions, it may be helpful to compare first their patterns with those of the primary passages; but they will need also to be compared with the patterns of the introductory redactional passages that follow.

We need to make some preliminary observations regarding the role that the redactional levels that we have defined in the previous chapter play within the passages on this second list. First, we should take due account of the fact that each of the three expansions with integral transitions that have been introduced at Level II of the redactional process (the earliest that is involved in passages of this type; passages of the first type all belong to Level I) provides a crucial link within early stages of the literary development of the respective books to which they belong. Jer 30:1-3 is the formal introduction to the "little book of consolation" (30:4–31:40), within which there is an early (or earlier) link at 30:23-24 (extracting the sharply negative material in 23:16-20) combined with a reaffirmation of the covenant promise in 31:1. Similarly, Ezek 24:25-27 is the redactional link between the oracles of judgment in chaps. 1–24 and the original collection of salvation oracles in chaps. 33–37. It is natural that each of these passages should pertain to the proximate future and date from the early exilic period.

At Level III, two expansions were introduced in the redaction of Jeremiah and of Ezekiel. These are Jer 4:11-12, a late preexilic passage, and Ezek 39:25-29, an early postexilic passage; thus both are from approximately the same period. These happen to be the two passages on this list that have *wĕʿattâ* as an integral transition, creating an impressive announcement of Yahweh's intention for the imminent or the proximate future, as the case may be.

The remaining expansions on this list belong to Level IV, except for Jer 33:15-16 (with transitional v 14), which paraphrases 23:5-6 and was introduced at Level VI. The Level IV expansions have predictions for the proximate or remote future. Those scheduled for the remote future are those in Isa 16:14 (with *wĕʿattâ* as transition), Isa 31:7 (with *kî bayyôm hahûʾ* as transition), and Zeph 3:11b (with *kî ʾāz* as transition), as well as the three in Ezekiel 38 (with a variant of *bayyôm hahûʾ*). It is to be noted that the formulas *bayyôm hahûʾ* with its variants and *hinnēh yāmîm bāʾîm* with its variant are just at this stage coming into prominence. One should note particularly that Jer 33:15f., Ezek 38:14ff., and Zeph 3:11b belong to expansive redactional structures.

1. Patterns

We offer accordingly a new list showing negative and positive content, the addressees, and the four types of images:

Negative images
1) Historical

   a) For the nations: Isa 16:14
2) Symbolic
   a) For individuals: Isa 22:24-25
   b) For Israel: Jer 7:32-34;
   19:6-9
   c) For the nations: Isa
   33:23b-24
3) Spiritual
   a) For Israel: Jer 30:24b

4) Cosmic
   a) For Israel: Isa 31:7
   b) For Israel and against the nations:
   Ezek 38:14b-16a, 16b, 19-23

Positive images
1) Historical
   a) For individuals: Isa 22:19-23
   b) For Israel: Jer 30:3

2) Symbolic

   a) For Israel: Ezek 24:27

3) Spiritual
   a) For Israel: Jer 31:1; 33:14-16;
   Ezek 39:25-29; Zeph 3:11b
4) Cosmic

It will be noted that in this group of passages those with a positive image begin to outnumber those with a negative image. Also, the proportion of historical images is much reduced as the symbolic and spiritual images increase. Apart from apocalyptic images expanding the Gog passage, it is only the historically oriented reflection in Isa 16:13-14 that pertains to the foreign nations.

The notable shift away from historical references toward the symbolic and the spiritual in this group of passages reveals a primary redactional concern for deeper meanings and more lasting effects, rather than for historical events in themselves. Appropriately, it is in the passages with a definite historical orientation that one finds the boldest and most innovative images, for they identify something new on the scene of human experience, whereas most of the other types of images tend to draw upon purely conventional images.

2. Imagery

"Restoring of fortunes" (Jer 30:3; Ezek 39:25), the destroying wind (Jer 4:12), the symbolic act of renaming and the baalistic associations of Tophet/Hinnom (Jer 7:32, 19:6),[12] the opening of the mouth (Ezek 24:27), the renewal of the covenant promise (Jer 31:1), the righteous Davidide and the typological renaming of Jerusalem (Jer 33:15-16), a panicky discarding of idols on the day of Yahweh (Isa 31:7), and the theme of Yahweh's self-vindication (Ezek 38:16b, 23)[13] are all drawn from metaphors and locutions in common parlance, and in some instances from the very book in which they are found.

One might be tempted to describe reflections on the meaning of Gog's coming and elaborations on the concept of devastating warfare in Ezekiel 38–39 as quite daring and innovative. They set the pattern for the uncontrolled speculation and bizarre imagery that one generally encounters in passages of the apocalyptic genre.

Isa 31:7, Jer 33:14-16, and the four Ezekiel passages on our list may properly be called eschatological as we have defined it (a term that includes those that are apocalyptic but not being limited to them). On the contrary, the remaining passages on this list, in spite of their imaginative symbolism and earnest spiritualizing, belong strictly within the realm of historical futurism.

a. Historical images

(1) In a private oracle

    Isa 22:19-23 (IV-A)[14]   Eliakim's investiture

(2) Punishment for the nations

    Isa 16:13-14 (IV-C)   A set time for Moab's humiliation
    Isa 33:23b-24 (IV-C)   Seizure of booty

A few words may be said about the peculiar imagery of Isa 16:13-14. It is not only in the sharp contrast it makes between the past (mē'āz) and the present moment ('attâ) that it is highly innovative,[15] but also in the fact that it schedules a future event for the end of a specific period of time. This is not to be interpreted as an example of proto-apocalyptic schematizing.[16] Nevertheless, we are entirely unaware of any symbolic meaning in the three years before Moab is brought into contempt and suffers drastic depopulation.[17] Unless "three years," like "three days," is entirely conventional — meaning a fairly lengthy but approximate duration — we must assume two things about the redactor who appended this reflection to Isaiah's oracles against Moab: (1) he was disturbed that the underlying oracles had not yet been fulfilled and (2) he believed that he could interpret the outcome of some special force upon the historical horizon, unknown to us but known to him.[18]

(3) Israel/Judah's restoration after exile

    Jer 30:3 (II)   Restoration and return
    Ezek 39:25-29 (III)   Return to secure dwelling place

A strikingly stereotyped locution appearing in these two passages is that involving the verb *šwb* (qal or hiph.) with the object *šĕbût* or *šĕbît*, a term with many nuances surrounding the idea of a reversal of fortunes or the restoration to one's accustomed state of being.[19] The content and the context of each passage determine its precise bearing. In Jer 30:3 it is the expected historical event of a return to the land of Judah and its repossession; this is scheduled for certain "coming days" that are not given a date, yet which for Jeremiah's redactor constitute the very next important thing to happen. In Ezek 39:25 the phrase includes — indeed, presupposes — the return from exile, but is occupied essentially with all that Yahweh's having pity and being jealous for his name would imply, that is, the spiritual blessings of being allowed to forget past shame and of receiving Yahweh's outpoured spirit.

2. *Symbolic images*

(1) Historical realities

Isa 22:24-25 (IV-A)   A peg's collapse

We must comment once again on the two redactional expansions to the private oracle in Isa 22:15-18. As has been explained, these two expansions are sequential to each other, and the second nullifies the effect of the first. We cannot but believe that they are indeed examples of *vaticinium ex eventu* — predictions made of an event already experienced. Reinforced by the oracle formula, v 25 affirms the downfall of Hilkiah, Shebna's successor, as Yahweh's final and conclusive intention; this is based on knowledge of what eventually happened, taking sequence as consequence. We need not comment on these two officials except to say that naming Shebna as *sōkēn*, "steward" (v 15), and Hilkiah simply as *'ebed*, "servant" (v 20), evidently reflects an arrangement different from that of Isa 36:3, 22, 37:2 par, where these two persons appear quite harmoniously together, though with different offices. The important thing about Isa 22:19-25 is its insinuation that it is a shift in Yahweh's intentions that effects a change of fortune for Hilkiah. Paralleling this is another shift in the symbolism of the word *yātēd*, given its usual meaning as tent-peg in v 23 but designating a wall-peg — something to hang things like clothes on — in v 25 (cf. Ezek 15:3).

(2) Spiritual realities

Jer 7:32-34, 19:6-9 (IV-C)   Renaming of Tophet/Hinnom
Ezek 24:27 (II)   Opening of the mouth

Jer 7:30-34 and 19:3-9 came rather late into their respective contexts (both at Level IV-C), and they play a somewhat different role in the separate passages. As has been stated, they are similar enough to each other to make ultimate derivation from Jeremiah a virtual certainty, yet they are sufficiently different from each other to reveal something of how different redactional traditions may work. Jer 19:3ff. has a close echo in Jer 32:34-35, which, like 19:5, may be making a tendentious mistake in identifying what went on at Tophet/Hinnom[20] as straightforward Baal worship. Relative priority goes, therefore, to 7:30ff. because it is more firmly anchored in its context and because it seems to share with Ezek 20:25-26 a horror of mentioning the name of the dreaded underworld god to which Israelite children were actually sacrificed.[21]

c. Spiritual images

(1) Subjective states

Jer 30:24b (II)	Prophecy brought to understanding

(2) Objective conditions

Jer 31:1 (II)	The covenant renewed
Jer 33:15-16 (VI)	Justice and security through an ideal Davidide
Ezek 39:25-29 (III)	Forgiveness and restoration
Zeph 3:11b (IV-C)	Removal of the proud

We have discussed Jer 33:14-16 on several occasions. The main thing that should finally be said about it is that it theologizes concerning a straightforward prediction that was at one time confidently made with regard to a still-to-reign Davidide (Jer 23:5-6). The original in Jeremiah 23 is not eschatological in the proper sense: it is imminently futuristic. The copy in chap. 33 is a clear examplar of what we do mean by "eschatology." Having noted the significance of the altered temporal formulas, we may observe two further items of ideological significance: (1) that the symbolic name *yāhwēh ṣidqēnû*, "Yahweh (is) our righteousness," is transferred from Judah and Israel directly to Jerusalem, reflecting the altered political circumstances, as well as ideology, of the postexilic period; and (2) the note of anxiety voiced in 33:14 that the promise of 23:5f. may yet — still in "coming days" — be fulfilled.

d. Cosmic images

(1) Nonapocalyptic

Isa 31:6-7 (IV-B)	Frantic discard of idols on the day of Yahweh

(2) Apocalyptic

Ezek 38:14b-16a (IV-C)	Approach of Gog's army
Ezek 38:16b (IV-C)	Yahweh's vindication
Ezek 38:19-23 (IV-C)	Cataclysmic vindication of Yahweh's honor

Secondary Predictions with Introductory Transitions

We come finally to what is by far the most extensive group of predictive passages, those with introductory temporal transitions, all of which have been created by redactors. To facilitate a comparison with the two foregoing lists, we show first the pattern of negativity and positivity, the addressees and the distinct types of images.

1. Patterns

Negative images
  1) Historical
    a) For individuals: 1 Sam 3:12-13
    b) For Israel: Jer 4:9-10; 5:18-19; 21:7; Hos 1:5; Mic 2:4-5; Zeph 1:10-11, 12-13
    c) For the nations: Isa 17:9; 19:16-17; Jer 9:24-25; Ezek 30:9
    d) For Israel and the nations: Mic 5:9-14
  2) Symbolic

Positive images
  1) Historical

    a) For Israel: Isa 11:11; Jer 3:18; 23:5-6; 31:38-40; Amos 9:11-12; Zeph 3:20
    b) For the nations: Isa 18:7; Jer 46:26b; 49:6, 39

  2) Symbolic

a) For Israel: Isa 3:18-23;
7:18-19, 20, 21-22, 23-25;
17:4-6; Jer 4:11-12; Amos
8:9-10, 11-12, 13-14

b) For the nations: Isa
23:15-16; 33:23b-24

3) Spiritual
   a) For Israel: Jer 8:1

   b) For the nations: Jer 3:17

a) For Israel: Isa 27:12, 13; Jer
16:14-15; 23:7-8; 30:8-9;
31:27-28; Ezek 29:21; Hos
2:18-22, 23-25; Joel 4:18;
Amos 9:13-15; Mic 4:6-7;
Zech 3:10; 13:1

b) For the nations: Isa 19:23

3) Spiritual
   a) For Israel: Isa 4:2-6;
   10:20-23; 17:7-8; 28:5-6; Jer
   31:29-30, 31-34; 33:14-16;
   50:4-5, 20; Joel 3:1-3; Zeph
   3:9-10, 11-13, 16-17

   b) For the nations: Isa 2:2-4;
   11:10; 19:18, 19-22, 24-25;
   Mic 4:1-4; Zech 8:23

   c) Liturgical: Isa 12:1-3, 4-6;
   25:9-10a; 26:1-6; 27:2-6

4) Cosmic
   a) For Israel: Isa 2:20-21
      b) For Israel and against the nations: Isa
   24:21-23; 38:10-13, 14-16, 18-23,
   39:11-16; Joel 4:1-3; Zech 12:3, 6, 7, 9,
   11-14; 13:1, 2-3, 4-6; 14:6-7, 8, 9b,
   13-14, 20-21

A comparison of this list with the two preceding shows a reduced proportion of predictions that are historical in their futurism, with a slight preponderance of negative over positive images. Mic 5:9-14 is unique in predicting judgment both for Israel and the nations. There is only one prediction to an individual, that in 1 Sam 3:12f. The positive begins to outweigh the negative in passages having a symbolic image, but with predictions for Israel far more numerous than those for the nations. Spiritual predictions are in a greater comparative proportion and are almost exclusively positive. Predictions for Israel with this type of images are dominant, especially when those verses in Zech 12:1ff. that refer to spiritual/cultic concerns are included. Comprehensive images are almost always expressed in cosmic terms.

We must remind ourselves that none of the passages on this list is authentic, that is, actually written by the prophet to whom it is ascribed. They are all redactional, from one of the levels indicated, II to VI, and with introductory temporal transitions.

Some comparisons of the types of redactional expansions that were made at the various levels may be helpful. All Level II expansions, those that entered along with initial collocation and reshaping, pertain to the proximate future and have to do with Israel/Judah/Jerusalem; of those with historical images, four are negative and only one is positive; of those with symbolic images, four are negative and four are positive; also, there is a single positive spiritual image.

All Level III occurrences, those that belong with the shaping of major tradition complexes, concern the proximate future (including the *vaticinium ex eventu* at Jer 21:7) except Isa 2:2-4, which pertains to a remote future. The balance between negative and positive predictions is about even. Historical images are more common than other types. The proportion between oracles for Israel and oracles for the nations is approximately two to one.

The Level IV passages are by far the most frequent, especially those that were composed after the major tradition complexes were formed and before definitive editing (IV-C). Outside the apocalyptic cycles (Ezekiel 38–39; Joel 3–4; Zechariah 12–13, 14), the nations are seldom in consideration. Historical images are infrequent in comparison with symbolic and spiritual images. A similar tendency toward more symbolic and spiritual images prevails also at Levels V and VI, and virtually all predictions added at these levels are positive. The predictions that were created at Levels IV to VI, except those in Jer 46:26a, 49:6, 39, refer to a proximate or remote future.

These observations show proportions and therefore trends, but our main concern at this point is to identify the respective traditional backgrounds for the various images. It is necessary to compare these with those found on our two previous lists, those in passages with integral transitions in primary and in secondary materials.

One thing we do not find here is any image that derives from myth — except in the apocalyptic scenes, which are a special case. What we do find is that most images are quite traditional, that is, drawn from the deposit of biblical imagery in general, and often from the book in question. In order to appreciate the full significance of this observation, we again need to discuss the four types of images (historical, symbolic, spiritual, and cosmic) separately.

2. Imagery

a. Historical images

Historical predictions appearing with introductory redactional transitions pertain to a variety of expectations, which we may arrange in logical, if not always chronological, order.

(1) In a private oracle

1 Sam 3:12-13abα[1] (V)   Deposition of the Elides

This prediction for Eli and the Elides is isolated from other private oracles on our lists in that it is introduced by *bayyôm hahû'* rather than by one of the other formulas and came into the Deuteronomistic History at redactional Level V. The imagery is conventional and unspecific. It depends entirely on the denunciations and announcements against the Elides as these appear in the previous chapter.

(2) Punishment on Israel/Judah/Jerusalem

Isa 17:9 (IV-C)	Despoiling of fortresses
Jer 4:9-10 (III)	The leaders' dismay
Jer 21:7 (III)	Execution of Zedekiah and citizens
Hos 1:5 (IV-C)	Defeat at Jezreel
Mic 2:4-5 (II)	Lament for despoilers
Mic 5:9-14 [E 10-15]	Judah's defeat, destruction of idols and nations
Zeph 1:10-11 (II)	Punishment of officials
Zeph 1:12-13 (II)	Plunder of Jerusalem

All except the *vaticinium ex eventu* at Jer 21:7 (which has *'aharê-kēn* as a transition) have *(wĕhāyâ) bayyôm hahû'*. Most are preexilic, but Jer 21:7 is early exilic and Isa 17:9 is early postexilic. Mic 5:9ff. and the verses in Zephaniah are from Level II; Jer 4:9f. and 21:7 are from Level III; the others are from Level V.

The theme of native peoples being driven by the Israelites from the territories which they originally inhabited is drawn from the Pentateuch, and especially from Deuteronomy, but it is rare to read of something analogous happening in the passages that we have been studying. In this regard the postexilic text Isa 17:9 is completely isolated from the mainstream of prophetic tradition.[22] It appears, therefore, to be ideological in nature even though it may reflect the physical desolation that was all too common during the imperial period.

Jer 4:9-10 realistically portrays the dismay and disillusionment of Jerusalem's leaders at an attack that Jeremiah views as inevitable but that they refuse to accept as possible. Jer 21:7 is a *vaticinium ex eventu* ostensibly referring to a realistically future disaster for the Judean king and the citizens of Jerusalem surviving the initial phases of Nebuchadrezzar's siege. Hos 1:5 employs a familiar military metaphor in reflection of such an event as Tiglath-pileser III's incursion into northern Israel in 734-732 (cf. 2 Kgs 15:19). Although it draws on the imagery of a serious social-economic crisis during the late monarchical period, Mic 2:4-5 has the background of Sennacherib's invasion in 701.

The traditional sources of Judah's military strength, horses and chariots, cities and strongholds, sorceries and soothsayers, images and standing stones and asherim, are rebuked in Mic 5:9ff., which probably originated during the latter years of Hezekiah's reign. It is especially innovative in its inclusion of foreign nations with Judah in the obligation to obey (šmʿ) Yahweh the Israelite god.

Although Zeph 1:10f., 12f. draw heavily on early traditions of the day of Yahweh, they show unparalleled familiarity with commonplace activities inside kingdom-period Jerusalem. These verses are innovative in depicting Yahweh as a grim searcher[23] and as being outraged by citizens who were behaving as though Yahweh's threats were idle.[24]

(3) Exile to a foreign land

Jer 5:18-19 (IV-C)   Survival of exiles in bondage

Since an indeterminate period of living as strangers in a foreign land is predicted in this deuteronomistically influenced passage as a punishment for forsaking Yahweh, the unique formula of transition, *wĕgam bayyāmîm hahēmmâ,* "but even in those days," seems understandable and appropriate. Furthermore, the theme of purposeful chastisement and the question and answer schema[25] have their basis in the language and ideology of the early exilic period.

(4) Punishment for the nations

Isa 19:16-17 (IV-C)   Judah's terrorizing of Egypt
Jer 9:24-25 (E 25-26) (III)   Punishment on coconspirators
Ezek 30:9 (IV-B)   Terror on Cush

As has been argued, Jer 9:24f. served originally to close off a major tradition block within the book of Jeremiah at redactional Level III. It serves to include the members of a conspiracy of Judah's near neighbors (cf. Jer 27:3) with Judah in the divine judgment.[26] This is commensurate with a highly developed prophetic theodicy making Yahweh universally sovereign.

The other two passages, which entered the text at Level IV, view Yahweh's punishment on Egypt as a means to the advancement of his universal sovereignty. Though Egypt had certainly been involved in abetting Judah's rebellion against Nebuchadrezzar, it escaped that king's immediate wrath, in spite of Ezek 29:17-20. Nevertheless, in Ezekiel's ideology its judgment was certain. Composed shortly after Jerusalem's fall, Ezek 30:1-9 predicts the day of Yahweh on Egypt and on neighbors like Cush that supported it. The late postexilic text, Isa 19:16f. (but not the series of redactional expansions that follow it), embraces a strongly chauvinistic image in depicting a Judahite military threat that would induce a womanlike terror among the Egyptians.[27] Both of these passages show rare theological sophistication in appealing to Yahweh's unseen purpose.

(5) Restoration for Judah/Jerusalem

Jer 23:5-6 (III)   Reign of a righteous Davidide

We have argued that this remarkable passage is early exilic and has a programmatic function in closing off the tradition complex to which it belongs. It has been especially influential in channeling a well-developed royalist ideology toward the spiritualizing reinterpretations of the postexilic period. As it stands, it must be understood strictly in the light of Zedekiah's failure. Especially noteworthy in a comparison of this early exilic passage with its very late adaptation in Jer 33:14-16 are the reference to "his days" (a specific historical period, that of the reign of the expected king) in contrast to the vaguely eschatological "in those days," and the statement that "he," not "she" (the city),will bear the symbolic name, *YHWH ṣidqēnû*.

(6) Return from exile with political reconstruction

Isa 11:11 (IV-C)	Second return from exile
Jer 3:18 (IV-C)	Reunification and repossession
Jer 31:38-40 (II)	Rebuilding and reconsecration of Jerusalem
Amos 9:11-12 (VI)	Jerusalem's restored dominion
Zeph 3:20 (IV-C)	Return and restoration

Jer 31:38-40, along with vv 27-28 and vv 31-34 and Amos 9:11-12, is early exilic, yet the Jeremiah verses and the Amos verses belong near or at opposite ends (Level II and Level VI) of the redactional processes coming to expression within the respective books. The remaining passages in this group are early postexilic and belong to Level IV-C, that of supplemental redaction just prior to final editing.

The locutions in Isa 11:11, "remnant" and "extend the hand," are common metaphors of the early postexilic period. The unparalleled list of specific countries of Jewish dispersion is historically instructive, to say the least. The word *senît*, "a second time," has been glossed into the text by someone dissatisfied with the meager return of persons during the time of Zerubbabel.

In Jer 3:18 references to a reuniting of the "house of Judah" and the "house of Israel," to the "north" as a source of invasion and a place of exile, and to the land of Israel as an ancestral heritage, are all firmly rooted within the book and in received tradition.

Although difficult to interpret because of the lack of information concerning the layout of Jerusalem from one period to another, Jer 31:38ff. seems to share the early Jeremianic redactors' horrified fascination with large numbers of the dead (cf. 7:33, 8:1-3, 33:5). The notion of Jerusalem's southern and eastern boundaries becoming "holy to Yahweh" is novel and innovative, but it is certainly more limited, and at the same time more metaphorical, than the highly schematized image in Ezekiel 40–48, which develops the concept of holiness as something with virtual independent status in application to the temple precincts, the city, and the entire land.

Amos 9:11-12 is a drastic reversal of the entire book to which it has been appended, not only in promising good fortune but also in focusing on Jerusalem, which has been of little concern to the book as a whole. Rooted in tradition are the aspiration of subduing Edom and the metaphor of Yahweh's putting his "name" upon foreign nations, a throwback to Solomonic imperialism.

Zeph 3:20, finally, repeats the familiar promises of a regathering, a return, and a reversal of fortunes. The theme of renown and praise for the returnees may echo the tradition of Gen 12:2-3.

(7) Restoration of the nations

Jer 46:26b (VI)	Restoration of Egypt
Jer 49:6 (VI)	Restoration of Ammon
Jer 49:39 (IV-B)	Restoration of Elam

(8) The nations bring tribute

Isa 18:7 (IV-C)	Egypt brings tribute to Yahweh

(9) Summary

Although we recognize some of the motifs in these historically specific predictions, certain concrete details must remain obscure to us because of a paucity of parallels. Some of the most highly idealistic aspirations incline in the direction of a full-blown eschatology as we have defined it, but on the whole this group of passages remains within the domain of historical futurism.[28]

b. Symbolic images

As was the case in the two lists of passages with integral temporal transitions (primary and secondary), predictions in passages with introductory transitions that employ symbolic images pertain either to anticipated historical events or to elements of spiritual transformation. It is the latter group that is moving toward fully developed eschatology.

(1) Historical realities

Isa 7:18-19 (II)	Destructive pests
Isa 7:20 (II)	A hired razor
Isa 7:21-22 (II)	Curds and whey
Isa 7:23-25 (II)	Briars and thorns
Isa 17:4-6 (II)	A lean harvest
Isa 23:15-16 (IV-A)	Tyre forgotten for seventy years
Isa 27:12 (VI)	Gathering of threshed grain
Isa 27:13 (VI)	A summoning trumpet
Isa 33:23b-24 (IV-C)	Seizure of booty
Jer 4:11-12 (III)	A destroying wind
Jer 30:8-9 (IV-C)	A broken yoke
Jer 31:27-28 (II)	Resowing and nurture
Ezek 29:21 (III)	Horn, opening of mouth

The predictions in Isaiah 7 and 17 came into the text in the initial process of collocation. Some scholars look for positive intentionality in some of the short expansions in Isa 7:18-25, but our argument for assigning them all to a single redactor (drawing them intact from a variety of traditions) has favored a consistently negative interpretation. The fly, the bee, the razor, the curds and whey, and the briars and thorns all point to the actual military threat of approaching Assyrian and Egyptian armies and its probable disastrous effects in Judah in the aftermath of the Syro-Ephraimite war.

Isa 17:4-6's graphic description of a sparse harvest in the territory of Ephraim belongs to the same historical situation. Though a spiritual famine similar to that of Amos 8:11 may also be implied, the main expectation is no doubt for a real catastrophe in the next following season.

The remaining passages in this list reflect a variety of redactional levels. Isa 23:15-16 (Level IV-A) employs the symbol of forgottenness and the schematic figure of seventy years of exile,[29] together with the metaphor of a king's captivity, to convey the expectation that Tyre, as Judah's co-conspirator, was to experience an analogous period of desolation.

The two Level VI additions in Isa 27:12-13 adopt innovative symbols, that of diaspora Jews being gathered individually as freshly harvested grain[30] and that of a summoning trumpet[31] for those still in "Assyria" and those driven from Egypt, expressing the hope of a more complete return of the Jews, apparently at a time long after the initial return under Zerubbabel.

Familiar symbols in Jeremiah and Ezekiel similarly stand for identifiable historical events or conditions. Jer 4:11-12 (Level III) employs the familiar image of a destroying wind from Yahweh to symbolize the calamity of an anticipated Neo-Babylonian invasion. Though exilic Jer 30:8-9 (Level IV-C) has certain spiritual dimensions, its main focus is on an idealistic but concrete event in the near future, the exchange of foreign servitude for service to Yahweh as God and to David as king. The resowing and nurture of "the house of Israel and the house of David" in Jer 31:27-28 (Level II) reapplies the signature image of the book as a whole (cf. 1:10) but adds a theological rationale in Yahweh's affirmation that it is the same divine watchfulness (cf. 1:12) that once determined their ruin that will now ensure their regrowth. On its part, Ezek 29:21 (Level III) uses the metaphors of a sprouting horn[32] and the opening of lips[33] as elements in an unspecified restoration.

To the persons for whom these predictions were intended, the images of doom on Israel were certainly unwanted, yet they were all too clear in their intent. On the other hand, the images of blessing were welcome and reassuring, but remained vague as to precisely what was to happen. It should be noted that folk wisdom may have furnished several of the negative images, but it was familiar themes from within the respective books themselves that have furnished the positive images in Jer 31:27f. and Ezek 29:21.

(2) Spiritual realities

Isa 3:18-23 (IV-A)	Confiscation of female adornments
Isa 19:23 (IV-C)	A highway between Assyria and Egypt
Jer 16:14-15 (IV-C)	A new oath
Jer 23:7-8 (VI)	A new oath
Hos 2:18-22 (E 16-20) (II)	Betrothal as husband
Hos 2:23-25 (E 21-23) (II)	Nature's responsiveness
Joel 4:18 (E 3:18) (IV-C)	Nature's bounteous flow
Amos 8:9-10 (V)	A dark and mournful day
Amos 8:11-12 (V)	Famine and drought
Amos 8:13-14 (V)	Languishing of youths
Amos 9:13-15 (VI)	Return of the lame
Mic 4:6-7 (VI)	Prolific fruitfulness
Zech 3:10 (IV-B)	Luxuriating hospitality

Expansions with this kind of symbol entered the text at a wide range of redactional levels. The Hosea passages are from Level II but Amos 8:9-10 is from Level V, and Isa 27:12, 13, Amos 9:13-15, and Mic 4:6-7 are from Level VI. The favorable passages concentrate on the subjective state of those who were to benefit from Yahweh's action on their behalf.

The confiscation of female adornments[34] in Isa 3:18-23 is meant as a rebuke to the general pride and luxuriating selfishness which they typify, for in spite of the specific female imagery, all human haughtiness is implied.

Isa 19:23, within the incremental series of favoring oracles for Egypt in chap. 19, offers the remarkable image of a highway *(měsillâ)* between Egypt and Assyria. Whether or not a specially constructed road existed, other than the ancient route of traders and armies, the intent of the image is to symbolize universal access to Yahweh in Jerusalem.[35]

The striking image in the parallel passages, Jer 16:14f. (Level IV-C) and 23:7f. (Level VI), of a new oath for identifying affirmation, venturing to substitute the return from Babylonian exile for the traditional exodus from Egypt, was almost certainly intended to be taken metaphorically (much in the vein of Jer 31:31-34), and certainly not prescriptively or programmatically.

The image of betrothal to a caring husband[36] is richly expounded in Hos 2:18-22 in terms of the benefits of a renewed covenant with Yahweh. Based on the catchword "answer,"[37] the following two verses (23-25) employ the responsiveness of nature to Yahweh's creative command as a symbol of a more trusting and responsive relationship between Yahweh and his people.

The ruin and the renewal of nature is another familiar theme. In Joel 4:18 (Level IV-C) and Amos 9:13-15 (Level VI), nature's bountifulness is the symbol of a great multitude of spiritual blessings. On the other hand, the dark day of Amos 8:9-10,[38] the famine and drought in vv 11-12, and the languishing of idolatrous youths (a rebuke to their fervent naturism) symbolize the spiritual doom of those who remain in rebellion and apostasy.

The return of the lame in Mic 4:6-7[39] draws upon the recollection of a past event as a symbol of anticipated spiritual benefits still to be experienced.

Finally, the image of luxuriating hospitality in Zech 3:10 (Level IV-B), a positive rather than negative symbol, draws upon a popular expression from the age of Solomonic imperialism to symbolize the spiritual blessings that were to follow from Joshua's purification and consecration.[40]

When these symbols were put to use in predictions of the type under study, they were immediately understandable, either because they were rooted in tradition or because the books to which they belong had partially developed them. Those with a negative implication must be explained as imaginative applications of the announcement of divine justice. It is not they that should be called eschatological. They do no more than make more graphic what had already been announced and predicted, namely, the effects of divine wrath. The passages with positive images, on the other hand, announce something perhaps hoped for but no longer confidently expected. They employ metaphors of radical transformation, either in nature or in human existence. They assume a drastically new basis for humankind's life within God's world, no longer the *quid pro quo* of Mosaic obligation but an existence in which all the ambiguities of historical experience give way to the certainties of God's unconditional favor and of perfect human obedience to God.

We still need to take up those symbolic elements that appear in apocalyptic scenes, in which they become elements in a comprehensive image. We defer this to the section on cosmic images that follows.

Of temporal formulas employed in this group of passages, *bayyôm hahû'* with its variant is by far the most common.[41] Other formulas of transition are *bā'ēt hahî'* and *hinnēh yāmîm bā'îm*.[42] Usually the prediction is for the proximate future, but it is for the remote future in Isa 19:23, 27:12-13; Jer 23:7,[43] 30:8; Joel 4:18; Amos 9:13; Mic 4:6; and Zech 3:10. It is predictions for the remote future that most often employ symbols of spiritual transformation.

c. Spiritual images

The predictions placed into this category are those of spiritual realities, which may be viewed as an extension of the symbolic images having a spiritual rather than historical focus. Inescapably, several of them contain elements of symbolism, but the distinction is that these are kept as subsidiary elements. It is remarkable that only one of these spiritual images, that in Jer 8:1-3, is negative; all the rest are positive. Seven (eight counting a parallel occurrence) offer salvation for the nations. The rest of the positive predictions offer benefits for Israel.

The predictions in this category have been designated as "oracles," but this is not meant in terms of a strict form-critical definition since very few (Jer 31:31-34, 33:14-16, 50:20; Joel 3:1-3 [E 4:1-3]; Zeph 3:9-10, 11-13) are actually structured as speeches by Yahweh.[44] As a matter of fact, very few of these predictions (Isa 2:2-4 par Mic 4:1-4; Isa 28:5-6; Joel 3:1-3; Zeph 3:9-10, 11-13, 16-17) are cast in poetic form. All the rest are entirely in prose, with the exception of Jer 31:31-34, which is prose containing elements of poetry.

We are beginning to encounter here a noteworthy loosening of traditional forms and structures, just what one might expect from the relatively late dating. Except for Isa 28:5-6 (early preexilic), Jer 31:31-34 (early exilic), and Jer 8:1-3 (also early exilic), all occurrences are postexilic. Furthermore, most of them derive from late levels within the redactional process. Jer 31:31ff. is from Level II, Isa 2:2ff. is from Level III, Mic 4:1ff. is from Level V, and Isa 4:2ff. and Jer 33:14ff. are from Level VI. All the rest are from Level IV — that of the free expansion of individual passages without special concern for redactional collocations and prior to definitive editing.

In the first two sections of this chapter it was useful to divide the passages with spiritual images between the more subjective and the more objective, but that division is of little significance here because virtually all the symbols used are objective. The thematic content of this group of predictions may better be studied, therefore, by dividing them between the relatively simple and the relatively complex. Even though the precise boundaries between the two groups may sometimes be uncertain on the basis of this criterion, it will prove nevertheless to be a decisive difference. The reason is that simple predictions tend to be intuitive while complex predictions tend to be reflective. This is perhaps one of the most significant insights of our present study.

Another reason for making this division is that, in moving from the simple type to the complex type, we are able to identify those that belong securely within the category of the eschatological.

(1) Simple

Isa 11:10 (IV-C)	The Davidides' cosmic appeal
Isa 17:7-8 (IV-C)	Exclusive worship of Yahweh
Isa 19:18 (IV-C)	Worship of Yahweh in five Egyptian cities
Isa 19:24-25 (IV-C)	Egypt and Assyria as Yahweh's people
Isa 28:5-6 (IV-A)	Yahweh's glory, justice, and strength
Jer 3:17 (IV-C)	A throne in Jerusalem for all nations
Jer 31:29-30 (IV-C)	Limiting of responsibility
Jer 50:4-5 (IV-A)	Reunification, repentance, and return
Jer 50:20 (IV-A)	Pardon and purging
Joel 3:1-3 (E 2:28-29) (IV-C)	Inspiration on every class
Zeph 3:9-10 (IV-C)	Worshipful speech
Zeph 3:16-17 (IV-C)	Yahweh rejoices over Zion
Zech 8:23 (IV-B)	Jews as agents in the world's conversion

Three special points of focus among the spiritual predictions have a simple development: (1) Yahweh, (2) Israel, and (3) the nations. Some passages have two of these foci, but none has more than two.

We must comment first on the Isaiah passages. Isa 11:10 promises that the "root" *(šōreš)* of David will stand as a beacon *(nēs)* for foreign nations and peoples. Isa 17:7-8 promises that *hā'ādam* (humankind in general or the covenant people as human) will pay attention to *(š'h)* the God who made them in the place of the cult objects that they have fabricated. Isa 19:18 predicts something that probably had already happened, the speaking of Canaanite (that is, Hebrew) in order to allow for the swearing of allegiance to Yahweh in five Egyptian cities, including Heliopolis. Isa 19:24-25 is venturesome beyond all bounds in predicting that Egypt and Assyria will form a holy trio with Israel both in bearing a blessing and in being blessed by Yahweh. Isa

28:5-6 (the earliest text in this group) foretells the aspects and hypostases in which Yahweh will be glorified.

There is an impressive array of predictive passages in Jeremiah with a spiritual image, most of which are simple both in structure and in focus. Jer 3:17 announces two things: that Jerusalem will become Yahweh's throne for all nations and that those nations will no longer be stubbornly in rebellion against it; this early postexilic passage is the only one in this category in Jeremiah that offers salvation to the nations. In a contemplative vein, Jer 31:29-30 predicts the reinterpretation of the sour-grapes proverb, limiting moral responsibility to those who have actually done the sinning and thereby promoting hope among those who have not participated in it. According to Jer 50:4-5, the repentant and reunited people will seek the way back to Zion while expressing the hope of being rejoined to Yahweh in an ever enduring, never to be forgotten, covenant. In Jer 50:20 Yahweh declares that no sin or iniquity whatever will be found in Israel or Judah because he will forgive those whom he has allowed to survive the exile.

The book of the Twelve Prophets has an interesting variety of spiritual symbols. The Yahweh speech in Joel 3:1-3 announces the outpouring of the divine spirit on "all flesh," including some who normally would not be included among the prophets: sons and daughters, old men and young men, even male and female slaves.[45] In a similar vein, Yahweh declares in Zeph 3:9-19 that he will purify the speech of the nations so that they may properly invoke and worship him, enabling the most distant of the diaspora faithful to resume offerings to him.[46] Following the victory song in vv 14-15, Zeph 3:16-17 affirms that Yahweh will be in the midst of Zion preparing to rejoice, renew, and deliver. Zech 8:23 has perhaps the most startling prediction of all: that foreigners will plead to be allowed to walk (hlk)[47] with Jews because they have heard that Yahweh is with them.

Although this group of predictive passages draws upon a traditional stock of ideas current for their respective ages, they are remarkable for their imagination and bold innovativeness. In common circulation were the "I am with you" theme (Zeph 3:17; Zech 8:23),[48] a rationalized polemic against idols (Isa 17:7-8),[49] the idea of the reaffirmation of Yahweh's covenant with Israel (Jer 50:5), the image of Yahweh as warrior (Zeph 3:17),[50] and the identification of Jerusalem as world-center (Jer 3:17; cf. Zech 8:23). These are all common stock within the biblical tradition and are not eschatological in the sense that they assume a drastic transformation within mankind or in the world. However, the presence of random eschatological motifs is to be noted in several of these passages.

The ideal Davidic king[51] is not a new idea in the late passage, Isa 11:10. What is new in this passage is the universalizing of this image, an idea that does not take root again until the development of Christian messianism. In general, the attitude of this group of passages toward the foreign nations is remarkably generous. Zech 8:23 retains an element of balance in its insistence that Jews must serve as the agents of the world's salvation because God is definitely with them. It goes beyond the reasonable expectations of historic futurism, however, in declaring that "nations of every tongue," and in strict proportion of ten foreigners to each Jew, will be allowed to walk to the city where they may share this marvelous "togetherness." This schematizing stretching of the proper limits of metaphor is definitely an eschatological trait, as are the passages that insist on a changing or purification of foreign speech (Isa 19:18; Zeph 3:10-11), along with the comprehensive gift of the divine spirit announced in Joel 3:1-3.

A persistent problem for the early postexilic community was the continuing presence of sin (cf. Zech 3:1-9, 5:1-4, 5-11). Often biblical eschatology, and especially its apocalyptic variety, endeavors to resolve this problem by simply treating sinners as non-sinners. The redactor who composed Jer 31:29-30 did not adopt this solution, but he did show some daring in his challenge to the dictum of guilt solidarity, as implied in the all-too-popular sour-grapes proverb (cf. Ezek 18:1-3). He was explicating an essential principle of biblical anthropology, not resorting to eschatological speculation.

On the contrary, Jer 50:4-5, 20 apply a drastic eschatological solution, the first in announcing that Judah and Israel, collectively and comprehensively, would seek Yahweh in Zion in expectation that the conditions of an eternal covenant would be fulfilled,[52] the second in announcing that sin and iniquity would simply not exist any more, either in Israel or in Judah, because Yahweh grandly pardons the survivors of the exile. These two predictions are ideological and schematic, and they certainly fail to allow for the vagaries of the human spirit, which essentially create the problems of history. It seems appropriate that they were scheduled in these verses not only for future days, but for a radically altered situation or condition of human existence, coming to expression in the peculiar temporal formula *bayyāmîm hahēm ûbāʿēt hahîʾ*.

Finally, Isa 19:24-25 carries eschatological idealism to its farthest bound in applying the foundation promise of Gen 12:2-3 to gentile nations on an equal basis with Israel. Unquestionably the most radical expression of universalism in the entire Old Testament, this final expansion within an incremental series of predictions for Egypt in Isaiah 19 affirms that Israel will be no more than a third partner, *primus inter pares,* alongside Egypt and Assyria, in bringing a blessing *(běrākâ)* in the midst of the earth (v 24), for Yahweh has already given his blessing[53] in making Egypt his people *(ʿammî),* Assyria the work of his hands *(maʿăśeh yāday),* and Israel his heritage *(naḥălātî).*

The temporal formulas used as introductory transitions in this group of passages are *kî ʾāz* (Zeph 3:9), *(wěhāyâ) bayyôm hahûʾ* (Isa 11:10, 17:7, 19:18, 24, 28:5; Zeph 3:16), *bayyāmîm hahēm(mâ)* (Jer 31:19; Zech 8:23), *bāʿēt hahî᾽* (Jer 3:17), *bayyāmîm hahēm ûbā῾ēt hahî᾽* (Jer 50:4, 20), and *wĕhāyâ ᾽aḥărê-kēn* (Joel 3:1 [E 2:28]). As we recall, the units with these formulas used as transitions are all relatively late passages, dating from late exilic to late postexilic. They project either a proximate (Isa 28:5f.; Jer 3:17, 31:29f., 50:4-5, 20) or a remote future (Isa 11:10, 17:7f., 19:18, 24f.; Joel 3:1ff.; Zeph 3:9f., 16f.; and Zech 8:23).

(2) Complex

Isa 2:2-4 (III)	Law and justice for the nations in Jerusalem
Isa 4:2-6 (VI)	Glory, cleansing, and protection
Isa 10:20-23 (IV-C)	Reliance on Yahweh
Isa 19:19-22 (IV-C)	A Yahweh altar in Egypt
Jer 8:1-3 (IV-C)	The embracing of death
Jer 31:31-34 (II)	A new covenant
Jer 33:14-16 (VI)	Fulfillment of the promise of a righteous Davidide
Mic 4:1-4 (V)	Law and justice for the nations in Jerusalem
Zeph 3:11-13 (IV-C)	Exaltation of the humble

This more complex group of predictions either touch upon more than two points of focus or draw together themes from an unusual variety of traditions.

In spite of the editorial superscription in v 1, Isa 2:2-4 does not directly deal with "Judah and Jerusalem" but concerns (1) the temple mount as a world center, (2) a motive for the Gentiles coming to it and the effect of this coming upon their inclination for making war, and (3) Yahweh's act of judging them *(špṭ)* and adjudicating their disputes *(ykḥ* hiph.)

Isa 4:2-6 casually mentions Yahweh's *ṣemaḥ*, "branch,"[54] but its main concern is for those who will have survived the exile and now reside in Jerusalem.[55] It announces the elimination of spiritual uncleanness through "a spirit of judgment and a spirit of burning," then goes on to predict the creation of a protecting cloud like the numinous pillar in the desert[56] or like the *shekinah* over the tabernacle,[57] serving as a shelter from heat and storm.[58]

Isa 10:20-23 is another confused medley of prognostications in which prior elements are made to follow as afterthoughts to the primary affirmation, which is that those who survive will confidently lean on Yahweh, even though they are only a remnant out of the innumerable horde that are to be included in Yahweh's immutable decree of destruction.[59]

Isa 19:19-22 similarly proceeds in a confused order from a central affirmation about the testimonial significance of a Yahweh altar and pillar in

Egypt *(vaticinium ex eventu)*. When the Egyptians appeal to Yahweh he will deliver them; they will worship at this altar and pillar to show that they "know" him through just such a deliverance; though Yahweh may smite Egypt, he will give heed to the supplications of those in Egypt who honor him.[60]

The book of Jeremiah also has several such complex predictions. The grim forecast of an all-embracing death in 8:1-3 is as confused in its structure and ideology as some of those seen in Isaiah. It announces that the bones of all classes of people in Jerusalem will be disinterred, then spread as dung as a testimony to the heavenly deities of their ineffectiveness. At the end (v 3) it reveals this redactor's despondency in the announcement that such a death would be preferable to the conditions of the exile that in fact awaits "this evil family" *(hammišpāḥâ hārā'â hazzō't)*.[61]

Jer 31:31-34 has a logical but unchronological arrangement: Yahweh will make a brand-new covenant, entirely different from the covenant that was made and broken.[62] It will provide a law written on the people's hearts. It will establish the ideal condition in which Yahweh is truly their god and they his people. This means that it will be unnecessary any longer to provide religious instruction, because everybody will know Yahweh. The premise of all this is that Yahweh will forgive and forget sin.

Jer 33:14-16 is a remake of the historical prediction in Jer 23:5-6. It not only includes affirmations that David's righteous "branch" will bring justice and righteousness, that Judah/Jerusalem will be preserved, and that the city will receive a symbolic name, but also affirms that these things will yet be fulfilled "in coming days."

Finally, there is Zeph 3:11-13. Yahweh is speaking here to his people — evidently the restored community — promising that former deeds will no longer shame them, and for two reasons: (1) the removal of the proudly exultant from "my holy mountain,"[63] and (2) the survival and security of a "people humble and lowly" who seek refuge in Yahweh's name and refrain from lies and deceit.[64] Though there is general thematic unity in this passage, it shares elements of the eclecticism seen in the other passages within this group.

As steeped as these complex predictions are in the traditions of their peculiar times, they are remarkable both for their innovativeness and for the highly schematic nature of their futuristic speculation.

The only negative prediction in this group, that at Jer 8:1-3, not only contradicts such passages as Jer 31:40 and Ezek 37:1-14 in embracing death as more significant than life, but incorporates a medley of confused ideas regarding death. The redactor of this passage lifts grim death to a level above what is normal and experiential. Indeed, it gives death an almost mythical significance.

Isa 2:2-4 par Mic 4:1-4, the only poetically structured prediction in this group, is quite remarkable in its idyllic imaging; yet the affirmations to the effect that all or many foreign nations will come to Jerusalem seeking law and justice, and that this will bring perpetual peace and eradicate the very inclination to warfare, transcend all the actualities of historical existence, even going beyond the high lyricism of Deutero-Isaiah. In Isa 4:2-6, being holy, being recorded for life, being thoroughly purged of sin, and finding protection under a specially created cloud of glory are meant as permanent features of the ideal future state. In Isa 19:19-22 the altar and pillar are made to serve as an enduring sign and witness to Yahweh's readiness to rescue those who confess him. In Jer 31:31-34 the new covenant and the new law, based on a blessed state of perfect forgivenness, are meant as permanent and perpetual. Finally, the traditional blessings mentioned in Jer 33:14-16 are designated for the time of the fulfillment of the promise for a perfect reign of righteousness.

Each of these complex spiritual predictions is eschatological in the fullest sense. The main reason is that for them all the realities of history as we know it will have been transformed. To be sure, they do manifest a heightened level of transcendentalism; but it is not merely a matter of the wondrous and the unexpected coming to pass, for even the historical and the symbolic predictions announce what is marvelously unexpected within the normal course of human events, and this is because Yahweh is at work to bring them about. But in these more complex predictions everything becomes the work of Yahweh, leaving no place at all for human effort. There is a significant difference in the fact that certain of them focus on the more external and objective elements of spiritual transformation (Isa 2:2ff. par, 10:20ff., 19:19ff.; Jer 8:1ff., 33:14ff.), while others are concerned with the more internal and subjective elements of this transformation (Jer 31:31ff.; Zeph 3:11ff.).

It is not surprising that virtually all of these complex spiritual predictions are postexilic — even late postexilic. They come very close to expressing the ideology of apocalyptic without actually becoming apocalyptic.

The temporal formulas introducing this group of passages are *bayyôm hahû'* (Isa 4:2, 10:20, 19:19; Zeph 3:11), *bāʿēt hahî'* (Jer 8:1), *hinnēh yāmîm bāʾîm* (Jer 31:31, 33:14), and *wĕhāyâ bĕʾaḥărît hayyāmîm* (Isa 2:2; Mic 4:1). Only Jer 8:1ff. and 31:31ff. predict the proximate future (significantly, both passages are early exilic), while all the others refer to a remote future.

(3) Liturgical elements (Level V)

Isa 12:1-3	Praise for forgiveness and salvation
Isa 12:4-6	Praise for Yahweh's universal greatness
Isa 25:9-10a	Praise for timely help
Isa 26:1-6	Praise for Zion's restoration
Isa 27:2-6	Praise for Yahweh's protection

It is to no truly future event that these passages refer, but to an ever-renewable, liturgical present/future in which pious individuals or the community are invited to experience once again (that is, for themselves) the joy and comfort that have come whenever Yahweh is present with his people.[65] Isa 12:1-3 is structured as individual declaration of praise; Isa 12:4-6, 25:9f., and 26:1-6 are descriptive praise hymns offered by the community; Isa 27:2-6 is an allegorical hymn. They are all late postexilic and have entered the text as part of the editing process (Level V).

d. Cosmic images

The predictive passages with cosmic motifs may embody elements of other types, but something new and distinctive has been created in them.

First of all, there is an historical element in the quasi-historical concept of a military attack on Israel and Jerusalem, but everything has been blown up to immense proportions to include the foreign invaders *en masse* in an all-out, last-ditch assault.

Second, there are elements of metaphor and symbolism. As in some of the other types of prediction, symbolic elements abound in Zech 12:2–13:6: the heavy stone (12:3), a pot on the fire and a torch in dry sheaves (12:6), a strengthening shield (12:8), a pagan funeral (12:11), a cleansing fountain (13:1), and a prophet's wounds (13:6). The dominant motif of miraculous intervention in the holy war (cf. Ezek 38:19-22; Zech 14:6-7) embodies symbolic elements as well.

Third, a spiritual concern saturates the entire scene. A programmatic effort toward spiritual transformation — partially based on historical circumstances and embodying a strongly parenetic interest — underlies the ritual mourning of Zech 12:10, 12-14, the cleansing of sin in 13:1, and the censuring of idols and of prophecy in 13:2-6. However, these are only incidental facets within an elaborate panorama.

It makes little sense to focus on individual negative or positive elements when analyzing this type of prediction. We may speak of the images employed in this type of composition as comprehensive for two reasons: (1) historical, symbolic, and spiritual elements, negative or positive, have been intertwined and (2) the defeat and/or judgment of foreign nations has been made ancillary to the salvation of God's people.

There is no longer a reason for judgment both on Israel and on the nations, or for salvation for Israel in distinction from salvation for the nations.[66] All historical paradoxes and ambiguities have been set aside: Israel is no longer sinful but perfectly righteous; the nations are now absolutely, finally, and definitively wicked, fully ripe for destruction. Everything has been prepared for the final showdown. An awesome suspense hangs over the entire world as it approaches its final moment. Israel may seem to be in extreme peril, but it will soon be rescued. The nations may have no qualms at all about their purpose to destroy Israel but will soon be defeated.

It is well to be reminded that this type of speculation belongs to the entire postexilic period, not just to its latter years. Certainly there is internal development within this period, but we must remember that the apocalyptic solution was put forth already in Ezekiel's Gog pericope. A drastic futurism and a radical separatism go hand in hand as hallmarks of apocalyptic in its fully developed form, but the roots of each are in evidence in Ezekiel 38–39, Joel 3–4, Zechariah 12–13, and Zechariah 14. This suggests that neither historical futurism nor nonapocalyptic eschatological speculation was able to satisfy those within the postexilic community who had yielded to despair that Yahweh ever would (or even could) do something decisive within history to resolve ambiguities, uncertainties, and dangers. For them, this could only happen beyond time and outside history. It is this anxiety that created the comprehensive imagery of early apocalyptic.

As has been seen, cosmic images are present already in non-apocalyptic eschatology; specifically, in embroidery upon the day of Yahweh concept. To judge from classical prophetic texts such as Isa 2:10-17, 24:1-23; Ezek 7:2-19; Amos 5:18-20; and Zeph 1:2-18, this was designed to resolve everything that was offensive and contradictory within human existence. This "day of Yahweh" was to be the single day among all of Yahweh's special "days"[67] when he would set everything right that had been wrong — especially Israel's own vacillation and apostasy.

At least in Ezekiel (7:21-27), it is made clear that foreign enemies were to become the instrument of divine wrath on this awesome day. Ezekiel awaited, and eventually witnessed, its coming in the event of Jerusalem's fall. Thus the day of Yahweh might come to be equated with a climactic historical event which the survivors of such an event would come to view as chronologically past (see our discussion of Ezek 34:12 in Chapter Seven).

But the older view was that it was the nations that were destined to be judged on the day of Yahweh. This was what was assumed by Amos's hearers, and it is made explicit in Joel 4:2 (E 3:22), along with Obad 15-16. It is this view of the day of Yahweh, rather than the more mature notion of judgment on Israel and on the nations together, that is reinstated in the apocalyptic pericopes under study here.

(1) Nonapocalyptic

Isa 2:20-21 (IV-A)   Frantic discard of idols on the day of
                            Yahweh

This is a preexilic expansion that is connected by *bayyôm hahû'* to the same expression at the end of v 17, and hence to the entire oracle of vv 10-17. Along with Isa 31:7, which has integral *bayyôm hahû'* following *kî* and quotes directly from it, this short expansion develops the image of the throwing away of silver and golden idols as useless sources of succor in a time of panic. It also reproduces the motif of hiding in caverns from v 10. The discard of objects of value is seen also in Ezek 7:10 and Zeph 1:18, but here it is the uselessness of the heathen gods made from precious metals, rather than the uselessness of the precious metals as such, that comes to expression. Though early preexilic in date, this expansion came into the text after chaps. 2–4 were formed into a single unit at redactional Level IV-A. Its prediction is for the same proximate future as that of the original day-of-Yahweh oracle to which it is attached.

(2) Apocalyptic

Isa 24:21-23 (IV-A)	Yahweh's cosmic judgment
Ezek 38:10-13 (IV-C)	Gog's evil plan
Ezek 38:14-16 (IV-C)	Attack on unsuspecting returnees
Ezek 38:18-23 (IV-C)	Arousal of Yahweh's wrath
Ezek 39:11-16 (IV-C)	A valley for vast burial
Joel 4:1-3 (E 3:1-3) (IV-C)	Restoration for Israel's oppressed and the gathering of the nations
Zech 12:3a (IV-A)	Jerusalem as a heavy stone
Zech 12:6-7 (IV-A)	Judah's clans a pot/torch
Zech 12:8 (IV-A)	A shield about Jerusalem
Zech 12:9 (IV-A)	Destruction of enemies
Zech 12:11 (IV-A)	Mourning in Jerusalem
Zech 13:1 (IV-A)	A cleansing fountain
Zech 13:2-3 (IV-A)	Riddance of idols and prophets
Zech 13:4-6 (IV-A)	Repudiation of prophets
Zech 14:6-7 (VI)	Obliteration of nature's cycles
Zech 14:8, 10-11 (VI)	Living waters from Jerusalem
Zech 14:9b (VI)	Yahweh's absolute sovereignty
Zech 14:13-14 (VI)	Panic on attackers
Zech 14:20-21 (VI)	Comprehensive holiness

We have identified Isa 24:21-23 as one of two incremental expansions (including 25:6-8) to the day-of-Yahweh oracle in 24:1-20. It is late postexilic in date and belongs to the Level IV-A redaction for this section of the book. It employs comprehensive and sometimes self-contradictory imagery: that of Yahweh punishing the forces of heaven and earth (21), which will be imprisoned and punished *mērōb yāmîm,* "after many days/years" (22), and that of the moon and sun succumbing before Yahweh Sebaoth in Jerusalem (23). Its early expansion in 25:6-8 develops the cosmic imagery, going so far as to

exclude death and tears from a projected eschatological banquet while including "all peoples/nations" within the universal sway of divine salvation.[68]
Although *wĕhāyâ bayyôm hahû'* is the introductory formula for this expansion,
the future that it predicts is remote.

All the remaining apocalyptic expansions on this list similarly have
(wĕhāyâ) bayyôm hahû' and refer to a remote future. This turns out to be one
among several features that clearly differentiates apocalyptic expansions from
that which came directly out of the classical prophetic tradition.

The apocalyptic expansions to the original Gog apocalypse (Ezek 38:1-9,
39:1-5, 17-20) are early postexilic and were introduced in the Level IV-C
redaction of the book. In comparison with the poetic and relatively simple
imagery of Isa 24:21-24 (with 25:6-8), important differences are apparent.
One difference is that these Gog expansions are both prosaic in form and
reflective in style. Although they show incremental development from the
respective sections of the original apocalypse to which they attach, they are
mainly atomistic with relationship to one another.

There are two main sources for the lurid imagery of these expansions.
One is the highly stylized inventory of quasi-holy-war events, for which there
is no more expressive parallel than that of 2 Chronicles 20.[69] Another is the
theme of Yahweh's self-vindication, drawn mainly from the book of Ezekiel
itself.

The motif of innocent helplessness on the part of those who have
resettled in Palestine is clearly apologetic. Not only does it accentuate the
unmotivated ferocity of the mythical attacker, but it unmistakably betrays a
deep anxiety that the historical return from exile may not, after all, guarantee
the permanent safety of God's people, thereby throwing an additional weight
of emphasis on the prospect of an irruptive supernatural intervention in order
to resolve these anxieties once for all.

Apocalyptic imagery is relatively undeveloped in Joel 4:1-3 (E 3:1-3),
an expansion to two previous eschatological expansions at 3:1-3, 4-6 (E
2:28-29, 30-32). Doubtless this remarkable new expansion, introduced by the
unparalleled and awkward formulation *kî hinnēh bayyāmîm hahēmmâ ûbā'ēt
hahî'*, presupposes the imagery of the materials to which it is attached. It
includes a short clause with the stereotyped expression *'ăšer ['āšîb] 'et šĕbût
yĕhûdâ wîrûšālayim*, "when I shall restore the fortunes of Judah and Jerusalem," indicating a vaguely defined act of divine favor that is to be integral
to, or synchronous with, the gathering and judging of the nations. This expansion is designedly programmatic in its demand for retribution on the part
of all of Israel's persecutors — those who may have been and those who may
yet be.

The main historical elements in Zech 12:2–13:6 are an innuendo of
rivalry between Jerusalem and the outlying districts, a cryptic reference to

"one whom they have pierced," and vague insinuations of spiritual or ritual imperfection. All the rest is speculative and highly imaginative. The enemy in question has not been mythified as in Ezekiel 38–39. Nevertheless, the battle is Yahweh's and therefore conclusive. Priestly concerns come to manifestation in references to mourning and cleansing — all on a monumental scale and highly schematic. The pericope as a whole aims to construct an image of absolute and undisturbed sinlessness within the community. It is not strange within this artificial construct that prophecy is to be banned, for apocalyptic claims to unfold the secrets that prophecy can only hint at (cf. Dan 9:1-2, 20-22), and unrestricted manticism threatens to disturb the tranquility of the ideologically perfect community of saints that has neither sins nor internal problems.

As has been argued, Zechariah 12–13 entered the text at Level IV-A of the book's redaction while Zechariah 14 entered it at Level VI — after the definitive editing. The imagery of chap. 14 is comparatively more comprehensive, variegated, and speculative. The verses introduced by temporal formulas belong to successive though roughly contemporaneous stages of ideological elaboration. As we have seen, competing interests are at work here to modify an original day-of-Yahweh oracle. Vv 6-7 and vv 13-14 draw directly upon images from the holy-war tradition. V 9b is a theological reflection based on the preceding affirmation of Yahweh's cosmic kingship (9a). Vv 8 and 10-11 describe a marvelous transformation of the land, much as in vv 4-5, and equally under the influence of Ezekiel 40–48. The demand for worldwide worship at Jerusalem during the Feast of Booths, with specification of punishment for noncompliance (vv 16-19), and a description of a state of comprehensive holiness (vv 20-21) betray more of the attitude of Qumranian perfectionism than of the program of a late priestly theocracy within the Old Testament itself.

(3) Summary

There can be no question but that the cosmic imagery of these apocalyptic scenes is far more bold and innovative than the cosmic imagery of the non-apocalyptic predictions. These scenes occasionally draw upon mythological motifs; however, mythological figures have been transported from the *Urzeit* to the *Endzeit* (Gunkel). The possibilities of simple metaphor and symbol have been transcended and the ideal of a complete spiritual transformation has given way to a radical program in which the righteous alone may live. In this drastic way, all the old ambiguities and paradoxes have been resolved. The faithful, tired out in the historical struggle, are reaching out for an image that is at the same time simple in conception and comprehensive in application.

With an eye to the use of the temporal formulas that have been employed in bringing this type of speculation to its fullest development, one must note first that each of the more nuanced formulas has been discarded. The Gog apocalypse employs its unparalleled formula, *bĕ'aḥărît haššānîm* (Ezek 38:8), to express an awareness of a more remote future beyond what is already remotely future. Its expansions settled for the remote future but drastically extended the framework of the last day in their stereotyped reemployment of *(wĕhāyâ) bayyôm hahû'* as a formula of transition. This gave a pseudo-contemporaneity to the apocalyptic drama. Joel's peculiar formulations are notably inventive, but stereotyping is the general trend here as well.

In each of these passages, everything happens "on that day." Yahweh's special day of conclusive revelation has been stretched out to include every-body's image of what perfection ought to be.

Conclusion

When we compare this third group of predictions, those that are redactional and have introductory temporal transitions, with the first and second groups, we are impressed not only with the wide variety of images employed, but also with a high degree of independence among the images themselves and in comparison with traditional images outside the prophetic corpus.

Only two themes present themselves in all three groups of predictions: (1) the return and restoration of the exiled community (group one: Isa 35:5-6, 58:8; Jer 31:13; Hos 3:5; Zech 8:11-13; group two: Jer 30:2-3; Ezek 39:25-29; group three: Isa 11:11, 27:12-13; Jer 3:18, 16:14-15 par 23:7-8, 30:8-9, 31:27-28, 50:4-5, 20; Hos 2:18-22, 23-25; Joel 4:1; Amos 9:11-12; Mic 4:6-7; Zeph 3:20) and (2) the defeat of enemy nations (group one: Ezek 38:8-9; Zech 12:4; Dan 10:20; group two: Ezek 38:14b-16a, 19-23; group three: the remaining expansions in Ezekiel 38–39; Zechariah 12–13, 14).

There are, however, three images or themes that appear in two of these groups: (1) the theme of Yahweh's day as a threat to Israel, found in group one (Isa 31:6-7; Ezek 7:3-4) and group three (Isa 2:20-21; Amos 8:9-10; Zeph 1:10-11, 12-13); (2) the theme of an ideally righteous Davidide, found only in group two (Jer 33:14-16) and group three (Isa 11:10; Jer 23:5-6); and (3) the covenant, which is rarely mentioned but in two group one passages (Jer 31:1, 50:4-5) is held to be still valid, while in one group three passage (Jer 31:31-34) it constitutes an entirely new arrangement that is to be established by an act of divine grace and power.

Other prominent themes appear only in group three passages, that is, those that are redactional and have introductory temporal transitions. Negative images within this group are those of nature's restraint (Isa 7:18-25, 17:4-6; Amos 8:11-14) and of cosmic judgment (Isa 24:21-23; Joel 4:1-3). Positive images are those of nature's transformation (Hos 2:23-25; Joel 4:18; Amos 9:13-15; Zech 3:10, 14:8, 10-11), of the conversion of the nations (Isa 2:2-4 par Mic 4:1-4; Isa 11:10, 19:18-25; Jer 3:17; Zech 8:23), of the removal of sin and impurity (Jer 31:38-40, 50:4-5; Zech 12:11, 13:1, 2-3, 14:20-21), of Yahweh's glory (Isa 10:20-23, 18:7, 24:21-23, 28:5-6; Zech 14:9 [cf. 16]) and of the glory of Jerusalem (Isa 4:2-6; Jer 31:38-40; Zeph 3:16-17).

It may seem surprising that the law or *Torah,* so dominant in postbiblical Judaism, is scarcely mentioned in these predictions. In Isa 2:3 par it has an entirely new function, while in Jer 31:33 it is completely spiritualized and is no longer written or taught.

The important point to observe is not that individual themes in predictions of this kind are isolated from their peculiar literary context or from their ideological tradition, but that they are essentially isolated from one another. This is the place to recall a tentative conclusion that emerged from our examination of cluster arrangements in Chapter Five, namely, that most of the individual units within such clusters are thematically atomistic, even in cases where several of them are placed as a group into the text by a single redactor. Now what we were able to conclude with respect to clusters proves to be generally true of all individual predictions of this sort, even when they are attached singly to their respective contexts.

Certainly, every important theme touched upon in one or more of this type of prediction invites careful study beyond what we have been able to give it. We await future special studies of many of them. As a matter of fact, monographs have already been devoted to some of them (as, e.g., the righteous Davidide or messiah figure, the new covenant, the final attack). It should be comparatively easy to make extensive comparisons of the passages that are plainly dependent on each other, such as the Jeremianic doublets or Isa 2:2-4 in comparison with Mic 4:1-4. Certainly it makes sense to compare the writings of a later period with similar writings of an early period.

Apart from these obvious leads, it would be hazardous to suggest a comprehensive diachronic and synchronic correlation for all the futuristic images found in the type of predictive passages that we have been studying (syndetic: those with temporal transitions) with those appearing asyndetically in other types of prophetic predictions. The correlations that we have identified are meant to be suggestive and paradigmatic, rather than definitive or prescriptive. In any event, it is safe to predict that their far-ranging significance will not be overlooked in future studies of prophetic eschatology and redaction.

CHAPTER THIRTEEN

The Tradition of Expanding Revelation

Introduction

We turn from our examination of individual images, themes, and motifs to a discussion of that element of redactional tradition which is perhaps more important than all the others combined: the liberty enjoyed by redactors allowing them — even inviting them — to expand upon that which had been received and laid down by the recognized prophets, offering it as equally authoritative revelation from God.[1]

This has been our primary concern from the beginning. As has been argued, self-conscious and deliberate intentionality must have been involved in the attachment of new predictions introduced by a temporal formula. We will make the point once again that the use of such formulas ought not to be interpreted as casual or conventional in any way. It may be convenient for modern scholars in their haste to disregard such a formula or interpret a passage as though it were either accidental or functionless, but such assumptions beg the question to be solved.

If our lengthy and complex study has shown anything, it is that each of the temporal connectives does have a distinct function, and that they have a purpose that goes beyond mere asyndetic addition. This forces us to ask about the ideology that lay behind the use of temporal transitions. Is their use indirect evidence that the attached materials are not actually from the prophet in question?

We must be wary of making this deduction. To be sure, virtually none of the expansions with introductory temporal transitions has proven to have a claim to authenticity with the probable exception of Jer 4:11-12, in which Jeremiah himself may have been involved as the redactor of his own prerecorded material. But proving authenticity has not been an important aspect of our study.

We have seen evidence that a given prophet's sentiments may come to expression when a disciple's hand has been at work. This is especially probable in such summarizing predictions as those in Jer 31:27-28, 31-34, 38-40. Also, the frequent use of the oracle formula *ně'um YHWH* throughout the book of Jeremiah may shed some light on this: either Jeremiah or one of his disciples was affirming that predictions with this formula (especially when it directly follows the temporal formula) were verily the word of Yahweh. This is what matters because it is not so important that a given passage may be the word of a particular prophet as that it is presented as the veritable word of Yahweh. Jeremiah may be a special case, but, on the other hand, the recognition of such phenomena in this book requires us to allow for the possibility of it occurring in the other prophetic books as well.

Thus the use of introductory temporal connectives need not in itself indicate remoteness of derivation. We come back, therefore, to our previous contention that those who employed a temporal formula as a connecting element definitely intended to establish some kind of synchronism or sequencing between the prediction of the underlying material and the new prediction. With regard to particular passages we have had some success in determining the intended time-relationship. This depended largely, but not exclusively, on the patent meanings of the various formulas. In some passages a transition formula creates a move from the past to the present, in others from the present or imminent future to a proximate future, and so forth. But as we have seen, the formulas in themselves are not so important as our ability to recognize whether a particular prediction is for the historical future or for a new, ongoing condition in which the normal course of human events has been transcended or transformed.

This may explain the "how," but it does not explain the "why." We need to know the ideology behind the use of temporal connectives. Why were the redactors of these passages not content simply to lay these new predictions alongside others without a temporal connective, as was generally done?

Our final effort in this lengthy investigation will be to suggest an answer to this question. In preparation for it, however, we have still to analyze two special matters: (1) the actual techniques used by the redactors and (2) special indications of ideology in the various styles of transforming or extending the image of future events.

Technique in Redactional Supplementation

Some attention has been paid to the matter of technique along the way, first in our linguistic and exegetical examination of the various formulas and then in our survey of the respective books. It is important to distinguish between the two distinct methods of connecting new materials to old materials: by catchword/phrase and by thematic association. To be sure, these may sometimes be combined, and both these methods are generally common throughout Scripture; but it will be helpful to review them now with reference to the special kind of passages under consideration here.

Connection by use of a catchword or phrase seizes upon an element in the underlying text that may not actually be central or crucial. It is sufficient that it has stimulated the redactor into announcing his new insight. Wherever this new insight modifies the underlying prediction in any significant way, it has the effect of expanding the revelational content and extending the revelational authority of the new prediction. As has been noted, this is not often by way of flat contradiction, but usually through explication or supplementation.

1. With catchwords or phrases

a. Thematically related predictions

Isa 2:20-21: thematically related to 4:12-17, this prediction picks v 17's closing phrase for use as its introduction.

Isa 11:10: thematically related to v 1, its subject, *šōreš yišay*, "root of Jesse," has been suggested by that verse's phrase *miššārāšâw*, "from its roots," and the synonyms that follow.

Jer 3:18: though suggested by the pattern, "one-two to Zion," in v 14, its ending, which contains the phrase *hā'āreṣ 'ăšer niḥaltî*, "the land that I gave as heritage," is influenced by *'ereṣ* and *naḥălat* in v 19.

Jer 5:18-19: a thematic association is with the concept of divine leniency; but *kālâ*, "complete finish," in v 18 is clearly influenced by the same word in v 10.

Joel 4:18 (E 3:18): though the thematic connection is tenuous, this independent salvation saying with the key word *hehārîm*, "the mountains," is linked to the phrase "my holy mountain" in v 17.

Zeph 1:10-11, 12-13: provided by the earliest redactor in anacrusis to poetic doom oracles, *wĕhāyâ bayyôm hahû'* in vv 10 and 12 (LXX) is used as a thematic phrase drawn from *wĕhāyâ bĕyôm zebaḥ YHWH* in v 8.

b. Thematically unrelated predictions

Isa 10:20-23: referring to those who have survived the exile, *šĕ'ār,* "remnant," in vv 20, 21 *bis,* 22 is picked up from the phrase *šĕ'ār 'ēṣ,* "remaining trees," in v 19, transforming a scene of desolation into a paean of bliss.

Isa 28:5-6: the positive image of Yahweh as an *'aṭeret ṣĕbî,* "glorious crown," is suggested by a key phrase that is used negatively in vv 1 and 3 with reference to Ephraim's drunkards, *'aṭeret gē'ût,* "crown of pride."

Jer 30:8-9: the phrase *kî gādôl hayyôm hahû',* "for great is that day," in the lament of vv 5-7 directly stimulates vv 8-9's opening phrase, *wĕhāyâ bayyôm hahû'.*

Mic 5:9-14 (E 10-15): suggested by *yikkārētû,* "shall be cut off," in v 8, a fourfold *wĕhikrattî,* "and I will cut off," specifies four objects of divine judgment in vv 9-12.

To a greater or lesser degree, every one of these passages intends to bring a new perspective to the predictions that have provided these catchwords or phrases, either positively or by way of negation and counteraction, and to that extent they are epexegetical and not merely thematic. They illustrate the commonly observed phenomenon of exposition by association. In any event, it is significant that either *(wĕhāyâ) bayyôm hahû'* or *bayyāmîm hahēmmâ* is the temporal formula used in these passages. This implies that the predicted extension or transformation is in temporal contiguity with the event predicted in the underlying passage. In a passage such as Isa 10:20-23 this must mean that Israel's punishment and Israel's salvation exist together within Yahweh's plan for the future.

2. Without catchwords or phrases

As we indicate, many of the passages with catchwords or phrases are in fact related thematically to their respective contexts. We have separated them from the remaining passages having a thematic connection without such a catchword or phrase. Thematic connections in this category may be, however, either epexegetical or topical. On the assumption that the epexegetically thematic passages show greater ideological intentionality, we have listed them first, indicating the nature of the exposition intended.

a. Epexegetical

1 Sam 3:12-13abα[1]: this is the deuteronomistic historian's programmatic interpretation of 2:27-36 with regard to the fate of the
house of Eli, reaffirming that the prediction in that passage is about
to be fulfilled.

Isa 3:18-23: this enumeration of female adornments to be confiscated
is intended as a comment on vv 16-17, 24, in particular the mention
of garments and beauty.

Isa 17:4-6: because v 3 mentions Ephraim alongside Damascus/Syria,
vv 4ff. explains how the downfall of the one ally is extended to
the other.

Isa 19:16-17: the redactor who added this prediction purported to be
privy to *'ăṣat YHWH ṣĕbā'ôt 'ăšer-hû' yô'ēṣ*, "the scheme that
Yahweh Sabaoth devised," against Egypt; cf. v 12.

Isa 19:18, 19-22, 23, 24-25: this is incremental epexegesis upon v 17 in
which each successive expansion enlarges upon what has previously been set down, but in terms of Egypt's salvation rather than
doom.

Isa 23:15-16: reflecting the belief that Tyre should be desolate for the
same typological period as her anti-Babylonian ally, Judah, the
redactor of this expansion adds forgottenness to the images of
desolation and ruin mentioned in the foregoing context.

Isa 24:21-23: the day-of-Yahweh poem in vv 1-20 has been universal
in its scope; this expansion gives it a firm Yahweh/Zion orientation.

Isa 27:12, 13: the verdict of the lament in vv 7-11 is so grim that it
cannot remain standing without these countering affirmations of
Yahweh's eventual purpose.[2]

Jer 3:17: the promise given to the *bānîm šôbābîm*, "wayward sons," of
their return to Zion in v 14 is interpreted in v 17 as a prediction
of universal submission to Yahweh's rule.

Jer 4:9-10: a call to mourning in the face of Yahweh's fierce anger let
loose in the coming invasion (vv 5-8) is immediately interpreted
in terms of the dismay and consternation of the leaders who are
responsible for making it come.

Jer 4:11-12: the above is further expounded as a fulfillment of a saying
about a hot wind that will destroy, rather than simply annoy and
harass.

Jer 8:1-3: the saying in 7:32-34 about the dead being buried in
Tophet/Hinnom is expanded to include the grim image of their
bones being disinterred and spread on the ground as a testimony
to the astral deities that their help has proven vain.

Jer 16:14-15: in a question-and-answer schema similar to that of Jer
  5:18-19, it is made emphatically clear that Israel's experience of being
  forsaken by Yahweh is due to their own forsaking of him; this
  realization strengthens the effect of an oath of self-identification in
  v 15 affirming that the miracle of divine grace in the return from
  Babylon is even greater than the exodus from Egypt.[3]

Jer 21:7: though delivered to Zedekiah, vv 4-6 is spoken to the inhabitants of Jerusalem in the 2mp; in the following 3mp prediction
  Zedekiah's personal fate and that of "his servants" and the other
  survivors are made more specific and final.

Jer 31:29-30: the reversal of fortunes predicted for Israel and Judah
  seems so marvelous that the redactor of these verses adds a rationale for it in terms of a refocusing of responsibility for the people's
  calamity.

Jer 46:26b, 49:6, 39: these *vaticinia ex eventu* modify predictions of
  doom for Egypt, Ammon, and Elam in terms of their eventual
  recovery from misfortune.

Jer 50:4-5, 20: Yahweh's action against Babylon within each context is
  interpreted in terms of its effects for Israel/Judah.

Ezek 29:21: originally at the very end of the oracular collection concerning Egypt, this salvation saying announces a divine purpose
  for Israel, coming to manifestation in Egypt's downfall.

Ezek 30:9: Kush had been mentioned as Egypt's ally in the underlying
  doom-oracle (4-5); the prediction *wĕnāpĕlû sōmĕkê miṣrayim,*
  "and those supporting Egypt will fall" (6), suggested to a redactor
  that Kush was also destined to suffer in Egypt's doom.

Ezek 38:10-13, 18-23, 39:11-16: beginning with a stereotyped *wĕhāyâ
  bayyôm hahû',* these initial expansions to the original Gog apocalypse (38:1-9, 39:1-6, 17-20) expound individual elements within
  it.

Ezek 38:14-16: this is an exposition of the motif of the unsuspecting
  people in v 11.

Hos 2:18-22, 23-25 (E 16-20, 21-23): the promise of Gomer/Israel's
  eventual restoration in vv 16-17 (E 14-15) is expounded in spiritual
  terms in each of these early expansions.

Joel 3:1-3 (E 2:30-32): the promise of the spirit in the preceding expansion is interpreted in terms of a cosmic upheaval and the ultimate
  survival of the faithful.

Joel 4:1-3 (E 3:1-3): this last of three expansions adds judgment upon
  the persecuting nations to the foregoing announcement regarding
  the penultimate days just prior to the ultimate "great and terrible
  day of Yahweh" (3:5 [E 2:31]).

Amos 8:9-10, 11-12, 13-14: according to our interpretation, these three expansions came into the text as part of the definitive editing of the book (before the addition of chap. 9) and are by separate redactors but added together as incremental epexegesis to 8:4-8, and perhaps to the entire book as it stood at that juncture.

Amos 9:11-12, 13-15: these exilic expansions, made by separate redactors, have the intention of counteracting not only 9:1-10 (itself a post-editing expansion) but the entire book.

Mic 2:4-5: added at an early level of redaction, this mock lament has the effect of dramatizing the woe-saying of vv 1-3.

Mic 4:6-7: seen as probably the latest addition, this expansion stands as a virtual motto for the book, as seen from the perspective of Yahweh's ultimate intention to restore the exiles "from this time forth and forevermore."

Zeph 3:9-10, 11-13: these are incremental salvation sayings announcing Yahweh's ultimate purpose over against the woe oracle in 3:1-8.

Zeph 3:16-17, 20: two salvation oracles interpret the victory hymn of vv 14-15 and thereby the entire book.

Zech 3:10: this expansion interprets vv 1-9 in terms of the eschatological bliss that is to result from it.

Zech 8:23: though it is an oracular précis to others in this chapter (at vv 2, 3, 4-5, 6, 7-8, 9-13, 14-16, 19, 20-22), its effect is to refocus the universalism of vv 20-22 in terms of the crucial role of the Jewish people in the salvation of Gentile converts.

Zech 12:3–13:6: in several stages, the original day-of-Yahweh oracle in vv 2, 3b-4a is expounded with respect to the spiritual restitution that is to result from Yahweh's victory.

Zech 14:6-8, 9, 12-21: mainly with *(wĕhāyâ) bayyôm hahû'* as transition formula, incremental expansions to the day-of-Yahweh oracle in vv 1-5, 9a predict various aspects of that final day: of victory over enemies, Yahweh's godship, a liturgical opportunity offered to survivors among the hostile nations, and comprehensive holiness.

b. Topical

Isa 4:2-6: this fairly late, exceedingly complex prediction of universal bliss among the remnant of Israel has absolutely nothing to do with the preexilic judgment sayings in the preceding context. It cannot be regarded as epexegetical in any sense. At most one may call the arrangement topical, that is, as predictive in a general way of Israel's ideal future.[4]

Isa 7:18-19, 20, 21-22, 23-25: an early redactor added unrelated symbolic images from various sources on the general topic of Judah's
peril before Assyria following the Syro-Ephraimite war, which
provides the background of the original material (1-17) in this
chapter.[5]

Isa 11:11: there is no thematic connection between this postexilic expansion and v 10; the association is merely topical.

Isa 17:7-8, 9: there is no thematic connection here either; the arrangement is topical (divine judgment on those who despise Yahweh
and Israel).

Jer 23:7-8: the general topic of salvation for Israel connects this symbolic
saying with vv 5-6, the redactional conclusion to chaps. 21–23.[6]

Jer 33:14-16: this very late addition, missing in the LXX, paraphrases
23:5-6; its placement at the head of a collection of "David" oracles
in 33:17-18, 19-22, 23-25 is topical, but fulfills an apologetic
function with respect to Yahweh's ultimate purpose regarding the
Davidic kingship.

c. Editorial

Isa 2:2-4 par Mic 4:1-4: each of these pericopes functions in a similar
way to create a bridge between originally separate blocks of material and they have a similar editorial purpose within their respective
contexts, that of expressing Yahweh's final intention in works of
judgment, namely, universal salvation through Israel, through
Zion, and through adherence to Yahweh.

Jer 9:24-25 (E 25-26): this enigmatic prediction regarding the fate of
Judah's co-conspirators was added for the editorial purpose of
closing off the grim prophecies against Judah in chaps. 7–9 in
combination with the wisdom saying of vv 22-23 (E 23-24).[7]

Jer 23:5-6: this has the editorial function of closing off the complex unit
21:1–23:4, pointing to Yahweh's eventual purpose in judging the
line of Davidic kings concluding with Zedekiah.

Jer 31:27-28, 31-34, 38-40: these predictions were drawn together as an
editorial summary to the "little book of consolation" to indicate
the ultimate outcome of the astounding reversal of fortunes announced in the editorial introduction at 30:1-3.

3. Conclusion

In most of the passages lacking temporal transitions, there is no similar intent
to expound. The most familiar pattern within the biblical literature is the piling
up of new assertions with no explicit purpose beyond that of producing an
expanding body of thematically or topically related materials, the only element
of explication being the aspect of increasing completeness.

With or without the use of catchwords or phrases, the dominant intention
of redactional predictions introduced by a temporal transition is to expound
and (re)interpret the predictions to which they are attached. This is an important conclusion because the same may seldom be stated with respect to the
merely asyndetic arrangement that generally prevails within the prophetic
collection.

The connections that we have identified as editorial have the additional
purpose of providing a general theological rationale for a specific grouping
of traditional materials. The connections that we have found to be merely
topical add little by way of reinterpretation, and the use of temporal transitions
tends toward the completely conventional. But this is an exception that has
the effect of demonstrating the general rule.

The Ideology of Expansion with Temporal Connectives

Having observed the various ways in which reductional supplements with
temporal transitions may be joined to the materials they intend to modify and
reinterpret, we need also to look once more at the ideology that is implicit in
making such connections, that is, the ways in which the underlying predictions
have been redirected by the attachment of these expansions.

Often oracles of judgment on Israel are expanded in terms of still further
judgment, while oracles of judgment for the nations are similarly expanded
in further announcements of judgment against them. It also happens that
oracles of salvation for Israel are extended as predictions of further blessings,
and the same may happen with respect to salvation oracles for the nations.
These are what we may call congruent patterns: those in which both sets of
terms (judgment *versus* salvation; Israel over against the nations) are preserved
in the expansion. Within these congruent patterns, God's attitude is assumed
to remain what it was, and the prospect for the addressees remains the same.
There is extension without significant variation. But we observe that incongruent patterns may also occur; in other words, there is divergence with respect
to the two sets of terms in comparison with their counterparts in the underlying
prediction. The most common shift is one in which only one of the factors

has been replaced by its opposite; we may call this single incongruency. Double incongruency, in which both factors have been changed to their opposites, is virtually nonexistent outside the apocalyptic passages.

We need to arrange our passages once more in a schematic pattern in order to display these possibilities. For this purpose we shall employ special sigla, as follows: PI = Punishment on Israel; PN = Punishment on the nations; SI = Salvation for Israel; SN = Salvation for the nations.[8]

It is possible to conceive hypothetically of the following arrangements:

- Congruent: PI > PI; SI > SI; PN > PN; SN > SN
- Singly incongruent: PI > SI; SI > PI; PN > SN; SN > PN; PI > PN; PN > PI; SI > SN; SN > SI
- Doubly incongruent: PI > SN; SN > PI; SI > PN; PN > SI.

The fact is, however, that not all these hypothetical possibilities actually occur in the texts under study here. We shall arrange occurrences in the above order with an indication of the redactional levels that have been established, using additional symbols for the special type of connection: CW for catchword (phrase), EpX for epexegesis, Top for topical.[9]

1. PI > PI (Israel's punishment extended as Israel's punishment)

- Level II: Isa 7:18-19 (Top), 20 (Top), 21-22 (Top), 23-25 (Top); Mic 2:4-5 (EpX); Zeph 1:10-11 (CW), 12-13 (CW)
- Level III: Jer 4:9-10 (EpX), 11-12 (EpX), 21:7 (EpX)
- Level IV-A: Isa 2:20-21 (CW), 3:18-23 (EpX)
- Level IV-C: Jer 5:18-19 (CW), 8:1-3 (EpX); Hos 1:5 (CW)
- Level V: 1 Sam 3:11-12 (EpX); Amos 8:9-10 (EpX), 11-12 (EpX), 13-14 (EpX)

All these are preexilic except Jer 5:18f. and 8:1ff., which are early exilic. The effect of the connection is to confirm the image of doom and counteract the dominant optimistic prophecy of the period while rebuking the people's unyielding hardness of heart. In the nature of the case, the images are either directly historical or symbolic with a historical reference (except in Isa 2:20-21, which simply confirms the cosmic imagery of the day-of-Yahweh poem in vv 10-17). It is significant that the strengthening oracle formula *nĕ'um YHWH* follows the temporal formula in Jer 4:9, 5:18, 8:1, 21:7; Amos 8:9, 11, 13. The passages with this formula are from various levels of redaction but they all have the same purpose, that of affirming that an intensification of the image of punishment on Israel is as much Yahweh's will as is that of the original prediction.

2. SI > SI (Israel's salvation extended as Israel's salvation)

- Level II: Hos 2:18-22 (E 16-20) (EpX), 23-25 (E 21-23) (EpX)
- Level IV-B: Zech 3:10 (EpX)
- Level IV-C: Isa 11:11 (Top); Jer 3:18 (CW), 31:29-30 (EpX); Joel 3:1-3 (E 2:28-29) (EpX), 4:18 (E 3:18) (CW); Zeph 3:9-10 (EpX), 11-13 (EpX), 16-17 (EpX), 20 (EpX)
- Level VI: Isa 27:13 (EpX); Jer 23:7-8 (Top), 33:14-16 (Top); Amos 9:13-15 (EpX); Mic 4:6-7 (EpX)

Of these passages, only the two in Hosea (both Level II) are preexilic; otherwise they are early (Level IV-C) or late (Levels IV-C and VI) postexilic.

In contrast to the PI > PI passages, these passages have images that are either spiritual or symbolic with a spiritual reference. The intention and effect are to affirm an extension and intensification of divine judgment upon Israel. In this group of passages as well, *nĕ'um YHWH* is common following the temporal transition. Its purpose is to confirm that this is indeed Yahweh's plan. This occurs in the two Hosea passages, in Jer 23:5f. and 7f., and in Zech 3:10,[10] all of which belong at fairly early redactional levels (II, III, and IV-B); also in the four Level VI passages, Jer 23:7f., 33:14; Amos 9:13-15; and Mic 4:6-7. The more numerous Level IV-C passages in this list, on the other hand, do not have the oracle formula.

3. PN > PN (the nations' punishment extended as the nations' punishment)

- Level IV-A: Isa 23:15-16 (EpX), 24:21-23 (EpX)
- Level IV-B: Ezek 30:9 (EpX)
- Level IV-C: Isa 17:9 (Top), 19:16-17 (EpX)

The Tyre prediction in Isaiah 23 and the Kush prediction in Ezekiel 30 are early exilic, while the remaining three on this list are postexilic. Only the Level IV redaction is represented here. Except for the cosmic image in Isa 24:21ff., the images are either spiritual or symbolic with a spiritual reference. None of these passages is a Yahweh speech, and the oracle formula is not found. These predictions are mainly prose statements reflecting on fore-given poetic oracles. The intention in Isa 24:21ff. is to redirect the day-of-Yahweh symbolism in the preceding context, but in the remaining passages it is to open up unexpected facets of Yahweh's judgment or to offer special insights into its meaning.

4. SN > SN (the nations' salvation extended as the nations' salvation)

- Level IV-B: Zech 8:23 (EpX)
- Level IV-C: Isa 19:19-22, 23, 24-25 (all EpX)

These postexilic prose predictions expand underlying prose and employ either spiritual images or symbolic images with a spiritual reference. They are not styled as Yahweh speeches, and the oracle formula is not used. The effect is to create incremental extensions of the underlying affirmations.

5. PI > SI (Israel's punishment transformed into Israel's salvation)

- Level IV-A: Isa 28:5-6 (CW)
- Level IV-C: Isa 17:7-8 (Top); Jer 16:14-15 (EpX), 30:8-9 (CW)
- Level VI: Isa 4:2-6 (Top),[11] 27:12 (EpX); Amos 9:11-12 (EpX)

This singly incongruent kind of arrangement must be seen as God's great surprise (cf. Isa 28:21). Its intention and effect are to overrule preliminary negative predictions in favor of Yahweh's ultimately beneficent purpose. Most but not all of the predictions in this category represent the Level IV redaction and they range in date from late preexilic (Isa 28:5f.) to late postexilic (Isa 4:2ff.). The images employed are all symbolic with a spiritual reference. The two Jeremiah predictions are strengthened by the addition of the oracle formula.

6. SI > PI (Israel's salvation transformed into Israel's punishment)

- Level IV-B: Mic 5:9-14 (E 10-15) (CW)

This is another of Yahweh's surprises, antedating the ideology of the PI > SI pattern. The one passage is early preexilic and requires něʾum YHWH in support of what must have been an unwelcome new revelation. The image is strictly historical in its futurism. The effect is to rebuke the triumphalist attitude of Judahites ungrateful for the great victory announced in 4:8–5:3 (E 4).

7. PN > SN (the nations' punishment transformed into the nations' salvation)

- Level IV-B: Jer 49:39 (EpX)
- Level IV-C: Isa 18:7 (EpX), 19:18 (EpX)
- Level VI: Jer 46:26b (EpX), 49:6 (EpX)

These predictions are all short prose statements, all postexilic. The three Jeremiah passages are late (49:39) or very late (46:26b, 49:6) historically oriented predictions that are, in fact, *vaticinia ex eventu*. It is clear that Jer 46:26b and 49:6 were added under the influence of Jer 49:39. The purpose of all three is to record already occurred reversals of fortune for the three nations mentioned. The two Isaiah passages, on the contrary, employ images that are either spiritual or symbolic with a spiritual reference; they are genuinely predictive as well as authentically eschatological.

8. PN > PI (the nations' punishment transformed into Israel's punishment)

- Level II: Isa 17:4-6 (EpX)

If Ephraim were to be viewed as a foreign enemy *vis-à-vis* Judah,[12] this would be another PN > PN passage. We have argued that it is authentically Isaianic and that it is early preexilic. It employs symbolic language, but with patent historical reference. Strengthened by the oracle formula at the end, its effect is to sharpen the somewhat casual mention of Ephraim in v 3 as coresponsible for Damascus' ruin.

9. SI > SN (Israel's salvation transformed into the nations' salvation)

- Level IV-C: Isa 11:10 (CW); Jer 3:17 (EpX)

Both of these passages are early postexilic and employ spiritual images or symbolic images with a spiritual reference. The intended effect is to extend and redirect Israel's salvation for the benefit of all nations. Remarkable as the universalistic idealism of these two passages may be, it may be equally remarkable that this particular theme appears so seldom.

10. SI > PN (Israel's salvation transformed into the nations' punishment)

- Level IV-C: Joel 4:1-3 (E 3:1-3) (EpX)

In this postexilic apocalyptic prediction the imagery is negative for the nations and positive for Israel, but with an order opposite to that of the other apocalyptic passages. Instead of making the defeat of the nations the premise for Israel's salvation, it extends the image of Israel's restoration in 3:5 (E 2:32) as the premise for the nations' summons to judgment. The effect is to finalize the tentative images of the two preceding predictions in the Joelian text (3:1-3 [E 2:28-29], 4-6 [E 2:30-32]), indicating the ultimate outcome of the upheavals that lie in Yahweh's future purpose. Thus, in addition to the fact that the Joelian redactor creates an idiosyncratic transition formula *(kî hinnēh bayyāmîm hahēmmâ ûbā'ēt hahî'),* this passage is special for its ideology and for the process of its composition.

11. PN > SI (the nations' punishment transformed into Israel's salvation)

- Level III: Ezek 29:21 (EpX)
- Level IV-A: Jer 50:4-5, 20; Zech 12:3, 6-7, 8, 9, 11-14, 13:1, 2-3, 4-6 (all EpX)
- Level IV-C: Isa 10:20-23 (CW); Ezek 38:10-13 (EpX), 14-16 (EpX), 18-23 (EpX), 39:11-16 (EpX)
- Level VI: Zech 14:6-7, 8, 9b, 13-14, 20-21 (all EpX)

The effect of this final group of passages is to interpret judgment on the nations as ancillary to Israel's salvation (in opposite order from that of Joel 4:1-3), but there is an important difference between the nonapocalyptic passages (Isa 10:20ff.; Jer 50:4-5, 20; Ezek 29:21) and the apocalyptic passages.

In the nonapocalyptic passages, this connection remains a mystery of Yahweh's beneficent purpose. Also, the foreign enemy is specifically identified in the context: Assyria (typological for Babylon) in Isaiah 10, Babylon in Jeremiah 50, and Egypt in Ezekiel 29. In each passage, oracular material against one of these nations is like similar material elsewhere, the only difference being the pleasant surprise that Israel/Judah will be saved as a result of the nations' ruin.

It is entirely different in the three apocalyptic series, those of Ezekiel 38–39, Zechariah 12–13, and Zechariah 14. Here the effect is to specify punishment on the nations as the necessary means toward Israel's ultimate salvation. Israel/Judah (including Jerusalem) is unified and complete; it is threatened now by a menace that renders meaningless all Yahweh's saving acts of the past, including the return from captivity. The identification of the enemy has also changed; it is no longer a specific historical antagonist but a completely dehistoricized, even mythical, foe. This enemy not only menaces the chosen people and their city but defies Yahweh himself. Yahweh no longer has any intention for the nations except to destroy them.[13] This ideology involves a complete reversal of the normative prophetic outlook concerning Yahweh's will for the nations' salvation. It is also a reversal of the classic ambivalence in Israel's attitude toward Yahweh and its imperfect obedience to Yahweh's will.

The Special Role of Predictions with Introductory Temporal Transitions

From the foregoing analysis it is apparent that the main concern of the prophetic redactors who supplemented the literary deposit that had come into their hands was for the future of the chosen people beyond what had already been laid down in the text. To this concern, a concern for further revelation regarding the foreign nations is unmistakably secondary. We can see this clearly in a numerical breakdown of the various types of extensions that we have been studying:

1) Congruent: PI > PI, 19 passages; SI > SI, 17 passages; PN > PN, 6 passages; SN > SN, 4 passages
2) Singly incongruent: PI > SI, 7 passages; SI > PI, 1 passage; PN > SN, 5 passages; PN > PI, 1 passage; SI > SN, 2 passages
3) Doubly incongruent: SI > PN, 1 passage; PN > SI, 2 passages[14]

This analysis shows that it was more natural for the redactors in question to extend the underlying elements (seen in the congruent patterns) than to transform them (seen in the incongruent patterns).

This brings us to the final question of what actually motivated these redactors to extend and expand the prophetic tradition as they did. If our long and complex study has made anything clear, it is that the employment of temporal transitions as introductory formulas to redactional expansions is both significant and purposeful, but we wish to know precisely why this occurred.

1. The dynamism of prophetic tradition

There are two parts to an answer to the preceding question. The first part lies in the reasonable suggestion that the prophetic redactors introduced new predictions from the example of similar shifts created by integral temporal transitions. It was with a good purpose that we consistently discussed integral temporal transitions alongside introductory temporal transitions. We have studied the integral transitions as they occur both in primary and in secondary materials with a view to the possibility that they might furnish the appropriate model for the introductory transitions that are employed in the redactional expansions, and this proves to be the case.

It is important to know that the prophetic redactors were quite familiar from their literary sources with the concept of a temporal shift within futuristic prediction. As they studied the sacred text already available to them they learned that God's purpose could in principle be extended from the past to the present and from the present to an imminent future, a proximate future, and even a remote future. Thus their notion of how Yahweh works within history was anything but static. They saw examples of how human behavior in response to God's demands may be filled both with variety and with ambivalence, requiring repeatedly new revelations of Yahweh's reactions both to compliant and to defiant behavior.

Thus the redactors who introduced their own expansions with temporal transitions were doing nothing without precedent. The conclusion that we must draw is that they considered themselves to be legitimate perpetuators and readapters of the former revelations. This is borne out by the observation that their new predictions encompass many of the same shifts in time relationships and in imagery as appear in the older deposit.

A major difference appears in the preponderance of historical images in the primary and *ad hoc* redactional predictions using integral temporal transitions, in comparison with the preponderance of spiritual and cosmic images in the redactionally attached predictions. This is altogether what we should expect in consideration of two important facts: (1) the redactors introducing the new predictions had comparatively little opportunity to be involved in the kind of dramatic historical crises that the original prophets had been engaged in; and (2) they apparently had more opportunity to engage in reflection — even speculation — than the prophets had enjoyed.

This shift had very much to do with the chronology of prophetic activity. Postexilic prophecy and redaction were engaged in dialogue with preexilic and exilic prophecy, developing imposing typologies from it to suit new crises and challenges. Crucial as the Assyrian and Neo-Babylonian invasions had been — in a particular way the destruction of Jerusalem in 586 — the event of the return (or returns) from exile was equally crucial, refocusing the futuristic expectations of the postexilic prophets and prophetic redactors.

Over the centuries, Israel/Judah had been exposed to a succession of foreign threats. Assyria and Babylon were menaces, but they came to be viewed by the prophets as instruments toward Israel's well-deserved punishment. At the end of the exile, the Achaemenid empire became an instrument of deliverance. However, the people of the postexilic period eventually became deeply disillusioned about the possibility of any further benefit from the foreign powers that continued to dominate them, and the tendency developed to drop distinctions and combine all foreign peoples within the image of one last great enemy. Through all these shifts of attitude, the claim of revelational authority remained alive, adding to the received tradition by reinterpreting it and refocusing it.

Thus we are able to understand why and how the tradition of redactional expansion developed from crisis to crisis; what we do not understand so well is how the tradition first originated. Nevertheless, one undeveloped item from our numerous probings may suggest how this may actually have begun. This is the function of the temporal formula *wĕʿattâ* in the prophet Amos's announcement of Yahweh's judgment on the priest of Bethel.

In a search for precedents it is well to go back to the primary material that is both negative in its prognostication and has a strongly historical orientation, for these attributes seem to characterize the most original predictions. Going back to the earliest of the prophetic books, we take note of the fact that the narrative of the encounter with Amaziah (Amos 7:10-17) is elemental within the structure of Amos, occupying as primitive a place as the initial collocation of "call" visions in 7:1-9, 8:1-3, into which it has been embedded. This pithy narrative is in fact absolutely basic to Amos's self-understanding as a prophet commissioned by Yahweh; it is accordingly programmatic to all of Amos's messages as well as to all later prophetic messages inspired by Amos's example.

The structure of the Amaziah episode in Amos is that of the apothegm, defined by H. W. Wolff as follows:

> Die klare Form eines Apophthegma (Memorabile), in dem ein Geschichtsausschnitt nur dazu vorgeführt wird, um das Hervorwachsen eines gezielten Prophetenspruchs verständlich zu machen und den Spruch auf diese Weise zu erklären.[15]

The exposition of this apothegm lies in the framework narrative at vv 10-13, presenting a situation in which the priest reports Amos's alarming message to Jeroboam, then passes on that king's prohibition against Amos preaching any longer within his realm.[16] Amos responds with a legitimating self-definition in which he first states what he is not — a professional or hereditary prophet — (vv 14-15a) and then proceeds to cite the content of Yahweh's summons to him (v 15b). V 16 is introduced by *wĕ'attâ*, "and now," establishing an initial sequence from the report of Yahweh's summons in v 15b and Amos's summons to Amaziah, and it is only at this point that the actual content of Amos's message is reported.

Early on we observed a structural and ideological parallel for this in 1 Sam 15:1-2; in each passage, a shift from a report of appointment by Yahweh and the event of the prophetic announcement is basic (see in Chapter Two). Within the Amos narrative there is a temporal sequence as well as a logical shift from a past to a present situation, and from this to the imminently future event of Amaziah's exile.

We certainly do not propose that all the prophetic redactors were consciously imitating this Amos passage, or that it was specifically this passage that established the theology of Yahweh's purpose amid ever-changing events. What we mean is that this passage illustrates the principle by which an earlier situation lies open to change and adaptation under the will of God. Because the Amaziah episode is primitive within the Amos tradition and because the book of Amos occupies initial position within the prophetic collection, this legitimating narrative of how Yahweh adapts his message to new situations has special weight and programmatic significance.[17]

2. *Intuition* versus *reflection in redactional creativity*

The second part of the answer to the question of the specific tradition behind redactional expansion lies in an analysis of the various impulses for this type of redactional expansion. Predictions introduced by temporal formulas appear to have been produced by three distinct kinds of impulse: (1) intuitive, (2) reflective, and (3) pragmatic. We set the third kind aside because it is restricted to such a completely formal procedure as inserted the liturgical responses in the late additions to Isaiah in 12:1-3, 4-6, 25:9-10a, 26:1-6, 27:2-6. The distinction between the intuitive and the reflective impulse is, however, basic.

a. *The intuitive impulse*

Let us look first at the kinds of prediction that were inspired intuitively. These may be explained as arising from a redactor's urge to express a conviction of immediate relevance. Usually the content is very brief, from a single verse to no more than three verses.

Among the intuitive predictions, distinct styling or structuring goes along with different types of images. A familiar fragment of poetry may come into the redactor's mind, inducing an impulse to cite all or some of it due to its peculiar aptness for the situation. Or the redactor may recall a particular liturgical technique as an appropriate vehicle for expressing a thought he has in his mind. Both these situations involve recalling something already established in tradition, either appropriate material or a suitable form. The opposite impulse may lead a redactor to formulate a new insight in his own words, appropriate to the occasion; it does not surprise us that such nontraditional, forward-looking insights are uniformly couched in prose.

Poetic expansions always have the introductory temporal formula in anacrusis. We have weighed opposing possibilities with respect to this phenomenon. The temporal formula is, as we have said, the redactor's in almost every instance, but we cannot be so sure that the rhythmic content is always his. On balance, it seems probable that in most instances the rhythmic material has been derived from tradition. The redactor's creativity is restricted therefore to his recognition of the aptness of this material as an appropriate expression for the special new insight that he intends to convey.

There is no essential difference in the redactor's intention in shorter or in longer poetic predictions. Shorter poetic fragments might appropriately express his intuition, but if he had a longer poem he might very well wish to cite it in its entirety, even out of sheer aesthetic appreciation. In many instances, he adds the oracle formula (almost always immediately after the temporal transition) to strengthen his claim of revelational authority. This happens with five of the fifteen shorter poems and with seven (eight counting a parallel) of the longer poems.[18]

The short prose expansions that appear to have arisen from intuitive impulses are about equal in number to all the poetic expansions combined.[19] Among these short prose expansions, the oracle formula is added following the temporal formula in seven Jeremiah passages and in Zeph 3:10-11. The important difference in comparison with the poetic expansions seems to be, not that the prose predictions are entirely intuitive (since many of them do actually preserve traditional materials or reproduce traditional images), but rather that the creative impulse in them is notably stronger.

b. The reflective impulse

This leaves us with the lengthier or more complex prose passages, which turn out to derive from quite a different impulse, that of theological reflection and speculation. This characterization does not involve a denial of revelational authority as such, but it may be significant that the oracle formula never appears after the temporal formula in these lengthier and more complex prose additions. Apparently the redactors who were responsible for this type of expansion were less directly caught up in intuitive insights and more devoted to patient (though hardly cautious!) reflection. Their expansions of traditional materials are taken up less with fresh insights concerning Yahweh's purpose in critical moments of Israel's history than with a general concern for the meaning and purpose of history in general — indeed, of the course of the entire created universe.[20]

Elements of the mentality of apocalyptic may be seen already in the single early passage of this type, Isa 3:18-23. It reveals a fascination with detail that one usually associates with priestly speculation, as in Ezekiel 40–48. The urge to make a complete inventory of confiscated items is what gives this Isaiah passage a level of complexity.

The apocalyptic passages generally have a higher level of complexity in their urge to describe every aspect of the ultimate state of being with lurid and even bizarre details. The tendency here is to create an elaborate panorama in which various facets of the predicted situation are explored. Not only does logic suffer in the process, but there is little concern for internal coherence. In apocalyptic passages where a primary compositional level has remained relatively undeveloped, it may nevertheless offer an open invitation for redactional successors to develop rococo scenes based upon it, or even to step aside momentarily from these scenes to interject something purely frenetic like Ezek 38:17's query, "Are you he of whom I spoke in former days (etc.)?"[21]

In the heaping up of introductory temporal transitions, there is an important distinction between the structure of the expansions to the Gog apocalypse and the expansions within the Zechariah apocalypses. While several of Ezekiel's expansions are elaborate in structure, the Zechariah expansions are mainly short, creating complexity mainly through their intricate combinations of atomistic and incremental supplementations. In both kinds of apocalyptic composition/redaction, "that day" comes to be loaded with everyone's futuristic agenda.

3. From old revelation to new revelation

Whether the redactional expansions that we have been studying express intuitive insights or processes of reflection and speculation, they lack one important thing in comparison with the original preaching of the prophets, a sense of immediacy. In spite of the fact that the genuine prophetic utterances came to be written down (the activity of redactional Level I), in virtually every instance it is highly probable that they were first delivered orally. Also, they were addressed to real, live audiences who were deeply concerned — or should have been concerned — with what the prophets in question had to say.

Furthermore, they tended to forecast new events within a realistically conceived future immediately impinging on the situation in which the audiences
found themselves.

On the contrary, it is hardly conceivable that the redactors — even those
who were personal disciples of the prophets — had any audience in mind
other than their own intimate circle and a succession of learned persons who
might have later access to the expanding deposit of revelatory words. It is
understandable that their new predictions tended to employ images of other
kinds than the strictly historical kind. At early redactional levels the historical
element is maintained in prominence, but at more remote levels this gives
way to the spiritualizing and the eschatological. The redactors were now
forecasting new situations or conditions rather than unitary events. Their
concern was less for the immediate future and more for an eventual new state
of being lying in the remote future.

If original prophecy enjoys the advantage of immediacy, redactional
expansion has the advantage of proceeding from a wider perspective than
that in which original prophecy was delivered. Redactors may compare
prophecy with prophecy and create cycles and collections of prophecy.
Redactors may interject complimentary or counterbalancing considerations
of their own. The essential fact is that they are involved in the process of
developing a self-conscious theology of prophecy, and this means that their
understanding of God's nature and work is both broader and richer than what
may be reflected in the word, or words, of one — or even all — of the
original prophets.

Among the redactors, however, an important difference is that those who
are motivated intuitively are often reacting to a new situation of crisis of their
own age, and they are doing so in the same way as their mentors did — by
delivering what they conceive God's word to be for this time and for this
place, *hic et nunc*.

Certainly the entire process of prophetic redaction adds a significant
dimension of subjectivism, but this varies between the more intuitive and the
more reflective types of expansion. Reflective expansion is more subjective
in that it relies heavily on private mental processes. But the intuitive may also
be subjective. Who can say what comes from within and what comes from
without? Who would claim that he is able to dissect the aesthetic, moral, and
cognitive dimensions of creative thought that have produced any one of the
redactional expansions that we have studied? Precisely where the divine and
the human meet within the process of predictive imagination must remain an
unexplorable mystery.

As we take seriously the avowed or implied claim of prophetic redaction
to expand the revelatory deposit and extend the revelatory situation, we must
agree that openness to alteration or expansion is of the essence of revelation.

Revelation once given is open to further revelation; therefore no message from God's inspired spokesmen may claim to say the final word except in the sense that it may offer an insight into an ultimate (and in this sense final) dimension of truth as it pertains to one special situation. It may happen that there will be a new "final" and "ultimate" word in a new situation as God continues to respond to human development and interaction.

This is true for Scripture as a whole and for individual prophecies within Scripture. The composite deposit of revelation that is given in Scripture does not claim to be generally and unalterably true for every conceivable situation, but first for the specific situations into which it was first delivered, and then only by appropriate analogy for all similar situations.[22]

If the present study were to be summarized in a few words, it would be this:

Biblical revelation is not static but dynamic.

It is not for one time and one place and one people; it is for new times and places, and for all peoples. Biblicism enshrines it but makes the twin errors of abstracting scriptural truth in isolation from exegetical contexting and of applying this to modern spirituality without translation.

For this conclusion we have gone not to the church theologians but to Scripture, studying what the prophets themselves believed concerning revelation. If anything has been established in our intensive exploration of how new revelation expands and extends old revelation, it is that a revelation that may be appropriate for our times must first be grounded in the old revelation, and then be open to God's emerging truth as it is revealed for today and for the future.

The more intuitive predictions show an intense involvement in the imaging of future events. The more reflective predictions reveal an attitude of relative detachment from such events. Both types agree, however, that Yahweh is sovereignly free, in interaction with humankind, to bring new things to pass according to his will. There can be no restraints on his possibilities except those that are imposed by his own character as a righteous, holy, and yet merciful God, as well as by the commitments that he has made as the creator of the world and the redeemer of his people.

There remains a mystery in God's control of future events that the human mind cannot fathom. The oracles of the prophets and the reinterpretations of the prophetic redactors range far and wide for appropriate analogies, but after all has been said and done, there are reaches of potentiality beyond all dimension in God's interaction with his world.

Definitely, a deity who claims lordship over the entire creation must possess unrestrained power over the future. When the chosen people transgress and despise his covenant, he is free at one time to punish them and at another time to bring them to repentance and reverse their ill fortunes. If they find themselves incapable of repentance, he is able to create a new heart and a new spirit.

If God is so free in dealing with Israel, what is to restrain him from opening his hands to all mankind? Surely, if there is only one God in the universe, he must offer himself as God to all his human creatures.

Whether we are disposed to believe or deny this, the revelations of the prophetic redactors surely assume that they must make room for it. Human beings have the tendency to create boundaries and make separations, but there can be no boundaries or separations in the possibilities that remain open for the God who reveals himself in Scripture.

> O the depth of the riches and wisdom and knowledge of God! How unsearchable are his judgments and how inscrutable his ways!
>
>> "For who knows the mind of the Lord,
>>   or who has been his counselor?"
>> "Or who has given a gift to him
>>   that he might be repaid?"
>
> For from him and through him and to him are all things. To him be glory forever. Amen (Rom 11:33-36).

Notes

NOTES TO CHAPTER 1

1. *Jeremiah 1–2* (Hermeneia) (Philadelphia: Fortress, 1986-89).

2. *Jeremiah: A Commentary* (OTL) (London: SCM, and Philadelphia: Westminster, 1986).

3. *A Critical and Exegetical Commentary on Jeremiah* (ICC), vol. I (Edinburgh: T. & T. Clark, 1986).

4. *Ibid.,* pp. lxii, lxxv-lxxvi, 176, 443-59.

5. (Wege der Forschung, 180; Darmstadt: Wissenschaftliche Buchgesellschaft); see especially Preuss's "Einleitung," pp. 1-19, and Wolfgang Köhler, "Prophetie und Eschatologie in der neueren Alttestamentlichen Forschung," pp. 259-92.

6. SVT I (1953), 199-229.

7. H. Gressmann, *Der Ursprung der israelitisch-jüdischen Eschatologie* (Göttingen, 1905); S. Mowinckel, *Psalmenstudien II* (Kristiana, 1922); idem, *He That Cometh,* trans. G. W. Anderson (New York-Nashville, 1954).

8. In other words, it was occasioned by the gap between what Israel ought to have been and might yet be, and what it actually was. Making a tentative survey of past and contemporary usage, Vriezen proposed that the term "eschatology" be retained, at least in a larger sense, for "the doctrine of the last things," without specific limitation to a cataclysmic world end. He went on to discuss in detail the specific ways in which the prophets from Amos to Second Isaiah projected a future salvation in relationship to the anticipated judgment. He identified two culminating points: (1) Isaiah (with Amos, Hosea, and Micah) at the entrance to a dark tunnel through which Israel must pass, creating a tension of expectation, and (2) Second Isaiah at the end of this tunnel, characterized by the tension of fulfillment. Noting that "the secret of the prophetic activity is the double aspect of Israel: the empirical Israel as the people of God" (220), he approved of B. D. Eerdmans's insight that Israel expected salvation because of their faith in the power of God, while disapproving of Gressmann's view that eschatology in Israel was a remnant of ancient oriental "eschatology." "We must never forget that *everything* [V's emphasis] that happens to Israel in the course of history is only viewed in a religious light; for the prophets there exists . . . no such thing as profane history, and practically . . . history in its entirety, which is directed by Yahweh, is viewed in connection with Israel" (221).

In his conclusion Vriezen outlined four general stages of development in Israel's eschatological expectation (225ff.): (1) pre-eschatological — before the classical prophets; (2) proto-eschatological — Isaiah and his contemporaries; (3) actual eschatological — as realized in Second Isaiah and his contemporaries; and (4) transcendentalizing eschatology — the form in which salvation is no longer expected in this world, but either spiritually in heaven or following a cosmic catastrophe in a new world. "The life of Israel came to have a double aspect: on the one hand, judgment is near at hand; on the other hand, however, salvation lies in the future. . . . People begin to think in terms of a near future and a more distant future" (228f.). "The eschatological vision was *possible* because Israel knew its God as the active Creator-God, who in his holiness does not abandon this world and goes on acting in history; this vision becomes *reality* because the prophets, penetrating into the knowledge of God's holy being, more and more experienced the discrepancy between what was and what ought to be. The final break in the ancient-Israelitic totalitarian philosophy of life . . . is the point where eschatology breaks through; and eschatology is the form in which the critical realism of the faith of the prophets maintained its confession of Yahweh, the Lord of the World" (229) [V's emphasis].

9. J. Lindblom, *Prophecy in Ancient Israel* (Philadelphia, 1962), pp. 360ff.; G. von Rad, *Old Testament Theology,* trans. D. G. M. Stalker (Edinburgh-New York, 1965), pp. 99ff. Lindblom attempts to list every relevant passage, though without extensive exegetical analysis, making a distinction between what he calls eschatological and noneschatological predictions. Von Rad's special service lies in the way in which he relates eschatological prediction to salvation history.

10. The salient points of this penetrating analysis deserve to be summarized here: there are three basic concepts that show a dimension of ultimacy: (1) God's intervention in human history, (2) God's blessing and curse, and (3) the covenant between Yahweh and Israel; the ultimacy of God's present intervention resides in his transcendence but is limited by the contingencies of place and time, the ultimacy of present blessing or curse imposes a transcendental dimension but is limited by relativities, and the ultimacy of the present covenant resides in its personal-juridical character but is limited by human unpredictability; present divine intervention is limited by its provisionality, present blessing and curse are subject to the limits of applicability, and the present covenant is limited both by human vacillation and by the secrets of the divine will; God's eschatological intervention is subject to the uncertainties of future events, eschatological blessing becomes a unique event rather than a general condition, and the eschatological covenant eliminates the risk factor of human unpredictability; these receive cosmic dimensions in the absolutism of apocalyptic; in all this the dominant concept is that of Yahweh's unique character as a God who acts in the world while remaining transcendent above it.

11. E.g., G. Pidoux, *Le Dieu qui vient* (Neuchâtel, 1947), pp. 14-15; H. Wildberger, "Jesajas Verständnis der Geschichte," *VT* 9 (1960), 12; J. Carmignac, "La notion d'eschatologie dans la Bible et à Qumran," *RQ* 7 (1967), 17ff.; J. M. P. van der Ploeg, O.P., "Eschatology in the Old Testament," *OTS* 17 (1972), 89ff.; Donald E. Gowan, *Eschatology in the Old Testament* (Philadelphia, 1986; Edinburgh, 1987).

12. (Philadelphia, 1972). Sanders coins a new term, "canonical criticism," by which he means an analysis of the processes by which the biblical canon grew to its present shape, with emphasis on the forces and events that determined the selection. Essentially, Sanders's "canonical criticism" is equivalent to what most scholars call tradition history or tradition criticism.

13. ET by D. M. G. Stalker, vol. II (New York-Evanston, 1965), pp. 410-29.

14. *TLZ* 88 (1963), 402ff.

15. (New York: Seabury, 1979).

16. *Jeremiah* (see note 2); *From Chaos to Covenant. Prophecy in the Book of Jeremiah* (New York: Crossroad, 1981); cf. Carroll, "A Non-cogent Argument in Jeremiah's Oracles Against the Prophets," *ST* 30 (1976), 43-51.

17. (Oxford: Clarendon Press, 1985); cf. p. 445, n. 2.

18. See S. J. De Vries, "The Land's Sabbath in 2 Chronicles 36:21," *Proceedings, Eastern Great Lakes and Midwest Biblical Societies* 6 (1986), 96-103.

19. In my article "Observations on Qualitative and Quantitative Time in Apocalyptic," J. G. Gammie et al., eds., *Israelite Wisdom, Theological and Literary Essays in Honor of Samuel Terrien* (New York: Union Theological Seminary, 1978), pp. 263-76, I have argued that prophecy was the "mother" of apocalyptic even while wisdom was its "father." The most elemental difference between prophecy and apocalyptic is the latter's rationalistic speculativeness, embodying a radical divergence in its understanding of time (cf. von Rad).

20. *The Hermeneutical Quest. Essays in Honor of James Luther Mays on his Sixty-Fifth*

Birthday (etc.), Donald G. Miller, ed. (PTM 4; Allison Park, PA.: Pickwick Publications, 1986), pp. 59-76. See also Clements, "Patterns in the Prophetic Canon," G. W. Coats and B. O. Long, eds., *Canon and Authority* (Philadelphia: Fortress, 1977), pp. 42-55.

21. Cf. H. W. Hertzberg, "Die Nachgeschichte alttestamentlicher Texte innherhalb des Alten Testaments," BZAW 66 (1936), 110-21.

22. Specific ways in which authors acting as their own redactors may have expanded original compositions are suggested in W. Zimmerli, "Das Phänomen der 'Fortschreibung' im Buche Ezechiel," J. A. Emerton, ed., *Prophecy* (Fohrer Fs.; BZAW 150 [1980]) 174-91.

23. Virtually all dating formulas pertain to past rather than future events. Although past dating is rather widely distributed in the Old Testament, we may note that it appears mainly in exilic or postexilic passages; cf. 2 Kgs 18:13 par Isa 36:1; Isa 6:1, 7:1, 14:28, 20:1-2; Jer 1:1-3, 3:6, 25:1, 26:1, 27:1, 28:1, 32:1, 35:1, 37:16, 42:7, 47:1; Ezek 1:1-2, 3:16, 8:1, 20:1, 24:1, 26:1, 29:1, 17, 30:20, 31:1, 32:1, 17, 33:21; Hag 1:1, 2:1, 10, 18, 20; Zech 1:1, 7, 7:1; Dan 1:1, 2:1, 5:30, 6:19, 7:1, 8:1, 9:1-2, 10:1, 11:1. The comparatively rare futuristic use of dating formulas is typological or schematic: *haššānâ,* "this year"; *baššānâ haššēnît,* "in the second year"; *baššānâ haššĕlîsît,* "in the third year" (2 Kgs 19:29 par Isa 37:30), *wĕhāyâ kimlôʾt šibʿîm šānâ,* "and it will happen after seventy years" (Jer 25:12); *miqqēṣ ʿarbāʿîm sanâ,* "at the end of forty years" (Ezek 29:13; cf. time-identifying "forty years" in v. 11).

24. In the Qumran literature, temporal terms including or similar to those being studied here are regularly given a purely eschatological (i.e., other-era) meaning; these include *bāʿēt hahîʾ* in 1QS 9:5, 1QM 18:3; *ʾaḥar passim; bĕʾaḥărît hayyāmîm* in 1QSa 1:1, 4QIsᵃ D:1, 4QF1 1:19, CD 4:4, 6:11; *lĕʾaḥărît hayyāmîm* in 1QpHab 2:5, 9:6, 14/6:2, 4QIsᵃ A 8, 4QIsᵇ 2:1, 4Q Isᶜ 10, 4QF1 1:15.

25. Since the tabulating of opinions on specific passages by various scholars seldom leads in itself to better understanding, no attempt will be made here to compile a comprehensive survey of the exegetical literature.

26. *The Expression Bajjôm Hahûʾ: Is It an Eschatological Terminus Technicus?* (AUNVAO, II. Hist-Filos. Klasse, 1936, no. 2) (Oslo, 1936); cf. p. 6.

27. *Yesterday, Today and Tomorrow. Time and History in the Old Testament* (Grand Rapids and London, 1968) (hereinafter abbreviated *YTT*)

28. E.g., the NEB translates *bayyôm hahûʾ* with "that day," "in that day," "on that day," "when that day comes," "at that time," "when that time comes," "then," and even "it will be too late" (1 Sam 8:18).

29. The term "integral" is applied in this study to internal syntactical links within redactional as well as primary units.

NOTES TO CHAPTER 2

1. Cf. Shemaryahu Talmon, "Waiting for the Messiah: The Spiritual Universe of the Qumran Covenanters," J. Neusner et al., eds., *Judaisms and Their Messiahs* (Cambridge: Cambridge University Press, 1988), pp. 11-37, where relevant passages are cited and other writings by Talmon on this subject are cited.

2. "'t ēt Zeit," E. Jenni and C. Westermann, eds., *Theologisches Handwörterbuch zum Alten Testament* (Munich-Zürich, 1976), II, 370-85.

3. *wʾth* > G.

4. We accordingly set aside from present consideration nontransitional temporal uses of *ʿattâ* and *wĕʿattâ;* that is, those that do no more than identify time when. Within the prophetic literature, these are found at Isa 37:26, 43:19, 48:7, 49:19; Jer 27:16; Hos 4:16, 5:3, 8:8, 10, 10:2, 3; Mic 5:3 [E 4], 7:4, 10; Zech 9:8; and Mal 3:15. The occurrence at Jer 32:36, a non-Septuagintal gloss, is omitted from our consideration because *wĕʿattâ lākēn* establishes an erroneous connection between an already complete judgment speech in 32:27-35 and the standard introduction to a new speech in 32:37-41.

5. I. Aharoni, *Arad Inscriptions* (Jerusalem: Bialik, 1975).

6. H. Torczyner et al., eds., *The Lachish Letters* (London 1938).

7. Despite its structural weakness, there is no clear evidence of redactional expansion within Isa 30:1-14. The Deity first speaks an oracle of woe against the pro-Egyptian party, who are characterized as *bānîm sôrĕrîm,* "treacherous sons" (vv 1-7); he next instructs the prophet to write down these words as a perpetual witness (v 8), then he appends new oracular material regarding *'am mĕrî,* "rebellious people" (vv 9ff.), probably the same group. Its situational transition with *wĕ'attâ* marks v 8 as the structural climax of this pericope.

8. *w'th* > G.

9. *w'th,* with additional words, is missing in G.

10. The day of Yahweh poem, concluding in the ominous declaration, "for the day of Yahweh is great and exceedingly terrifying, who can endure it?" provides a situational background for the call to repentance in vv 12-14, introduced by the unusual formulation, *wĕgam 'attâ,* "but even now."

11. This analysis fails to sustain the claim of A. Laurentin that the primary life-setting for this formula is juridical and liturgical (*Bib* 45 [1964] 168-95, 413-32). For further discussion, see H. A. Brongers, "Bemerkungen zum Gebrauch des adverbialen *Wĕ'attah* im Alten Testament," *VT* 15 (1965), 289-99; E. Jenni, "Zur Verwendung von *'attâ* 'jetzt' im Alten Testament," *TZ* 28 (1972), 5-12; I. Lande, *Formelhafte Wendung der Umgangsprache im Alten Testament* (Leiden, 1949), pp. 46-52; L. Kohler, "Archäologisches. Nr. 19 (12)," *ZAW* 40 (1922), 45-46.

12. On the literary analysis of 1 Samuel 2-3, see S. J. De Vries, *YTT,* 287f. The structure of the judgment oracle in 2:27-36 may be outlined as follows:

I. Accusation (invective), 27-29: herald formula, 27bα; historical review and divine appointment, 27bβ-28; complaint, 29.

II. Announcement (threat), 30-36: oracle formula, 30aα[1]; divine forswearing, 30aα2β; announcement proper, 31-33; prediction, 34; appointment, 35; new prediction, 36.

Most of vv 27-28, 31-33, 35 has poetic meter.

13. On the documentary analysis of 1 Samuel 15 see *YTT,* 87.

14. See S. J. De Vries, "The Forms of Prophetic Address in Chronicles," *HAR* 10 (1986), 18-20.

15. Cf. H. Wildberger, BKAT X/2, p. 631.

16. There are two possible identifications of the speaker: Yahweh or Jeremiah. If the clause with *'attâ* is taken as part of the citation, Yahweh is identifying himself as speaking judgment in the very process of predicting the hot wind — in which case the meaning is that Yahweh interprets his predication as a communication of judgment. This would mean that the time word *'attâ* is to be subordinated to the citation formula with *bā'ēt hahî',* rather than placed in contrast to it.

The other, more attractive, possibility is that Jeremiah, brought into the foreground by the emphatic *gam 'ănî,* is commenting on his own oracle in vv 5-8, 13-17 (with or without the first redactional expansion in vv 9-10). In this interpretation Jeremiah must be seen as his own redactor. He is interpreting the original prediction in terms of the hot-wind image, which in the proximate future will be seen as pertinent to the threat of a military attack and confirmative of the prophet's legitimation as an authoritative spokesman of revelation.

17. Cf. Holladay, comm., I, 425.

18. The second verb is not represented in G.

19. Cf. W. Zimmerli, BKAT XIII/1, 160.

20. The most likely interpretation of this allegory is that the mother is either Judah or Josiah and that the strong stem is Jehoiachin.

21. Cf. BKAT XIII/2 *in loco;* also p. 184 in Zimmerli's article mentioned in Chapter One, note 22.

22. Cf. Zimmerli, BKAT XIII/2, 610.

23. Cf. Zimmerli, BKAT XIII/2, 968-71.

24. In Ezekiel *lākēn* with the herald formula is a familar locution; cf. 5:7, 8, 23:22, 24:9, 39:25.

25. On this difficult text see H. W. Wolff, BKAT XIV/1, 120, taking *'attâ* as parallel to nonsequential *'attâ* in v 3.

26. See Chapter Ten for further discussion of this crucial passage.

27. Latin for a prediction based on an event already known. See the excursus in Chapter Three on revelatory authority in *vaticinium ex eventu*.

28. Very similar structurally is Jeremiah's address to the princes and people with use of a situational *'attâ* in 26:13.

29. In the present study an undifferentiated "Israel" will be regularly used for premonarchic Israel, the kingdom of northern Israel ("Ephraim"), the erstwhile kingdom of Judah, or the postexilic restoration community when spoken of primarily in ethnological or religious terms. Only when the specific political entity is intended will such terms as "Judah" and "Jerusalem" be used.

30. Following *(wĕ)'attâ* as a situation formula in prophetic passages, one finds legitimation formulas such as *nĕ'um YHWH* (Jer 7:13; Joel 2:12; Hag 2:4), *yō'mar YHWH* (Isa 33:10), and *kōh-'āmar YHWH* (Isa 43:1).

31. Because *'āz* is not regularly used in biblical narrative in a move from one event to the next, we may be certain that special emphasis is being placed on the transition whenever it is employed. Biblical Hebrew has rich resources for making temporal connections between events in the narrative past, particularly the use of temporal phrases with *be* or *ke* prefixed to the infinitive absolute, or the ubiquitous narrative aorist (commonly known as the *waw*-consecutive imperfect). Biblical Aramaic as found in Daniel and Ezra reveals a comparative paucity of literary sensibility in its constant reliance on *bĕdayin* or *'ĕdayin*, "then," for making temporal transitions; cf. Jouön, *Bib* 21, 56ff.

32. With regard to past durations cf. also *min-'āz*, Jer 44:18; *mē'āz*, Gen 39:5; Exod 5:23; 9:24; Josh 14:10; 2 Sam 15:34; Isa 14:8, 16:13; Ps 76:8 [E 7]; Ruth 2:7.

33. In this unique passage the temporal sequence is in reverse, from the effect to the cause.

34. Omitting Jer 11:15, where the text is too uncertain to allow confident analysis; see the commentaries.

35. On the confused text, cf. H. Wildberger, BKAT X/3 1220-21; also H. Barth, *Die Jesaja-Worte in der Joziazeit* (WMANT 48; Neukirchen 1977), pp. 46-48.

36. *Contra* KBL[3], p. 26, suggesting stylistic emphasis. Cf. past usage in Josh 22:31; Judg 5:19, 22; future usage in Isa 33:23; Hab 1:11; Ps 96:12.

37. Cf. Isa 1:20, 40:5, Mic 4:4. M. Fishbane, *op. cit.,* pp. 478f. discusses this passage as exegesis on Deut 32:9, 13.

38. On the complex redaction of this section, see our analysis of Ezekiel in Chapter Eight; cf. Zimmerli, BKAT XIII/2, 772.

39. Cf. Wolff, BKAT XIV/4, 70-71; A. S. van der Woude, *Micha* (De Prediking van het Oude Testament; Nijkerk 1976), pp. 104f.

40. The MT of this passage is very corrupt; cf. *BHS*[mg], 1QHab iv 9-10.

NOTES TO CHAPTER 3

1. Gressmann, *Der Ursprung der israelitisch-judäischen Eschatologie;* FRLANT 6 (Göttingen, 1905); Munch, *The Expression Bajjôm Hahû'* (see Chapter One, n. 27). Because of defective methodology, Munch's work should no longer be cited as authoritative on this subject. In my book *Yesterday, Today and Tomorrow* (publication date in Chapter One, note 27), I subjected this time-designative to intensive independent study, first discussing past occurrences and at the end, futuristic (see in Chapter One). Although I have changed my mind in a few instances, the general results may stand with regard to past and present time; but I welcome the opportunity to consider again the application of this expression to future time. Only, now I see the need to study it within the context of the range of similar expressions as I restrict the examination to the transitional function.

2. *YTT,* 57-136; see the tables on pp. 127-31, 134f.

3. Cf. *YTT,* 137-277.

4. *YTT,* 144-46; cf. 346-50.

5. *YTT,* 284-85.

6. Cf. *YTT,* 286, 289-90, 292-95.

7. For a general discussion of the function of past, present, and future epitomes, see *YTT*, 136, 253, 261, 274, 276.

8. Cf. *YTT*, 314-22.

9. Cf. *YTT*, 296.

10. Cf. *YTT*, 297, 312. On *hălō'-bĕyôm qahtî . . . yābō' happālîṭ* see Zimmerli, BKAT XIII/1, 568, 570.

11. See pp. 71, 77, 82, 92, 102, 136, 163. The casualty report as epitome occurs in Exod 32:28; Josh 8:25; Judg 3:29, 20:21, 35; 1 Sam 22:18, 31:6; 2 Sam 18:7; 1 Macc 5:34, 60, 9:49, 11:74.

12. Reading MT *tēda'* rather than LXX *tē'ōr* (cf. *BHS*^mg, RSV).

13. Cf. *YTT*, 311.

14. Persons are addressed in the 2mp, shifting from the 3mp. Apparently the persistent tendency to idol worship constituted a grave concern — even while the redactor predicted its extirpation (cf. 2:20, 17:8, 27:9, 30:22) — as it did also for Trito-Isaiah (Isa 65:2-7, 66:3).

15. Vv 1-4, touched up by a redactor at the beginning of v 4, may be Isaianic, while vv 5, 8-9, affirming Yahweh's intent to protect Jerusalem from the Assyrians, is a preexilic expansion (so O. Kaiser, comm., p. 409; cf. H. Barth, *op. cit.*, pp. 83-89 (assigning vv 5, 8b-9 to his "Assyrian redactor").

16. Cf. *YTT*, 297, 312.

17. *BHS*^mg gloss.

18. *Contra YTT*, 320-21.

19. *Contra YTT*, 321-22.

20. Cf. Wildberger, BKAT X/3, 1572.

21. On the influence of Exodus 15, cf. M. Sweeney, *Isaiah 1–4 and the Post-Exilic Understanding of the Isaianic Tradition* (BZAW 171; Berlin-New York, 1988), p. 19; also P. A. Ackroyd, "Isaiah 1–12: Presentation of a Prophet," *Studies in the Religious Tradition of the Old Testament* (London: SCM Press, 1987), pp. 94-98.

22. 1QIs^a, Syr, correcting MT 3ms.

23. This has commonly been recognized as a positive reimaging of the love song found in Isa 5:1-7, which was written by Isaiah himself as a stern reprimand to the nation's apostasy.

24. Cf. *BHS*^mg.

25. The MT has the advantage over LXX, *en tō kairō ekeinō*, because elsewhere introductory rubrics have *bayyôm hahû'* rather than *bā'ēt hahî'*.

26. More often than not, the additional poetry is from traditional material rather than from fresh composition.

27. According to H. Barth, *op. cit.*, pp. 30-32, 80-81, all of vv 1-6 belongs to the "Assyrian recension." Most commentators (cf. Kaiser, Hertzberg) view at least vv 1-3 as Isaianic. *Contra* Hertzberg, BKAT X/1, 640, *wĕhāyâ bayyôm hahû' nĕ'um YHWH* is not a gloss. For further discussion see De Vries, *YTT*, p. 300, n. 58.

28. Isa 25:6ff. develops apocalyptic imagery that is significantly different from that of 24:21ff. and is probably an early expansion of it. 25:16ff., with its introductory perfect-consecutive verb, attaches to 24:23 rather than to the intrusive hymn of declarative praise in 25:1-5.

29. Cf. *YTT*, 309; on "rest" see the comments in following sections on Isa 10:20 and 11:11.

30. Cf. *YTT*, 317-18. Holladay, comm., identifies *wĕhāyâ bayyôm hahû'* in v 9 and *bā'ēt hahî'* in v 11 as structural parallels — an arbitrary claim completely unsubstantiated by the evidence examined in the present study.

31. In this instance the formula *wĕhāyâ bayyôm hahû'* has a direct referent in the underlying text, viz., v 7's "that day *(hayyôm hahû'),"* defined as "a time of distress *('ēt ṣārâ)"* for Jacob. Cf. *YTT*, 309.

32. Cf. *YTT*, 303.

33. V 7b, composed in the third person, is from an editor.

34. Because of the Isaianic parallel, it is not probable that this pericope has been directly influenced by Deuteronomy, although its influence on Deuteronomy is very probable.

35. *BYWM HH'* at the end of v 9a is a gloss disturbing meter and syntax.

36. The reading is to be preferred to MT's *wĕhāyâ bā'ēt hahî'* because the word *yôm* is thematic here while *'ēt* appears only in redactional materials (the LXX confirms MT's *bā'ēt hahî'* in 3:19, 20; but cf. *'ēt* for *yôm* in 3:16). A further reason for following the LXX reading in 1:12 is that the locution *bā'ēt hahî'* does not appear elsewhere in the Old Testament with *wĕhāyâ*.

37. *YTT,* 287-89.

38. Cf. *YTT,* 298. Vv 20-21 is in prose except in part of v 21, where v 19 is reproduced.

39. The obvious referent is the phrase *bayyôm hahû'* in v 17. Vv 20f. is epexegetical to the epexegesis of vv 18f., hence dates to late within the Isaianic stream of tradition. Commentators generally call attention to the great complexity of the compositional process in this passage; cf. Sweeney, *op. cit.;* Kaiser, comm.

40. Cf. *YTT,* 298. *Contra* Sweeney, *op. cit.,* pp. 155-58, claiming compositional unity. Kaiser, comm., pp. 82-84, joins 4:1 to 3:25-26, but verses with the third personal feminine plural belong together.

41. Barth, *op. cit.,* p. 282, n. 33, gives it a pre-Josianic date.

42. Sweeney, *op. cit.,* pp. 159-60, 179-81, separates vv 3-6 from v 2. However, late redactors often combine disparate *topoi* from various, even rival, traditions. This passage will receive special attention in Chapter Eleven.

43. Our position is in marked contrast to that of Barth, *op. cit.,* 199f., 287, who dates vv 1-17 to Isaiah's early activity but assigns vv 18-20 to an early redaction (with "Assyrian recension" glosses in v 17 and v 20), while identifying vv 21f. and vv 23-25 as exilic glosses.

44. Cf. the complex analysis in Kaiser, comm., pp. 172-77. On the view that a single redactor drew these separate sayings from a variety of traditions, the shift from Yahweh's action in vv 18f. and 20 to the following panoramic scenes does not require separate redactional levels (*contra* Barth).

45. Barth, *op. cit.,* pp. 40-41, argues for a date in the Persian or Seleucid period. Cf. *YTT,* 305.

46. Hertzberg, comm., 413f. argues that it combines Isaianic themes but cannot be from Isaiah himself. Cf. *YTT,* 315, regarding *'ôd mĕ'āṭ* and epitomizing *wĕhāyâ bayyôm hahû'* in v 27.

47. On "remnant" in 10:20, 11:11, 28:5 cf. Herrmann, *op. cit.,* pp. 127-30.

48. *Contra* Kaiser, Hertzberg, and most others, who assign these two verses to separate redactors.

49. Cf. *BHS*mg.

50. Cf. Barth, *op. cit.,* pp. 58-64; *YTT,* 302.

51. LXX, influenced by vv 10-11, alters the reading to 3fs.

52. *Contra* Barth, *op. cit.,* p. 207, n. 26, arguing that v 9 is exilic and that vv 7-8 are postexilic.

53. Hertzberg, BKAT X/2, 698-726, has an extensive analysis of this chapter, identifying vv 1b-4, 11-14 as original.

54. Cf. BKAT X/2, 727-47.

55. This is more probable than the supposition of a single redactor because of the rather remarkable synthetic development from pericope to pericope.

56. Cf. the tendentious rereadings of LXX and Tg.

57. Cf. BKAT X/2, 362-65.

58. The tradition of a seventy-year exile is almost certainly borrowed from Jer 25:12. The expression *kîmê melek 'eḥād* remains without satisfactory explanation.

59. On "in days to come" in v 6, cf. BKAT X/2, 1013-18.

60. It has been brought forward along with 29:17-29 from its original position in the early collection.

61. After Zimmerli, BKAT XIII/2, 933-54; for a full discussion, see below in Chapter Six.

62. The messenger formula precedes the temporal formula in 38:10, 14. 38:18 has *nĕ'um YHWH* following the transition with an explicative temporal phrase.

63. *Contra BHS*mg; RSV; Wolff, BKAT XIV/1, 6, 20-21.

64. One should take special note of the striking epitome with *běyôm 'eḥād* in v 9, as well as the divine name "Yahweh Sebaot"; cf. v 6.

65. *Contra YTT,* 321-22.

66. Cf. *YTT,* 307.

67. See especially pp. 343-47.

68. Cf. O. Cullmann, *Christus und die Zeit* (Zollikon-Zürich, 1946; rev. ed., 1962; also J. Barr, *The Semantics of Biblical Language* (Oxford, 1961), chap. 4; also idem, *Biblical Words for Time* (SBT 33; Naperville, 1962).

69. See *YTT,* pp. 340-42, " 'Yahweh's day,' past, present, and future."

70. The first passage predicts the termination of an appointment to office and the second, a new appointment to office, in each instance as the outflowing of Yahweh's imminently future action.

71. Cf. *YTT,* pp. 343-50.

72. For Near Eastern parallels, cf. Michael Fishbane, *op. cit.,* pp. 474-75.

73. See our special treatment of this passage in Chapter Six.

74. "Der Phänomen der 'Fortschreibung' im Buche Ezechiel," J. A. Emerton, ed., *Prophecy* (Fohrer Fs., BZAW 150 [1980]), pp. 174-91.

75. The apocalyptic use of known events in ostensible predictions of the future must be viewed as a special case, but the principle is the same. The seer presumes to stand with Yahweh in his control and prognostication of the future, as it were attempting to look over his shoulder. On *ex eventu* prophecy in apocalyptic, see further J. J. Collins, *Daniel, With an Introduction to Apocalyptic,* FOTL XX (1984), 11-12.

76. This is not to deny that prophecy has a futuristic orientation and was often understood as prognostication. As my colleague David Carr reminds me, Isaiah 40–55 definitely views prophecy as future telling.

77. See De Vries, *Prophet against Prophet* (Grand Rapids: Eerdmans, 1978), pp. 144-51.

78. Cf. GKC 112[b]; S. R. Driver, *A Treatise on the Use of the Tenses in Hebrew* (Oxford: Clarendon, 1892), pp. 139-42.

79. In terms of syntactical function, *wěhāyâ* preceding *bayyôm hahû'* must be seen as parallel to those structures in which *wěhāyâ* is followed either by a circumstantial phrase or another temporal phrase, and then by the main verb (futuristic imperfect or *waw*-consecutive perfect). Passages with *wěhāyâ* and a circumstantial phrase are the following:

Isa 10:12, *wěhāyâ kî-yěbaṣṣa' 'ǎdōnāy . . . epqōd* [LXX *yipqōd*] . . . , "And it will happen when the Lord has finished . . . that he will punish . . .";

Isa 16:12, *wěhāyâ kî nir'â kî nil'â* [cf. BHS[mg]] *mô'āb . . . ûbā' . . . wělō' yûkal,* "And it will happen when Moab appears, when he wearies himself . . . and comes . . . that he will not prevail";

Jer 3:16, *wěhāyâ kî tirbû ûpěrîtem bā'āreṣ bayyāmîm hahēmmâ . . . lō' yōměrû 'ôd . . . ,* "And it will happen when you have multiplied and increased in the land in those days . . . that they will no longer say . . .";

Jer 5:19, *wěhāyâ kî tō'měrû . . . wě'āmartā . . . ,* "And it will happen when they say . . . that you will say . . .";

Jer 51:63, *wěhāyâ kěkallōtěkā . . . tiqšōr . . . ,* "And it will happen when you have finished . . . that you shall bind . . ."; (cf. also Jer 3:9 past).

Passages with *wěhāyâ* followed by a temporal phrase are the following:

Isa 14:3-4, *wěhāyâ běyôm hānîǎḥ YHWH lěkā . . . wěnāśātā . . . ,* "And it will happen when Yahweh has given you rest . . . that you will take up . . .";

Isa 23:17, *wěhāyâ miqqēṣ šib'îm šānâ yipqōd YHWH . . . ,* "And it will happen after seventy years that Yahweh will visit . . .";

Isa 66:23, *wěhāyâ middê . . . ûmiddê . . . yābô . . . ,* "And it will happen from . . . and from . . . that shall come . . .";

Jer 12:15, *wěhāyâ 'aḥǎrê nātšî 'ôtām 'āšûb . . . ,* "And it will happen after I have plucked them up that I shall again . . .";

Jer 25:12, *wĕhāyâ kimlō't šib'îm šānâ 'epqōd . . .* , "And it will happen at the completion of seventy years that I shall punish . . . ";

Zeph 1:8, *wĕhāyâ bĕyôm zebaḥ YHWH ûpāqadtî . . .* , "And it will happen on the day of Yahweh's sacrifice that I shall visit . . .";

I Chr 17:11, *wĕhāyâ kî mālĕ'û yāmékā lāleket 'im-'abōtêkā wahăqîmôtî . . .* , "And it will happen when your days are full for walking with your fathers that I shall raise up. . . ." (Cf. par 2 Sam 7:12, omitting *wĕhāyâ*.)

80. Cf. also past, Jer 3:9.

81. On the syntax of the form *wĕhāyâ*, see G. C. Ogden, "Time and the Verb *hyh* in Old Testament Prose," *VT* 21 (1971) 451-69.

82. Those passages with the simple form predicting a radically changed condition are the most numerous: Isa 4:2-6, 17:7-8, 9, 19:16-17, 18, 19-22, 23, 24-25, 25:9, 26:1-6, 27:2-6, 28:5-6; Ezek 24:27; Amos 8:13-14; Zeph 3:16-18; Zech 3:10, 12:6-7, 8, 11-14, 13:1, 14:9, 20-21. In some passages certain actions lead to a resulting condition: 1 Sam 3:12; Isa 2:20-22, 31:7; Ezek 29:21; Amos 9:11-12; Mic 2:4, 4:6-7; Zech 12:11-14. Passages that predict a decisive event with no special attention to the resulting condition are: Isa 7:20, 22:25; Ezek 30:9, 38:14-16, 19; Hag 2:23; Zech 12:4.

83. One should note the striking epitome with *hyh* in Zech 14:21; see *YTT,* 322; cf. 343.

84. Cf. F. Baumgärtel, "Die Formel *'ne'um jahwe',*" *ZAW* 73 (1961) 277-90; also R. Rendtorff, "Zum Gebrauch der Formel, *ne'um Jahwe,* im Jeremiabuch," *ZAW* 66 (1954) 23-37.

85. See also *bayyôm hahû'* as a time identifier in a private oracle at Jer 39:17.

NOTES TO CHAPTER 4

1. Also Zeph 1:12 MT has *bā'ēt hahî',* but it is not listed here because of the prior claim of the LXX reading, *bayyôm hahû';* see above in Chapter Three.

2. S. Herrmann, *op. cit.,* p. 219, argues that 30:22 and 31:1 are deuteronomistic insertions, independent of their respective contexts; R. P. Carroll, *From Chaos to Covenant,* p. 208, takes the position that 30:23-24 and 31:1 were used by redactors to build up the tradition of future restoration, false to Jeremiah's own expectation; W. Holladay, comm., II, 179f. believes that 31:1, without *bā'ēt hahî',* is a redactional closure for 30:21b (but does *nĕ'um YHWH* ever stand alone at the beginning of a redactional insertion?), and that vv 23-24 is another redactional insertion, while v 22 is a non-Septuagintal gloss.

3. Though he dates all of vv 14-26 to the postexilic period, Holladay (comm., II, 228f.) makes no detailed comparison of vv 14-16 with 23:5-6.

4. See also Lam 5:7. Carroll, *From Chaos to Covenant,* p. 214, claims that this text differs ideologically from the Ezekiel citation in arguing that in the future the saying will no longer apply, for the reason that its application pertains only to the period of its popular use.

5. Cf. Wildberger, BKAT X/2, 681ff., dating vv 1b-2, 4-6a to the seventh century.

6. Cf. B. Gosse, "L'ouverture de la nouvelle alliance aux nations en Jérémie iii 14-18," *VT* 39 (1989), 387-92.

7. LXX reads *bayyāmîm hahēm ûbā'ēt hahî'.*

8. See in his commentary, pp. lxii, 767.

9. Cf. McKane, comm., pp. 126f.

10. LXX *whyh* is not likely because elsewhere *wĕhāyâ* does not appear with *bayyāmîm hahēm(mâ)* (cf. Zeph 1:12).

11. *Contra* Holladay, comm., p. 184, v 19 depends syntactically and ideologically upon v 18.

12. McKane, comm., pp. lxiii, 126-27, states that *wĕgam* indicates the modification and reinterpretation of the *kalah.* Both W. Thiel, *Die deuteronomischen Redaktion von Jeremia 1–25* (WMANT 41; Neukirchen, 1973), p. 97, and Carroll, *From Chaos to Covenant,* pp. 76f., opt for deuteronomistic authorship; Carroll claims that the passage speaks about judgment rather than salvation; but the judgment may be seen as instrumental toward salvation (cf. 31:29-30).

13. On *hinnēh yāmîm bāʾîm* in v 32, see the following section on this formula.

14. LXX omits this formula in both verses.

15. Holladay, comm., II, 391-403, rescues these two passages for Jeremiah by an unmotivated excision of the doubled temporal expression. It is not clear whether he would also remove the oracle formula, which occurs in the MT of both v 4 and v 20.

16. *Contra* Carroll, *Jeremiah*, p. 823, claiming that vv 4 and 20 form the closure for a unified composition.

17. *Ûbāʿēt qabṣî ʾethem*, "even at the time when I gather you," explicates *bāʿēt hahîʾ* (*contra BHS*mg, the doubling of the same phrase would be unparalleled as well as inexplicable).

18. Anomalously using the feminine perfect with the masculine subject.

19. Cf. P. Humbert, "La formule hébraïque en *hineni* suivi d'un participe," *Opuscules d'un Hébraïsant* (Mémoires de l'Université de Neuchatel, 26; Neuchatel, 1958), pp. 54-59; also *ibid.* in *REJ*, 58-64.

20. In material for use in the Forms of the Old Testament Literature (FOTL) project, Erhard von Waldow has given this formula the name, "Introduction to the announcement of future events." B. O. Long uses this rather unwieldy name for it in *2 Kings* (FOTL X; Grand Rapids: Eerdmans, 1991).

21. Vv 2-19 has been designated as a special type of prophet legend in S. J. De Vries, *Prophet against Prophet* (Grand Rapids, 1978), p. 55; cf. B. O. Long, *2 Kings*, FOTL X (1991) *in loco.*

22. Holladay, comm., II, 160-62, identifies it as original; 30:1-3 and 31:27-28 are framework material for what he calls the "recension for the South"; before Jerusalem's fall Jeremiah reused a "recension of the North" (p. 156) with three sequences of new material (30:10-11, 16-17, 31:7-9a). Thiel, *Die deuteronomische Redaktion von Jeremia 26–45*, WMANT 52 (1981), p. 249, and Herrmann, *op. cit.*, p. 218, assign it to the deuteronomist.

23. Some MSS add *nʾm yhwh;* cf. Syr.

24. Holladay, comm., I, 265, claims that both 7:32 and 19:6 are authentic, though the latter is the passage that occupies an original position. Thiel, *op. cit.*, pp. 222-23, 245, assigns 7:1–8:3 to the D school. McKane, comm., pp. lxiii, 176, identifies 7:29a as a snatch of original poetry that has attracted vv 29b and 30-34 as epexegesis, vv 30-34 being credited as a "skilful little composition in their own right"; cf. 16:9, 25:10. The image of battle casualties in v 33 is characteristic of a late redactional level in Jeremiah; cf. 8:1-3, 25:33, 51:47, 52, along with 19:7.

25. Holladay, comm., I, 268-69 follows von Rad in describing this unit as "theological reflection"; he also claims that 19:1–20:6 constitutes a "unit of prophetic biography" (pp. 537ff.). McKane, comm., pp. lxxv-lxxvi, 443-59, identifies parts of vv 1-2, 10-11 as the original core of this section; the epexegesis in vv 5-6 was triggered by the reference to Tophet in vv 12-13.

26. Even if 48:12-13 are to be read as prose, vv 11-13 must be seen as a unitary composition, for the reason that v 11 cannot stand alone as a complete literary unit. It is better to assign 48:11-13 and 49:1-2 to a redactor (probably the same as that of 51:41-53) than to accede to Holladay's attempt (comm., II, 342, 366) to rescue these verses for Jeremiah by an arbitrary identification of the transition formulas as glosses (cf. *BHS*mg).

27. The phrase *gm . . . gm* in vv 44b-49a has been omitted in the LXX due to homoiarchton.

28. It is important to see that vv 41-53 constitutes a single compositional unit in five strophes, as follows:

Taunt against fallen Babylon, 41-44
Summons to flee, 45-46
Threat, 47-49
Summons to flee, 50-51
Threat, 52-53.

Holladay (comm., II, 400ff.) exerts notable effort toward claiming much of Jer 50:1–51:58 for the prophet; it constitutes the "longest unified sequence of material in the book" (401). Eighty-two verses are held to be genuine to Jeremiah, while 51:47-48 is to be recognized as a "less convincing" doublet to vv 52-53; a tenth unit within this section is 51:49-58. Holladay's rationale for assigning this material to the prophet is the questionable assumption that he would have expected Babylon to fall eventually, in spite of Judah's need to be sorely punished (cf. 29:28).

29. Holladay, comm., I, 316, claims that both vv 22-23 and vv 24-25 are Jeremianic, even though they are both late insertions within their context. McKane, comm., p. lii, identifies v 24b as secondary.

30. Holladay (comm., I, 476, 621-22) claims that 16:14-15 is secondary in its context, while 23:7-8 is in its original setting (Holladay and S. G. Janzen, *Studies in the Text of Jeremiah*, HSM 6 [Cambridge, MS 1973], *in loco*, would place 23:7f. before v 5). Although other scholars (e.g., Carroll, *From Chaos to Covenant*, p. 148) agree that 16:14-15 is out of context, we shall argue that it is 23:7f. that is out of place. McKane, comm., pp. lxxiii, 373-76, argues that 16:14-15 fits better in the context of 23:1-8. Though most scholars agree that one or both of these passages is secondary, dates assigned to them vary from the exilic to the late postexilic period. On the text, see McKane, comm., p. xix. See further S. Herrmann, *op. cit.*, pp. 169-72; A. Marx, BZAW 150 (1980), 110; M. Fishbane, *op. cit.*, pp. 471-74.

31. Scholars generally agree on the priority of 23:5f. over against 33:14ff. Holladay, comm., I, 616-20, assigns 23:5f. to the end of Zedekiah's reign; it is an apologia for this king's legitimacy following Jehoiachin's deportation; 23:14ff. is a secondary reflex. McKane, comm., p. 561, interprets 23:5f. against the background of the same decisive break in the Davidic monarchy, which either was about to take place or had recently occurred. For Carroll, *From Chaos to Covenant*, pp. 148, 202, 23:5f. could have been designed for celebrating Zedekiah's accession in 597, or it was the program of an exilic restoration movement, as in Jer 33:19-26, Ezek 37:24-28. Cf. Herrmann, *op. cit.*, pp. 210-12, anchoring this passage in Isa 9:5 while denying the play on the name "Zedekiah."

32. Mainly because 33:14-26 is missing in the LXX, we date this revision to a time very late in the postexilic period (see in Chapter Thirteen).

33. In 31:38 the *kethibh* omits *bā'îm,* which is rightly supplied in the *qere* and in many manuscripts and translations.

34. Thiel, *op. cit.*, pp. 249, and Carroll, *From Chaos to Covenant*, pp. 213-23, assign the first two pericopes to the D school; cf. Herrmann, *op. cit.*, pp. 166-67, 179-85, 200-201.

35. Comm., II, 170, 196-99. Vv 27f. close the scroll of hope for the South; vv 31ff. deliberately copies deuteronomistic language, but is from Jeremiah himself, having been composed for the ceremony of the recitation of the law at the Feast of Booths in the fall of 587 B.C.E., after the fall of Jerusalem.

36. Comm., II, 199-200. Holladay claims that these verses are from the time of Nehemiah because of the reference to the "tower of Hananel," mentioned in Neh 3:1, 12:39; Zech 14:10. However, we shall argue for the insufficiency of this claim, dating vv 38-40 to the same period as the other sections.

37. Breaking the sequence are late exilic vv 29-30 (see in the preceding section on *bayyāmîm hahēmmâ*) and late postexilic vv 35-37. Antecedently, it is more likely that all three units were added together, having been drawn from random traditions, than that only vv 31-34 are original, and that first early vv 27f., and then very late vv 38ff. came to be successively attached to it, as Holladay claims. Similar collocations elsewhere reflect either a single redactional procedure incorporating thematically similar traditions (cf. Isa 7:18-25) or a successive reinterpretation of underlying material at the hands of a unified school of redactions (cf. Isa 19:16-25; Ezek 38:10–39:20). See our further observations on clusters in Chapter Five.

38. This passage is poetic but in irregular meter.

39. Cf. A. Marx, "A propos des doublets du livre de Jérémie. Réflexions sur la formation d'un livre prophétique," BZAW 150 (1980), 106-20, arguing that the latter of each respective doublet was designedly adapted and inserted by a redactor (or redactors) as an expression of his ideology concerning the nature and intent of God.

40. Cf. P. R. Ackroyd, "An Interpretation of the Babylonian Exile: A Study of II Kings 20 and Isaiah 38–39," *Studies in the Religious Tradition of the Old Testament* (London: SCM Press, 1987), pp. 152-71, republished from *SJT* 27 (1974), 329-52.

41. "Samuel und Silo," *VT* 13 (1963), 390-400.

42. This redactor has left his mark especially in the expression "oracle of Yahweh god of Israel," and in his notable emphasis on the word "house."

43. One passage with *hinnēh yāmîm bā'îm* remains in uncertainty because of its radically asyndetic attachment: Jer 9:24 (E 25); see Chapters Seven and Eleven.

44. Cf. E. Jenni, "*'ḥr danach*," *THAT* I, 110-18; H. Seebass, "*'acharîth*," *TDOT* I, 207-12.

45. So Wildberger, BKAT X/1, p. 58; Barth, *op. cit.*, p. 52; Sweeney, *op. cit.*, pp. 131-32.

46. From this feature, Kaiser, comm., pp. 40-45, argues for postexilic dating; but one should note that the emphasis on righteousness is characteristic of Isaiah.

47. Cf. G. C. Aalders, "The Fishers and the Hunters," *EvQ* 30 (1958), 133-39. Holladay, comm., I, 477-79, assigns this passage to Jeremiah, dating it to 609-605. Many others (e.g., Thiel) assign it to D. McKane, comm., pp. xix, lxxiii, 377-79, identifies vv 16-18 as an original independent unit.

48. This is true prediction rather than *vaticinium ex eventu*. The prose verses, 3:3-4 (E 2:30-31), may have been added by the same redactor, or they may have been already attached when vv 1-2 (E 2:28-29) were added. 4:1-3 (E 3:1-3) is from a still later redactor (see above on *bayyāmîm hahēm ûbā'ēt hahî*').

49. Comm., pp. xlxvii, 491-504.

50. The date is early exilic; cf. Holladay, comm., II, 323-24.

51. "*b'ḥjrt hjmjm dans les textes préexiliques*," *VT* 20 (1970), 445-50.

52. Jer 48:45-47 is not attested in G.

53. We must comment briefly about each of these passages. The patriarch Jacob's recital of *'et ǎšer yiqrā' 'etkem bě'aḥǎrît hayyāmîm*, "that which shall happen to you in the sequel of days" — which is the series of tribal sayings to follow in Gen 49:2-27 (R^JE) — refers in fact to conditions that are already past for the writer, with effects continuing into the present.

Balaam's *māšāl* concerning *'ǎšer ya'ǎśeh hā'ām hazzeh lě'ammĕkā bě'aḥǎrît hayyāmîm* (Num 24:14), "what this people will do to your people in the sequel of days," is tantamount to the utterance about the doings of the mysterious "star" and "sceptre" (vv 15-19), no doubt already fulfilled according to the understanding of the preexilic redactor.

The prediction of return in Deut 4:30bβ is set at a time already present to the exiles addressed in the foregoing vv 25-29; the event that is to occur at a time indicated by the phrase *ûmēṣā'ûkā kōl haddĕbārîm hā'ēlleh*, "when all these things encounter you" (v 30aβ), is parallel to, and synonymous with, *baṣṣar lĕkā*, "in your distress" (v 30aα).

The time following Moses' death mentioned in Deut 31:29 covers the long period of Israel's apostasy that precedes an event contemplated in the expression, *wĕqārā't 'etkem hārā'â bě'aḥǎrît hayyāmîm*, "when the disaster will meet you in the sequel of days" (v 29b). This is already past/present in the experience of the speaker.

The restoration of Moab's fortunes that Yahweh promises in Jer 48:47, set for a time *bě'aḥǎrît hayyāmîm*, is already an accomplished fact for the late postexilic redactor (or redactors) who added this and 49:6, 39. All this material is missing in the LXX.

In Dan 2:28 (Aramaic), the expression *māh dî lehĕwē' bě'aḥǎrît yômayyā'*, "what will happen in the sequel of days," refers to all the past and future events symbolized in the vision of vv 29-45.

The past and future events symbolized in the vision of Dan 11:2–12:4 correspond to *'et 'ǎšer yiqrāh lě'ammĕkā bě'aḥǎrît hayyāmîm*, "that which is to happen to your people in the sequel of days," revealed by Michael to Daniel in 10:14.

54. Cf. Holladay, comm., I, 631-36, referring to a crisis of controversy *ca.* 600 B.C.E. A possible consideration against authenticity might be the appearance of a temporal transition that usually appears in *vaticinium ex eventu* passages; see above. See also A. Marx, *op. cit.*, p. 113.

55. Final *kynh* is not attested in G; cf. 30:24.

56. "Observations on Quantitative and Qualitative Time in Wisdom and Apocalyptic" (publication data in Chapter One, note 19), pp. 264-66.

57. Defending the minority position, Hans Wildberger in BKAT X/1, pp. 75-90, argues for Isaianic authorship in the Isaiah passage; cf. further his detailed study, "Die Völkerwallfahrt

zum Zion," *VT* 7 (1957), 65-81. For the extensive literature and a detailed discussion of the problem see Sweeney, *op. cit.,* pp. 164-74.

58. It is scarcely possible that the peculiar temporal formula introducing these two units would have come independently into the separate texts. This formula is a clearly identifiable redactional device used to introduce the entire poem in vv 2-5 as a preface to the rest of Isaiah 2-4, a distinct unit within the original book, chaps. 2–31. The editor of Micah, who used the unit, including the identical temporal transition, as the primary link within his book, almost certainly drew his material from Isaiah.

59. Apart from minimal orthographic variances, noteworthy differences are the following:
1) Isaiah places the thematic participle *nākôn,* before, and Micah, after the clause *yihyeh har bêt-YHWH;*
2) Following the verbs in parallel, *nāhărû* and *hālĕkû,* Isaiah has the respective subjects in the sequence *kol-haggôyim* and *'ammîm rabbîm;* Micah has *'ammîm . . . gôyîm rabbîm;*
3) Following the parallel verbs *wĕšāpaṭ* and *wĕhôkiăḥ,* Isaiah has the prepositional phrases in sequence, *bēn gôyim* and *lĕ'ammîm rabbîm,* while Micah has *bēn 'ammîm rabbîm* and *lĕgôyyîm 'ăṣumîm;*
4) Isaiah has the singular verb *yiśśā',* treating *gôy* in v 4 as a collective subject, while Micah has the plural verb, taking *gôy* distributively;
5) Isaiah has the prepositional phrase *'elâw* for Micah's *'alâw* and the preposition *'el* for Micah's *wĕ'el;*
6) Micah adds *'ad-rāhôq* in v 3, disturbing the parallelism.

There is little basis for choosing which text is (more) original except in noting that Isaiah employs *'ammîm rabbîm* more consistently and that Micah's *'ad-rāhôq* is clearly explicative. Also, Micah's additional grounding clause in v 4b and its drastic reshaping of Isaiah's exhortation in v 5 as an apologia provide evidence that the version that came into the Mican text is indeed derivative from the Isaianic version.

60. So C. Rietzschl, *Das Problem der Urrolle, Ein Beitrag zur Redaktionsgeschichte der Jeremiabuches* (Gütersloh, 1966), p. 91.

61. *Ibid.,* pp. 79-80; cf. W. Rudolph, HAT 3, p. 296.

62. Cf. *BHS*mg.

NOTES TO CHAPTER 5

1. This observation should serve as a caution for a recent movement toward emphasizing the redactional unity between these three major parts of Isaiah, as seen, e.g., in M. A. Sweeney, *Isaiah 1–4 and the Post-Exilic Understanding of the Isaianic Tradition* (BZAW 171; Berlin-New York, 1988); P. A. Ackroyd, "Isaiah 1-12: Presentation of a Prophet," *Studies in the Religious Tradition of the Old Testament* (London: SCM, 1987), pp. 79-104 (reprinted from *SJT* 27 [1974], pp. 328ff.); and R. Rendtorff, *Die theologische Stellung des Schöpfungsglaubens bei Deutero-jesaja* (ThB 57; Munich, 1975). We shall return to this question in the following chapter.

2. Cf. Wildberger, BKAT X/3, p. 1572.

3. E.g., H. Barth; see Chapter Three, note 43.

4. Though this unparalleled articulation of unbounded universalism has been drastically weakened in the ancient translations, it has not escaped the appreciative notice of Egyptian Islam.

5. See further the treatment of 16:14 in the following chapter on Jeremiah.

6. It might seem appropriate to define a "schema of prophetic confrontation" for each of the narrative passages listed. Inasmuch as Amos 7:8-16 occupies a centrally significant position within the book's structure, it may be viewed as the prime examplar for the other, less organically connected, passages. For further discussion of this crucial passage, see Chapter Thirteen.

NOTES TO CHAPTER 6

1. Cf. J. Vermeylen, *Du prophète Isaïe à l'apocalyptique. Isaïe I XXXV, Miroir d'un demi-millénaire d'expérience religieuse en Israël,* 2 vols. (Paris: Librairie Lecoffre, 1977-78).

2. *Op. cit. passim.*

3. See De Vries, *Prophet against Prophet,* pp. 145-46.

4. *Die prophetische Heilserwartungen im Alten Testament, Ursprung und Gestaltwandel* (BWANT 15; Stuttgart, 1965), pp. 126-44.

5. Cf. H. Wildberger, "Jesajas Verständnis der Geschichte," *VT* 12 (1962), 83-117; O. Kaiser, "Geschichtliche Erfahrung und eschatologische Erwartung," *NZSRP* 15 (1973) 272-85.

6. (WMANT 48; Neukirchen-Vluyn: Neukirchener, n.d.); subtitle: *Israel und Assur als Thema einer produktiven Neuinterpretation des Jesajaüberlieferung.* Influential scholars, such as R. E. Clements and G. T. Sheppard, have been favorable to Barth's effort.

7. On more precarious ground is O. Kaiser's dating of the polemical materials against Assyria to the end of the fifth century (*Isaiah 1-12* [Old Testament Library], 2nd ed.; Philadelphia, 1983), p. 5.

8. Barth includes all passages in Isaiah 1-35 in a "schematische Übersicht" on pp. 299-300. His translation of the contribution of the "Assur-Redaktion" appears as an appendix on pp. 311-36, with explicit identification of this redaction's verbal content.

9. We may agree on the following details: 1:21-26 is eighth century; 2:2-5 is from a postexilic editor; 2:20-23 is a postexilic expansion to eighth-century 2:2-17 (18-19); 3:18-23 is a pre-Josianic addition to eighth-century 3:1-17, 24, 4:1; 4:2 is a postexilic addition to 4:1 (but we identify vv 3-6 as part of the same expansion); 7:18-19, 20 are eighth-century expansions to eighth-century 7:10-17; 11:10, 11 are postexilic additions to eighth-century 11:1-9; 28:5-6 is a redactional expansion to eighth-century 28:1-4, 7a; 29:17-24 is late postexilic; 31:6-7 is a postexilic expansion to eighth-century 31:1-5, 8-9 (Barth assigns vv 5, 8b-9 to his "Assyrian recension).

We disagree with Barth's identifications with regard to the following: He claims that 7:10-20 is eighth-century material glossed in by the redactor who was responsible for the "Assyrian recension," while vv 21-22 are exilic and vv 23-25 are postexilic, but we date all of vv 18ff. to the preexilic period. He claims that 10:5-15 is eighth-century, that vv 16-19 are part of the "Assyrian recension," and that vv 20-23 are postexilic; we agree about vv 20-23, but date vv 12-19 to the seventh century. He views 17:1b-6 as an Isaianic piece worked into the "Assyrian recension," while vv 7-8 are late exilic or early postexilic, and v 9 is exilic; we identify all of vv 7-9 as postexilic and assign vv 4-6 to Isaiah's earliest redactor. He sees 18:1-6 as Isaianic material worked into the "Assyrian recension," with a postexilic gloss at v 7; we assign v 3, and possibly v 6b, to an intermediate level of redaction. He claims that 19:1-15 is exilic, while vv 16-25 are expansions dating from *ca.* 400; we agree about the expansions but see no reason for denying vv 1ff. to Isaiah.

10. Publication data in note 1.

11. A separate section on pp. 603-52 analyzes the woe-oracle as a ritual-liturgical act.

12. It is clear that Vermeylen intends to relate these stages successively. He does not allow for the possible contemporaneity of rival expectations, except in the final stage.

13. Vermeylen's work seems to exemplify the assumptions of much modern Roman Catholic biblical scholarship in denying anything normative. All is process and fluidity. There is no essential logic or necessity in the canonization process; only chance and erratic choice. In any event, Vermeylen's treatment stands at opposite poles with relation to the model proposed by J. W. Watts in his recent commentary on Isaiah 1-33 (Word Biblical Commentary, 24) delineating even more redactional stages than in Vermeylen's treatment, interpreting them as successive stages within a twelve-part dramatic presentation that are supposed to have actually occurred about 435 B.C.E.

14. Publication data in Chapter Five, note 1.

15. Pp. 27-133.

16. Pp. 134-83.

17. Cf. Chap. II, "The Redactional Unity of the Book of Isaiah," pp. 11-25.

18. *Contra* Barth and Vermeylen, there were no further preexilic expansions (cf. Wildberger, pp. 1562-63).

19. "Nicht die sekundären Abschnitte von 13-23 sind in eine jesajanische Sammlung eingefügt worden, sondern jesajanische Stücke werden in eine solche Sammlung von Fremdvölkerorakeln eingeschoben" (p. 1561).

20. 32:9-14 is possibly authentic (p. 1571).

21. Cf. Sweeney, *op. cit.*, pp. 131-33.

22. 17:9, 27:12; cf. 17:3 in reference to the northern Israelites.

23. *Contra* De Vries, *YTT,* 298, 31:7 is drawn from 2:20 rather than the other way around.

24. Also in the secondary verses, 19:18, 21 and 30:23.

25. Also, from Isaiah's disciples, in 20:6, and in other secondary passages (10:27, 27:1, 52:6).

26. See our examination of cluster arrangements in Chapter Five.

27. *Op. cit.,* p. 31.

28. Cf. Sweeney's summary on p. 187. On chaps. 2–4 see also Sweeney, "Structure and Redaction in Isaiah 2–4," *HAR* 11 (1987) 407-22.

29. On vv 6-11 and vv 12-17, see De Vries, *YTT,* pp. 314-15.

30. Cf. the integral occurrence at 31:7.

31. Further expansions in 3:25, 26, 4:1, 2-6 explicate various elements within the Isaianic prophecy. These additions make no reference to 3:18-23. Though 4:2-6 is clearly postexilic, the other verses could have preceded or followed 3:18-23 into the text.

32. See our discussion in Chapter Twelve.

33. See our analysis of clusters in Chapter Five.

34. Assigned by Barth, *op. cit.,* pp. 35-41, to the "Assyrian recension."

35. Wildberger correctly argues in BKAT X/1, 412-16 that this complex description of the "remnant's" eventual condition has little affinity with the prophet's own idea that the survival of a remnant only magnifies the grim image of Israel's comprehensive judgment to come.

36. In the original text of v 23, as preserved in some Greek manuscripts, it is the awesome *'ădōnāy,* "Lord," who is in process *('ōśeh)* of preparing the whole earth's (not land's) *kālâ wĕnehĕrāṣâ* ("final form and decreed design").

37. Positive promises for a "remnant" do not occur in authentic passages; cf. Wildberger, BKAT X/3, p. 1664; Herrmann, *op. cit.,* pp. 127-30. Nevertheless, aspirations for judicial integrity and military strength fit best the late preexilic period, specifically the time of Josiah's successors.

38. The latter always in clusters.

39. Ephraim is treated as a foreign enemy, in parallel with Damascus.

40. Except in material from the deuteronomistic history at 39:6.

41. BKAT X/3, 1563.

42. On the crucial role played by chap. 35 in the redactional growth of this book, see O. H. Steck, *Bereitete Heimkehr: Jesaja 35 als redaktionelle Brücke zwischen dem Ersten und Zweiten Jesaja* (SBS 121; Stuttgart, 1985). Chaps. 36–39 of Isaiah are not strictly in consideration, because they have been drawn from 2 Kings.

43. Amsterdam: Vrije Universiteit Uitgeverij, 1987.

44. Cf. Sweeney, *op. cit.,* pp. 11-25; C. R. Seitz, "The Divine Council: Temporal Transition and New Prophecy in the Book of Isaiah," *JBL* 109 (1990), 229-47.

NOTES TO CHAPTER 7

1. Cf. C. Rietzschl, *Das Problem der Urrolle. Ein Beitrag zur Redaktionsgeschichte des Jeremiabuches* (Gütersloh: Gerd Mohn, 1966), pp. 127-36; N. Lohfink, "Der junge Jeremia als propagandist und Prophet. Zum Grundstock von Jer 30–31," P.-M. Bogaert, ed., *Le livre de Jérémie* (Leuven, 1981), pp. 351-68.

2. *Jeremiah* (see Chapter One, note 2); cf. *From Chaos to Covenant* (Chapter One, note 16)

3. Comm., I, 1-10; II, 24-35.

4. Cf. Herrmann, *op. cit.,* pp. 139-241.

5. On 31:31ff., *op. cit.,* pp. 179-85, 195-204, 215-22.

6. This is a tenacious theme in the biographical section; cf. 39:17 on Ebed-melech, 45:1-5 on Baruch.

7. Kristiana, 1914.

8. WMANT 41; see also his second volume on chaps. 26ff., WMANT 53 (Neukirchen 1981).

9. BZAW 132.

10. Old Testament Library (Philadelphia: Westminster, and London: SCM).

11. Philadelphia and Minneapolis: Fortress.

12. See especially his article "Prototype and Copies: A New Approach to the Poetry-Prose Problem in the Book of Jeremiah," *JBL* 79 (1960), 351-67.

13. International Critical Commentary (Edinburgh: T. & T. Clark).

14. Publication data in Chapter Six, note 4.

15. Cf. Carroll, *From Chaos to Covenant,* pp. 9f.: "I am not denying that Jeremiah . . . spoke prose in everyday life. My point is rather that a major poet . . . does not use banal prose for the majority of his most important statements. . . . If the poetic tradition as the basis of Jeremiah's work is to be maintained, then to saddle the prophet with the infelicities of the repetitive and banal pieties of the prose sections is to call in question his poetic abilities and make of him more of an inferior scribe than a poet. Such a reduction of ability cannot be ruled out, but if it is to be maintained, then the poetic material must be attributed to some other poet. . . . It is not simply a question of whether he only wrote poetry or wrote prose as well! It is a matter of whether he wrote this kind of prose.

16. Although not exhaustive, Holladay's listing (comm., II, 16-24) is extensive and complex. Virtually everything is attributed either to Jeremiah or Baruch. The successive expansions, as Holladay outlines them, are as follows: (1) the first scroll (before 605); (2) the second scroll (605); (3) a fresh scroll in 594, expanding the already expanded second scroll; (4) four prose passages subsequently added; (5) new collections made after 594; (6) material added during the final siege; (7) a fresh collection made after Jeremiah purchased the field, in several stages; (8) a foreign-nations scroll added during 594-587; (9) Baruch's narrative in two stages; (10) exilic additions; (11) late sixth-century additions; (12) fifth-century additions.

17. For publication data, see note 1.

18. For an extensive classified bibliography, showing past and recent research, see Holladay, comm., II, 447-61.

19. The same formula in v 16 is a gloss (see in Chapter Three).

20. Major internal transitions in chaps. 1–24 are *wayhî děbar-YHWH 'ēlāy lē'mōr,* "and Yahweh's word happened to me, as follows," 1:4, 2:1, 16:1; *wayyō'mer YHWH 'ēlāy,* "and Yahweh spoke to me," 3:6, 11, 11:6, 9, 14:11, 15:1; *kōh 'āmar YHWH 'ēlāy,* "thus spoke Yahweh to me," 17:19; and *hir'ănî YHWH wěhinnēh,* "Yahweh showed me, and lo," 24:1.

21. Cf. Holladay, comm., I, 594.

22. Assigned by Holladay, comm., I, 477-79, to Jeremiah during the years 609-605; it refers to Egypt, then Babylon, not to the two deportations of 597 and 587; cf. also McKane, comm., pp. lxxiii, 377-79, viewing vv 16-18 as an original unit.

23. Holladay, comm., I, 594, assigns it to Jeremiah following 594.

24. Holladay, comm., I, 631-36, dates this passage after 594 and assigns it to Jeremiah. One should observe the abbreviated reprise in 30:24, by a redactor (see below).

25. As has been mentioned, *bayyôm hahû'* in v 16b is part of a gloss, no doubt influenced by the same expression in v 17.

26. See in Chapter Four on *hinnēh yāmîm bā'îm.*

27. It is assigned by Holladay, comm., I, 132-38, to Jeremiah's second scroll.

28. Holladay, comm., I, 265f., 536-39, identifies Jeremianic material both in 7:29-34 and in 19:1ff.

29. Jer 33:14-26 is missing in the LXX translation. Holladay, comm., II, 228-31, assigns 23:5f. to Jeremiah and dates it to 587, while assigning 33:14-16 to the postexilic period.

30. Holladay, comm., II, 162, assigns vv 1-3, 4, 5-9, 10-21 to Jeremiah.

31. Holladay, comm., II, 179f., assigns 31:1 to Jeremiah while identifying 30:23-24 as an intrusive gloss.

32. But *bĕʾaḥărît hayyāmîm,* so expressive in 23:20 (see above), is dangling and functionless in this context.

33. Otherwise Jeremianic passages with citations are relatively late; cf. 3:16, 7:32 par 19:6, 16:14 par 23:7. We have seen in Isaiah that passages with a temporal formula in anacrusis, or as part of a liturgical rubric, reproduce preexisting materials. In Jeremiah the anacrusis construct implies the quotation of preexisting materials, and so apparently also with the citation rubric. The parallel with Ezek 18:2 assures that the saying about sour grapes had an existence in common parlance, and this seems very likely also with regard to the saying about the hot wind. The prose additions, however, are fresh compositions.

34. MT *tōʾmĕrû* should be retained over against the emendation to *yōʾmĕrû* (*BHS*mg, RSV) because Yahweh is asking a question to follow up the promise of survival.

35. In the place of MT "Judah," the LXX substitutes "Edomites," an apologetic move that ignores the singular gentilics. Judah would never have appeared in this list were it not original; furthermore, if it were an insertion, it would most likely have been placed at the end of the list. However, both v 24bβ and v 25b are to be suspected as explicative glosses; the first may have come into the text as a rationalization for the judgment, and the second may have entered the text as a later effort to explain why Judah, among "all the house of Israel," had to be included.

36. But see integral *lākēn hinnēh yāmîm bāʾîm nĕʾum YHWH* in 19:6.

37. Though Holladay, McKane, and Carroll, among recent commentators, are in agreement that 23:7-8 is the original setting for this saying, and that 16:14-15 is entirely out of context, *lākēn* has a function here that it completely lacks at 23:7. Furthermore, the original LXX reading has 23:7f. at the very end of chap. 23, where it modifies a threat equally dire in v 40.

38. Though the genre "report of a prophetic word" prevails elsewhere in the narrative sections of the book (20:1-6, 24:1-10, 29:1-14, 32:1-44, 34:1-7, 8-22, 35:1-19, 37:3-10, 39:15-18, 40:1-6, 43:8-13), Jer 21:1ff. belongs to the rare genre "report of an oracular inquiry," similar to that found in 2 Kgs 22:11-20; Ezek 14:1-11, 20:1-21.

39. To death by pestilence (v 6) the threats of sword and famine have been added. The option of surrender in order to save one's life as a prize of war is reminiscent of Jeremiah's words to Ebed-melech (39:18) and Baruch (45:5).

40. Zedekiah is identified as "king of Judah" (cf. vv 1, 4). The expression "pestilence, sword, and famine" combines the great "pestilence *(deber)*" of v 6 and the "sword and famine" of v 9 (LXX; MT adds "and pestilence").

41. As in Holladay, comm., II, 22-23.

42. Probable dates are as follows: chap. 26: 609; chap. 27: 597; chap. 28: 593; chap. 29: 597-588; chap. 34: 588-586; chap. 35: 609-598; chap. 36: 605. In defense of 586 rather than 587 as the year of Jerusalem's fall, see our discussion in Chapter Eight (Ezekiel).

43. The best explanation of the fact that 33:14-26 is missing in the LXX would be that, even though some of the content of this section may be relatively early, these verses were added following the definitive editing.

44. The three blessings expressly identified in 30:3, namely, restoration of fortunes, return from exile, and repossession of the land, are here given more specific explication. In chap. 32 the purchase of ancestral land guarantees return (v 37), repossession of the land (vv 41-44), and an everlasting covenant (vv 38-40), all of which is summarized in the promise of restored fortunes (v 44b).

45. Pp. 166-67, 179-85, 200-201.

46. P. 249.

47. Pp. 213, 215-23.

48. Comm., II, 170, 196-99.

49. Thomas M. Raitt, in his book *A Theology of Exile, Judgment/Deliverance in Jeremiah and Ezekiel* (Philadelphia 1977), has made a substantial contribution to the discussion by showing (see especially pp. 112ff.) that the shift from prophecies of judgment to words of salvation may

be observed in a number of prose Yahweh-speeches in Jeremiah (24:4-7, 29:4-7, 10-14, 31:31-34, 32:6-15, 42-44, 32:36-41, 33:6-9) that contain all or most of nine parallel elements: (1) address to the exiles; (2) the remembrance of severe and recent judgment, (3) a God-given new spirituality, (4) the covenant formula, (5) the themes of knowing and obeying Yahweh, (6) the promises of restoration and/or return, (7) the consequent repentance, (8) the priority of Yahweh's volition, and (9) the nonmotivation of Yahweh's action (see the diagram on p. 116). Raitt identifies all of these passages as Jeremianic. Although, for the reasons given, we cannot directly attribute 31:31-34 to the prophet, Raitt's analysis is sufficiently evidential to substantiate the claim that this passage does indeed have an authentic background in the Jeremianic tradition. We do not know whether Jeremiah would have tried to stop his disciples, had he been aware of how they were reshaping his ideas; but it is at least clear that they sincerely believed, on their part, that their new message was somehow compatible with his, and that he would speak as they spoke under drastically altered circumstances.

50. Holladay, comm., II, 170, identifies vv 31-33aα as prose and vv 33aβb-34 as poetry.

51. Time-identifying *bayyôm hahû'* appears in an identifying characterization at 25:33 under the influence of the day of Yahweh ideology and the casualty report styling (see in Chapter Three and in De Vries, *YTT,* 301).

52. So also with time-identifying *bayyôm hahû'* in Jer 39:17.

53. See the literature on this formula mentioned in Chapter Three, note 83.

NOTES TO CHAPTER 8

1. Cf. J. Miller, *Das Verhältnis Jeremias und Hesekiels sprachlich und theologisch untersucht, mit besonderer Berücksichtigung der Prosareden Jeremias* (Assen, 1955).

2. Cf. Herrmann, *op. cit.,* p. 290: "Bei Jeremia dominiert die Geschichte, die Einsicht in ihren Ablauf, die tiefere Erkenntnis ihres rätselhaften Wesens, auf dessen Grunde aber dennoch der gnädige Gott wartet; bei Ezechiel dominiert das Recht, das juristisch umschreibbare Verhältnis zwischen Gott und Volk, und darum auch der Gott, dessen Prestige gewahrt bleiben will, der nich aus Gnade rettet, sondern um seines heilgen Namens willen."

3. G. A. Cooke, *A Critical and Exegetical Commentary on the Book of Ezekiel* (ICC; Edinburgh, n.d.); W. Eichrodt, *Der Prophet Hesekiel* (ATD 22/1-2, Göttingen [ET 1970]); W. Zimmerli, *Ezechiel* (BKAT XIII/1-2, Neukirchen-Vluyn).

4. For a complete survey of genres and formulas, see R. Hals, *Ezekiel* (FOTL XIX; Grand Rapids: Eerdmans, 1989).

5. Because the dating formula differs significantly (cf. also that of 40:1) from the stereotyped formula in 1:2, 8:1, 20:1, Zimmerli treats the dating in 24:1 as secondary, though accurate; according to him, it was added by a redactor from Ezekiel's immediate school not long after the event.

6. Against many scholars, I maintain August 15, 586, as the date of Jerusalem's second capture and destruction. The reasons are summarized in my article "Chronology of the Old Testament," *IDB,* I, 596-98:

> Now . . . that Jehoiachin's surrender is definitely dated in Adar, 597, a 587 date for Jerusalem's destruction can be defended only on the unlikely supposition that II Kings (and parallel sources) dated Zedekiah's reign by Nisan years. . . . It is true that we find Jeremiah reckoning by a Nisan new year (25:1; 46:2). This is true also of Ezekiel, but this fact cannot be adduced as support for 587, because if 587 were the year of Jerusalem's fall, Ezekiel's chronology would have to be based on Tishri years (this being the only likely explanation of Ezek. 33:21). . . . There is no sufficient reason to suppose that the writer or writers of the books of Kings, who had so long and consistently stuck to a Tishri reckoning for Judah, and who continued to reckon on this basis even for the date of Jehoiachin's release (II Kings 25:27), would at this one point in the records change to Nisan reckoning. There is then no reasonable escape from a 586 date for Jerusalem's fall. This is demanded by Ezek 33:21, which employs Nisan reckoning to date the arrival

of a messenger in Babylon with the tragic news of Jerusalem's fall, presumably only a few months after this event, in the twelfth year of Jehoiachin's captivity.

7. Since Ezekiel could not have actually spoken to these nations in person, he either had to have been holding a mock recital before an audience representing these nations (an unlikely assumption), or he had to be composing them in writing. Once written down, they became material for the same kind of redactional expansion that has been applied elsewhere in the book.

8. An oracle against Egypt dated to the twenty-seventh year appears out of sequence at 29:17-20.

9. On the terminology and phenomenology of the "day of Yahweh," see De Vries, *YTT*, 47-50, 340-42.

10. LXX "eleventh."

11. See our analysis of 24:27 in Chapter Three and in our ensuing discussion.

12. Publication data in Chapter One, note 13.

13. *Wächter über Israel: Ezechiel und seine Tradition* (BZAW 82; Berlin, 1962).

14. Cf. Amos 8:2.

15. See Zimmerli's extensive discussion in BKAT XIII/1, 155-65.

16. Cf. Ronald Hals, FOTL, XIX, 41-45.

17. "Erkenntnis Gottes nach dem Buch Ezechiel," *Gottes Offenbarung* (ThB 19 [1963]), pp. 41-119; cf. BKAT XIII/1, 55*-61*.

18. *'attâ* at the beginning of v 8 functions purely as a "situation formula" (see in Chapter Two).

19. Though Nebuchadrezzar's thirteen-year siege (585-572) resulted in important concessions, Tyre was not occupied by a military power until after Alexander's victory in 333.

20. LXX "eleventh" reflects an effort to correct the date given in the MT at 33:21 on the basis of 2 Kgs 25:2 par Jer 52:5 (cf. 39:2), where it is correct because Zedekiah's reign included an accession year.

21. As has previously been mentioned, the entirety of v 26 and the words *'et happālît* in v 27 are glosses.

22. Othmar Keel, *Wirkmäsige Siegeszeichen im Alten Testament* (Göttingen, 1974), pp. 123f., 142, shows that a horned helmet worn by a king is a symbol of godhead in widely attested Near-Eastern iconography.

23. In spite of Zimmerli's misgivings, this can best be explained as an allusion to 33:22 and associated texts, but the emphasis may be on the new availability of revelation as an ongoing blessing, rather than on Ezekiel's psychological state.

24. In the original composition it is the land, not specifically the returnees occupying the land, that is the butt of Gog's attack. This focus changes in the secondary expansions, which, while mentioning "my [Yahweh's] land" (38:16) and "the land of Israel" (38:18-19), otherwise refer to "a quiet people who dwell securely" (38:11, 14), "those gathered . . . who dwell at the center of the earth" (38:12), "my people Israel" (38:14, 16, 39:7), "those who dwell in the cities of Israel" (39:9), "the house of Israel" (39:12, 22-23, 29), "Jacob, the whole house of Israel" (39:25), and "the people of the land" (39:13). These variations represent a significant shift in ideology. Similarly, a focus on Gog and on military terminology eventually changes to purely ethnic terminology: "many peoples" (*'ammîm rabbîm* in 38:9, 15, 22; *gôyim rabbîm* in 38:23) or simply "the nations" *(haggôyim)*" in 38:16, 39:7, 21, 23, 28. These shifts reveal that postexilic Judaism had come to see itself less as a nation with a political structure and occupying a specific territory, and more as a distinct people threatened by other peoples. The concept of nationhood has given way to that of pure ethnicity.

25. I have commented as follows on Zimmerli's observation in my essay "Observations on Quantitative and Qualitative Time in Wisdom and Apocalyptic," in J. G. Gammie, et al., eds., *Israelite Wisdom: Theological and Literary Essays in Honor of Samuel Terrien* (Missoula, 1978), p. 265: "Here is an unprecedented level of objectifying the future, completely bypassing the crisis of the present condition of deportation and exile. Time has been radically quantified

and categorized; apocalyptic is beginning to form in the place of traditional prophetic eschatology. . . . We must disagree with Zimmerli in identifying this manner of speaking as merely "a first step on the way to apocalyptic." . . . What we have here is apocalyptic itself — embryonic no doubt, yet unmistakably alive and irreversibly different from anything that had previously been seen. Prior to this, Israel's prophets had prognosticated the future deliverance on two factors: (1) their knowledge of the past and the present; (2) their conception of Yahweh's character and purpose. But now we see something truly new: within a single, unredacted context, the forecast of the coming restoration is no longer the climax of the prediction, but has become a premise upon which a distant, fresh peril — the condition for an ultimate deliverance — is posited."

26. *Contra* Paul D. Hanson, *The Dawn of Apocalyptic* (Philadelphia, 1975); cf. De Vries, "Observations," pp. 272, 275f.

NOTES TO CHAPTER 9

1. Cf. S. Herrmann, *Heilserwartungen,* pp. 105-18.
2. Cf. M. Buss, *The Prophetic Word of Hosea, A Morphological Study* (BZAW 111; Berlin, 1969).
3. Had the book been composed as late as 745, when the Assyrian king Tiglath-Pileser III first began his aggressive actions, or as late as 742, when that king invaded the northern kingdom (cf. 2 Kgs 15:19-20), it almost certainly would have alluded to this. We cannot rely on the editorial superscription (1:1), dating the book to the reigns of Uzziah and Jeroboam, nor can we date the famous earthquake (cf. Zech 14:5). The convergence of evidence, however, places Amos's ministry during the affluent Jeroboam era, hence before 752, prior to the tumultuous politics of the immediately ensuing years (cf. Hos 7:5-7).
4. Cf. Herrmann, *Heilserwartungen,* pp. 118-26.
5. See De Vries, *YTT,* pp. 318-20.
6. *Contra* RSV, one should translate, "Therefore, now they shall go into exile at the head of the exiles (etc.)."
7. See in Chapters Three, Four, and Five.
8. Proportions of anacrusis to prose occurrences in the books where the former do occur are as follows: Isaiah, 4 to 21; Jeremiah, 2 to 18; Hosea, 2 to 1; Joel, 1 to 2; Amos, 4 to 1 (or 5 to 0); Micah, 3 to 0; Zephaniah, 4 to 1.
9. 4:18 (E 3:18); Mic 4:6-7 is a postexilic addition.
10. Temporal transitions in anacrusis are *kî 'āz* in Zeph 3:9; *bayyôm hahû'* in Isa 28:5; Amos 8:13, 9:11; Mic 4:6 (with *nĕ'um YHWH*); Zeph 3:11; *wĕhāyâ bayyôm hahû'* in Isa 17:4, 24:21; Zeph 1:12 LXX, and with *nĕ'um YHWH* in Jer 4:9, 30:8; Hos 2:18, 23 (E 16, 21); Amos 8:9; Mic 5:9 (E 10); Zeph 1:10; *hinnēh yāmîm bā'îm* with *nĕ'um [   ] YHWH* in Amos 8:11, 9:13; *wĕhāyâ bĕ'aḥărît hayyāmîm* in Isa 2:2 par Mic 4:1.
11. *'āz* performs the same function in 3:1-4. At 5:2 (E 3) *lākēn* links the announcement of salvation through a ruler from Bethlehem to a prediction of wide-ranging restoration. On these two passages, see below.
12. This element is specific to this genre; cf. H. W. Wolff, "Die Begründung der prophetischen Heils- und Unheilssprüche," *ZAW* 52 (1934), 1-22; C. Westermann, *Basic Forms of Prophetic Speech* (Philadelphia, 1967), pp. 129ff.; K. Koch, *The Growth of the Biblical Tradition* (New York, 1969), pp. 210ff.
13. In Jer 3:17, 4:11, and 30:1 it is *bā'ēt hahî'* that explicates other time expressions. Cf. Amos 8:11, where *hinnēh yāmîm bā'îm* explicates *yôm mar* in v 10.
14. This would make *biqhal YHWH,* "in Yahweh's congregation," in v 5 more realistically relevant, as over against the strained and attenuated explanations that are usually offered in the commentaries.
15. MT *lĕkā* (2ms), confirmed by LXX, should not be amended to 2mp. Whatever may have been the redactor's intent in shifting from the 2mp address of v 3, the singular stands here as tenacious evidence of compositional complexity.

16. See the commentaries. Difficult readings in the MT are *nihĕyâ* after *nĕhî*, the following *'āmar*, the verb *yāmîr*, and the expression *'êk yāmîš lî lĕsôbēb* (cf. LXX).

17. Cf. A. Alt, "GES ANADASMOS in Juda," *Kleine Schriften zur Geschichte des Volkes Israel*, III (Munich, 1968), pp. 373-81.

18. *Bā'ēt hahî'* in v 4 is a gloss that mars the poetic rhythm.

19. Cf. Isa 1:20, 40:5, 58:14, 62:2, Jer 9:11.

20. One should take appreciative notice of the very late poem in 7:11-13, "A day for the building of your walls." *Yôm libnôt gĕdērāyik* in v 11 and *yôm hû'* in v 12 are substantives; the repetition of key words (especially *wĕyām miyyām wĕhar hāhār*) and strong alliteration are special stylistic features.

21. Cf. A. van der Woude, *Micha* (De Prediking van het Oude Testament; Nijkerk, 1976), pp. 152ff.

22. It is likely that alliteration with thematic *'attâ* is intended.

23. Cf. Isa 7:14.

24. Cf. Herrmann, *Heilserwartungen*, pp. 149-53.

25. Cf. S. J. De Vries, "The Acrostic of Nahum in the Jerusalem Liturgy," *VT* 16 (1966), 476-81.

26. Following 1QpHab, we should translate, "Then like the wind he shall sweep by and pass through, and so he will make his might his god."

27. In calling for divine judgment upon his fellow Judahites, Habakkuk seems to stand very much on the same ground as the redactor of Mic 5:9-14. However, that redactor did not neglect to include the foreign instrument of that judgment; in the conclusion of his expansion he has Yahweh declare: "And in anger and wrath I will execute vengeance upon the nations that did not obey." The same impulse leads Habakkuk to call for divine judgment also on "the wicked who swallows up the man more righteous than he," which must mean the Chaldeans in comparison with the Judahite nobility (1:13).

28. Although Herodotus mentions that this wild and ferocious people were sweeping over western Asia as far south as Egypt *ca.* 626, and they were giving trouble to the Medes and Assyrians *ca.* 612, there is nothing in the text of Zephaniah that requires the looming enemy to be the Scythians rather than the Neo-Babylonians after 605.

29. *Bayyôm hahû'* in v 9 is a gloss that disturbs the meter; see in Chapter Three.

30. 3:5 is a later gnomic saying glossed into the text.

31. In 18α LXX "as on a feast day" should be read in place of the difficult Hebrew text.

32. In v 19 *bā'ēt hahî'* is a gloss that disturbs the meter.

33. The same redactor may be responsible for the gloss in v 19 and the change of temporal formula in 1:12 MT.

NOTES TO CHAPTER 10

1. The priests are no longer put under censure, as in Mal 1:6–2:9.

2. The designation of the priests and other clergy as *mĕšartîm* is restricted to the late writings, Deuteronomy, P in Exodus and Numbers, Ezekiel 40ff., Psalms, Esther, Ezra-Nehemiah, and Chronicles.

3. See the excursus in Chapter Two.

4. This is the only section outside chaps. 1–2 that makes concrete historical predictions.

5. The dates are in the sixth to ninth months (August to December) of this king's second year of reign. With dates added redactionally, the original first oracle is in 1:2, 5-6, 8, 12, 14b (with epexegetical elements in vv 3-4, 7, 9-11, 13-14a); the second is in 2:2-9; the third is in 2:11-19; the fourth is in 2:20-23.

6. Cf. K. Koch, "Haggais unreines Volk," *ZAW* 79 (1967), 52-66; O. R. Hildebrand, "Temple Ritual: A Paradigm for Moral Holiness in Haggai II 10-19," *VT* 39 (1989), 154-68.

7. Two interpretive glosses are added in v 18b.

8. The intermingling of cosmic day-of-Yahweh imagery and historically oriented Yahweh-

war imagery supports von Rad's derivation of the former from the latter (*Der heilige Krieg im alten Israel* [Zürich, 1949]; *ibid.*, "The Origin of the Concept of the Day of Yahweh," *JSS* 4 [1959], 97ff.; cf. De Vries, *YTT* 36f., 50, 340).

9. 2:21-22 goes beyond 2:6-7 in its mention of "thrones," "kingdoms," and "power (*ḥōzeq*)."

10. *YTT* 320f.

11. As in vv 6-7, '*ănî mar'îš*, "I am shaking," defines the present and imminently future divine activity that leads to effects defined in a sequence of imperfects and/or perfect *wāw*-consecutive perfects.

12. Cf. Zech 6:9-14.

13. On the question of this person's "investiture," cf. P. R. Ackroyd, *Exile and Restoration* (Philadelphia, 1968), pp. 164-66.

14. The original formula for introducing oracular pericopes is a stereotyped *wayhî dĕbar YHWH [   ] lē'mōr* (6:9, 7:4, 8:1), while that which regularly introduces visions is *rā'îtî hallaylâ wĕhinnēh* (1:8, 2:1, 4:1, 5:1, 6:1). Redactional introductory formulas are, for oracles, the date with *hāyâ dĕbar YHWH 'el zĕkaryâ* (etc.) and, for visions, *wayyar'ēnî . . . wayyō'mer;* cf. integral *wayhî dĕbar YHWH 'el zĕkaryâ lē'mōr* at 7:8. 7:1 commences in original Zecharian style, but the oracular material does not begin until v 4; thus the date provided is original even though it introduces just the narrative situation set forth in vv 1-3.

15. "Die Exilswende in der Sicht des Propheten Sacharja," *Studien zur Geschichte Israels im persischen Zeitalter* (Tübingen, 1964), pp. 109-26; cf. "Serubbabel und der Hohepriester beim Wiederaufbau des Tempels in Jerusalem," *idem,* pp. 127-48.

16. The dating on the same day of the month — though of a different month — is tantalizingly coincidental. Apart from the possibility that the month-number may have been corrected in either text, it does not seem unreasonable to suggest that Zechariah's date may have been intended as a symbolic replication of Haggai's.

17. Since Wellhausen, the first four words of Zech 6:10b, *ûbā'tā 'attâ bayyôm hahû'*, have generally been taken as a gloss, but a purpose for such a gloss is not apparent. More probably, the second *ûbā'tā* is a dittography (cf. De Vries, *YTT* 313).

18. MT '*ătārôt* in v 11 results from the alteration of the singular form, and the name and title of Joshua ben Jehozadak have been substituted for the name of Zerubbabel. Whether or not this textual alteration implies that Zerubbabel had been forcibly removed from the community, it is apparent that it was burgeoning pro-priestly ideology that eventually led to this rereading. On the significance of the ceremony in question, see Galling, *op. cit.,* pp. 121-23.

19. For further discussion of the question of shifting expectations for Zerubbabel, see Carroll, *When Prophecy Failed,* pp. 162-68.

20. *Contra BHS*mg, *hahēm* is not to be amended to *hā'ēlleh* since it refers to a period earlier than that of v 9.

21. 3:1-9, which has been secondarily inserted into the original night-vision cycle, comes to a climax in an unmistakable epitome with the temporal expression, *bĕyôm 'eḥād* (cf. 1 Kgs 20:29, Isa 10:17), declaring that the land's guilt — the concern of the pericope as a whole — will be removed (see *YTT* 233, 304f.).

22. The labeling of chaps. 12–14 as "Trito-Zechariah" depends on the answer to the question whether they arose within a redactional process separate from that of chaps. 9–11.

23. See pp. 245f., 321, 123-26, and 322, respectively. I have given up my identification of *bayyôm hahû'* in 12:4 as belonging to an epitome, treating it here as an integral transition.

24. *Introduction to the Old Testament as Scripture* (Philadelphia, 1979), p. 483.

25. See the excursus "Additional futuristic transitions in Daniel," in Chapter Four; cf. also *YTT* 343.

26. It is this in particular that associates Daniel with Zechariah 12–14; cf. the sixty-two weeks of Dan 9:25.

27. (WMANT 34; Neukirchen: Neukirchener Verlag, 1969).

28. The significance of the "shepherd" passages as part of a definitive redaction is echoed in a recent study by Paul L. Redditt, "Israel's Shepherds: Hope and Pessimism in Zechariah

9-14," *CBQ* 51 (1989), 631-42. Unaware of Saebø's study, Redditt claims that "the principal redactor/author" drew together the elements of six independent collections (the "shepherd" pericopes being one of the six), allowing the subsections 10:2-3a, 11:1-17, 12:6-7, 10-12, 13:1-9 to present his personal panorama of the future, in contrast to those of the individual collections. Unfortunately, Redditt's treatment undertakes no independent study of the biblical text and therefore can be of little service in our present analysis.

29. *Theocracy and Eschatology* (Richmond, 1968; ET of *Theocratie und Eschatologie* [1959]), p. 801.

30. For title, see below.

31. K. Elliger, *Die Propheten Nahum, Habakkuk, Zephanje, Haggai, Sacharja, Maleachi,* pp. 174-76.

32. Lamarche, Paris: Libairie Lecoffre; Otzen, Copenhagen: Munksgaard; Lutz, WMANT 27; Neukirchen: Neukirchener Verlag; Willi-Plein, BBB 42, Cologne: Hanstein.

33. The most effective textual treament is that of Saebø in *op. cit.,* pp. 58-105, 108-27. Saebø bases his critical methodology on a systematic evaluation of the *Tendenz* of the MT and VSS as a whole, rather than on *ad hoc* preferences.

34. *Op. cit.,* pp. 72-103. He views 12:1–13:6 and 14:1ff. as cohesive compositions within themselves, in which the temporal expressions are the main keys to the internal arrangement. Otzen, *op. cit.,* pp. 213-29, enthusiastically endorses this concept.

35. This objection also pertains to Tournay's suggestion that typological numerology has led a single composer (Zechariah?) to employ specific quantities of each variant (R. Tournay, O.P., "Zacharie XII–XIV et l'histoire d'Israel," *RB* 81 [1974], 359).

36. For an appreciative evaluation of Saebø's work, see Douglas U. Knight, *The Rediscovery of the Traditions of Israel* (Missoula, 1973), pp. 367-82.

37. *Op. cit.,* pp. 254-76.

38. *Op. cit.,* pp. 282-309.

39. The shift from *hā'ammîm* to *gôyê* may be taken as evidence of v 3b's literary independence; one should note that the expansion comprising vv 3a, 5, 7, 8b also has the locution *hā'ammîm.* Cf. *kol-haggōyim sābîb* in 14:14.

40. On this passage as a reinterpretation of Deut 28:28, see Fishbane, *op. cit.,* p. 501.

41. On the structural patterns of ancient holy-war narratives, cf. von Rad, *Der Heilige Krieg im alten Israel* (4th ed.; Göttingen, 1965).

42. Possibly to be amended to *'alpê yĕhûdâ,* "Judahite clans"; cf. *BHS*mg.

43. *Wĕyāšĕbâ yĕrûšālaim 'ôd taḥtéhā.* The following *bîrûšālim* makes no sense and should probably be omitted.

44. On the relationship of this to the previous expansion, cf. Saebø, *op. cit.,* pp. 275-76.

45. Cf. 13:3.

46. *Ṭum'â* is a cultic term not used elsewhere to modify *rûăḥ,* "spirit." This is a clue that the redactor in question may have been condemning prophesying specifically as a cultic offense.

47. See his summary in *op. cit.,* pp. 308f.

48. *Op. cit.,* pp. 287-88.

49. Cf. Lutz, *op. cit.,* pp. 30-32.

50. See the extended discussion in *op. cit.,* pp. 289-98.

51. Saebø, *op. cit.,* pp. 300-303.

52. *Bākem* in v 13 refers back to the nations of vv 1-3.

53. The locution is *haggōyim,* drawn from vv 2-3 (cf. 14), in distinction from *hā'ammîm* in v 12.

54. The clause, "and there shall no longer be (never again shall be) a trader in the house of Yahweh Sebaoth on that day," epitomizes the entire pericope (cf. De Vries, *YTT* 322); that is, it pinpoints the thrust of the predicted pansacrality polemically, as an attack on the presence of foreign merchants within the temple precincts.

55. On the text of this difficult verse, see Saebø, *op. cit.,* pp. 116, 299-300.

56. *Neged yĕrûšālaim* is the glossator's transition. The antecedent of *wĕyāšĕbû bāh* may be *hā'āreṣ;* but cf. *BHS*mg.

57. The normal meaning of *lḥm* niph. followed by a prepositional phrase with *bě* is "fight against," not "with (alongside)."

58. Cf. De Vries, *The Achievements of Biblical Religion* (Lanham MD: University Press of America, 1983), pp. 340-42.

59. See H. G. M. Williamson, "Eschatology in Chronicles," *TynBul* 28 (1977), 115-54; *ibid., Israel in the Books of Chronicles* (Cambridge, 1977); DeVries, *1-2 Chronicles* (FOTL XI; Grand Rapids, 1989), pp. 114-15.

60. *Op. cit.,* pp. 78-96.

61. *Op. cit.,* pp. 205-12; cf. Daniella Ellul, "Variations sur le thème de la Guerre Sainte dans le Deutero-Zecharie," *ETR* 56 (1981), 55-71.

62. *The Dawn of Apocalyptic* (Philadelphia, 1975).

63. "Observations on Quantitative and Qualitative Time in Wisdom and Apocalyptic," pp. 263-76.

64. It is evident that the idealism of vv 16ff. is tempered by a painful awareness of Gentile indifference toward Judaism's appeal. The reference to the recalcitrant "families of Egypt" in vv 18-19 probably reflects the conditions of the Ptolemaic period, 323-198 B.C.E. The notion of comprehensive holiness goes beyond the normative Jewish concept during the late postexilic period; it is best illustrated in sectarian writings such as the Temple scroll and the Book of Discipline from Qumran.

65. Cf. M. Delcor, "Les sources du Deutero-Zacharie et des procédées d'emprunt," *RB* 59 (1952), 385-411.

66. This is a defect in Willi-Plein's treatment (*op. cit.;* cf. especially pp. 105-21).

67. Cf. De Vries, *YTT,* pp. 124-26.

68. In 38:12 "those who dwell at the center of the earth" is a term for the inhabitants of the land rather than for the citizens of Jerusalem.

NOTES TO CHAPTER 11

1. Cf. N. Perrin, *What Is Redaction Criticism?* (Philadelphia: Fortress, 1969). The term is generally more applicable to the Gospels because the "Evangelists" were basically involved in collecting, reshaping, and amplifying blocks of source material, making the redactional level the most creative.

2. The aim of scribal glossation is to produce a more consistent and ideologically acceptable text. The purpose of canonical ordering is to select a list of authoritative books, neutralize random passages from a normative viewpoint, and establish a theologically authoritative text. The writings of Scripture came to constitute a sacrosanct book that required exegesis and interpretation but did not allow redactional alteration. Prophetic tradition came to an end and redactional expansion ceased. There could be no further levels of predictive prophecy leading to new visions of the divine purpose. (See the concluding section of this chapter, "Beyond Redaction.")

3. On the special motives that led to the recording to prophetic material, see the illuminating discussion in R. E. Clements, "Prophecy as Literature" (1986), analyzed in Chapter One.

4. *Das Problem der Urrolle;* see the summary on p. 125.

5. *Wěhāyâ bayyôm hahû'* with *ně'um YHWH* belongs to secondary material in Jer 30:8, where it likewise stands in anacrusis to a poetic fragment.

6. We have argued that "and they will say," read by the LXX, is to be preferred in 4:10 rather than MT "and I will say"; the leaders, not Jeremiah, are responsible for the complaint about Yahweh's deceiving the people (*contra* H. Graf von Reventlow, *Liturgie und prophetisches Ich bei Jeremia* [Gütersloh, 1966], pp. 110f., 124). The renowned "confessions" (11:18-20, 12:1-4, 15:10-12, 15-18, 17:14-18, 18:19-23, 20:7-12, 14-18) — which are certainly not secondary — are the main evidence of the prophet's willingness to record his personal reactions to what he was proclaiming.

7. Such as the late postexilic insertion, drawn from 16:14-15, at 23:7-8 (see in Chapter Seven).

8. See the discussion in Chapter Eight.

9. As will be shown, its parallel in Mic 4:1-5 belongs to Level V, that of definitive editing.

10. These chapters contain authentic Isaianic materials, but the formation of the redactional unit is relatively late. Sweeney (*op. cit.,* p. 107) dates the redactional formation of Isaiah 2-4 to the late sixth or early fifth century.

11. In a significant number of passages entering the text at this level, catchwords or phrases in the underlying materials have occasioned the expansion (Isa 2:20f., 10:20ff., 11:10, 11, 18:7, 22:24f., 28:5f.; Jer 3:18, 5:18f., 16:14f., 30:8f.; Ezek 30:9, 38:10ff., 14ff.; Hos 1:5; Mic 5:9ff.). Even without such a catalyst, almost all the passages on this list have been designed as epexegesis to the underlying material. It is only in Isa 17:7-8, 9; Jer 3:17; Joel 3:18; and Zeph 3:16-17, 20 that this intent is not in evidence. In these exceptional passages the thematic inclusion of preexisting materials has motivated the expansion. (See our further discussion in Chapter Thirteen.)

12. Cited in Isa 31:6-7, a Level IV addition made at stage B (see below).

13. Introductory *bayyôm hahû'* self-consciously explicates "the day" of vv 2-4, in particular its emphasis on the coming "day of Egypt's doom."

14. *Bayyôm hahû'* introduces an image that is epexegetical to this epitomizing formula.

15. Cf. G. W. Tucker, "Prophetic Superscriptions and the Growth of the Canon," G. W. Coats and B. O. Long, eds., *Canon and Authority* (Philadelphia, 1977), pp. 56-70.

16. Cf. Sweeney, *op. cit.,* pp. 11-25.

17. As I have argued in *Yesterday, Today and Tomorrow,* pp. 287-89, 1 Sam 3:2-11, 13bα^{2}β-18 is one of three originally independent narratives in 1 Samuel 1-3. The other two are in 1:1-28, 2:11, 19-21 and 2:12-17, 22a, 23-25. Along with chap. 4, these were combined into a new ark narrative through use of linking material in 3:1, 19-20. With deuteronomistic expansions, 2:27-36 belongs to a Zadokite polemicist, but 3:12f. is a programmatic insertion from the deuteronomistic redactor. Though this insertion points ostensibly to an imminently future event, to the deuteronomist this is long past. Within the independent narrative of 3:2ff., the vision oracle of vv 11, 13bα^{2}β-14 has a formal accusation in the last seven words of v 13, *kî-mĕqalĕlîm lāhem bānâw wĕlō' kihâ bām,* "because his sons were bringing a curse on themselves while he did not restrain them." The formal announcement (threat), with *lākēn* and the oath formula, predicts the imminent termination of a priestly office for the Elides. In his expansion, the deuteronomist means to summarize all the complaints against the Elides, including those of *n's,* "contempt" (2:17), *dĕbārîm rā'îm,* "evil doings" (2:23), *b't,* "kicking (?)" (2:29), and *qll* "bringing a curse" (3:13bα^{2}β) mentioned in the text as it lay before him. Contrary to 2:23-25, the deuteronomist implicates Eli (*ba'ăwōn 'ăšer-yādā',* "because of the iniquity of which he was aware") along with his sons in this guilt.

18. The liturgical insertions bracket the foreign-oracle section, chaps. 13-23. They celebrate victory over the nations from a postexilic perspective.

19. The situation is analogous to that which created the liturgical rubrics in Hab 3:1, 3, 9, 13, 19. It may be imagined that a lector might read portions of the underlying text while the congregation would respond with the appropriate hymn.

20. These very late predictions differ from those inspired by the initial return in laying emphasis on the theme of delay and disappointment (cf. "one by one" and the image of threshing in v 12, "lost" and "driven out" in v 13).

21. Because 33:14-16, 17-18, 19-22, 23-26 are united in their Davidic interest, it may be inferred that they were added as a unit. The reference to *kōhănîm halĕwiyyim* in v 18, to *halĕwiyyim hakōhănîm* in v 21, and to *halĕwiyyim mĕšarĕtê 'ōtî* in v 22 suggests also a dominant Levitical interest, as in the Chronicles tradition (cf. S. J. De Vries, "Moses and David as Cult-Founders in Chronicles," *JBL* 107 (1988), 619-39.

22. *Biblical Theology in Crisis* (Philadelphia, 1970), pp. 97-122; "The Old Testament as Scripture in the Church," *CTM* 43 (1972), 709-22; "The Exegetical Significance of Canon for the Study of the Old Testament," Congress Volume, Göttingen 1977 (SVT 29; Leiden, 1978), pp. 66-80; *Introduction to the Old Testament as Scripture* (Philadelphia, 1979); *Old Testament Theology in a Canonical Context* (Philadelphia, 1985).

23. *Torah and Canon* (Philadelphia, 1972); *Canon and Criticism. A Guide to Canonical Criticism* (Philadelphia, 1984); "Text and Canon. Concepts and Method," *JBL* 88 (1979), 5-29.

24. Cf. Seeligmann, "Voraussetzungen der Midraschexegese," Congress Volume (SVT

1; Leiden, 1953), pp. 150-81. Properly speaking, midrash is a "literature about a literature" (A. G. Wright, *The Literary Genre Midrash* [New York, 1967], p. 74). Although there are prerabbinical examples of midrash, there are none within the Old Testament apart from the two examples of what I call "proto-midrash" in 1 Chr 5:1-2 and 17:23-24 (*1 and 2 Chronicles* (FOTL XI; Grand Rapids, 1989), pp. 54-56, 212-15.

25. See our discussion of this work in Chapter One.

26. *Jahrbuch für Biblische Theologie* 3, "Zum Problem des biblischen Kanons" (Neukirchen: Neukirchener Verlag, 1988), pp. 115-33.

27. The fact that the Pentateuch, which contains approximately as much narrative as law, came now to be referred to as the Torah reveals that the law as interpreted and applied within the late Jewish community was the authoritative point of reference from which even the biblical story was to be judged.

28. On the development of the concept of a scriptural canon, see further P. R. Ackroyd, "The Open Canon," *Studies in the Religious Tradition of the Old Testament* (London: SCM, 1987), pp. 208-24. Particularly useful is Ackroyd's distinction between (1) the historic canon, (2) the canon within the canon — sections chosen in various traditions of especially authoritative value — and (3) the "open canon" — the influence of various sections of Scripture upon the interpretation of others.

29. See in Chapter Three. Their formal functionlessness is the clearest indication that they are in fact nothing but random glosses.

NOTES TO CHAPTER 12

1. Cf. also the Egyptians as "fishers" in Jer 16:16a.

2. Cf. *BHS*mg.

3. Pp. 281-82, 341.

4. *TLZ* 85 (1960), 401-20; also *BZAW* 99 (1967), 32-58. Reprinted in H. D. Preuss, ed., *Eschatologie im Alten Testament* (Darmstadt, 1978), pp. 147-80.

5. See our discussion of Carroll's book, *When Prophecy Failed,* in Chapter One.

6. "Er erkündet für die Jerusalemer Gemeinde einen Wendepunkt, den der gegenwärtige Tag als Grenzscheide zweier Zeitalter bildet" (147).

7. Pp. 111-37 in J. Neusner et al., eds., *Judaisms and Their Messiahs.*

8. See G. Wanke, " 'Eschatologie'. Ein Beispiel theologischer Verwirrung," *KuD* 16 (1970), 300-12; reprinted in Preuss, *op. cit.,* pp. 342-60.

9. This is in any event the position to which most scholars are moving; cf. G. Habets, "Eschatologie-eschatologisches," H.-J. Fabry, ed., *Bausteine biblischer Theologie* (BBB 50; Botterweck Fs., Cologne-Bonn: Hanstein, 1977), pp. 351-69.

10. Recently Magne Saebø has argued that the etymological element in *eschatos/eschaton* might be made more determinative by reserving "eschatology/eschatological" for events that make a decisive difference in what is expected for the future ("Eschaton und Eschatologia im Alten Testament in traditions-geschichtler Sicht," J. Hausmann and H.-J. Zobel, eds., *Alttestamentlicher Glaube und Biblische Theologie* [Preuss Fs, Stuttgart-Berlin-Köln, 1992], pp. 321-30), in disregard of ideological content. The difficulty of applying this definition to the passages under study here is that virtually all passages — not only those that announce a drastic reversal of fortunes — imply a decisive change of one sort or another.

11. See the definition offered in De Vries, "Observations on Quantitative and Qualitative Time," pp. 273f.

12. See Zimmerli (BKAT *in loco*) for arguments in favor of a symbolic meaning for this act in preference to the commonly preferred psychological explanation.

13. This theme is especially well developed in Ezek 35:11-13, 36:20-24, 32. It provides the ideological basis for the stereotyped "recognition formula" *wîda'tā(tem) kî 'ănî YHWH,* "So you will know that I am Yahweh," occurring frequently in the book of Ezekiel.

14. In this section and in the next (those concerning secondary passages), redactional levels are indicated in parentheses.

15. This is rarely seen in the prophetic literature; cf. Isa 48:16; Ezek 39:23-29; Zech 8:9-13).

16. As in Wildberger, BKAT X/2, 631.

17. Cf. M. Cogan, "Three Years as a Typological Period," in J. H. Tigay, ed., *Empirical Models for Biblical Criticism* (Philadelphia: University of Pennsylvania Press, 1985), pp. 207-9.

18. A *śākîr* (cf. Job 7:1-2) may be a hired laborer (Lev 25:53) or a mercenary soldier (Jer 46:21). Since the first might be hired by the day and the second for as long as needed, the evident *tertium comparationis* is the sense of obligation to fulfill a pre-agreed period of service. Though we have no basis for ascribing the notion of predetermined history to this redactor, he clearly believes that Yahweh has set forces in motion and is controlling them toward their destiny.

19. The literature on this expression is fairly extensive; cf. W. L. Holladay, *The Root śûbh in the Old Testament* (Leiden, 1958), pp. 110-14. In addition to these two passages, it is found in Deut 30:3; Jer 29:14, 30:18, 31:23, 32:44, 33:7, 11, 48:47, 49:6, 39; Ezek 16:53, 29:14; Hos 6:11; Joel 4:1; Amos 9:14; Zeph 2:7, 3:10; Ps 14:7 par 53:7 (E 6), 85:2 (E 1), 126:1, 4; Job 42:10; Lam 2:14.

20. See J. Simons, *Jerusalem in the Old Testament* (Leiden, 1952), pp. 10-12, 52.

21. These were probably the enigmatic "Rephaim" (Ug: RPU), surreptitiously worshiped in Jerusalem as Malk (= MT Molech); cf. 2 Kgs 23:10, Jer 32:35. On the Rephaim, see J. Gray, "The Rephaim," *PEQ* 84 (1949), 127-39; G. R. Driver, *Canaanite Myths and Legends* (Edinburgh, 1956), pp. 9-10, 67-71, 155. On Malk, see E. Eissfeldt, *Molk als Opferbegriff im Persischen und Hebräischen* (Halle, 1935); also H. Gese, *Die Religionen Altsyriens* (Stuttgart, 1970), pp. 139, 214f.

22. The recent effort to explain the patriarchal promises in the Genesis J material (in particular 12:1-3 and 15:1-6) as propaganda for the late-sixth-century return of Jewish exiles to the land of Israel (cf. J. van Seters, "The So-Called Deuteronomistic Redaction of the Pentateuch," *Congress Volume* [SVT 43; Leiden: Brill, 1991], pp. 58-77) encounters a fatal flaw in the fact that the ideology of prophetic redaction seems completely unaware of the presence of inhospitable natives threatening to resist being displaced by newcomers. On the contrary, this ideology assumes that the land lies quite empty, and that all that is needed is sufficient faith and courage to make the effort to reestablish residence in a land that has now grown unfamiliar. The predictive texts that show the returnees in anxiety for foreign hostility are proto-apocalyptic. They depict the Jews as potential victims rather than as aggressors, and the enemies are outside, rather than within, the land.

23. This is the biblical source of the *dies irae* theme in Christian penitential liturgies.

24. This must be appreciated as an insightful extension of a high prophetic view of the divine nature.

25. Cf. Jer 13:12-14, 23:33; Ezek 21:12, 37:18-19. See B. O. Long, *1 Kings* (FOTL IX), pp. 110, 258; idem, "Two Question and Answer Schemata in the Prophets," *JBL* 90 (1971), 129-39.

26. A later hand is responsible for identifying uncircumcision, physical or spiritual, as the specific reason for including Judah with these nations.

27. Most other biblical references to Judah as a military aggressor hail from the first-temple period, leaving us to wonder whether any postexilic Jews actually did aspire to become such a threat to their neighbors.

28. The temporal formulas employed are *wĕhāyâ bayyôm hahû'* (10x), *bā'ēt hahî'* (2x), *bayyāmîm hāhēmmâ* (2x), *hinnēh yāmîm bā'îm* (3x), *'aḥarê-kēn* (3x), and *bĕ'aḥărît hayyāmîm* (1x). Predictions are for the proximate future except in one passage referring to the imminent future (1 Sam 3:12f.) and seven passages that refer to a remote future (Isa 11:11, 17:9, 19:16; Jer 46:26b, 49:6, 39; Ezek 30:9).

29. Cf. Jer 25:12; Dan 9:2, 24ff.; 2 Chr 36:21.

30. Cf. Isa 17:5.

31. In the prophetic tradition the blowing of a trumpet is almost always a symbol of incipient military destruction. As a symbol of imminent blessing for the faithful, it appears only here, in Isa 58:1, and in Zech 9:14 (cf. Joel 2:15-16).

32. Cf. O. Keel, *Wirkmäsige Siegeszeichen im Alten Testament* (Göttingen, 1981), pp. 123f., 142.

33. Cf. Ezek 24:27, 33:22. On possible mythological associations, see J. M. Kennedy, "Hebrew *pithōn peh* in the Book of Ezekiel," *VT* 41 (1991), 233-35.

34. Cf. Ezek 16:10-13, 17-18, 39, 23:26, 42.

35. Cf. Isa 11:16, 35:8, 40:3, 62:10.

36. Cf. Ezek 16:8.

37. Cf. Isa 58:9.

38. Although the allusion is to the welcome/unwelcome day of Yahweh announced in Amos 5:18-20, this motif becomes dominant in apocalyptic texts viewing Yahweh's day as a threat to Israel's enemies, rather than to herself.

39. Cf. Isa 35:6.

40. Cf. 1 Kgs 4:25; 2 Kgs 18:31 par Isa 36:16; Joel 2:22; Mic 4:4.

41. Alone in Isa 3:18, 7:20, 17:4, 19:23; Ezek 29:21; Amos 8:13; Mic 4:6; Zech 3:10; with preceding *wĕhāyâ* in Isa 7:18, 21, 23, 23:15, 27:12-13; Jer 30:8; Hos 2:18, 21; Amos 8:8; Joel 4:18.

42. Jer 4:11, 16:14, 23:7, 31:27; Amos 8:11, 9:13.

43. This passage refers to the remote future in spite of the fact that its doublet at Jer 16:14 refers to the proximate future. It is the context that determines the difference.

44. Reinforcement by use of the oracle formula, common in the Jeremiah passages, may occur in third-person as well as in first-person address (cf. Jer 4:9-10, 8:1-3, 31:31-34, 50:4-5, 20).

45. Cf. Isa 32:15, 44:3; Ezek 36:26-27.

46. Cf. Isa 19:18.

47. The verb *hlk* frequently stands for moral and religious life or practice, but in this passage an actual pilgrimage or return to Jerusalem may be implied, its most notable feature being Gentile participation.

48. The "assistance formula," a graphic expression for Yahweh's saving help, is used in numerous Old Testament passages; cf. H. D. Preuss, " 'Ich will mit dir sein,' " *ZAW* 80 (1968), 139-73.

49. Cf. Isa 2:8, 20, 44:20, and numerous similar passages.

50. Cf. Zeph 1:14. See further O. Keel, *The Symbolism of the Biblical World* (New York, 1978), pp. 219-22.

51. Cf. the classic treatment of the theme of a universal Davidic kingship by S. Mowinckel, *He That Cometh* (New York-Nashville, 1954).

52. Cf. Jer 3:18; Ezek 37:15-23; Hos 2:2 (E 1:11).

53. MT *bĕrākô*, "blessed him," is an ideological correction (LXX *bĕrēkāh*). The LXX tendentiously alters "Egypt" and "Assyria" to "those in Egypt" and "those in Assyria." On the question of reinterpretive ideology in the LXX and Aramaic Targum of this passage, see Carroll, *When Prophecy Failed*, pp. 127-28.

54. Together with the "fruit of the land" *(pĕrî hā'āreṣ)*, it brings the ideal blessings of beauty *(ṣĕbî)*, glory *(kābôd)*, and distinction *(tip'eret)* for "Israel's refugees" *(pĕlēṭat yiśrā'ēl)*; cf. Isa 10:20; Ezra 9:8, 13-15; Neh 1:2; 2 Chr 30:6.

55. This significant shift away from the hope of return to a situation of residence in Jerusalem is chacteristic of late postexilic ideology (cf. Zechariah 12–14). The faithful are declared "holy" (cf. Zech 14:20-21) and are recorded in a "book of life" (cf. Mal 3:16).

56. Exod 13:21-23, 14:19-20.

57. Exod 40:34-38.

58. For this familiar symbol cf. Ps. 91:1, 121:5; Isa 25:4-5, 32:2.

59. This is intended as a grim warning to apocalyptic enthusiasts who dream of total restoration (cf. Hertzberg, BKAT X/1, 415-16).

60. This is evidence alongside the Elephantine papyri that the Deuteronomic prohibition against extraneous shrines was not observed (if even known) among the Egyptian diaspora (cf. Hertzberg, BKAT X/2, 736-42).

61. This runs contrary to Ezekiel's effort to resist such despondency (cf. 33:10-11, 37:11-14). In threats, the derogatory use of *mišpāḥâ* in reference to Israel and/or Judah appears at Amos 3:1 and Mic 2:3; cf. the plural in Jer 2:4, 33:24.

62. In contrast to Jer 30:22, 31:1, 50:5, which predict the continuing validity of the traditional covenant.

63. The locution includes the word *qadšî*, established in the preexilic liturgy as a fond metaphor for the temple site (Ps 2:6, 15:1, 43:3), which becomes a general term for the city in postexilic salvation sayings (Isa 11:9, 56:7, 57:13).

64. This is meant as an apologia for the restoration community *vis-à-vis* those being denounced in Zeph 1:5-6, 8-9, 12, 3:1-7.

65. They express what I have described as the cultic present/future in *YTT* 46f., 284f.

66. Elsewhere the punishment of the nations and the salvation of Israel are presented as transcendental acts of Yahweh, with no instrumental connection of the one to the other.

67. Cf. De Vries, *YTT* 43.

68. This hint of universalism, usually eliminated in apocalyptic ideology, reappears in Zech 14:16 following a parallel affirmation of Yahweh's cosmic rule in v 9.

69. Cf. De Vries, *1-2 Chronicles* (FOTL XI), pp. 323-39; idem, "Temporal Terms as Structural Elements in the Holy War Tradition," *VT* 25 (1975), 103-5.

NOTES TO CHAPTER 13

1. In his valuable treatment of various modes of reinterpreting biblical prophecy in the postbiblical (including New Testament, patristic, and rabbinical) literature, John Barton emphasizes how the definition of prophecy has been extended in the synagogue and church beyond recognition in comparison with original ecstatic prophecy (*Oracles of God. Perceptions of Ancient Prophecy in Israel after the Exile* [London: Darton, Longman & Todd, 1986]; cf. especially pp. 266-73). It must be maintained, nevertheless, that, however much inner-biblical prophetism may have evolved as seen from a religion-phenomenonological point of view, within the Old Testament itself each new expansion of the type we have been studying was fully intentional in its claim to have come as new authoritative revelation.

2. Cf. Carroll, *When Prophecy Failed,* p. 148.

3. This is the original setting for this remarkable salvation saying. By contrast, its paraphrase in 23:7-8 is not epexegetical but merely topical with relation to its context.

4. This is intended as a paradigm of eschatological bliss. Since the similarly complex salvation saying in 2:2-4 functions as an editorial introduction to chaps. 2–4, a tantalizing possibility might be that Isa 4:2-6 was placed here with the purpose of closing the unit editorially. But this remains unlikely because of the apparent lateness of this prediction.

5. The gloss at the end of v 17, *'et melek 'aššûr,* "the king of Assyria," could be viewed as a catch-phrase for the attachment of the following sayings only on the highly unlikely assumption that it would have been in the text prior to the entrance of these Level II expansions.

6. It is more loosely connected to its context than is 16:14-16, the passage which it paraphrases, because the latter passage is directly epexegetical of its fore-given material. The similar introductory formulas made it natural to attach 23:7f. to vv 5f., but we must keep in mind that this arrangement was created in a Hebrew text younger than the *Vorlage* of the LXX, which places it at the end of v 40.

7. Chap. 10 is an independent addition to this tradition complex.

8. The symbol > means "becomes" or "is transformed into."

9. Editorial connections are excluded because they are formal and not directly ideological.

10. It has Zechariah's usual strengthening appellative, *şĕbā'ôt,* added to Yahweh's name.

11. Also editorial; see above.

12. Reference to the valley of Rephaim outside Jerusalem is intended only as a metaphor from nature; any mythological innuendo that may be intended remains obscure.

13. Even the tentative universalism of Zech 14:16 is brought into question by the suggestion that most if not all foreigners will decline Yahweh's offer.

14. Among the passages we are studying, there are no occurrences of the hypothetical combinations, SN > PN, PI > PN, SN > SI, PI > SN, SN > PI, or SI > PN.

15. BKAT XIV/2, 354. Wolff finds further examples of the genre in Hos 1:2-9, 3:1-5 (BKAT XIV/1, 9-10, 71-72). His definition is similar to that of G. W. Coats in FOTL I, 86-88, 317 with reference to a nonprophetic passage (Gen 9:20-27): "A short and pointed saying pertaining to the addressee and supported by a narrative framework, the saying being primary with relation to the framework."

16. Cf. P. A. Ackroyd, "A Judgment Narrative Between Kings and Chronicles? An Approach to Amos 7:9-17," *Studies in the Religious Tradition of the Old Testament* (London: SCM, 1987), pp. 195-208; reprinted from G. W. Coats and B. O. Long, eds., *Canon and Authority, Essays in Old Testament Religion and Theology* (Philadelphia, 1977), pp. 71-81. Judging from the fact that this pericope does not fit well with the content of Amos's authentic oracles, Ackroyd suggests that it was inserted editorially from a separate narrative source (possibly about an anonymous prophet) for the express purpose of legimating Amos's ministry. See also G. M. Tucker, "Prophetic Authority. A Form-Critical Study of Amos 7:10-17," *Int* 27 (1973), 423-34.

17. It may be very meaningful that this earliest collection of prophetic oracles has evolved from a prophet narrative since this suggests a possible link to the earlier prophet legends that play an important role within the Deuteronomistic History. On the urgent concern for personal legitimation among the prophetic figures of the preclassical legends, see De Vries, *Prophet against Prophet*.

18. The shorter poetic predictions that we are studying are the following: Isa 17:4-6, 28:5-6; Jer 4:9 (v 10 is in prose), 30:8-9; Joel 3:1-3, 4:18; Amos 8:9-10, 11-12, 13-14. In addition, quasi-liturgical rubrics introduce short sections of poetry in Mic 2:4-5 and Zeph 3:16-17. The lengthier poetic materials are in Isa 2:2-4 par Mic 4:1-4, 24:21-23; Hos 2:18-22, 23-25; Amos 9:13-15; Mic 5:9-14; and Zeph 3:11-13.

19. These relatively short expansions are the following: 1 Sam 3:12-13abα[1]; Isa 2:20-21, 3:18-23, 7:18-19, 20, 21-22, 23-25, 11:10, 11, 17:7-8, 9, 18:7, 19:18, 23, 24-25, 23:15-16, 27:12, 13, Jer 3:17, 18, 5:18-19, 9:24-25, 16:14-15, 21:7, 23:5-6, 46:26b, 49:6, 39, 50:4-5, 20; Ezek 29:21, 30:9; Hos 1:5; Zeph 3:20; Zech 3:10, 8:23. We add to this list two prose predictions styled as interpretations of special citations, Jer 4:11-12 and 31:29-30.

20. Nonapocalyptic passages revealing this impulse are Isa 4:2-6, 19:16-17, 19-22; Jer 8:1-3, 31:27-28, 31-34, 38-40, 33:14-16. Apocalyptic passages with this motivation are Joel 4:1-3 and the literary complexes, Ezekiel 38–39; Zech 12:2–13:6, 14:1ff.

21. In disregard of the opening messenger formula, the apocalyptic redactor displays a weakening sense of what revelation should be by allowing God himself to wonder about the typology of Scripture. According to Daniel I. Block, the Deity is asking a rhetorical question, to which a negative answer is presupposed ("Gog in Prophetic Tradition," *VT* 42 [1992], 154-72).

22. Although the canonizing decision, already implicit in unannounced moves to close off the deposit of authoritative Scripture and made official and explicit in the conciliar declarations, may have been historically inevitable, its effect was to damp down the dynamism of redactional tradition (see "Beyond Redaction" in Chapter Eleven). One perceives that the canonizing moves that put a stop to the growth of the Old and New Testaments were essentially in the interest of ecclesiastical institutions. It is in the very nature of institutions that they tolerate only such creativity as can be managed and controlled to the profit of the institution, and that they are constantly suspicious of unrestrained freedom within the communities or organizations they seek to control.

Index of Authors

363

Index of Scripture Passages

366